standard catalog of®

2nd Edition

CORVETTE 1953-2005

John Gunnell

Published by

700 East State Street • Iola, WI 54990-0001
715-445-2214 • 888-457-2873
www.krause.com

Our toll-free number to place an order or obtain
a free catalog is (800) 258-0929.

Library of Congress Catalog Number: 2004093895

ISBN: 0-87349-907-7

Edited by Brian Earnest

Designed by Brian Brogaard

Printed in the United States of America

CONTENTS

Wieck Media and Nicky Wright

ACKNOWLEDGMENTS

I would like to thank numerous people for helping with this book. Automotive journalist and photographer Jerry Heasley, of Pampa, Texas, supplied many of the color photographs. Other color images came from the Nicky Wright Collection, which is maintained by the National Automobile and Truck Museum of the United States (NATMUS) in Auburn, Indiana. The late Mr. Wright was a good friend and his beautiful photographs of collectible American cars are a tribute to his passion for great automobiles. Special thanks to NATMUS founder John Martin Smith and the staff members of the museum for making Nicky Wright's photographs available for this book. In addition, thanks go to Don Williams and Kenneth Behring and the staff of the Blackhawk Automotive Museum, of Danville, California, for photographs of cars from the Blackhawk Collection. Thanks also to Brian Brogaard for the book's graphic design, Karen O'Brien for editing this project, and everyone at Krause Publications. Finally, thanks to Mike Yager and his crew at Mid America Direct, in Effingham, Illinois, for their efforts in proofreading the text and photo captions.

- John Gunnell

John Gunnell

The Mid America Direct staff, (from left to right) David Saunders, Mike Yager, Butch Claar, and Frank Burk, proofreading the manuscript for this book.

INTRODUCTION

The 1953 Corvette was based on the 1952 EX-122 show car. It was one of the few Motorama dream cars to actually go into production with the styling virtually unchanged.

The Corvette was created as an economical sports car for young adults. It was also something that could be used as a performance-image builder while Chevrolet waited for its V-8. The car's fiberglass body was not only novel, but practical. It lowered the cost of production in limited numbers and expedited the Corvette's debut. Steel-bodied models were originally planned for later model years.

Sports-car enthusiast and television celebrity Dave Garroway heaped a lot of praise on the pretty new Corvette in the Chevrolet sales promotion film Halls of Wonder. Yet, many of the sports-car fans it was meant for snubbed it. They harbored a prejudice that nothing good could come out of Detroit and certainly not from Chevrolet. Remember, at the time, a "Chevy" was the car mothers drove to the grocery store to pick up peanut butter and jelly for children's lunches. The marque did not have a hot-car image yet. The fact that Corvettes used standard "family car" mechanical components and came with a Powerglide automatic transmission were other points of criticism.

Most of the people who knocked the 'Vette never drove one. As Road & Track said of the 1954 version, "The outstanding characteristic of the Corvette is probably its deceptive performance."

The car looked the same in 1955, but the 265-cid V-8 made it much hotter. Unfortunately, like a beautiful debutante with a black belt in karate, its appearance belied its power. Sales were so bad Chevrolet management was on the verge of killing the Corvette. However, when Ford came out with its two-passenger Thunderbird, the company was forced to continue production for competitive reasons.

Sales shot up dramatically in 1956. The Corvette now had the looks to match its performance that sparked the increase. A manual transmission, roll-up side windows, and lockable doors also added to its appeal. And several prestigious racing victories contributed to its performance image.

With the introduction of fuel-injection in 1957, advertising proclaimed, "For the first time in automotive history—one horsepower for every cubic inch." Chrysler 300 fans knew better, but it did make good copy, and sales once again increased.

The clean, classic styling of 1956 and 1957 was

Nicky Wright

David McLellan and his 1995 ZR-1 at home

considerably jazzed up in 1958. Although the basic design was attractive, the chrome-laden 1958 is generally considered the gaudiest Corvette. But, apparently, that's what the public wanted and sales climbed significantly over the previous year's model.

Some of the excess glitter was removed in 1959. In 1961, the Corvette received a new "duck tail" rear-end treatment. Two years later, in a major restyling, the 1963s were an immediate hit. Demand was so great many customers had to wait two months or more to take delivery of their new Sting Ray coupe or ragtop. By now, Corvette's reputation as a powerful sports car was firmly established on the track and street.

A four-passenger Corvette was considered for 1963. It might have been quite successful. Thunderbird sales soared when the T-bird went that route in 1958. However, the T-bird never really claimed to be a true sports car; it was a "sporty" personal car. Putting a back seat in the Corvette might have hurt its image.

The basic aerodynamic styling introduced in 1968 would remain until 1983. After the early 1970s, Corvettes became significantly tamer. Still, when you mention performance, the American car that comes first to most peoples' minds is the Corvette. By 1976, Corvette's shapely aerodynamic body was eight years old. Yet it would remain in this form for half a dozen more years, attracting performance-minded drivers even though the engine choices were far milder than they had been. After all, what else was there? As Chevrolet proclaimed, Corvette was "America's only true production sports car."

Only the Sting Ray coupe body remained for 1976, when convertible Corvettes temporarily became extinct. Removable roof panels would be the closest one could come to open-topped motoring. Corvettes remained fiberglass-bodied, of course; but this year a partial steel underbody was added. Customers had a choice of wide- or close-ratio four-speed gearboxes and the standard or special (L82) 350-cid V-8 engine. The latter engine, installed in 5,720 cars, had finned aluminum rocker covers and special cylinder heads. Sales hit a record level.

The Sting Ray name faded away for 1977, but not much else changed. Less than 16 percent of Corvettes came with either the close-ratio or wide-ratio four-speed transmission . . . a figure typical of this period. Most customers, it seemed, wanted Corvette's performance, but didn't wish to shift for themselves. The L82 V-8 engine was installed in 6,148 cars.

An aerodynamic restyling of the basic body arrived for Corvette's 25th anniversary year in 1978, adding a fastback roofline and large wraparound back window. The high-performance (L82) V-8 added horsepower with a new dual-snorkel air-intake system and lower-restriction exhaust components. Nearly one-third of this year's Corvettes sported optional Silver Anniversary two-tone Silver paint. Even more striking were the Indy Pace Car replicas with Black-over-Silver paint and a host of extras. They sold for well above retail at the time and remain among the most desirable Corvettes today.

Some Indy Pace Car features found their way onto standard models for 1979, including bolt-on spoilers and lightweight bucket seats. Both the base and special V-8s now had the dual-snorkel intake. Production slid upward for the model year, but sales slipped a bit. Another modest restyling came in 1980, lowering the hood profile, recessing the grille and taking off some weight. Lift-off roof panels were made of microscopic glass beads. Front and rear spoilers were now molded into place. Corvette 350-cid V-8s produced as much as 230 hp, but speedometers now peaked at 85 mph.

In another weight-cutting move, a fiberglass-reinforced Monoleaf rear spring was installed on automatic transmission models in 1981. A new 190-hp, 350-cid or 5.7-liter engine had cast magnesium rocker covers and stainless steel exhaust manifolds. In an attempt to keep up with a rising problem, the theft alarm added a starter interrupt.

A new Corvette was in the works, but the 1982 version had some strong points of its own: essentially, a strong new drivetrain in the last of the old bodies. The "Cross Fire" fuel-injected V-8 used throttle-body injectors, but produced only 10 more horsepower (200) than the former version. For the first time since 1955, all Corvettes had automatic transmission. A built-to-order Collector Edition featured Silver Beige Metallic paint and a frameless glass hatch. This was the first 'Vette to carry a price tag above $20,000. Sales sagged dramatically, perhaps because customers were waiting for the coming fourth-generation Corvette.

No Corvettes at all were built for the 1983 model year, but the aerodynamic '84 edition (debuting in the spring of 1983) was worth the wait. The car buff books fawned

Nicky Wright

Zora Arkus-Duntov (left) enjoying his work

over it with superlatives. Technical changes included an aluminum drive shaft and fiberglass springs. A new four-speed manual transmission with automatic overdrive in the top three gears was offered, but only one in eight Corvettes carried it. The overdrive was locked out during hard acceleration. This year's dual-injector V-8 produced 205 hp. One other little change: Corvette's price tag soared past the $23,000 mark.

Horsepower jumped by 25 for 1985, with a new TPI (tuned-port-injected) 350-cid V-8. The next year a convertible arrived. It was the first open-top Corvette since 1975. Anti-lock braking also became standard, as did a new VATS anti-theft system. A four-speed overdrive automatic transmission was standard, but a four-speed manual (overdrive in the top three gears) cost no more. A switch to aluminum heads for the TPI engine produced a few problems, so early models kept the old cast-iron heads. All convertibles (a.k.a. roadsters) were sold as Indy Pace Cars.

It can easily be said that all Corvettes are collectible, yet some more so than others. The 1978 Indy Pace Car Replica is one example and the '82 Collector Edition is another. Neither qualifies as rare, though, as quite a few were produced. No doubt, strong demand will also keep the '86 convertible on the desirable list.

Though little changed from the previous model, the 1987 Corvette Y-body coupe and convertible highlighted state-of-the-art technology throughout. From an electronic instrument panel with eight possible gauge readouts in four locations to aluminum cylinder heads and a high-performance stereo speaker system, the Chevrolet luxury sports car was aimed at buyers who wanted the latest in automotive features, regardless of cost.

Some early 1987 Corvettes experienced problems with cracking of their new aluminum cylinder heads. The problem was ultimately solved, but did have a negative effect on production operations. The 5.7-liter Corvette V-8 was also fitted with new roller lifters, which reduced friction and bumped horsepower to 240. Also new for the year was an optional Z52 suspension setup, a low-tire-pressure indicating system and Bosch four-wheel anti-lock braking. In the works was a change to recently developed Goodyear 17-inch tires with a racing-style 45 percent aspect ratio, plus a much-desired gearbox change.

At a plant in Brewer, Maine, the North American branch of Germany's Zahnrad Fabrik Friedrichshafen AG (better known to car buffs as ZF) was busy developing a new six-speed manual transmission for the Corvette. Unfortunately, the new transmission was not ready in 1987, when 86 percent of Corvettes came with Turbo Hydra-Matic drive and 14 percent had four-speed manual transmissions.

Corvette production continued to be housed in Chevrolet's Bowling Green, Kentucky, factory. Model-year production totaled 30,632 (including 10,625 convertibles) although model-year sales of 25,266 units fell short of the 35,969 sold in 1986.

Nicky Wright

David McLellan (left) and the 1978 Corvette Indianapolis 500 Pace Car

For 1988, the Corvette remained available as a hatchback coupe or a roadster, with prices starting just below $30,000. Increased excitement was generated by a new 5.7-liter V-8 that jumped horsepower from 240 to 245. The 17-inch tires were now made available for cars with the Z52 option. However, the ZF six-speed remained on the 'Vette owners' "wish list" and 81.2 percent of the cars had a four-speed manual transmission with lock-up overdrive.

Production of 1988 Corvettes began on August 24, 1987 and stopped on July 28, 1988. During that period, 'Vettes were built on a single shift at the Bowling Green, Kentucky, factory with workers cranking out an average of 11 cars per hour. Output totaled 22,789 units, of which 7,407 were ragtops. Model-year sales of 25,425 units again accounted for a .03 percent share of the domestic automobile market.

A reaction-injected-molded (RIM) structural composite front bumper beam was new for all 1989 Corvettes and all models were available with the long-awaited ZF gearbox. The Corvette was one of the few American cars to start offering air bags this season. Both coupes and roadsters were powered by a 5.7-liter tuned port-injected V-8, which produced 245 hp at 4300 rpm in coupes and 240 hp at 4000 rpm in convertibles. A much-heralded ZR-1 "King-of-the-Hill" Corvette was scheduled for mid-1989 release, but its delivery date was ultimately delayed.

Model-year output went in the right direction in 1989, rising to 26,412 units, of which 9,749 were open cars. Transmission attachments ran a bit higher for automatics (84.4 percent) despite the availability of the six-speed transmission. Nearly all 1989 Corvettes came loaded with options including a Bose sound system used in 91.4 percent, a rear window defogger in 63.1 percent, and power seats in 96.9 percent.

An exciting addition to the 1990 Corvette lineup was the ZR-1 coupe, which was engineered in conjunction with Lotus of England and the Mercury Marine Division of Brunswick Corporation, in Stillwater, Oklahoma. It bowed in September 1989 as a 1990 model and production of 3,000 copies was scheduled for Bowling Green, Kentucky.

The ZR-1's prime attraction was a special high-performance 5.7-liter aluminum double-overhead-cam V-8 (RPO LT5) that featured four valves per cylinder and 375 hp. This motor was mated to the ZF transmission. The car's body also had a wider rear roof bow and quarter panel section made of traditional SMC plastic materials produced by GenCorp at its Reinforced Plastics Division plant in Marion, Indiana. A price tag of $59,495 made the ZR-1 America's most expensive production car.

To go along with the ZR-1 performance image, power output on standard L98-powered coupes and convertibles was 245 hp (or 250 hp with sport mufflers). The basic price for a Corvette increased $434 to $32,479. New for 1990 convertibles was an optional removable hardtop.

During the 1987-1990 period, Chevrolet Motor Division operated as a branch of General Motors Corporation, with its headquarters in Warren, Michigan. Robert D. Burger was general manager through mid-1989 when Jim C. Perkins, an enthusiast and Classic Chevy collector, took over the command post.

The most talked about change for 1991 Corvettes was the restyling of the coupe's and convertible's rear to more closely resemble the ZR-1, the price of which increased $4,643 to $64,138 for what was essentially a carry-over model from 1990.

This same scenario occurred in 1992 as the ZR-1 did not change drastically, but its price climbed to $65,318. The standard Corvette models received a more potent (300 horsepower) 5.7-liter V-8. Acceleration Slip Regulation was also a new feature on 'Vettes this year.

It was the 40th Anniversary of the Corvette in 1993. The occasion was marked by Chevrolet offering an optional special appearance package, available on all models, that included "Ruby Red" exterior and interior, anniversary badging on the hood, deck and side-gills, and seat headrests embroidered with the anniversary logo. The ZR-1s LT5 V-8 received a power boost improving it's rating to 405 hp, which was an increase of 20 hp over the previous powerplant. The '93 'Vette also introduced GM's Passive Keyless Entry System, and was the first North American automobile to use recycled sheet-molded-compound body panels.

Some "tweaking" was done to 1994 Corvettes, with several safety and ride-enhancing items installed. The price of a ZR-1 was now $67,443. Corvettes now offered brake-transmission shift interlock, dual airbags, sequential fuel injection and a refined interior including new carpeting and door panel trim. The ZR-1 received new wheels. The 4L60-E electronic four-speed overdrive automatic transmission standard in Corvettes was also refined to provide smoother shift points.

The ZR-1, now priced at just over $68,000, made its final appearance in 1995. The biggest change on Corvettes this year was a new gill panel located behind the front wheel openings that instantly identified these 'Vettes as '95 models. Changes included the addition of heavy-duty brakes with larger front rotors and the use of deCarbon gas-charged shock absorbers for improved ride quality. A Corvette paced the 1995 Indianapolis 500, the third time (1978 and 1986, previously) for America's sports car to lead the pack at Indy.

Chevrolet constructed this 1979 Turbo-Corvette with fuel injection as an "idea" vehicle. The production Corvette with a 5.7-liter V-8 engine got a boost from its regular 195 hp to an estimated 260 hp by adding the special equipment. Chevrolet engineers were testing the potential for performance with smaller engines that is possible by turbocharging. Air came in through the air cleaner, traveled through the turbocharger, up through the chrome pipe to the manifold and intake ports for each cylinder, where the air was mixed with metered injected fuel.

1996 was a year of transition at Bowling Green, Kentucky, with the fourth-generation Corvette in its final year. With the ZR-1 now history, Chevrolet introduced two special versions of the Corvette in the form of a Grand Sport Edition and Collector Edition. The Grand Sport, in its Admiral Blue, White Stripe, and Red "hash mark" on the left front fender finish, evoked memories of the brutish racing Corvettes from 1962-63 and raced by legends including A.J. Foyt and Roger Penske. The modern version was powered by the 330-hp LT4 V-8 coupled to a T56 six-speed manual transmission. The Collector Edition Corvette was finished in Sebring Silver and featured badging and embroidered seat headrests with the Collector Edition logo. Also available was a Z51 Performance & Handling Package offered only on the Corvette coupe for enthusiasts who wanted to run their cars in autocross or gymkhana events.

The fifth-generation Corvette of 1997 received rave reviews in the press, and after a mid-model year (January 1997) launch sold over 9,000 copies in coupe form only. Everything was new about this Corvette including the frame construction and blunt tail styling. The LS1 5.7-liter V-8 was more compact and more potent, producing 350 hp and 345 lb.-ft. of torque. The cockpit was reminiscent of the original Corvette of 1953 in that it utilized a twin-pod design. It was the first all-new Corvette in 13 years and only the sixth major change in the car's 44-year history.

Observing its 45th year in 1998, the Corvette lineup added a convertible to go with the coupe launched the year previous. The refinements included magnesium wheels with a bronze tint and daytime running lamps. Price of a coupe reached $37,995 with the ragtop costing $44,425. For the fourth time, a Corvette was selected to be the pace car for the Indianapolis 500. The 1998 pace car 'Vette was finished in Purple and Yellow.

David Hill, Corvette's chief engineer

The fifth-generation Corvette, in its third model year in 1999, added a hardtop to the lineup. The fixed-roof Corvette was the first offered since the legendary second-generation Sting Rays of 1963-1967. The new hardtop Corvette featured body lines unique to that model, that subtly set it apart from its coupe and convertible counterparts. A Corvette C5 was the official pace car of the 1999 24 Hours of LeMans in France. Additionally, Chevrolet introduced the Corvette C5-R, a General Motors-engineered and factory-backed GT2-classed sports car that competed in select U.S. and international sports car races.

Rumors of the demise of the Corvette have been steady in recent years, but after 46 years of production and with it being a proven image-enhancing product for Chevrolet, the Corvette's future cannot be dismissed so easily.

DAVID C. HILL

David C. Hill was named vehicle line executive for General Motors Performance Cars in November 1995.

Hill is responsible for the Cadillac luxury roadster, Chevrolet Corvette, Chevrolet Camaro and Pontiac Firebird.

Within GM, vehicle line executives have full responsibility for assuring the success of vehicles in the marketplace, as well as their profitability. This requires integrating expertise from a variety of functions, including styling, engineering, purchasing, finance, manufacturing, merchandising and sales.

In addition to his role as a vehicle line executive, Mr. Hill has served as the Chevrolet Corvette chief engineer since November 1992.

Hill began his GM career with Cadillac Motor Car Division in 1965. From 1965 to 1973 he served as senior project engineer in the Cadillac engine lab.

In 1973 Hill became a staff project engineer for Cadillac engine design and release. He held that position until becoming the general supervisor of the Cadillac body and chassis lab in 1976.

From 1978 to 1981, Hill served as staff engineer for Cadillac car development. In 1982 he became a Cadillac staff engineer for emissions and transmissions. Later that year he was promoted to vehicle chief engineer for the Cadillac Allante.

In 1988 Hill's responsibilities were expanded as he was named chief engineer for the Cadillac DeVille and Concours. He held that position until becoming the engineering program manager for Cadillac in May 1992. He was named chief engineer for the Corvette in November 1992.

Born January 15, 1943, Hill received a bachelor of science degree in mechanical engineering from Michigan Technological University in 1965 and a master of science degree in mechanical engineering from the University of Michigan in 1970.

Wieck Media

Nicky Wright

1953 Corvette roadster

1953

CORVETTE (Six-cylinder) SERIES E2934

The new 1953 Corvette had a fiberglass body, chrome-framed grille with 13 heavy vertical chrome bars, rounded front fenders with recessed headlights with wire screen covers, no side windows or outside door handles, a wraparound windshield and protruding, fender-integrated taillights. The interior featured a floor-mounted shifter for the Powerglide two-speed automatic transmission and oil pressure, battery, water temperature and fuel gauges, plus a tachometer and clock. Each 1953 Corvette was virtually hand-built and a lot of minor changes were made during the production run. All of the first-year cars were Polo White with Sportsman Red interiors. All had black canvas convertible tops which manually folded into a storage space behind the seats. Other 1953-only features included special valve covers, a one-piece carburetor linkage and a small trunk mat. Short exhaust extensions were used on all '53s (and early '54s) because they were prone to drawing exhaust fumes into the car through the vent windows. A black oilcloth window storage bag was provided to protect the 1953 Corvette's removable plastic side windows when stowed in the trunk.

I.D. NUMBERS

The Corvette used the standard Chevrolet Vehicle Identification Number (VIN) coding system. A tag located on the left-hand front door hinge pillar consisted of 10 symbols. The first symbol was an E for 1953 models. The second and third symbols indicated the model year, for example 53 = 1953. The fourth symbol identified the assembly plant as follows: F = Flint, Michigan. (All 1953 Corvettes were made in Flint). The last six symbols were digits representing the sequential production number. Corvettes for 1953 were numbered E53F001001 to E53F001300. Engine numbers were found on the right-hand side of the crankcase behind the distributor. The

Nicky Wright

1953 Corvette roadster, one of only 300 built

Nicky Wright

1953 Corvette roadster; note the factory mesh-covered headlights.

engine numbers for 1953 models used the prefix LAY. Since the Corvette bodies were virtually handmade, they did not carry standard Fisher Body Style Numbers as did other GM cars. The Corvette model number consisted of the four digits 2934, which also served as the body style number for the early production years.

ENGINE

Inline. Six-cylinder. Overhead valve. Cast iron block. Displacement: 235.5 cid. Bore and stroke: 3.56 x 3.96 in. Compression ratio: 8.0:1. Brake hp: 150 at 4200 rpm. Single breaker-point ignition. Carburetor: Three Carter Type YH one-barrel Model 2066S (early models); Model 2055S (later models).

CHASSIS FEATURES

Wheelbase: 102 inches. Overall length: 167 inches. Front tread: 57 inches. Rear tread: 58.8 inches. Steel disk wheels. Tires: 6.70 x 15. Front suspension: Coil springs, tubular shock absorbers and stabilizer bar. Rear suspension: Leaf springs, tube shocks and solid rear axle. Drum brakes. Axle ratio: 3.55:1.

OPTIONS

Signal-seeking AM radio ($145.15). Heater ($91.40). White sidewall tires.

Jerry Heasley

1953 Corvette 235.5-cid 150-hp inline six-cylinder engine

Jerry Heasley

1953 Corvette roadster interior

HISTORICAL FOOTNOTES

The first Corvette was built on June 30, 1953 at the Flint, Michigan, assembly plant. In addition to being the first, it is the rarest Corvette. Model year production peaked at 300 units. About 200 of the 300 Corvettes made in 1953 are known to exist today, although the first two cars built are missing. The '53s were constructed in an area at the rear of Chevrolet's customer delivery garage on Van Slyke Ave., in Flint, Michigan. Calendar-year sales of 300 cars was recorded. By early 1954, Chevrolet announced that 315 Corvettes had been built and that production of the model had been shifted to the assembly plant in St. Louis, Missouri. Programming, at that point, called for production of 1,000 Corvettes per month in St. Louis by June 1954. The company predicted that 10,000 per year could be built and sold. Zora Arkus-Duntov joined Chevrolet Motor Division in 1953 and would become chief engineer of the Corvette.

1953 CORVETTE

Model Number	Body/Style Number	Body Type & Seating	Factory Price	Shipping Weight	Production Total
2934	2934	2-dr Rds-2P	3498	2705	300

Nicky Wright

1953 Corvette roadster, all models came with whitewall tires and two-spinner hubcaps

Jerry Heasley

1953 Corvette roadster, all models were Polo White with Sportsman Red interiors

Nicky Wright

1953 Corvette roadster, all models came with AM radios

Jerry Heasley

1954 Corvette roadster with Powerglide transmission

CORVETTE (Six-cylinder) SERIES E2934

For all practical purposes the 1953 and 1954 Corvettes were the same. Minor changes were made to the window storage bag, air cleaners, starter and locations of the fuel and brake lines. Unlike the previous year's model, 1954s were available in Pennant Blue, Sportsman Red and Black, in addition to Polo White. The soft top was now offered in beige. A new style of valve cover was used. It was held on by four bolts through the outside lip instead of two center studs. The valve cover decals were different with larger lettering. The optional radio had Conelrad National Defense System icons on its face. In early 1954, the original two-handled hood latch was changed to a single-handle design. Six-cylinder Corvettes after serial number E54S003906 had integrated dual-port air cleaners. A clip to hold the ventipanes closed was added in late 1954 and also used on all 1955 models.

I.D. NUMBERS

The Corvette used the standard Chevrolet Vehicle Identification Number (VIN) coding system. A tag located on the left-hand front door hinge pillar consisted of 10 symbols. The first symbol was an E for Corvette. The second and third symbols indicated the model year, for example 54 = 1954. The fourth symbol identified the assembly plant as follows: S = St. Louis, Mo. The last six symbols were digits representing the sequential production number. Corvettes for 1954 were numbered E54S001001 to E54S004640. Engine numbers were found on the right-hand side of the crankcase behind the distributor. The engine numbers for 1954 models used the suffix YG. Since the Corvette bodies were virtually handmade, they did not carry standard Fisher Body Style Numbers as did other GM cars. The Corvette model number consisted of the four digits 2934, which also served as the body style number for the early production years.

ENGINE

Inline. Six-cylinder. Overhead valve. Cast-iron block. Displacement: 235.5 cid. Bore and stroke: 3.56 x 3.96 in.

Nicky Wright

1954 Corvette interior, the speedometer reached 140 mph

Nicky Wright

1954 Corvette roadster, note the exhaust extensions not found on 1953 models.

Compression ratio: 8.0:1. Brake hp: 150 at 4200 rpm. Single breaker-point ignition system. Four main bearings. Carburetor: Three Carter Type YH one-barrel Model 2066S.

NOTE: Later in the model year a new camshaft upped horsepower to 155.

Nicky Wright

1954 Corvette dual-fin, bullet taillights

CHASSIS FEATURES

Wheelbase: 102 inches. Overall length: 167 inches. Front tread: 57 inches. Rear tread: 58.8 inches. Tires: 6.70 x 15. Front suspension: Coil springs, tube shocks and stabilizer bar. Rear suspension: Leaf springs, tube shocks and solid rear axle. Drum brakes. Steel disk wheels. Axle ratio: 3.55:1.

OPTIONS

RPO 102A Signal-seeking AM radio ($145.15). RPO Directional signals ($16.75). RPO 101A Heater ($91.40). RPO 422A windshield washer ($11.85). RPO 420A parking brake alarm ($5.65). RPO 313M Powerglide automatic transmission ($178.35). RPO 290B 6.70 x 15 white sidewall tires. RPO 421A Courtesy light ($4.05)

Nicky Wright

1954 Corvette roadster retained the 1953 grille and mesh-covered headlights

HISTORICAL FOOTNOTES

Production of 1954 Corvettes began December 23, 1953. Approximately 80 percent of 1954 Corvettes were painted White. About 15 percent had a Pennant Blue exterior with Shoreline Beige interior. About three percent were Red with a Red interior and some Black cars with Red interiors were built. In addition, Metallic Green and Metallic Brown cars are thought to have been built. The 1954 Corvette did not achieve its sales target of 10,000 cars. In fact, over 1,100 were unsold when the year ended. A 1954 Corvette could go from 0 to 60 mph in 11 seconds and from 0 to 100 mph in 41 seconds.

1954 CORVETTE

Model Number	Body/Style Number	Body Type & Seating	Factory Price	Shipping Weight	Production Total
2934	2934	2-dr Rds-2P	$2,774	2,705 lbs.	3,640

Jerry Heasley

1954 Corvette roadster, all models were built with windshield washers

Jerry Heasley

1954 Corvette roadster, all models were available with beige tops

Jerry Heasley

1955 Corvette roadster, one of only 700 built

CORVETTE – (Six/V-8) – SERIES E2934 –

Corvette styling remained the same as last year's model. The big news was the availability of a V-8 engine. An enlarged gold "V" within the word "CheVrolet" on the front fenders was a quick way to tell the V-8 powered (12-volt electrical system) cars from those with a six-cylinder engine (and six-volt electrical system). On the 1955 V-8 cars the frame was modified to allow room for the fuel pump.

I.D. NUMBERS

The Corvette used the standard Chevrolet Vehicle Identification Number (VIN) coding system. A tag located on the left-hand front door hinge pillar consisted of 10 symbols. The first symbol was an E for Corvette. The second and third symbols indicated the model year, for example 55 = 1955. The fourth symbol identified the assembly plant as follows: S = St. Louis, Mo. The last six symbols were digits representing the sequential production number. Corvettes for 1955 were numbered VE55S001001 to VE55S001700 (1955 six-cylinder cars had no "V" prefix). Engine numbers were found on the right-hand side of the crankcase behind the distributor. The engine numbers for 1955 six-cylinder cars used the same YG suffix as 1954 models. The engine numbers for 1955 V-8 cars used the suffix FG (Powerglide automatic transmission) or GR (manual transmission). Since the Corvette bodies were virtually handmade, they did not carry standard Fisher Body Style Numbers as did other GM cars. The Corvette model number consisted of the four digits 2934, which also served as the body style number for the early production years.

NOTE: Total production of both models was 700. At least a half dozen six-cylinder Corvettes were built as 1955 models.

ENGINES

SIX: Inline. Six-cylinder. Overhead valve. Cast-iron block. Displacement: 235.5 cid. Bore and stroke: 3.75 x 3.00 in. Compression ratio: 8.0:1. Brake hp: 155 at 5000 rpm. Single breaker-point ignition system. Four main bearings. Solid valve lifters. Carburetor: Three Carter one-barrel Model 3706989.

V-8: Inline. Overhead valve. Cast-iron block. Displacement: 265 cid. Bore and stroke: 3.56 x 3.96 in. Compression ratio: 8.0:1. Brake hp: 195 at 4200 rpm. Single breaker-point ignition system. Five main bearings. Solid valve lifters. Carburetor: Rochester four-barrel Model 7008005.

TRANSMISSIONS

MANUAL TRANSMISSION: A three-speed manual transmission became standard late in the model year. A single dry-plate clutch was used with manual transmission.

AUTOMATIC TRANSMISSION: A two-speed Powerglide automatic transmission was optional.

CHASSIS FEATURES

Wheelbase: 102 inches. Overall length: 167 inches. Front tread: 57 inches. Rear tread: 58.8 inches. Tires: 6.70 x 15. Frame: Welded steel box-section type. Front suspension: Coil springs, tube shocks and stabilizer bar. Rear suspension: Leaf springs, tube shocks and solid rear axle. Drum brakes. Steel disk wheels. Axle ratio: 3.55:1.

OPTIONS

RPO Directional signals ($16.75). RPO 101A Heater ($91.40). RPO 102A Signal-seeking AM radio ($145.15). RPO 422A windshield washer ($11.85). RPO 420A Parking brake alarm ($5.65). RPO 313M Powerglide automatic transmission ($178.35). RPO 290B 6.70 x 15 White sidewall tires ($26.90). RPO 421A Courtesy light ($4.05).

HISTORICAL FOOTNOTES

Production of 1955 Corvettes began October 28, 1954. New-for-1955 Corvette colors included Copper with a Beige interior and Harvest Gold (yellow) with a Green and Yellow interior. Cars with a Red exterior now featured a Light Beige interior. The interior material was called Elascofab. Soft convertible tops were offered in canvas and vinyl. New top colors included White and Dark Green. A V-8 powered 1955 Corvette could go from 0-to-60 mph in 8.7 seconds; from 0-to-100 mph in 24.7 seconds.

1955 CORVETTE

Model Number	Body/Style Number	Body Type & Seating	Factory Price	Shipping Weight	Production Total
Six-Cylinder					
2934	2934	2-Rds-2P	$2,774	2,705 lbs.	Note 1
V-8					
2934	2934	2-dr Rds-2P	$2,909	2,870 lbs.	Note 1

NOTE: Total production of both models was 700. At least a half dozen six-cylinder Corvettes were built as 1955 models.

Jerry Heasley

1955 Corvette roadster with 265-cid 195-hp V-8 engine

Jerry Heasley

1956 Corvette hardtop with 210-hp standard V-8

CORVETTE SERIES (V-8) SERIES E2934

In 1956, the Corvette began to define itself as a true American sports car. A lot of people would have been perfectly content if Chevrolet had frozen Corvette styling with the 1956 model. The same basic grille styling was kept intact, but the grille teeth looked a bit slimmer. Chevrolet styling studio chief Clare MacKichan directed the 1956 redesign, which was somewhat inspired by the thrusting headlamps and twin-bulge hood of the Mercedes-Benz 300SL gullwing coupe. There were new front fenders with chrome-rimmed headlights; glass windows; external door handles; chrome-outlined concave side body coves and sloping, taillight-integrated rear fenders. The dash layout remained the same as in the past. The 1956 rear view mirror, located on the center of the top of the dash, was adjusted by using a thumbscrew. Improved-fit soft convertible tops were standard and a power top was optional, as was a removable fiberglass hardtop. Upholstery colors were limited to Beige or Red, but seven nitro-cellulose lacquer body colors were available. They were Onyx Black with a Silver panel (Black or White soft top); Polo White with a Silver panel (Black or White soft top); Venetian Red with a Beige panel (Beige or White soft top); Cascade Green with a Beige panel (Beige or White soft top); Aztec Copper with a Beige panel (Beige or White soft top); Arctic Blue with a Silver panel (Beige or White soft top) and Inca Silver with an Imperial Ivory panel (Black or White soft top).

I.D. NUMBERS

Numbers were the same as for previous models with the number symbols changed as follows: E56S001001 to E56S004467. All Corvettes were V-8 powered and all Chevrolets with V-8 engines used a V serial number prefix. The first symbol E indicates Corvette. The second and third symbols (56) indicate the model year. The fourth symbol identifies the assembly plant S = St. Louis, Mo. The last six symbols indicate the sequential production number. The beginning engine numbers were 0001001 and up at each assembly plant with F = Flint, Mich. and T = Tonawanda, N.Y. Suffixes were as follows: GV for 265-cid 210-hp V-8 with Powerglide; GU for 265-cid 240-hp V-8 with two

Nicky Wright

1956 Corvette

Jerry Heasley

1956 Corvette convertible with one of only 887 Beige interiors

four-barrel carburetors, high-lift "Duntov" camshaft and three-speed manual transmission; GR for regular 265-cid 225-hp V-8 with dual four-barrel carburetor, and three-speed manual transmission; FK for 265-cid 210-hp V-8 with three-speed manual transmission and FG for 265-cid 225-hp V-8 with Powerglide.

NOTE: Powerglide adds 95 pounds to weight.

ENGINES

BASE ENGINE: V-8. Overhead valve. Cast-iron block. Displacement: 265 cid. Bore and stroke: 3.75 x 3.00 inches. Compression ratio: 9.25:1. Brake hp: 210 at 5600 rpm. Five main bearings. Solid valve lifters. Carburetor: Carter Type WCFB four-barrel Model 2419S.

OPTIONAL ENGINE: V-8. Overhead valve. Cast-iron block. Displacement: 265 cid. Bore and stroke: 3.75 x 3.00 inches. Compression ratio: 9.25:1. Brake hp: 225. Five main bearings. Solid valve lifters. Carburetor: Two four-barrel carburetors.

OPTIONAL ENGINE: V-8. Overhead valve. Cast-iron block. Displacement: 265 cid. Bore and stroke: 3.75 x 3.00 inches. Compression ratio: 9.25:1. Brake hp: 240 at 5200 rpm. Five main bearings. Solid valve lifters. High-lift camshaft. Carburetor: Two four-barrel carburetors.

Jerry Heasley

1956 Corvette convertible, 1,259 of 3,467 had two-toned paint

TRANSMISSIONS

MANUAL TRANSMISSION: A close-ratio three-speed manual all-synchromesh transmission with floor-mounted gear shifter was standard equipment.

AUTOMATIC TRANSMISSION: A two-speed Powerglide automatic transmission was optional equipment.

CHASSIS FEATURES

Wheelbase: 102 inches. Overall length: 168 inches. Overall height: 51.9 inches. Overall width: 70.5 inches. Front tread: 57 inches. Rear tread: 59 inches. Ground clearance: Six inches. Tires: 6.70 x 15. Frame: Welded steel box-section, X-braced type. Front suspension: Independent; unequal-length A-arms; coil springs, tube shocks. Steering: Saginaw worm-and-ball, 16:1 ratio, 37-foot turning circle. Rear suspension: Live axle on semi-elliptic leaf springs, anti-roll bar, tubular shock absorbers. Rear axle type: Hypoid semi-floating. Brakes: Four-wheel hydraulic, internal-expanding, 11-inch diameter drums, 157 square inches effective lining area (121 square inches with optional sintered metallic linings). 15-inch steel bolt-on wheels. Standard rear axle ratio with three-speed 3.70:1; with Powerglide: 3.55:1. Optional axle ratios: 3.27:1, 4.11:1 and 4.56:1.

OPTIONS

RPO 101 Heater ($115). RPO 102 Signal-seeking AM radio ($185). RPO 107 Parking brake signal ($5). RPO 108 Courtesy lights ($8). RPO 109 Windshield washer ($11). RPO 290 White sidewall tires 6.70 x 15 ($30). RPO 313 Powerglide automatic transmission ($175). RPO 419 Auxiliary hardtop ($200). RPO 426 Electric power windows ($60). RPO 449 Special high-lift camshaft. ($175). RPO 469 Dual four-barrel carburetor equipment ($160). RPO 473 Hydraulic folding top mechanism ($100).

HISTORICAL FOOTNOTES

Production of 1956 Corvettes began November 4, 1955. Chevrolet general manager Ed Cole and Corvette chief engineer Zora Arkus-Duntov decided it was time for the Corvette to go racing in 1956. Zora drove one car to a two-way average of 150.583 mph at Daytona's Flying Mile. John Fitch also set a record of 90.932 mph for the standing-start mile at Daytona and 145.543 mph in the production sports car class. In the spring of 1956, at Pebble Beach, Calif., dentist Dr. Dick Thompson finished second overall and first in class in a sports car road race. Thompson went on to take the Sports Car Club of America (SCCA) 1956 championship with his Corvette. A 225-hp 1956 Corvette could go from 0-to-60 mph in 7.3 seconds; from 0-to-100 mph in 20.7 seconds.

1956 CORVETTE

Model Number	Body/Style Number	Body Type & Seating	Factory Price	Shipping Weight	Production Total
2934	2934	2-dr Rds-2P	$2,900	2,730 lbs.	3,467

Jerry Heasley

1956 Corvette ragtop

Jerry Heasley

1957 Corvette with fuel injection

CORVETTE SERIES (V-8) SERIES E2934

The 1957 Corvette looked the same as the previous year's model. The thumb-screw-adjusted rearview mirror of 1956 was replaced with a lock-nut type that required a wrench to adjust. The big news was the availability of a 283-cid 283-hp fuel-injected V-8. Among the standard features were: dual exhaust; all-vinyl bucket seats; three-spoke competition-style steering wheel; carpeting; outside rearview mirror; electric clock and tachometer. Corvettes were now available in seven colors: Code 704 Onyx Black (Black, White or Beige top); Code 718 Polo White (Black, White or Beige top); Code 709 Aztec Copper (White or Beige top); Code 713 Arctic Blue (Black, White or Beige top); Code 712 Cascade Green (Black, White or Beige top); Code 714 Venetian Red (Black, White or Beige top) or Code 804 Inca Silver (Black or White top). White, Silver, and Beige were optional color choices for the side cove.

I.D. NUMBERS

Numbers were the same as for previous models with the number symbols changed as follows: E57S100001 to E57S106339. All Corvettes were V-8 powered and all Chevrolets with V-8 engines used a V serial number prefix. The first symbol (E) indicates Corvette. The second and third symbols (57) indicate the model year. The fourth

Nicky Wright

1957 Corvette convertible in Venetian Red

1957 Corvette "Fuelie," Onyx Black was 1957's most popular color

symbol identifies the assembly plant S = St. Louis, Mo. The last six symbols indicate the sequential production number. The beginning engine numbers were 0001001 and up at each assembly plant with F = Flint, Mich. and T = Tonawanda, N.Y. Suffixes were as follows: EF four-barrel/synchromesh; EG dual four-barrel/high-lift cam/synchromesh; EH dual four-barrel/synchromesh; EL fuel-injection/high-lift cam; EM fuel-injection/synchromesh; EN fuel-injection/high-lift cam; FG Powerglide/dual four-barrel; FH Powerglide and FK Powerglide/fuel-injection.

ENGINES

BASE ENGINE: V-8. Overhead valve. Cast iron block. Bore and stroke: 3.87 x 3.00 inches. Displacement: 283 cid. Compression ratio: 8.50:1. Brake hp: 185 at 4600 rpm. Taxable hp: 48.00. Torque: 275 at 2400. Five main bearings. Crankcase capacity: 4 qt. (Add 1 qt. for filter). Cooling system capacity: 16 qt. (Add 1 qt. for heater). Dual exhaust. Carburetor: Carter Model 3744925 four-barrel.

BASE ENGINE: V-8. Overhead valve. Cast iron block. Displacement: 283 cid. Bore and stroke: 3.87 x 3.00

1957 Corvette with 283-cid 283-hp fuel-injected V-8

inches. Compression ratio: 9.50:1. Brake hp: 220 at 4800 rpm. Five main bearings. Carburetor: Carter four-barrel Model 3744925.

OPTIONAL ENGINE: V-8. Overhead valve. Cast iron block. Displacement: 283 cid. Bore and stroke: 3.87 x 3.00 inches. Compression ratio: 9.50:1. Brake hp: 245. Five main bearings. Carburetor: Four-barrel carburetor.

OPTIONAL ENGINE: V-8. Overhead valve. Cast iron block. Displacement: 283 cid. Bore and stroke: 3.87 x 3.00 inches. Compression ratio: 9.50:1. Brake hp: 250. Five main bearings. Induction: Rochester fuel injection.

OPTIONAL ENGINE: V-8. Overhead valve. Cast iron block. Displacement: 283 cid. Bore and stroke: 3.87 x 3.00 inches. Compression ratio: 9.50:1. Brake hp: 270. Five main bearings. Carburetor: Two four-barrel carburetors.

OPTIONAL ENGINE: V-8. Overhead valve. Cast iron block. Displacement: 283 cid. Bore and stroke: 3.87 x 3.00 inches. Compression ratio: 10.50:1. Brake hp: 283. Five main bearings. Induction: Rochester fuel injection.

NOTE: A solid lifter camshaft was used with EL and EG engines; hydraulic lifters with others.

TRANSMISSIONS

STANDARD MANUAL TRANSMISSION: A close-ratio three-speed manual all-synchromesh transmission with floor-mounted gear shifter was standard equipment.

AUTOMATIC TRANSMISSION: A two-speed Powerglide automatic transmission was optional equipment.

OPTIONAL MANUAL TRANSMISSION: A close-ratio four-speed manual all-synchromesh transmission with floor-mounted gear shifter was optional equipment after May.

CHASSIS FEATURES

Wheelbase: 102 inches. Overall length: 168 inches. Overall height: 51.9 inches. Overall width: 70.5 inches. Front tread: 57 inches. Rear tread: 59 inches. Ground clearance: Six inches. Tires: 6.70 x 15. Frame: Welded steel box-section, X-braced type. Front suspension: Independent; unequal-length A-arms; coil springs, tube shocks. Steering: Saginaw worm-and-ball, 16:1 ratio, 37-foot turning circle. Rear suspension: Live axle on semi-elliptic leaf springs, anti-roll bar, tubular shock absorbers. Rear axle type: Hypoid semi-floating. Brakes: Four-wheel hydraulic, internal-expanding, 11-inch diameter drums, 157 square inches effective lining area (121 square inches with optional sintered metallic linings). 15-inch steel bolt-on wheels. Standard rear axle ratio with three-speed 3.70:1; with Powerglide: 3.55:1. Optional axle ratios: 3.27:1, 4.11:1 and 4.56:1.

Jerry Heasley

1957 Corvette, one of 1,040 fuel-injected models

1957 Corvette retained the 1956 body style

OPTIONS

RPO 101 Heater ($110). RPO 102 Signal-seeking AM radio ($185). RPO 107 Parking brake alarm ($5). RPO 108 Courtesy Lights ($8). RPO 109 Windshield washer ($11). RPO 276 Five 15 x 5.5-inch wheels ($14). RPO 290 White sidewall tires 6.70 x 15 ($30). RPO 313 Powerglide automatic transmission ($175). RPO 419 Auxiliary hardtop ($200). RPO 426 Power windows ($55). RPO 440 Optional cove color ($18). RPO 469A 283-cid 245-hp dual four-barrel carburetor V-8 engine ($140). RPO 469B V-8 283-cid 270-hp dual four-barrel carburetor engine with Duntov competition camshaft ($170). RPO 579A V-8 283-cid 250-hp fuel-injection engine ($450). RPO 579B V-8 283-cid 283-hp fuel-injection engine with Duntov competition camshaft ($450). RPO 579E V-8 283-cid 283-hp fuel-injection engine with cold-air induction system ($675). RPO 473 Power-operated folding top mechanism ($130). RPO 677 Positraction axle with 3.70:1 ratio ($45). RPO Positraction axle with 4.11:1 ratio ($45). RPO Positraction axle with 4.56:1 ratio ($45). RPO 684 Heavy-duty racing suspension ($725). RPO 685 Four-speed manual transmission ($175).

HISTORICAL FOOTNOTES

Production of 1957 Corvettes began October 19, 1956. The fuel-injected 1957 Corvette reached the magical one-horsepower-per-cubic-inch high-performance bracket. The Corvette's continuous-flow fuel-injection system was a joint effort of Zora Arkus-Duntov, John Dolza and General Motor's Rochester Division. Only 1,040 of the 1957 Corvettes were fuel-injected. A 283 hp fuel-injection 1957 Corvette could go from 0-to-60 mph in 5.7 seconds and from 0-to-100 mph in 16.8 seconds. It had a top speed of 132 mph. Another important option was the competition suspension package RPO 684 which included heavy-duty springs, shocks and roll bars, 16.3:1 quick-ratio steering; a Positraction differential; special brake cooling equipment; and Cerametallic brake linings. Dick Thompson and Gaston Audrey won the 12-hour Sebring Race in Corvettes and Thompson took the SCCA B-production championship for the second year in a row.

1957 CORVETTE

Model Number	Body/Style Number	Body Type & Seating	Factory Price	Shipping Weight	Production Total
2934	2934	2-dr Rds-2P	$3,176	2,730 lbs.	6,339

1958 Corvette design changes included dual headlights and hood louvers

CORVETTE SERIES (V-8) SERIES J800

Corvette styling was jazzed up for 1958. There were now four chrome rimmed headlights with fender length chrome strips running between each pair of lights. As if that weren't enough glitter, fake louvers were placed on the hood. The grille was similar to the previous year, but had four fewer vertical bars. Three horizontal chrome strips were added to the new cove. A couple of vertical chrome bars decorated the trunk. They detracted from an otherwise graceful rear-end treatment. The wraparound front and rear bumpers were larger. The interior changed dramatically. The gauges were clustered together in front of the driver, rather than spread across the dash as before. A center console and passenger assist (sissy) bar were added. Seat belts were made standard equipment. They had been a dealer-installed option in 1956 and 1957. There were six exterior body colors offered: Charcoal (Black or White soft top); Silver Blue (White or Beige soft top); Regal Turquoise (Black or White soft top); Signet Red (Black or White soft top); Panama Yellow (Black or White soft top) and Snowcrest White (Black, White, or Beige soft top).

I.D. NUMBERS

The Vehicle Identification Number (VIN) is located on a plate on the left front door hinge pillar post. For 1958 the numbers were: J58S100001 to J58S109168. The first symbol (J) indicates Corvette. The second and third symbols (58) indicate the model year. The fourth symbol identifies the assembly plant (S = St. Louis, Mo). The last six symbols indicate the sequential production number. Engine code suffixes were: CQ = three-speed manual transmission; CR = three-speed manual transmission and fuel injection; CS = three-speed manual transmission, high-lift camshaft and fuel injection; CT = three-speed manual transmission and dual four-barrel carburetors; CU = three-speed manual transmission, high-lift camshaft and dual four-barrel carburetors; DG = Powerglide automatic transmission; DH = Powerglide automatic transmission and fuel injection and DJ = Powerglide automatic transmission and dual four-barrel carburetors. Cars with optional four-speed manual transmissions used the same engine code suffixes as cars with three-speed manual transmissions. The beginning engine numbers were 0001001 and up at each assembly plant with F = Flint, Mich. and T = Tonawanda, N.Y. The body number plate was located on the engine side of the cowl. The Fisher Body Style Number 58-867 identifies a Corvette. The Body Number is the production serial number of the body. The Trim Number indicates the interior trim color and material. The pebble-grain vinyl upholstery was available in Red, Dark Gray or Turquoise. The Paint Number indicates the color combination. The six 1958 Corvette acrylic lacquer exterior colors offered

1958 Corvette

were No. 500A Charcoal; No. 502A Silver Blue; No. 504A Regal Turquoise; No. 506A Signet Red; No. 508A Panama Yellow; and No. 510A Snowcrest White. The body side cove could be painted Silver or White.

ENGINES

BASE ENGINE: V-8. Overhead valve. Cast iron block. Displacement: 283 cid. Bore and stroke: 3.87 x 3.00 inches. Compression ratio: 9.50:1. Brake hp: 230 at 4800 rpm. Five main bearings. Carburetor: Carter Type WCFB four-barrel.

OPTIONAL ENGINE: V-8. Overhead valve. Cast iron block. Displacement: 283 cid. Bore and stroke: 3.87 x 3.00 inches. Compression ratio: 9.50:1. Brake hp: 245. Five main bearings. Carburetor: Two four-barrel carburetors.

OPTIONAL ENGINE: V-8. Overhead valve. Cast iron block. Displacement: 283 cid. Bore and stroke: 3.87 x 3.00 inches. Compression ratio: 9.50:1. Brake hp: 250. Five main bearings. Induction: Rochester fuel injection.

OPTIONAL ENGINE: V-8. Overhead valve. Cast iron block. Displacement: 283 cid. Bore and stroke: 3.87 x 3.00 inches. Compression ratio: 9.50:1. Brake hp: 270. Five main bearings. Carburetor: Two four-barrel carburetors.

OPTIONAL ENGINE: V-8. Overhead valve. Cast iron block. Displacement: 283 cid. Bore and stroke: 3.87 x 3.00 inches. Compression ratio: 10.50:1. Brake hp: 290. Five main bearings. Induction: Rochester fuel injection.

TRANSMISSIONS

STANDARD MANUAL TRANSMISSION: A three-speed manual all-synchromesh transmission with floor-mounted gear shifter was standard equipment.

AUTOMATIC TRANSMISSION: A two-speed Powerglide automatic transmission was optional equipment.

OPTIONAL MANUAL TRANSMISSION: A four-speed manual all-synchromesh transmission with floor-mounted gear shifter was optional equipment.

CHASSIS FEATURES

Wheelbase: 102 inches. Overall length: 177.2 inches. Overall height: 51.6 inches. Overall width: 72.8 inches. Front tread: 57 inches. Rear tread: 59 inches. Ground clearance: Six inches. Tires: 6.70 x 15. Frame: Welded steel box-section, X-braced type. Front suspension: Independent; upper and lower A-arms, unequal-length wishbones; coil springs; anti-roll bar; tubular shocks. Steering: Saginaw recirculating ball, 17:1 ratio; 3.7 turns lock-to-lock; 38.5-foot turning circle. Rear suspension: Live axle on semi-elliptic leaf springs, tubular shock absorbers. Rear axle type: Hypoid semi-floating. Brakes: Four-wheel hydraulic, internal-expanding, 11-inch diameter drums, 157 square inches effective lining area

1958 Corvette design changes include dual headlights and hood louvers

(121 square inches with optional sintered metallic linings). 15-inch steel bolt-on wheels. Standard rear axle ratio with three-speed 3.70:1; with Powerglide: 3.55:1. Optional axle ratios: 4.11:1 and 4.56:1.

OPTIONS

RPO 101 Heater ($96.85). RPO 102 Signal-seeking AM radio ($144.45). RPO 107 Parking brake alarm ($5.40). RPO 108 Courtesy Lights ($6.50). RPO 109 Windshield washer ($16.15). RPO 276 Five 15 x 5.5-inch wheels (no charge). RPO 290 White sidewall tires 6.70 x 15 ($31.55). RPO 313 Powerglide automatic transmission ($188.30). RPO 419 Auxiliary hardtop ($215.20). RPO 426 Electric power windows ($59.20). RPO 440 Optional cove color ($16.15). RPO 469 283-cid 245-hp dual four-barrel carburetor V-8 engine ($150.65). RPO 469C V-8 283-cid 270-hp dual four-barrel carburetor engine ($182.95). RPO 579 V-8 283-cid 250-hp fuel-injection engine ($484.20). RPO 579D V-8 283-cid 290-hp fuel-injection engine ($484.20). RPO 473 Power-operated folding top mechanism ($139.90). RPO 677 Positraction axle with 3.70:1 ratio ($48.45). RPO 678 Positraction axle with 4.11:1 ratio ($48.45). RPO 679 Positraction axle with 4.56:1 ratio ($45). RPO 684 Heavy-duty racing suspension ($780.10). RPO 685 Four-speed manual transmission ($215.20).

HISTORICAL FOOTNOTES

Production of 1958 Corvettes began October 31, 1957. Almost 11 percent of 1958 Corvettes were powered by the 283-cid 290-hp fuel-injected V-8. A 1958 Corvette with the standard 230-hp V-8 and 4.11:1 rear axle could go from 0-to-60 mph in 9.2 seconds. It did the quarter mile in 17.4 seconds at 83 mph and had a top speed of 103 mph. A 1958 Corvette with the optional 250-hp fuel-injected V-8 and 3.70:1 rear axle could go from 0-to-60 mph in 7.6 seconds and from 0-to-100 mph in 21.4 seconds. It did the quarter mile in 15.7 seconds at 90 mph and had a top speed of 120 mph. A 1959 Corvette with the 290-hp fuel-injected engine took only 6.9 seconds to go from 0-to-60 mph and got slightly better gas mileage.

1958 CORVETTE

Model Number	Body/Style Number	Body Type & Seating	Factory Price	Shipping Weight	Production Total
J800	867	2-dr Rds-2P	$3,591	2,781 lbs.	9,168

The 1958 Corvette was similar in many ways to the 1958 model.

CORVETTE SERIES (V-8) SERIES J800

The 1959 Corvette was basically a cleaned-up 1958. The fake hood louvers and vertical chrome strips on the trunk were removed. Interior changes included redesigned bucket seats and door panels, a fiberglass package tray under the sissy bar and concave gauge lenses. A tachometer, outside rearview mirror, seat belts, dual exhaust and electric clock were among the standard features. Sunvisors became optional. New concave instrument lenses reduced reflections. The optional four-speed manual transmission had a T-shaped reverse-lockout shifter with a white plastic shifter knob. There were seven exterior body colors offered: Tuxedo Black (Black or White soft top); Classic Cream (Black or White soft top); Frost Blue (White or Blue soft top); Crown Sapphire (White or Turquoise soft top); Roman Red (Black or White soft top); Snowcrest White (Black, White, Tan or Blue soft top) and Inca Silver (Black or White soft top). Blue, Red, Turquoise, and (for the first time) Black interiors were available. The armrests and door handles were in a different position, the seats had a new shape and a shelf was added.

I.D. NUMBERS

The Vehicle Identification Number (VIN) is located on a plate on the left front door hinge pillar post. For 1959 the numbers were: J59S100001 to J59S109670. The first symbol (J) indicates Corvette. The second and third symbols (59) indicate the model year. The fourth symbol identifies the assembly plant (S = St. Louis, Mo). The last six symbols indicate the sequential production number. Engine code suffixes were: CQ = three-speed manual transmission; CR = three-speed manual transmission and fuel injection; CS = three-speed manual transmission, high-lift camshaft and fuel injection; CT = three-speed manual transmission and dual four-barrel carburetors; CU = three-speed manual transmission, high-lift camshaft and dual four-barrel carburetors; DG = Powerglide automatic transmission; DH = Powerglide automatic transmission and fuel injection and DJ = Powerglide automatic transmission and dual four-barrel carburetors. Cars with optional four-speed manual transmissions used the same engine code suffixes as cars with three-speed manual transmissions. The beginning engine numbers were 0001001 and up at each assembly plant with F = Flint, Mich. and T = Tonawanda, N.Y. The body number plate was located on the engine side of the cowl. The Fisher Body Style Number 59-867 identifies a Corvette. The Body Number is the production serial number of the body. The Trim Number indicates the interior trim color and material. The vinyl upholstery was available in Black, Blue, Red, or Turquoise. The Paint Number indicates the color combination. The 1959 Corvette acrylic lacquer exterior colors offered were No.

The 1959 Corvette listed at $3,875.

502A Frost Blue; No. 503A Tuxedo Black; No. 504A Crown Sapphire; No. 506A Roman Red; No. 508A Classic Cream; No. 509A Inca Silver and No. 510A Snowcrest White. The body side cove could be painted Silver or White.

ENGINES

BASE ENGINE: V-8. Overhead valve. Cast-iron block. Displacement: 283 cid. Bore and stroke: 3.87 x 3.00 inches. Compression ratio: 9.50:1. Brake hp: 230 at 4800 rpm. Five main bearings. Hydraulic valve lifters. Carburetor: Carter Type WCFB four-barrel Model 2816.

OPTIONAL ENGINE: V-8. Overhead valve. Cast-iron block. Displacement: 283 cid. Bore and stroke: 3.87 x 3.00 inches. Compression ratio: 9.50:1. Brake hp: 245. Five main bearings. Carburetor: Two four-barrel carburetors.

OPTIONAL ENGINE: V-8. Overhead valve. Cast-iron block. Displacement: 283 cid. Bore and stroke: 3.87 x 3.00 inches. Compression ratio: 9.50:1. Brake hp: 250. Five main bearings. Induction: Rochester fuel injection.

OPTIONAL ENGINE: V-8. Overhead valve. Cast-iron block. Displacement: 283 cid. Bore and stroke: 3.87 x 3.00 inches. Compression ratio: 9.50:1. Brake hp: 270. Five main bearings. Carburetor: Two four-barrel carburetors.

OPTIONAL ENGINE: V-8. Overhead valve. Cast-iron block. Displacement: 283 cid. Bore and stroke: 3.87 x 3.00 inches. Compression ratio: 10.50:1. Brake hp: 290. Five main bearings. Induction: Rochester fuel injection.

TRANSMISSIONS

STANDARD MANUAL TRANSMISSION: A three-speed manual all-synchromesh transmission with floor-mounted gear shifter was standard equipment.

AUTOMATIC TRANSMISSION: A two-speed Powerglide automatic transmission was optional equipment.

OPTIONAL MANUAL TRANSMISSION: A four-speed manual all-synchromesh transmission with floor-mounted gear shifter was optional equipment.

CHASSIS FEATURES

Wheelbase: 102 inches. Overall length: 177.2 inches. Overall height: 51.6 inches. Overall width: 72.8 inches. Front tread: 57 inches. Rear tread: 59 inches. Ground clearance: six inches. Tires: 6.70 x 15. Frame: Welded steel box-section, X-braced type. Front suspension: Independent; upper and lower A-arms, unequal-length wishbones; coil springs; anti-roll bar; tubular shocks. Steering: Saginaw recirculating ball, 17:1 ratio; 3.7 turns lock-to-lock; 38.5-foot turning circle. Rear suspension: Live axle on semi-elliptic leaf springs, tubular shock absorbers. Rear axle type: Hypoid semi-floating. Brakes: Four-wheel hydraulic, internal-expanding, 11-inch diameter drums, 157 square inches effective lining area (121 square inches with optional sintered metallic linings). 15-inch steel bolt-on wheels. Standard rear axle ratio with three-speed 3.70:1; with Powerglide: 3.55:1. Optional axle ratios: 4.11:1 and 4.56:1.

OPTIONS

Additional cove color ($16.15). RPO 101 Heater ($102.25). RPO 102 Signal-seeking AM radio ($149.80). RPO 107 Parking brake alarm ($5.40). RPO 108 Courtesy lights ($6.50). RPO 109 Windshield washer ($16.15). RPO 261 Sunshades ($10.80). 276 Five 15 x 5.5-inch wheels (No charge). RPO 290 White sidewall tires 6.70 x 15 ($31.55). RPO 313 Powerglide automatic transmission ($199.10). RPO 419 Auxiliary hardtop ($236.75). RPO 426 Electric power windows ($59.20). RPO 269 283-cid 245-hp dual four-barrel carburetor V-8 engine ($150.65). RPO 469C V-8 283-cid 270-hp dual four-barrel carburetor engine ($182.95). RPO 579 V-8 283-cid 250-hp fuel-injection engine ($484.20). RPO 579D V-8 283-cid 290-hp fuel-injection engine ($484.20). RPO 473 Power-operated folding top mechanism ($139.90). RPO 675 Positraction axle with optional ratio ($48.45). RPO 684 Heavy-duty brakes and suspension ($425.05). RPO 685 Four-speed

Jerry Heasley

1959 Corvette with 283-cid V-8

manual transmission ($188.30). RPO 686 Metallic brakes ($26.90)

HISTORICAL FOOTNOTES

A 250-hp fuel-injected 1959 Corvette with the 3.70:1 rear axle could go from 0-to-60 mph in 7.8 seconds. It did the quarter mile in 15.7 seconds at 90 mph and had a top speed of 120 mph. A 290-hp fuel-injected 1959 Corvette with the 4.11:1 rear axle could go from 0-to-60 mph in 6.8 seconds; from 0-to-100 mph in 15.5 seconds. It did the quarter mile in 14.9 seconds at 96 mph and had a top speed of 124 mph. Road & Track described the 1959 Corvette as "a pretty package with all the speed you need and then some."

1959 CORVETTE Model Number	Body/Style Number	Body Type & Seating	Factory Price	Shipping Weight	Production Total
J800	867	2-dr Rds-2P	3875	2912	9670

Jerry Heasley

1959 Corvette in Roman Red

1960 Corvette in Honduras Maroon

CORVETTE SERIES (V-8) SERIES 0800

The 1960 Corvette looked much the same as the previous year's model. A new rear suspension sway bar improved the car's handling. Aluminum cylinder heads and an aluminum radiator were introduced, but later withdrawn. Standard equipment included: tachometer, sun visors, dual exhaust, carpeting, seat belts, outside rearview mirror and electric clock. Buyers could choose from eight exterior finishes: Tuxedo Black (Black, White or Blue soft top); Ermine White (Black, White or Blue soft top); Tasco Turquoise (Black, White or Blue soft top); Horizon Blue (Black, White or Blue soft top); Sateen Silver (Black, White or Blue soft top); Cascade Green (Black, White or Blue soft top); Roman Red (Black or White soft top) and Honduras Maroon (Black soft top). A new aluminum clutch housing cut the Corvette's weight by 18 pounds. A larger-diameter front anti-roll bar and new rear bar enhanced ride and handling characteristics of the 1960 model.

I.D. NUMBERS

The Corvette VIN is embossed on a stainless steel plate welded to the top of the steering column mast under the hood. For 1960 the numbers were: 00867S100001 to 00867S110261. The first symbol (0) indicates the model year 1960. The second and third symbols identify the body series (08 = Corvette). The fourth and fifth symbols indicate the body style number (67 = convertible). The sixth symbol identifies the assembly plant (S = St. Louis, Mo). The last six symbols indicate the sequential production number. Engine code suffixes were: CQ = 283-cid 230-hp V-8 with 9.5:1 compression ratio, manual transmission and four-barrel carburetor; CR = 283-cid 275-hp V-8 with 11.0:1 compression ratio, manual transmission and fuel-injection; CS = 283-cid 315-hp V-8 with 11.0:1 compression ratio, manual transmission and fuel injection; CT = 283-cid 245-hp V-8 with 9.5:1 compression ratio, manual transmission and two four-barrel carburetors; CU =

Karen O' Brien

1960 Corvette interior with four-speed

1960 Corvette, one of 280 painted Sateen Silver with a white cove.

283-cid 270-hp V-8 with 9.5:1 compression ratio, manual transmission and two four-barrel carburetors; DG = 283-cid 230-hp V-8 with 9.5:1 compression ratio, Powerglide automatic transmission and four-barrel carburetor and DJ = 283-cid 245-hp V-8 with 9.5:1 compression ratio, Powerglide automatic transmission and two four-barrel carburetors. The beginning engine numbers were 0001001 and up at each assembly plant with F = Flint, Mich. and T = Tonawanda, N.Y. Corvette engines have the last six digits of the VIN stamped on the block next to the engine number. The body number plate was located on the engine side of the cowl. The Fisher Body Style Number 60-0867 identifies a Corvette. The Body Number is the production serial number of the body. The Trim Number indicates the interior trim color and material. The vinyl upholstery was available in Black, Blue, Red, or Turquoise. The Paint Number indicates the color combination. The 1960 Corvette exterior colors offered were No. 502A Horizon Blue; No. 504A Tasco Turquoise; No. 506A Roman Red; No. 509A Sateen Silver; No. 510A Ermine White; No. 517A Cascade Green and No. 523A Honduras Maroon. The body side cove could be painted Silver or White.

ENGINES

BASE ENGINE: V-8. Overhead valve. Cast-iron block. Displacement: 283 cid. Bore and stroke: 3.87 x 3.00 inches. Compression ratio: 9.50:1. Brake hp: 230 at 4800 rpm. Five main bearings. Hydraulic valve lifters. Carburetor: Carter Type WCFB four-barrel Model 3779178.

OPTIONAL ENGINE: V-8. Overhead valve. Cast-iron block. Displacement: 283 cid. Bore and stroke: 3.87 x 3.00 inches. Compression ratio: 9.50:1. Brake hp: 245. Five

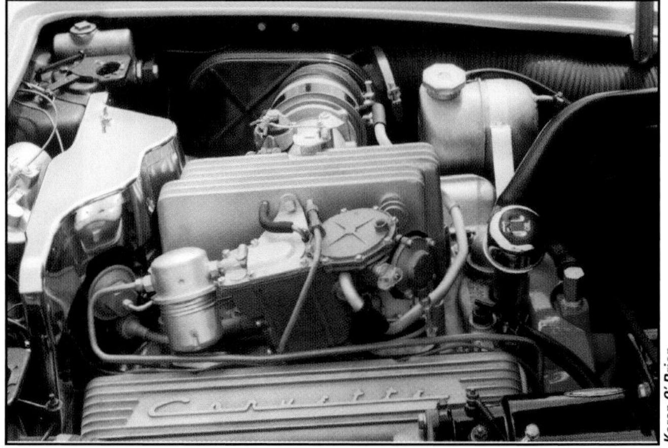

Karen O' Brien

1960 Corvette 283-cid fuel-injected V-8 engine

Karen O' Brien

1960 Corvette convertible, one of 65 in Cascade Green with white cove main bearings. Hydraulic valve lifters. Carburetor: Two four-barrel carburetors.

OPTIONAL ENGINE: V-8. Overhead valve. Cast-iron block. Displacement: 283 cid. Bore and stroke: 3.87 x 3.00 inches. Compression ratio: 9.50:1. Brake hp: 270. Five main bearings. Hydraulic valve lifters. Carburetor: Two four-barrel carburetors.

OPTIONAL ENGINE: V-8. Overhead valve. Cast-iron block. Displacement: 283 cid. Bore and stroke: 3.87 x 3.00 inches. Compression ratio: 11.00:1. Brake hp: 275. Five main bearings. Hydraulic valve lifters. Induction: Rochester fuel injection.

OPTIONAL ENGINE: V-8. Overhead valve. Cast-iron block. Displacement: 283 cid. Bore and stroke: 3.87 x 3.00 inches. Compression ratio: 11.00:1. Brake hp: 315 at 6200 rpm. Five main bearings. Solid valve lifters. Induction: Rochester fuel injection.

TRANSMISSIONS

STANDARD MANUAL TRANSMISSION: A three-speed manual all-synchromesh transmission with floor-mounted gear shifter was standard equipment.

AUTOMATIC TRANSMISSION: A two-speed Powerglide automatic transmission was optional equipment.

OPTIONAL MANUAL TRANSMISSION: A four-speed manual all-synchromesh transmission with floor-mounted gear shifter was optional equipment.

CHASSIS FEATURES

Wheelbase: 102 inches. Overall length: 177.2 inches. Overall height: 51.6 inches. Overall width: 72.8 inches. Front tread: 57 inches. Rear tread: 59 inches. Ground clearance: Six inches. Tires: 6.70 x 15. Frame: Welded steel box-section, X-braced type. Front suspension: Independent; upper and lower A-arms, unequal-length wishbones; coil springs; anti-roll bar; tubular shocks. Steering: Saginaw recirculating ball, 17:1 ratio; 3.7 turns lock-to-lock; 38.5-foot turning circle. Rear suspension: Live axle on semi-elliptic leaf springs, tubular shock absorbers. Rear axle type: Hypoid semi-floating. Brakes: Four-wheel hydraulic, internal-expanding, 11-inch diameter drums, 157 square inches effective lining area (121 square inches with optional sintered metallic linings). 15-inch steel bolt-on wheels. Standard rear axle ratio with three-speed 3.70:1; with Powerglide: 3.55:1. Optional axle ratios: 4.11:1 and 4.56:1.

OPTIONS

Additional cove color ($16.15). RPO 101 Heater ($102.25). RPO 102 Signal-seeking AM radio ($137.75). RPO 107 Parking brake alarm ($5.40). RPO 108 Courtesy Lights ($6.50). RPO 109 Windshield washer ($16.15). RPO 121 Temperature control radiator fan ($21.55). RPO 261 Sunshades ($10.80). RPO 276 Five 15 x 5.5-inch wheels (No charge). RPO 290 White sidewall tires 6.70 x 15, four-ply ($31.55). RPO 313 Powerglide automatic transmission ($199.10). RPO 419 Auxiliary hardtop ($236.75). RPO 426 Electric power windows ($59.20). RPO 469 283-cid 245-hp dual four-barrel carburetor V-8 engine ($150.65). RPO 469C V-8 283-cid 270-hp dual four-barrel carburetor engine ($182.95). RPO 579 V-8 283-cid 275-hp fuel-injection engine ($484.20). RPO 579D V-8 283-cid 315-hp fuel-injection engine ($484.20). RPO 473 Power-operated folding top mechanism ($139.90). RPO 675 Positraction axle with optional ratio ($43.05). RPO 685 Four-speed manual transmission ($188.30). RPO 686 Metallic brakes ($26.90). RPO 687 Heavy-duty brakes and suspension ($333.60). RPO 1408 Five 6.70 x 15 Nylon tires ($15.75). RPO 1625A 24-gallon fuel tank ($161.40).

HISTORICAL FOOTNOTES

The majority of 1960 Corvettes, 50.1 percent, were sold with a detachable hardtop. Most, 51.9 percent, also had a four-speed manual transmission. A 1960 Corvette with the 283-cid 230-hp V-8 could go from 0-to-60 in 8.4 seconds and did the quarter mile in 16.1 seconds at 89 mph. The Route 66 television series, featuring Martin Milner and George Maharis driving their 1960 Corvette across the country on the "Mother Road" debuted this season.

1960 CORVETTE

Model Number	Body/Style Number	Body Type & Seating	Factory Price	Shipping Weight	Production Total
0800	67	2-dr Conv-2P	$3,872	2,840 lbs.	10,261

Nicky Wright

The 1961 Corvette with redesigned grille

CORVETTE SERIES (V-8) SERIES 0800

The badge on the front of the 1961 Corvette was a crossed flag over a "V." A refined, thin, vertical and horizontal bar grille and duck-tail rear end treatment with four cylindrical taillights quickly set the new 1961 Corvette apart from its predecessor. This design was a predecessor to the Sting Ray coming in 1963 and added more space to the Corvette's trunk. The rear emblem had a spun silver background with the crossed flags over a "V" design and the words "Chevrolet Corvette." The exhaust now exited under the car, rather than through bumper ports. Standard equipment included: tachometer; seat belts; sun visors; dual exhaust; carpeting; electric clock, an outside rearview mirror, a lockable rear-seat storage area and a new aluminum radiator. A temperature-controlled radiator fan was also made standard. Seven exterior colors were available: Tuxedo Black (Black or White soft top); Ermine White (Black or White soft top); Roman Red (Black or White soft top); Sateen Silver (Black or White soft top); Jewel Blue (Black or White soft top); Fawn Beige (Black or White soft top); Honduras Maroon (Black or White soft top).

I.D. NUMBERS

The Corvette VIN is embossed on a stainless steel plate welded to the top of the steering column mast under the hood. For 1961 the numbers were: 10867S100001 to 10867S110939. The first symbol (1) indicates the model year 1961. The second and third symbols identify the body series (08 = Corvette). The fourth and fifth symbols indicate the body style number (67 = convertible). The sixth symbol identifies the assembly plant (S = St. Louis, Mo). The last six symbols indicate the sequential production number. Engine code suffixes were: CQ = 283-cid 230-hp V-8 with 9.5:1 compression ratio, manual transmission

Nicky Wright

Sun shades were standard.

1961 Corvette in Sateen Silver

and four-barrel carburetor; CR = 283-cid 275-hp V-8 with 11.0:1 compression ratio, manual transmission and fuel-injection; CS = 283-cid 315-hp V-8 with 11.0:1 compression ratio, manual transmission and fuel-injection; CT = 283-cid 245-hp V-8 with 9.5:1 compression ratio, manual transmission and two four-barrel carburetors; CU = 283-cid 270-hp V-8 with 9.5:1 compression ratio, manual transmission and two four-barrel carburetors; DG = 283-cid 230-hp V-8 with 9.5:1 compression ratio, Powerglide automatic transmission and four-barrel carburetor and DJ = 283-cid 245-hp V-8 with 9.5:1 compression ratio, Powerglide automatic transmission and two four-barrel carburetors. The beginning engine numbers were 0001001 and up at each assembly plant with F = Flint, Mich. and T = Tonawanda, N.Y. Corvette engines have the last six digits of the VIN stamped on the block next to the engine number. The body number plate was located on the engine side of the cowl. The Fisher Body Style Number 61-0867 identifies a Corvette. The Body Number is the production serial number of the body. The Trim Number indicates the interior trim color and material. The vinyl upholstery was available in Black, Red, Fawn or Blue. The Paint Number indicates the color combination. The 1961 "Magic Mirror" acrylic lacquer exterior colors were: No. 900 Tuxedo Black; No. 912 Jewel Blue; No. 920 Fawn Beige; No. 923 Roman Red; No. 936 Ermine White; No. 940 Sateen Silver and No. 948 Honduras Maroon.

ENGINES

BASE ENGINE: V-8. Overhead valve. Cast-iron block. Displacement: 283 cid. Bore and stroke: 3.87 x 3.00 inches. Compression ratio: 9.50:1. Brake hp: 230 at 4800 rpm. Five main bearings. Hydraulic valve lifters. Carburetor: Carter Type WCFB four-barrel Model 3779178.

OPTIONAL ENGINE: V-8. Overhead valve. Cast-iron block. Displacement: 283 cid. Bore and stroke: 3.87 x 3.00 inches. Compression ratio: 9.50:1. Brake hp: 245. Five main bearings. Hydraulic valve lifters. Carburetor: Two four-barrel carburetors.

OPTIONAL ENGINE: V-8. Overhead valve. Cast-iron block. Displacement: 283 cid. Bore and stroke: 3.87 x 3.00 inches. Compression ratio: 9.50:1. Brake hp: 270. Five main bearings. Hydraulic valve lifters. Carburetor: Two four-barrel carburetors.

OPTIONAL ENGINE: V-8. Overhead valve. Cast-iron block. Displacement: 283 cid. Bore and stroke: 3.87 x 3.00 inches. Compression ratio: 11.00:1. Brake hp: 275. Five main bearings. Hydraulic valve lifters. Induction: Rochester fuel injection.

OPTIONAL ENGINE: V-8. Overhead valve. Cast-iron block. Displacement: 283 cid. Bore and stroke: 3.87 x 3.00 inches. Compression ratio: 11.00:1. Brake hp: 315 at 6200 rpm. Five main bearings. Solid valve lifters. Induction: Rochester fuel injection.

TRANSMISSIONS

STANDARD MANUAL TRANSMISSION: A three-speed manual all-synchromesh transmission with floor-mounted gear shifter was standard equipment.

AUTOMATIC TRANSMISSION: A two-speed Powerglide automatic transmission was optional equipment.

Nicky Wright

1961 Corvette

OPTIONAL MANUAL TRANSMISSION: A four-speed manual all-synchromesh transmission with floor-mounted gear shifter was optional equipment.

CHASSIS FEATURES

Wheelbase: 102 inches. Overall length: 177.2 inches. Overall height: 51.6 inches. Overall width: 72.8 inches. Front tread: 57 inches. Rear tread: 58.8 inches. Ground clearance: Six inches. Tires: 6.70 x 15. Frame: Welded steel box-section, X-braced type. Front suspension: Independent; upper and lower A-arms, unequal-length wishbones; Coil springs; anti-roll bar; tubular shocks. Steering: Saginaw recirculating ball, 17:1 ratio; 3.7 turns lock-to-lock; 38.5-foot turning circle. Rear suspension: Live axle on semi-elliptic leaf springs, tubular shock absorbers. Rear axle type: Hypoid semi-floating. Brakes: Four-wheel hydraulic, internal-expanding, 11-inch diameter drums, 157 square inches effective lining area (121 square inches with optional sintered metallic linings). 15-inch steel bolt-on wheels. Standard rear axle ratio with three-speed 3.36:1.

OPTIONS

Additional cove color ($16.15). RPO 101 Heater ($102.25). RPO 102 Signal-seeking AM radio ($137.75). RPO 276 Five 15 x 5.5-inch wheels (No charge). RPO 290 White sidewall tires 6.70 x 15, four-ply ($31.55). RPO 313 Powerglide automatic transmission ($199.10). RPO 419 Auxiliary hardtop ($236.75). RPO 426 Electric power windows ($59.20). RPO 441 Direct-Flow exhaust system (no charge). RPO 469 283-cid 245-hp dual four-barrel carburetor V-8 engine ($150.65). RPO 468 V-8 283-cid 270-hp dual four-barrel carburetor engine ($182.95). RPO 353 V-8 283-cid 275-hp fuel-injection engine ($484.20). RPO 354 V-8 283-cid 315-hp fuel-injection engine ($484.20). RPO 473 Power-operated folding top mechanism ($161.40). RPO 675 Positraction axle with optional ratio ($43.05). RPO 685 Four-speed manual transmission ($188.30). RPO 686 Metallic brakes ($37.70). RPO 687 Heavy-duty brakes and suspension ($333.60). RPO 1408 Five 6.70 x 15 Nylon tires ($15.75). RPO 1625A 24-gallon fuel tank ($161.40).

HISTORICAL FOOTNOTES

Most 1961 Corvettes, 51.98 percent, came with a detachable hardtop and 64.1 percent had a four-speed manual transmission. This was the last year wide whitewall tires were available. A 1961 Corvette with a 283-cid 315-hp solid-lifter fuel-injected V-8 and the 3.70:1 rear axle could go from 0-to-30 mph in 2.6 seconds; from 0-to-60 mph in 6.0 seconds and from 0-to-100 mph in 14.2 seconds. It did the quarter mile in 15.5 seconds at 106 mph and had a maximum speed of 140 mph. This was the last year a contrasting color could be ordered from the factory for the side coves.

1961 CORVETTE

Model Number	Body/Style Number	Body Type & Seating	Factory Price	Shipping Weight	Production Total
0800	67	2-dr Conv-2P	$3,934	2,840 lbs.	10,939

Jerry Heasley

1962 Corvette Gulf Oil Race Car

CORVETTE SERIES (V-8) SERIES 0800

The most noticeable changes for 1962 were the removal of the side cove chrome trim, a blacked-out grille and ribbed chrome rocker panel molding. For the first time since 1955, Corvettes were offered in solid colors only. Standard features included: electric clock; dual exhaust; tachometer; heater and defroster; seat belts; outside rearview mirror and windshield washer. The wheels were available in Black, Beige, Red, Silver or Maroon. The last time buyers had a choice of wheel colors was in 1957. In following years, wheels would be offered in only a single color. Seven exterior colors were available: Tuxedo Black (Black or White soft top); Ermine White (Black or White soft top); Roman Red (Black or White soft top); Sateen Silver (Black or White soft top); Fawn Beige (Black or White soft top); Honduras Maroon (Black or White soft top); Almond Beige (Black or White top).

I.D. NUMBERS

The Corvette VIN is embossed on a stainless steel plate welded to the top of the steering column mast under the hood. For 1962 the numbers were: 20867S100001 to 20867S114531. The first symbol (2) indicates the model year 1962. The second and third symbols identify the body series (08 = Corvette). The fourth and fifth symbols indicate the body style number (67 = convertible). The sixth symbol identifies the assembly plant (S = St. Louis, Mo). The last six symbols indicate the sequential production number. Engine code suffixes were: RC = 327-cid 250-hp V-8 with 10.5:1 compression ratio, manual transmission and four-barrel carburetor; RD = 327-cid 300-hp V-8 with 10.5:1 compression ratio, manual transmission and four-barrel carburetor; RE = 327-cid 340-hp V-8 with 11.25:1 compression ratio, manual transmission and four-barrel carburetor; RF = 327-cid 360-hp V-8 with 11.25:1 compression ratio, manual transmission and fuel injection; SC = 327-cid 250-hp V-8 with 10.5:1 compression ratio, Powerglide automatic transmission and four-barrel carburetor and SD = 327-cid 300-hp V-8 with 10.5:1

Jerry Heasley

1962 Corvette with narrow whitewall tires

Jerry Heasley

1962 Corvette

compression ratio, Powerglide automatic transmission and four-barrel carburetor. The beginning engine numbers were 0001001 and up at each assembly plant with F = Flint, Mich. and T = Tonawanda, N.Y. Corvette engines have the last six digits of the VIN stamped on the block next to the engine number. The body number plate was located on the engine side of the cowl. The Fisher Body Style Number 62-0867 identifies a Corvette. The Body Number is the production serial number of the body. The Trim Number indicates the interior trim color and material. The vinyl upholstery was available in Black, Red or Fawn. The Paint Number indicates the color combination. The 1962 "Magic Mirror" acrylic lacquer exterior colors were: No. 900 Tuxedo Black; No. 920 Fawn Beige (Autumn Gold); No. 923 Roman Red; No. 936 Ermine White; No. 938 Almond Beige; No. 940 Sateen Silver and No. 948 Honduras Maroon.

ENGINES

BASE ENGINE: V-8. Overhead valve. Cast-iron block. Displacement: 327 cid. Bore and stroke: 4.00 x 3.25 inches. Compression ratio: 10.5:1. Brake hp: 250 at 4400 rpm. Five main bearings. Hydraulic valve lifters. Carburetor: Carter Type AFB four-barrel Model 3788246.

OPTIONAL ENGINE: V-8. Overhead valve. Cast-iron block. Displacement: 327 cid. Bore and stroke: 4.00 x 3.25 inches. Compression ratio: 10.5:1. Brake hp: 300. Five main bearings. Hydraulic valve lifters. Carburetor: Carter Type AFB four-barrel.

OPTIONAL ENGINE: V-8. Overhead valve. Cast-iron block. Displacement: 327 cid. Bore and stroke: 4.00 x 3.25 inches. Compression ratio: 11.25:1. Brake hp: 340. Five main bearings. Hydraulic valve lifters. Carburetor: Carter Type AFB four-barrel.

OPTIONAL ENGINE: V-8. Overhead valve. Cast-iron block. Displacement: 327 cid. Bore and stroke: 4.00 x 3.25 inches. Compression ratio: 11.25:1. Brake hp: 360. Five main bearings. Hydraulic valve lifters. Induction: Fuel injection.

TRANSMISSIONS

STANDARD MANUAL TRANSMISSION: A three-speed manual all-synchromesh transmission with floor-mounted gear shifter was standard equipment.

AUTOMATIC TRANSMISSION: A two-speed Powerglide automatic transmission was optional equipment.

OPTIONAL MANUAL TRANSMISSION: A four-speed manual all-synchromesh transmission with floor-mounted gear shifter was optional equipment.

CHASSIS FEATURES: Wheelbase: 102 inches. Overall length: 177.2 inches. Overall height: 52.1 inches with hardtop. Overall width: 72.8 inches. Front tread: 57 inches. Rear tread: 58.8 inches. Ground clearance: Six and 7/10 inches. Tires: 6.70 x 15. Hardtop weight: 55 pounds. Interior hip room: 59.6 inches. Hat room: 42.3 inches. Leg room: 46.5 inches. Shoulder room: 49.4 inches. Trunk room: 12.1 cubic feet. Frame: Welded steel box-section, X-braced type. Front suspension: Independent; upper and lower A-arms, unequal-length wishbones; coil springs; anti-roll bar; tubular shocks. Steering: Saginaw recirculating ball, 21:1 ratio; 3.7 turns lock-to-lock; 38.5-

foot turning circle. Rear suspension: Live axle on semi-elliptic leaf springs, tubular shock absorbers. Rear axle type: Hypoid semi-floating. Brakes: Four-wheel hydraulic, internal-expanding, 11-inch diameter drums, 327 square inches effective lining area. 15-inch steel bolt-on wheels. Standard rear axle ratio with three-speed 3.36:1.

OPTIONS

RPO 102 Signal-seeking AM radio ($137.75). RPO 276 Five 15 x 5.5-inch wheels (No charge). RPO 313 Powerglide automatic transmission ($199.10). RPO 419 Auxiliary hardtop ($236.75). RPO 426 Electric power windows ($59.20). RPO 441 Direct-Flow exhaust system (no charge). RPO 473 Power-operated folding top mechanism ($161.40). RPO 583 327-cid 300-hp V-8 engine ($53.80). RPO 396 327-cid 340-hp V-8 engine ($107.60). RPO 582 327-cid 370-hp fuel-injected V-8 engine ($484.20). RPO 675 Positraction axle with optional ratio ($43.05). RPO 685 Four-speed manual transmission ($188.30). RPO 686 Metallic brakes ($37.70). RPO 687 Heavy-duty brakes and suspension ($333.60). RPO 1832 Five 6.70 x 15 white sidewall tires ($31.55). RPO 1833 Five 6.70 x 15 Nylon tires ($15.75).

Jerry Heasley

1962 Corvette Gulf Oil Race Car

HISTORICAL FOOTNOTES

A 1962 Corvette with a 327-cid 360-hp fuel-injected V-8 and the 3.70:1 rear axle could go from 0-to-30 mph in 2.5 seconds; from 0-to-60 mph in 5.9 seconds and from 0-to-100 mph in 13.5 seconds. It did the quarter mile in 14.5 seconds at 104 mph and had an estimated maximum speed of 150 mph.

1962 CORVETTE Model Number	Body/Style Number	Body Type & Seating	Factory Price	Shipping Weight	Production Total
0800	67	2-dr Conv-2P	$4,038	2,925 lbs.	14,531

Jerry Heasley

1962 Corvette convertible

Nicky Wright

1963 Corvette split-window coupe with standard wheel covers

CORVETTE STING RAY SERIES (V-8) SERIES 0800

The Corvette received major restyling in 1963, including a divided rear window for a new "split-window" fastback coupe. The sides of the front fenders, behind the wheel openings, were decorated with two long, horizontal "wind split" indentations or louvers that were designed to look like brake cooling ducts, although they were not functional. The rear deck treatment resembled that of the previous year's model, but the rest of the car appeared totally new. The twin side-by-side headlights were hidden in an electrically-operated panel. This was more than a styling gimmick, as it added to the car's basic aerodynamic design. The recessed fake hood louvers were another matter. Front fender louvers, vents on the roof side panels (of the fastback "split-window" sport coupe) and ribbed rocker panel molding were styling features used on the sides of the new Corvette. The interior had circular gauges with black faces. There was storage space under the seats of early models. Among the standard equipment was windshield washer; carpeting; outside rearview mirror; dual exhaust; tachometer; electric clock; heater and defroster; cigarette lighter; and safety belts. Seven interior colors were offered: Black, White, Silver, Silver-Blue, Daytona blue, Red and Tan. For the first time since 1957, a Beige softtop was available. Seven exterior colors were available: Tuxedo Black; Ermine White; Riverside Red; Silver Blue; Daytona Blue; Saddle Tan and Sebring Silver. All were available with a Black, White, or Beige soft top.

I.D. NUMBERS

The Corvette VIN is embossed on a stainless steel plate welded to the right side hinge pillar cross-brace under the glove box. For 1963 the numbers were: [Convertibles] 30867S100001 to 30867S121513; [Coupes] 30837S100001

Nicky Wright

1963 was the first year for hidden headlights

to 30837S121513. The first symbol (3) indicates the model year 1963. The second and third symbols identify the body series (08 = Corvette). The fourth and fifth symbols indicate the body style number (67 = convertible; 37 = "split-window" coupe). The sixth symbol identifies the assembly plant (S = St. Louis, Mo). The last six symbols indicate the sequential production number. Engine code suffixes were: RC = 327-cid 250-hp V-8 with 10.5:1 compression ratio, manual transmission and four-barrel carburetor; RD = 327-cid 300-hp V-8 with 10.5:1 compression ratio, manual transmission and four-barrel carburetor; RE = 327-cid 340-hp V-8 with 11.25:1 compression ratio, manual transmission and four-barrel carburetor; RF = 327-cid 360-hp V-8 with 11.25:1 compression ratio, manual transmission and fuel injection; SC = 327-cid 250-hp V-8 with 10.5:1 compression ratio, automatic transmission and four-barrel carburetor and SD = 327-cid 300-hp V-8 with 10.5:1 compression ratio, automatic transmission and four-barrel carburetor. The beginning engine numbers were 0001001 and up at each assembly plant with F = Flint, Mich. and T = Tonawanda, N.Y. Corvette engines have the last six digits of the VIN stamped on the block next to the engine number. The body number plate was located on the engine side of the cowl. The Fisher Body Style Number 62-0867 identifies a Corvette Sting Ray convertible and the Fisher Body Style Number 62-0837 identifies a Corvette Sting Ray "split-window" coupe. The Body Number is the production serial number of the body. The Trim Number indicates the interior trim color and material. The vinyl upholstery was available in Black, Red, Saddle Tan and Dark Blue. Two Saddle Tan leather upholstery options were offered. Vinyl upholstery (codes) and color choices for coupes were (STD/BLK) Black; (490 A, 490 J) Dark Blue; (S, XE, XG) Dark Blue; (490 C, 490 L) Red; (Q, XA, XC) Red; (490 E, 490 N) Saddle Tan and (U, XJ, XL) Saddle Tan. Leather upholstery (codes) and color choices for coupes were (898A, 898E) Saddle Tan and (Q, G, S) Saddle Tan. Vinyl upholstery (codes) and color choices for convertibles were (STD/BLK) Black; (490 B, 490 K) Dark Blue; (T, XF, XH) Dark Blue; (490 D, 490 M) Red; (R, XB, XD) Red; (490 F, 490 P) Saddle Tan and (V, XK, XM) Saddle Tan. Leather upholstery (codes) and color choices for coupes were (898B, 898F) Saddle Tan and (R, H, T) Saddle Tan. The Paint Number indicates the color combination. The 1961 "Magic Mirror" acrylic lacquer exterior colors were: No. 900 Tuxedo Black; No. 912 Silver Blue; No. 916 Daytona Blue; No. 923 Riverside Red; No. 932 Saddle Tan; No. 936 Ermine White and No. 941 Sebring Silver.

ENGINES

BASE ENGINE: V-8. Overhead valve. Cast-iron block. Displacement: 327 cid. Bore and stroke: 4.00 x 3.25 inches. Compression ratio: 10.5:1. Brake hp: 250 at 4400 rpm. Torque: 350 lbs.-ft. at 2800 rpm. Five main bearings. Hydraulic valve lifters. Carburetor: Carter Type WCFB four-barrel Model 3501S.

OPTIONAL ENGINE: [RPO L75] V-8. Overhead valve. Cast-iron block. Displacement: 327 cid. Bore and stroke: 4.00 x 3.25 inches. Compression ratio: 10.5:1. Brake

Nicky Wright

1963 Corvette convertible

hp: 300 at 5000 rpm. Torque: 360 lbs.-ft. at 3200 rpm. Five main bearings. Hydraulic valve lifters. Carburetor: Carter aluminum Type AFB four-barrel.

OPTIONAL ENGINE: [RPO L76] V-8. Overhead valve. Cast-iron block. Displacement: 327 cid. Bore and stroke: 4.00 x 3.25 inches. Compression ratio: 11.25:1. Brake hp: 340 at 6000 rpm. Torque: 344 lbs.-ft. at 4000 rpm. Five main bearings. Mechanical valve lifters. Duntov camshaft. Carburetor: Carter aluminum Type AFB four-barrel.

OPTIONAL ENGINE: [RPO L84] V-8. Overhead valve. Cast-iron block. Displacement: 327 cid. Bore and stroke: 4.00 x 3.25 inches. Compression ratio: 11.25:1. Brake hp: 360 at 6000 rpm. Torque: 352 lbs.-ft. at 4000 rpm. Five main bearings. Mechanical valve lifters. Duntov camshaft. Induction: Ram-Jet fuel injection.

TRANSMISSIONS

STANDARD MANUAL TRANSMISSION: A three-speed manual all-synchromesh transmission with floor-mounted gear shifter was standard equipment.

AUTOMATIC TRANSMISSION: A two-speed Powerglide automatic transmission with floor-mounted gear shifter was optional equipment.

OPTIONAL MANUAL TRANSMISSION: A four-speed manual all-synchromesh transmission with floor-mounted gear shifter was optional equipment.

CHASSIS FEATURES: Wheelbase: 98 inches. Overall length: [Convertible] 175.2 inches [Coupe] 175.3 inches. Overall height: [Coupe] 49.8 inches. Overall width: 69.6 inches. Front tread: 56.3 inches. Rear tread: 57.0 inches. Ground clearance: Five inches. Tires: 6.70 x 15. Frame: Full-length ladder type with five cross members and separate body. Front suspension: Independent; upper and lower A-arms, unequal-length wishbones; coil springs; anti-roll bar; tubular shocks. Steering: Saginaw recirculating ball, 17:1 ratio; 3.4 turns lock-to-lock. Rear suspension: Independent with fixed differential; nine leaf springs; lateral struts and universally-jointed axle shafts; radius arms and direct-acting shock absorbers. Rear axle type: Hypoid semi-floating. Brakes: Hydraulic, duo-servo, self-adjusting with sintered iron linings and cast-iron drums. Drum diameter [Front]: 11 x 2.75 inches; [Rear]: 11 x 2.0 inches. Total swept area: 134.9 square inches. 15-inch five-lug steel disc wheels. Standard rear axle ratio 3.70:1.

OPTIONS

RPO 898 Genuine leather seat trim ($80). RPO 941 Sebring Silver exterior paint ($80.70). RPO A01 Soft-Ray tinted glass, all windows ($16.15). RPO A02 Soft-Ray tinted glass, windshield ($10). RPO 431 Electric power windows ($59.20). RPO C07 Auxiliary hardtop for convertible ($236.75). RPO C48 Heater and defroster deletion ($100 credit). RPO C60 Air conditioning ($421.80). RPO G81 Positraction rear axle, all ratios ($43.05). RPO G91 Special 3.08:1 "highway" ratio rear axle ($2.20). RPO J50 Power brakes ($43.05). RPO J65 Sintered metallic brakes

Jerry Heasley

1963 Corvette Z06 race car

Jerry Heasley

1963 Corvette coupe

($37.70). RPO L75 327-cid 300-hp V-8 ($53.80). RPO L76 327-cid 340-hp V-8 ($107.60). RPO L84 327-cid 370-hp fuel-injected V-8 ($430.40). RPO M20 Four-speed manual transmission ($188.30). RPO M35 Powerglide automatic transmission ($199.10). RPO N03 36-gallon fuel tank for "split-window" coupe only ($202.30). RPO N11 Off-road exhaust system ($37.70). RPO N34 Woodgrained plastic steering wheel ($16.15). RPO N40 Power steering ($75.35). RPO P48 Special cast-aluminum knock-off wheels ($322.80). RPO P91 Nylon tires, 6.70 x 15 black sidewall ($15.70). RPO P92 Rayon tires, 6.70 x 15, white sidewall ($31.55). RPO T86 Back-up lamps ($10.80). RPO U65 Signal-seeking AM radio ($137.75). RPO U69 AM-FM radio ($174.35). RPO Z06 Special performance equipment for "split-window" coupe ($1,818.45).

HISTORICAL FOOTNOTES

The Corvette Sting Ray evolved from a racing car called the Mitchell Sting Ray. William L. Mitchell had replaced Harley Earl as head of General Motors styling in 1958. Mitchell thought it was important for the Corvette to be associated with racing, so he persuaded Chevrolet general manager Ed Cole to sell him the chassis of the 1957 Corvette SS "mule" for $1 (to get around the corporate racing ban) so he could build a race car. Mitchell had designer Larry Shinoda create a body for the Sting Ray race car inspired by the sea creature of the same name. Shinoda came up with the "split-window" coupe design, which Mitchell loved although Zora Arkus-Duntov was against its vision-blocking look. The "split-window" was offered only one year and has become a very collectible item. Corvette "firsts" for 1963 included optional knock-off wheels, air conditioning and leather upholstery. Air conditioning was a rare option in 1963 because it was introduced late in the year. Only 1.3 percent of the 1963 Corvettes were so-equipped. However, 83.5 percent came with four-speed manual transmission. The L84-powered Corvette could go from 0-to-60 mph in 5.9 seconds and from 0-to-100 mph in 16.5 seconds. Five historic Corvette Grand Sports were constructed in 1963 before all GM racing programs were canceled. Grand Sports weighed 1,908 pounds and had a 377-cid version of the small-block Chevy V-8 equipped with an aluminum cylinder block and aluminum hemi-head cylinder heads. They also featured a twin ignition system and port fuel injection.

Jerry Heasley

1963 Corvette Grand Sport

1963 CORVETTE

Model Number	Body/Style Number	Body Type & Seating	Factory Price	Shipping Weight	Production Total
0800	37	2-dr FsBk Cpe-2P	$4,257	3,150 lbs.	10,549
0800	67	2-dr Conv-2P	$4,037	2,881 lbs.	10,919

Jerry Heasley

1964 Corvette coupe with optional cast-aluminum wheels

CORVETTE STING RAY SERIES (V-8) SERIES 0800

Styling was cleaned up a bit for 1964. The previous year's distinctive rear window divider was replaced by a solid piece of glass. The fake hood vents were eliminated and the roof vents were restyled. A three-speed fan was available in the coupe to aid in ventilation. Seven exterior colors were available: Tuxedo Black; Ermine White; Riverside Red; Satin Silver; Silver Blue; Daytona Blue and Saddle Tan. All were available with a Black, White or Beige soft top.

I.D. NUMBERS

The Corvette VIN is embossed on a stainless steel plate welded to the right side hinge pillar cross-brace under the glove box. For 1964 the numbers were: [Convertibles] 40867S100001 to 40867S122229; [Coupes] 40837S100001 to 40837S122229. The first symbol (4) indicates the model year 1964. The second and third symbols identify the body series (08 = Corvette). The fourth and fifth symbols indicate the body style number (67 = convertible; 37 = coupe). The sixth symbol identifies the assembly plant (S = St. Louis, Mo). The last six symbols indicate the sequential production number. Engine code suffixes were: RC = 327-cid 250-hp V-8 with 10.5:1 compression ratio, manual transmission and four-barrel carburetor; RD = 327-cid 300-hp V-8 with 10.5:1 compression ratio, manual transmission or high-performance manual transmission and four-barrel carburetor; RE = 327-cid 365-hp V-8 with 11.00:1 compression ratio, manual transmission or special high-performance manual transmission and four-barrel carburetor; RF = 327-cid 375-hp V-8 with 11.00:1 compression ratio, manual transmission and fuel injection; RP = 327-cid 250-hp V-8 with 10.5:1

Nicky Wright

1964 Corvette convertible, one of 13,925 produced

Nicky Wright

1964 Corvette convertible with standard wheel covers

compression ratio, manual transmission, four-barrel carburetor and air conditioning; RQ = 327-cid 300-hp V-8 with 10.5:1 compression ratio, manual transmission, four-barrel carburetor and air conditioning; RR = 327-cid 365-hp V-8 with 11.00:1 compression ratio, manual transmission or special high-performance manual transmission, four-barrel carburetor and air conditioning; RT = 327-cid 365-hp V-8 with 11.00:1 compression ratio, manual transmission and four-barrel carburetor; RU = 327-cid 365-hp V-8 with 11.00:1 compression ratio, manual transmission, four-barrel carburetor and air conditioning; RX = 327-cid 375-hp V-8 with 11.00:1 compression ratio, manual transmission and fuel injection; SC = 327-cid 250-hp V-8 with 10.5:1 compression ratio, automatic transmission and four-barrel carburetor; SD = 327-cid 300-hp V-8 with 10.5:1 compression ratio, automatic transmission and four-barrel carburetor. SK = 327-cid 250-hp V-8 with 10.5:1 compression ratio, automatic transmission, four-barrel carburetor and air conditioning; SL = 327-cid 300-hp V-8 with 10.5:1 compression ratio, automatic transmission, four-barrel carburetor and air conditioning. The beginning engine numbers were 0001001 and up at each assembly plant with F = Flint, Mich. and T = Tonawanda, N.Y. Corvette engines have the last six digits of the VIN stamped on the block next to the engine number. The body number plate was located on the engine side of the cowl. The Fisher Body Style Number 62-0867 identifies a Corvette Sting Ray convertible and the Fisher Body Style Number 62-0837 identifies a Corvette Sting Ray "split-window" coupe. The Body Number is the production serial number of the body. The Trim Number indicates the interior trim color and material. The Paint Number indicates the color combination. The 1964 "Magic Mirror" acrylic lacquer exterior colors were: No. 900 Tuxedo Black; No. 912 Silver Blue; No. 916 Daytona Blue; No. 923 Riverside Red; No. 932 Saddle Tan; No. 936 Ermine White and No. 940 Satin Silver.

Jerry Heasley

1964 Corvette coupe featured functional air-exhaust vents on the left rear pillar

Nicky Wright

1964 Corvette convertible in Silver Blue

VINYL UPHOLSTERY CODES

[St. Louis-built Coupe Body] (STD) Black; (490AA) Red; (490BA) Blue; (490CA) Saddle; (491AA) Silver and Black; (491BA) Silver and Dark Blue; (401CA) White and Black; (491GA) White and Dark Blue; (491DA) White and Red; and (491HA) White and Saddle.

[A.O. Smith-built Coupe Body] (STD) Black; (490H) Red; (490K) Blue; (490M) Saddle; (491AE) Silver and Black; (491N) Silver and Dark Blue; (491CB) White and Black; (491S) White and Dark Blue; (491Q) White; and Red and (491U) White and Saddle.

[St. Louis-built Convertible Body] (STD) Black; (490AB) Red; (490BB) Blue; (490CB) Saddle; (491AE) Silver and Black; (491BE) Silver and Dark Blue; (491CE) White and Black; (491GE) White and Dark Blue; (491DE) White and Red; and (491HE) White and Saddle.

[A.O. Smith-built Convertible Body] (STD) Black; (490G) Red; (490J) Blue; (490L) Saddle; (491AA) Silver and Black; (491M) Silver and Dark Blue; (491CA) White and Black; (491R) White and Dark Blue; (491P) White and Red; and (491T) White and Saddle.

LEATHER UPHOLSTERY CODES

[St. Louis-built Coupe Body] (898A) Black; (498EA) Red; (898JA) Blue; (898CA) Saddle; (899AA) Silver and Black; (899BA) Silver and Dark Blue; (899CA) White and Black; (899GA) White and Dark Blue; (899DA) White and Red; and (899HB) White and Saddle.

[A.O. Smith-built Coupe Body] (898A) Black; (898M) Red; (498B) Blue; (898H) Saddle; (899AE) Silver and Black; (899N) Silver and Dark Blue; (899CB) White and Black; (899S) White and Dark Blue; (899Q) White and Red; and (899U) White and Saddle.

[St. Louis-built Convertible Body] (898A) Black; (898EA) Red; (898JA) Blue; (898CA) Saddle; (899AE) Silver and Black; (899BE) Silver and Dark Blue; (899CE) White and Black; (899GE) White and Dark Blue; (899DE) White and Red; and (899HE) White and Saddle.

[A.O. Smith-built Convertible Body] (898A) Black; (898L) Red; (898N) Blue; (898G) Saddle; (899AA) Silver and Black; (899M) Silver and Dark Blue; (899CA) White and Black; (899R) White and Dark Blue; (899P) White and Red and (899T) White and Saddle.

ENGINES

BASE ENGINE: V-8. Overhead valve. Cast-iron block. Displacement: 327 cid. Bore and stroke: 4.00 x 3.25 inches. Compression ratio: 10.5:1. Brake hp: 250 at 4400 rpm. Torque: 350 lbs.-ft. at 2800 rpm. Five main bearings. Hydraulic valve lifters. Carburetor: Carter Type WCFB four-barrel Model 3501S.

OPTIONAL ENGINE: [RPO L75] V-8. Overhead

valve. Cast-iron block. Displacement: 327 cid. Bore and stroke: 4.00 x 3.25 inches. Compression ratio: 10.5:1. Brake hp: 300 at 5000 rpm. Torque: 360 lbs.-ft. at 3200 rpm. Five main bearings. Hydraulic valve lifters. Carburetor: Carter aluminum Type AFB four-barrel.

OPTIONAL ENGINE: [RPO L76] V-8. Overhead valve. Cast-iron block. Displacement: 327 cid. Bore and stroke: 4.00 x 3.25 inches. Compression ratio: 11.00:1. Brake hp: 365 at 6200 rpm. Torque: 350 lbs.-ft. at 4000 rpm. Five main bearings. Mechanical valve lifters. High-lift camshaft. Carburetor: Holley four-barrel Model 4150.

OPTIONAL ENGINE: [RPO L84] V-8. Overhead valve. Cast-iron block. Displacement: 327 cid. Bore and stroke: 4.00 x 3.25 inches. Compression ratio: 11.00:1. Brake hp: 375 at 6200 rpm. Torque: 350 lbs.-ft. at 4400 rpm. Five main bearings. Mechanical valve lifters. High-lift camshaft. Induction: Ram-Jet fuel injection.

TRANSMISSIONS

STANDARD MANUAL TRANSMISSION: A three-speed manual all-synchromesh transmission with floor-mounted gear shifter was standard equipment.

AUTOMATIC TRANSMISSION: A two-speed Powerglide automatic transmission with floor-mounted gear shifter was optional equipment.

OPTIONAL MANUAL TRANSMISSION: A four-speed manual all-synchromesh transmission with floor-mounted gear shifter was optional equipment.

CHASSIS FEATURES

Wheelbase: 98 inches. Overall length: [Convertible] 175.2 inches [Coupe] 175.3 inches. Overall height: [Coupe] 49.8 inches. Overall width: 69.6 inches. Front tread: 56.8 inches. Rear tread: 57.6 inches. Ground clearance: Five inches. Tires: 6.70 x 15. Frame: Full-length ladder type with five cross members and separate body. Front suspension: Independent; upper and lower A-arms, unequal-length wishbones; Coil springs; anti-roll bar; tubular shocks. Steering: Saginaw recirculating ball, 17:1 ratio; 3.4 turns lock-to-lock. Rear suspension: Independent with fixed differential; nine leaf spirings; lateral struts and universally-jointed axle shafts; radius arms and direct-acting shock absorbers. Rear axle type: Hypoid semi-floating. Brakes: Hydraulic, duo-servo, self-adjusting with sintered iron linings and cast-iron drums. Drum diameter [Front]: 11 x 2.75 inches; [Rear]: 11 x 2.0 inches. Total swept area: 134.9 square inches. 15-inch five-lug steel disc wheels. Standard rear axle ratio 3.70:1. Available rear axle gear ratios: 4.11:1; 4.56:1; 3.08:1; 3.36:1; 3.55:1; 3.70:1.

OPTIONS

RPO 898 Genuine leather seat trim ($80.70). RPO A01 Soft-Ray tinted glass, all windows ($16.15). RPO A02 Soft-Ray tinted glass, windshield ($10). RPO 431 Electric power windows ($59.20). RPO C07 Auxiliary hardtop for convertible ($236.75). RPO C48 Heater and defroster deletion ($100 credit). RPO C60 Air conditioning ($421.80). RPO F40 Special front and rear suspension ($37.70). RPO G81 Positraction rear axle, all ratios ($43.05) RPO G91 Special 3.08:1 "highway" ratio rear axle ($2.20). RPO J50 Power brakes ($43.05). RPO J56 Sintered metallic brakes ($37.70). RPO K66 Transistor ignition system ($65.35). RPO L75 327-cid 300-hp V-8 ($53.80). RPO L76 327-cid 365-hp V-8 ($107.60). RPO L84 327-cid 375-hp fuel-injected V-8 ($538.40). RPO M20 Four-speed manual transmission ($188.30). RPO M35 Powerglide automatic transmission ($199.10). RPO N03 36-gallon fuel tank for coupe only ($202.30). RPO N11 Off-road exhaust system ($37.70). RPO N40 Power steering ($75.35). RPO P48 Special cast-aluminum knock-off wheels ($322.80). RPO P91 Nylon tires, 6.70 x 15 black sidewall ($15.70). RPO P92 Rayon tires, 6.70 x 15, white sidewall ($31.85). RPO T86 Back-up lamps ($10.80). RPO U69 AM-FM radio ($174.35).

HISTORICAL FOOTNOTES

Only 3.2 percent of 1964 Corvettes were sold with the standard three-speed manual transmission. Most, 85.7 percent, were equipped with a four-speed manual transmission. An L84-powered 1964 Corvette could go from 0-to-60 mph in 6.3 seconds and from 0-to-100 mph in 14.7 seconds. It had a top speed of 138 mph.

1964 CORVETTE

Model Number	Body/Style Number	Body Type & Seating	Factory Price	Shipping Weight	Production Total
0800	37	2-dr FsBk Cpe-2P	$4,252	2,945 lbs.	8,304
0800	67	2-dr Conv-2P	$4,037	2,960 lbs.	13,925

Jerry Heasley

Only 168 1965 Corvette coupes came with blackwall tires

CORVETTE STING RAY SERIES (V-8) SERIES 9000

Three functional, vertical front, slanting louvers on the sides of the front fenders; a blacked-out, horizontal-bars grille and different rocker panel moldings were the main styling changes for 1965 Corvettes. A new hood without indentations was standard, but Corvettes with a newly optional 396-cid "big-block" V-8 used a special hood with a funnel-shaped "power blister" air scoop. Inside the car the instruments were changed to a flat-dial, straight-needle design with an aircraft-type influence. The seats had improved support and one-piece molded inside door panels were introduced. Standard equipment included: tachometer; safety belts; heater and defroster; windshield washer; outside rearview mirror; dual exhaust; electric clock; carpeting; manually-operated top (convertible) and sun visors. A four-wheel disc-brake system was standard, although drum brakes could be substituted for a $64.50 credit. Fuel injection was phased out at the end of the 1965 model year. New options included a nasty-looking side exhaust system and telescoping steering wheel. Eight exterior colors were available: Tuxedo Black; Ermine White; Nassau Blue; Glen Green; Milano Maroon; Silver Pearl; Rally Red and Goldwood Yellow. All convertibles came with a choice of a Black, White or Beige soft top. Interior colors were Black, Red, Blue, Saddle, Silver, White, Green, and Maroon.

I.D. NUMBERS

The Corvette VIN is embossed on a stainless steel plate welded to the right side dash pillar brace under the glove box. For 1965 the numbers were: [Convertibles] 194675S100001 to 194675S123562; [Coupes] 194375S100001 to 194375S123562. The first symbol (1) indicated Chevrolet. The second and third symbols identify the body series (94 = Corvette). The fourth and fifth symbols indicate the body style number (67 = convertible; 37 = coupe). The sixth symbol indicates the model year 5 = 1965. The seventh symbol identifies the assembly plant S = St. Louis. The last six symbols indicate the sequential production number. Engine code suffixes were: HE = 327-cid 250-hp V-8 with 10.5:1 compression ratio, manual transmission and four-barrel carburetor; HF = 327-cid 300-hp V-8 with 10.5:1 compression ratio, manual transmission and four-barrel carburetor; HG = 327-cid 375-hp V-8 with 11.00:1 compression ratio, manual transmission and fuel injection; HH = 327-cid 365-hp V-8 with 11.0:1 compression ratio, manual transmission or special-high-performance manual transmission and four-barrel carburetor; HI =

Four-wheel disc brakes were standard on the 1965 Corvette

327-cid 250-hp V-8 with 10.5:1 compression ratio, manual transmission and four-barrel carburetor; HJ = 327-cid 300-hp V-8 with 10.5:1 compression ratio, manual transmission and air conditioning; HK = 327-cid 365-hp V-8 with 11.0:1 compression ratio, manual transmission or special-high-performance manual transmission and four-barrel carburetor; HL = 327-cid 365-hp V-8 with 11.0:1 compression ratio, manual transmission and four-barrel carburetor. HM = 327-cid 365-hp V-8 with 11.0:1 compression ratio, manual transmission, four-barrel carburetor and air conditioning; HN = 327-cid 375-hp V-8 with 11.0:1 compression ratio, manual transmission and fuel injection; HO = 327-cid 250-hp V-8 with 10.5:1 compression ratio, fuel injection and automatic transmission; HP = 327-cid 300-hp V-8 with 10.5:1 compression ratio, fuel injection and automatic transmission; HQ = 327-cid 250-hp V-8 with 10.5:1 compression ratio, fuel injection, automatic transmission and air conditioning; HR = 327-cid 300-hp V-8 with 10.5:1 compression ratio, fuel injection, automatic transmission and air conditioning; HT = 327-cid 350-hp V-8 with 11.0:1 compression ratio, manual transmission or special high-performance manual transmission and fuel injection; HU = 327-cid 350-hp V-8 with 11.0:1 compression ratio, manual transmission or special high-performance manual transmission, air conditioning and fuel injection; HV = 327-cid 350-hp V-8 with 11.0:1 compression ratio, manual or special high-performance manual transmission and four-barrel carburetor; HW = 327-cid 350-hp V-8 with 11.0:1 compression ratio, manual or special high-performance manual transmission, four-barrel carburetor, and air conditioning. IF = 396-cid 425-hp V-8 with 11.0:1 compression ratio, manual transmission or special high-performance manual transmission, four-barrel carburetor. The beginning engine numbers were 0001001 and up at each assembly plant with F = Flint, Mich. and T = Tonawanda, N.Y. Corvette engines have the last six digits of the VIN stamped on the block next to the engine number. The body number plate was located on the engine side of the cowl. The Fisher Body Style Number 65-19467 identifies a Corvette Sting Ray convertible, and the Fisher Body Style Number 65-19437 identifies a Corvette Sting Ray coupe. The Body Number is the production serial number of the body. The Trim Number indicates the interior trim color and material.

Jerry Healsey

1965 Corvette convertible—15,376 were built

Jerry Healsey

1965 Corvette convertible, fender louvers are now three functional vertical slots

PAINT CODES

The Paint Number indicates the color combination. (AA) Tuxedo Black; (CC) Ermine White; (FF) Nassau Blue; (GG) Glen Green; (MM) Milano Maroon; (QQ) Silver Pearl; (UU) Rally Red; and (XX) Goldwood Yellow.

VINYL UPHOLSTERY CODES: (407) Red; (414) Blue; (420) Saddle; (426) Silver; (430) Green; (437, 443, 450) White; (435) Maroon.

LEATHER UPHOLSTERY CODES: (402) Black; (408) Red; (415) Blue; (421) Saddle; (427) Silver; (431) Green; (438, 444, 451) White; (436) Maroon.

ENGINES

BASE ENGINE: V-8. Overhead valve. Cast-iron block. Displacement: 327 cid. Bore and stroke: 4.00 x 3.25 inches. Compression ratio: 10.5:1. Brake hp: 250 at 4400 rpm. Torque: 350 lbs.-ft. at 2800 rpm. Five main bearings. Hydraulic valve lifters. Carburetor: Carter Type WCFB four-barrel Model 3846247.

OPTIONAL ENGINE: [RPO L75] V-8. Overhead valve. Cast-iron block. Displacement: 327 cid. Bore and stroke: 4.00 x 3.25 inches. Compression ratio: 10.5:1. Brake hp: 300 at 5000 rpm. Torque: 360 lbs.-ft. at 3200 rpm. Five main bearings. Hydraulic valve lifters. Carburetor: Carter Type AFB four-barrel.

OPTIONAL ENGINE: [RPO L79] V-8. Overhead valve. Cast-iron block. Displacement: 327 cid. Bore and stroke: 4.00 x 3.25 inches. Compression ratio: 11.00:1. Brake hp: 350 at 5800 rpm. Torque: 360 lbs.-ft. at 3600 rpm. Five main bearings. Hydraulic valve lifters. High-lift camshaft. Carburetor: Holley 4150 four-barrel.

OPTIONAL ENGINE: [RPO L76] V-8. Overhead valve. Cast-iron block. Displacement: 327 cid. Bore and stroke: 4.00 x 3.25 inches. Compression ratio: 11.00:1. Brake hp: 365 at 6200 rpm. Torque: 350 lbs.-ft. at 4000 rpm. Five main bearings. Mechanical valve lifters. High-lift camshaft. Carburetor: Holley 4150 four-barrel.

OPTIONAL ENGINE: [RPO L84] V-8. Overhead valve. Cast-iron block. Displacement: 327 cid. Bore and stroke: 4.00 x 3.25 inches. Compression ratio: 11.00:1. Brake hp: 375 at 6200 rpm. Torque: 350 lbs.-ft. at 4400 rpm. Five main bearings. Mechanical valve lifters. High-lift camshaft. Induction: Ram-Jet fuel injection.

1965 1/2 ENGINE

OPTIONAL ENGINE: [RPO L78] V-8. Overhead valve. Cast-iron block. Displacement: 396 cid. Bore and stroke: 4.094 x 3.76 inches. Compression ratio: 11.00:1. Brake hp: 425 at 6400 rpm. Torque: 415 lbs.-ft. at 4000 rpm. Five main bearings. Mechanical valve lifters. High-lift camshaft. Carburetor: Holley 4150 four-barrel.

TRANSMISSIONS

STANDARD MANUAL TRANSMISSION: A three-speed manual all-synchromesh transmission with floor-mounted gear shifter was standard equipment.

AUTOMATIC TRANSMISSION: A two-speed Powerglide automatic transmission with floor-mounted gear shifter was optional equipment.

OPTIONAL MANUAL TRANSMISSION: A high-performance all-synchromesh four-speed manual transmission with floor-mounted gear shifter was optional equipment.

OPTIONAL MANUAL TRANSMISSION: A special high-performance four-speed manual all-synchromesh close-ratio transmission with floor-mounted gear shifter was optional equipment.

CHASSIS FEATURES

Wheelbase: 98 inches. Overall length: [Convertible] 175.2 inches [Coupe] 175.3 inches. Overall height: [Coupe] 49.8 inches. Overall width: 69.6 inches. Front tread: 56.8 inches. Rear tread: 57.6 inches. Ground clearance: Five inches. Tires: 7.75 x 15. Frame: Full-length ladder type with five cross members and separate body. Front suspension: Independent; upper and lower A-arms, unequal-length wishbones; coil springs; anti-roll bar; tubular shocks.

Jerry Heasley

1965 Corvette in Nassau Blue with removable hardtop

Steering: Saginaw recirculating ball, 17:1 ratio; 3.4 turns lock-to-lock. Rear suspension: Independent with fixed differential; nine leaf springs; lateral struts and universally-jointed axle shafts; radius arms and direct-acting shock absorbers. Rear axle type: Hypoid semi-floating. Brakes: Hydraulic, four-wheel discs. Steel disc wheels. Standard rear axle ratio 3.36:1. Available rear axle gear ratios: 4.11:1; 4.56:1; 3.08:1; 3.55:1; 3.70:1.

OPTIONS

RPO 898 Genuine leather seat trim ($80.70). RPO A01 Soft-Ray tinted glass, all windows ($16.15). RPO A02 Soft-Ray tinted glass, windshield ($10.80). RPO 431 Electric power windows ($59.20). RPO C07 Auxiliary hardtop for convertible ($236.75). RPO C48 Heater and defroster deletion ($100 credit). RPO C60 Air conditioning ($421.80). RPO F40 Special front and rear suspension ($37.70). RPO G81 Positraction rear axle, all ratios ($43.05). RPO G91 Special 3.08:1 "highway" ratio rear axle ($2.20). RPO J50 Power brakes ($43.05). RPO J61 Drum brake substitution ($64.50 credit). RPO K66 Transistor ignition system ($75.35). RPO L75 327-cid 300-hp V-8 ($53.80). RPO L76 327-cid 365-hp V-8 ($129.15). RPO L78 396-cid 425-hp V-8 ($292.70). RPO L79 327-cid 350-hp V-8 ($107.60). RPO L84 327-cid 375-hp fuel-injected V-8 ($538.00). RPO M20 Four-speed manual transmission ($188.30). RPO M22 Close-ratio four-speed manual transmission ($236.95). RPO M35 Powerglide automatic transmission ($199.10). RPO N03 36-gallon fuel tank for coupe only ($202.30). RPO N11 Off-road exhaust system ($37.70). RPO N14 Side Mount exhaust system ($134.50). RPO N32 Teakwood steering wheel ($48.45). RPO N36 Telescopic steering wheel ($43.05). RPO N40 Power steering ($96.85). RPO P48 Special cast-aluminum knock-off wheels ($322.80). RPO P92 7.75 x 15, white sidewall tires ($31.85). RPO T01 7.75 x 15 gold sidewall tires ($50.05). RPO U69 AM-FM radio ($203.40). RPO Z01 Back-up lamps and inside Day/Night mirror ($16.15).

HISTORICAL FOOTNOTES

Most 1965 Corvettes (89.6 percent) were sold with a four-speed manual transmission; 8.6 percent had Powerglide automatic transmission; 69.5 percent had tinted glass; 10.3 percent had air conditioning and 13.7 percent had power steering. An L78-powered 1965 Corvette could go from 0-to-60 mph in 5.7 seconds; from 0-to-100 mph in 13.4 seconds.

1965 CORVETTE

Model Number	Body/Style Number	Body Type & Seating	Factory Price	Shipping Weight	Production Total
194	37	2-dr FsBk Cpe-2P	$3,947	3,570 lbs.	8,186
194	67	2-dr Conv-2P	$3,212	3,645 lbs.	15,376

1966 Corvette convertible with new egg-crate grill

CORVETTE STING RAY SERIES (V-8) SERIES 9000

A plated, cast-metal grille with an "egg crate" insert; ribbed rocker panel moldings; chrome-plated exhaust bezels; spoke-style wheel covers; a vinyl covered headliner and the elimination of roof vents helped set the 1966 Corvette apart from the previous year's model. The front fender sides again had thee slanting vertical air louvers. Inside, the seats had an extra amount of pleats. Corvettes equipped with the new 427-cid V-8 came with a power-bulge hood. The 10 lacquer exterior finishes offered were Tuxedo Black; Ermine White; Nassau Blue; Mosport Green; Milano Maroon; Silver Pearl; Rally Red; Sunfire Yellow; Laguna Blue and Trophy Blue. All convertibles came with a choice of a Black, White or Beige soft top. Interior colors were Black; Red; Bright Blue; White-Blue; Saddle; Silver; Green and Blue.

I.D. NUMBERS

The Corvette VIN is embossed on a stainless steel plate welded to the right side dash pillar brace under the glove box. For 1966 the numbers were: [Convertibles] 194676S100001 to 194676S127720; [Coupes] 194376S100001 to 194376S127720. The first symbol (1) indicated Chevrolet. The second and third symbols identify the body series (94 = Corvette). The fourth and fifth symbols indicate the body style number (67 = convertible; 37 = coupe). The sixth symbol indicates the model year 6 = 1966. The seventh symbol identifies the assembly plant (S = St. Louis, Mo). The last six symbols indicate the sequential production number. Engine code suffixes were: HH = 327-cid 300-hp V-8 with 10.5:1 compression ratio, manual transmission and four-barrel carburetor; HR = 327-cid 300-hp V-8 with 10.5:1 compression ratio, automatic transmission and four-barrel carburetor; HD = 327-cid 350-hp V-8 with 11.00:1 compression ratio, manual transmission and four-barrel carburetor; HO = 327-cid 300-hp V-8 with 10.5:1 compression ratio, four-barrel carburetor and automatic transmission; HT = 327-cid 350-hp V-8 with 11.0:1 compression ratio, four-barrel carburetor and manual transmission; HP = 327-cid 300-hp V-8 with 10.5:1 compression ratio, four-barrel carburetor and manual transmission; KH = 327-cid 350-hp V-8 with 11.0:1 compression ratio, four-barrel carburetor and manual transmission; IK = 427-cid 425-hp V-8 with 11.0:1 compression ratio and manual transmission; IL = 427-cid 390-hp V-8 with 10.25:1 compression ratio, four-barrel carburetor and manual transmission; IM = 427-cid 390-hp V-8 with 10.25:1 compression ratio, four-barrel carburetor and manual transmission; IP = 427-cid 425-hp V-8 with 11.0:1 compression ratio, four-barrel carburetor and manual transmission; IQ = 427-cid 390-hp V-8 with 10.25:1 compression ratio, four-barrel carburetor and automatic transmission and IR = 427-cid 390-hp V-8 with

Jerry Heasley

1966 Corvette coupe

10.25:1 compression ratio, four-barrel carburetor and automatic transmission. The beginning engine numbers were 0001001 and up at each assembly plant with F = Flint, Mich. and T = Tonawanda, N.Y. Corvette engines have the last six digits of the VIN stamped on the block next to the engine number. The body number plate was located on the engine side of the cowl. The Fisher Body Style Number 66-19467 identifies a Corvette Sting Ray convertible and the Fisher Body Style Number 66-19437 identifies a Corvette Sting Ray coupe. The Body Number is the production serial number of the body. The Trim Number indicates the interior trim color and material.

PAINT CODES

The Paint Number indicates the color combination: (900) Tuxedo Black; (972) Ermine White; (974) Rally Red; (976) Nassau Blue; (978) Laguna Blue; (980) Trophy Blue; (982) Mosport Green; (984) Sunfire Yellow; (986) Silver Pearl; (988) Milano Maroon.

VINYL UPHOLSTERY CODES: (STD) Black; (407) Red; (414) Bright Blue; (418) Dark Blue; (420) Saddle; (426) Silver and Black; (430) Green; (437) White and Black; (450) White and Blue.

LEATHER UPHOLSTERY CODES: (402) Black; (408) Red; (415) Bright Blue; (419) Dark Blue; (421) Saddle; (427) Silver and Black; (431) Green; (451) White and Blue.

ENGINES

BASE ENGINE: [RPO L75] V-8. Overhead valve. Cast-iron block. Displacement: 327 cid. Bore and stroke: 4.00 x 3.25 inches. Compression ratio: 10.5:1. Brake hp: 300 at 5000 rpm. Torque: 350 lbs.-ft. at 2800 rpm. Five main bearings. Hydraulic valve lifters. Carburetor: Holley four-barrel.

OPTIONAL ENGINE: [RPO L79] V-8. Overhead valve. Cast-iron block. Displacement: 327 cid. Bore and stroke: 4.00 x 3.25 inches. Compression ratio: 11.00:1. Brake hp: 350 at 5800 rpm. Torque: 360 lbs.-ft. at 3000 rpm. Five main bearings. Hydraulic valve lifters. High-performance camshaft. Carburetor: Holley four-barrel.

OPTIONAL ENGINE: [RPO L30] V-8. Overhead valve. Cast-iron block. Displacement: 427 cid. Bore and stroke: 4.251 x 3.76 inches. Compression ratio: 10.25:1. Brake hp: 390 at 5200 rpm. Torque: 460 lbs.-ft. at 3600 rpm. Five main bearings. Hydraulic valve lifters. High-performance camshaft. Carburetor: Holley four-barrel.

OPTIONAL ENGINE: [RPO L72] V-8. Overhead valve. Cast-iron block. Displacement: 427 cid. Bore and stroke: 4.251 x 3.76 inches. Compression ratio: 11.00:1. Brake hp: 425 at 5000 rpm. Torque: 460 lbs.-ft. at 4000 rpm. Five main bearings. Mechanical valve lifters. Special-performance camshaft. Carburetor: Large Holley four-barrel.

TRANSMISSIONS

STANDARD MANUAL TRANSMISSION: A three-speed manual all-synchromesh transmission with floor-mounted gear shifter was standard equipment.

AUTOMATIC TRANSMISSION: An automatic transmission with floor-mounted gear shifter was optional equipment.

OPTIONAL MANUAL TRANSMISSION: A

1966 Corvette coupe, one of 9,958 built this year

high-performance all-synchromesh four-speed manual transmission with floor-mounted gear shifter was optional equipment.

OPTIONAL MANUAL TRANSMISSION: A special high-performance four-speed manual all-synchromesh close-ratio transmission with floor-mounted gear shifter was optional equipment.

CHASSIS FEATURES: Wheelbase: 98 inches. Overall length: [Convertible] 175.2 inches. Overall height: [Coupe] 49.6 inches. Overall width: 69.6 inches. Front tread: 57.6 inches. Rear tread: 58.3 inches. Ground clearance: Five inches. Tires: 7.75 x 15 redwall or whitewall. Frame: Full-length steel ladder type with five cross members and separate body. Front suspension: Independent; unequal-length A-arms, coil springs; tubular shocks and anti-roll bar. Steering: Saginaw recirculating ball, 17.6:1 ratio; 2.9 turns lock-to-lock; turning circle 41.6 feet. Rear suspension: Independent; transverse leaf springs; transverse struts;

Jerry Heasley

This 1966 Corvette convertible came with the 427-cid V-8.

half shafts with universal-joints; trailing arms and tubular shock absorbers. Rear axle type: Hypoid semi-floating. Brakes: Hydraulic, vented four-wheel discs; 11.75-inch diameter; single calipers; total swept area 461 sq. in. Six-inch wide pressed steel disc wheels. Standard rear axle ratio 3.55:1. Available rear axle gear ratios: 3.08:1; 3.36:1; 3.55:1; 3.70:1; 4.11:1; 4.56:1.

OPTIONS

RPO 898 Genuine leather seat trim ($79). RPO A01 Soft-Ray tinted glass, all windows ($15.80). RPO A02 Soft-Ray tinted glass, windshield ($10.55). RPO 431 Electric power windows ($59.20). RPO A82 Headrests ($42.15). RPO A85 Shoulder harness ($26.35). RPO C07 Auxiliary hardtop for convertible ($231.75). RPO C48 Heater and defroster deletion ($97.85 credit). RPO C60 Air conditioning ($412.90). RPO F41 Special front and rear suspension ($36.90). RPO G81 Positraction rear axle, all ratios ($42.15). RPO J50 Power brakes ($43.05). RPO J56 Special heavy-duty brakes ($342.30). RPO K66 Transistor ignition system ($73.75). RPO L79 327-cid 350-hp V-8 ($105.35). RPO L36 427-cid 390-hp V-8 ($181.20). RPO L72 427-cid 427-hp V-8 ($312.85). RPO M20 Four-speed manual transmission ($184.30). RPO M21 Four-speed close-ratio manual transmission ($184.30). RPO M22 Heavy-duty close-ratio four-speed manual transmission ($237). RPO M35 Powerglide automatic transmission ($194.85). RPO N03 36-gallon fuel tank for coupe ($198.05). RPO N11 Off-road exhaust system ($36.90). RPO N14 Side Mount exhaust system ($131.65). RPO N32 Teakwood steering wheel ($48.45). RPO N36 Telescopic steering wheel ($42.15). RPO N40 Power steering ($94.80). RPO P48 Special cast-aluminum knock-off wheels ($326.00). RPO P92 7.75 x 15, white sidewall tires ($31.30). RPO T01 7.75 x 15 gold sidewall tires ($46.55). RPO U69 AM-FM radio ($199.10). RPO V74 Traffic hazard lamp switch ($11.60).

HISTORICAL FOOTNOTES

Only two percent of all 1966 Corvettes had a three-speed manual transmission; 89.3 percent came with a four-speed manual gearbox; 13.2 percent had a tilting steering wheel and 20.2 percent had power steering.

1966 CORVETTE

Model Number	Body/Style Number	Body Type & Seating	Factory Price	Shipping Weight	Production Total
194	37	2-dr FsBk Cpe-2P	$4,295	2,985 lbs.	9,958
194	67	2-dr Conv-2P	$4,084	3,005 lbs.	17,762

Jerry Heasley

1966 Corvette coupe

Jerry Heasley

1967 Corvette convertible

CORVETTE STING RAY SERIES (V-8) SERIES 9000

Some consider the 1967 the best looking of the early Sting Rays. Its styling, although basically the same as in 1966, was a bit cleaner. The same egg-crate style grille with Argent Silver finish was carried over. The same smooth hood seen in 1966 was re-used. Big-block cars had a large front-opening air scoop over the center bulge instead of the previous power blister. The crossed flags badge on the nose of the 1967 Corvette had a widened "V" at its top. On the sides of the front fenders were five vertical and functional louvers that slanted towards the front of the car. Minor changes were made to the interior. The most noticeable was the relocation of the parking brake from under the dash to the center console. The new headliner was cushioned with foam and fiber material. Four-way flashers, directional signals with a lane-change function, larger interior vent ports and folding seat-back latches were all new. At the rear there were now dual round taillights on each side (instead of a taillight and optional back-up light). The twin back-up lights were now mounted in the center of the rear panel, above the license plate. Standard equipment included: a new dual-chamber brake master cylinder; six-inch wide slotted rally wheels with trim rings; an odometer; a clock; carpeting and a tachometer. The optional finned aluminum wheels were changed in design and had a one-year-only, non-knock-off center. The 10 lacquer exterior finishes offered were: Tuxedo Black; Ermine White; Elkhart Blue; Lyndale Blue; Marina Blue; Goodwood Green; Rally Red; Silver Pearl; Sunfire Yellow and Marlboro Maroon. All convertibles came with a choice of a Black, White or Teal Blue soft top. The all-vinyl foam-cushioned bucket seats came in Black, Red, Bright Blue, Saddle, White and Blue, White and Black, Teal Blue and Green.

I.D. NUMBERS

The Corvette VIN is embossed on a stainless steel plate welded to the right side dash pillar brace under the glove box. For 1967 the numbers were: [Convertibles] 194677S100001 to 194677S122940; [Coupes] 194377S100001 to 194377S122940. The first symbol (1) indicated Chevrolet. The second and third symbols identify the body series (94 = Corvette). The fourth and fifth symbols indicate the body style number (67 = convertible; 37 = coupe). The sixth symbol indicates the model year (7 = 1967). The seventh symbol identifies the assembly plant (S = St. Louis, Mo). The last six symbols indicate the sequential production number. Engine code suffixes were: HE = 327-cid 300-hp V-8 with 10.0:1 compression ratio; four-barrel carburetor and manual transmission; HH = 327-cid 300-hp V-8 with 10.0:1 compression ratio, manual transmission and four-barrel carburetor; HR = 327-cid 300-hp V-8 with 10.0:1 compression ratio, automatic transmission and four-

1967 Corvette Sting Ray coupe with functional, five-slot fender louvers

barrel carburetor; HD = 327-cid 350-hp V-8 with 11.0:1 compression ratio, manual transmission and four-barrel carburetor; HO = 327-cid 300-hp V-8 with 10.0:1 compression ratio, four-barrel carburetor and automatic transmission; HT = 327-cid 350-hp V-8 with 11.0:1 compression ratio, four-barrel carburetor and manual transmission; HP = 327-cid 350-hp V-8 with 11.0:1 compression ratio, four-barrel carburetor and manual transmission; KH = 327-cid 350-hp V-8 with 11.0:1 compression ratio, four-barrel carburetor and manual transmission IL = 427-cid 390-hp V-8 with 10.25:1 compression ratio, four-barrel carburetor and manual or automatic transmission; JC = 427-cid 400-hp V-8 with 10.25:1 compression ratio, three two-barrel carburetors and manual transmission; JE = 427-cid 435-hp V-8 with 11.0:1 compression ratio, three two-barrel carburetors and manual transmission; IT = 427-cid 425-hp V-8 with 12.5:1 compression ratio, four-barrel carburetor and manual transmission; IU = 427-cid 435-hp V-8 with 11.0:1 compression, three two-barrel carburetors and manual transmission; IM = 427-cid 390-hp V-8 with 10.25:1 compression ratio, four-barrel carburetor and manual transmission; JF = 427-cid 400-hp V-8 with 10.25:1 compression ratio, three two-barrel carburetors and manual transmission; JH = 427-cid 435-hp V-8 with 11.0:1 compression ratio, three two-barrel carburetors and manual transmission; IQ = 427-cid 390-hp V-8 with 10.25:1 compression, four-barrel carburetor and automatic transmission; JD = 427-cid 400-hp V-8 with 10.25:1 compression ratio, three two-barrel carburetors and automatic transmission; IR = 427-cid 390-hp V-8 with 10.25:1 compression ratio, four-barrel carburetor and automatic transmission; JG = 427-cid 400-hp V-8 with 10.25:1 compression ratio, three two-barrel carburetors and automatic transmission; JA = 427-cid 435-hp V-8 with 11.0:1 compression ratio, three two-barrel carburetors and manual transmission. The beginning engine numbers were 0001001 and up at each assembly plant with F = Flint, Mich. and T = Tonawanda, N.Y. Corvette engines have the last six digits of the VIN stamped on the block next to the engine number. The body number plate was located on the engine side of the cowl. The Fisher Body Style Number 67-19467 identifies a Corvette Sting Ray convertible and the Fisher Body Style Number 67-19437 identifies a Corvette Sting Ray coupe. The Body Number is the production serial number of the body. The Trim Number indicates the interior trim color and material.

1967 Corvette Sting Ray coupe

PAINT CODES

The Paint Number indicates the color combination. [900] Tuxedo Black; [972] Ermine White; [974] Rally Red; [976] Marina Blue; [977] Lyndale Blue; [980] Elkhart Blue; [983] Goodward Green; [984] Sunfire Yellow; [986] Silver Pearl; [988] Marlboro Maroon.

VINYL UPHOLSTERY CODES: (STD) Black; (407)

1967 Corvette convertible

Red; (414) Bright Blue; (418) Teal Blue; (420) Saddle; (430) Green; (450) White and Blue; (455) White and Black.

LEATHER UPHOLSTERY CODES: (402) Black; (408) Red; (415) Bright Blue; (419) Teal Blue; (421) Saddle; (431) Green; (451) White and Blue.

ENGINES

BASE ENGINE: [RPO L75] V-8. Overhead valve. Cast-iron block. Displacement: 327 cid. Bore and stroke: 4.00 x 3.25 inches. Compression ratio: 10.0:1. Brake hp: 300 at 5000 rpm. Torque: 360 lbs.-ft. at 3400 rpm. Five main bearings. Hydraulic valve lifters. Holley four-barrel Model R3810A or R3814A.

OPTIONAL ENGINE: [RPO L79] V-8. Overhead valve. Cast-iron block. Displacement: 327 cid. Bore and stroke: 4.00 x 3.25 inches. Compression ratio: 11.0:1. Brake hp: 350 at 5800 rpm. Torque: 360 lbs.-ft. at 3600 rpm. Five main bearings. Hydraulic valve lifters. High-performance camshaft. Carburetor: Holley four-barrel.

OPTIONAL ENGINE: [RPO L36] V-8. Overhead valve. Cast-iron block. Displacement: 427 cid. Bore and stroke: 4.251 x 3.76 inches. Compression ratio: 10:25:1. Brake hp: 390 at 5400 rpm. Torque: 460 lbs.-ft. at 3600 rpm. Five main bearings. Hydraulic valve lifters. High-performance camshaft. Carburetor: Holley four-barrel.

OPTIONAL ENGINE: [RPO L68] V-8. Overhead valve. Cast iron block. Displacement: 427 cid. Bore and stroke: 4.251 x 3.76 inches. Compression ratio: 10.25:1. Brake hp: 400 at 5400 rpm. Taxable hp: 57.80. Torque: 460 at 3600 rpm. Five main bearings. Hydraulic valve lifters. Special-performance camshaft. Crankcase capacity: 5 qt. (Add 1 qt. for filter). Cooling system capacity: 21 qt. (Add 1 qt. for heater). Carburetor: Three Holley two-barrel. Sales code: L68.

OPTIONAL ENGINE: [RPO L71] V-8. Overhead valve. Cast-iron block. Displacement: 427 cid. Bore and stroke: 4.251 x 3.76 inches. Compression ratio: 11.0:1. Brake hp: 435 at 5800 rpm. Torque: 460 lbs.-ft. at 4000 rpm. Five main bearings. Mechanical valve lifters. Special-performance camshaft. Carburetor: Three Holley two-barrels.

OPTIONAL ENGINE [RPO L72]: V-8. Overhead valve. Cast iron block. Displacement: 427 cid. Bore and stroke: 4.251 x 3.76 inches. Compression ratio: 11.0:1. Brake hp: 425 at 5600 rpm. Taxable hp: 57.80. Torque: 460 at 3800 rpm. Five main bearings. Mechanical valve lifters. Special-performance camshaft. Crankcase capacity: 5 qt. (Add 1 qt. for filter). Cooling system capacity: 21 qt. (Add 1 qt. for heater). Carburetor: Four-barrel. Sales code: L72.

OPTIONAL ENGINE: [RPO L89] V-8. Overhead valve. Cast-iron block. Displacement: 427 cid. Bore and stroke: 4.251 x 3.76 inches. Compression ratio: 11.0:1. Brake hp: 435 at 5800 rpm. Torque: 460 lbs.-ft. at 4000 rpm. Five main bearings. Mechanical valve lifters. Aluminum cylinder heads. Extra-large exhaust valves. Special-performance camshaft. Carburetor: Three Holley two-barrels.

1967 1/2 ENGINE

OPTIONAL ENGINE: [RPO L88] V-8. Overhead

valve. Displacement: 427 cid. Bore and stroke: 4.251 x 3.76 inches. Compression ratio: 12.50:1. Brake hp: 560 at 6400 rpm. Five main bearings. Mechanical valve lifters. Special ultra-high-performance camshaft with .5365-inch intakes. Carburetor: Single Holley 850CFM four-barrel.

TRANSMISSIONS

STANDARD MANUAL TRANSMISSION: A three-speed manual all-synchromesh transmission with floor-mounted gear shifter was standard equipment.

AUTOMATIC TRANSMISSION: An automatic transmission with floor-mounted gear shifter was optional equipment.

OPTIONAL MANUAL TRANSMISSION: A high-performance all-synchromesh four-speed manual transmission with floor-mounted gear shifter was optional equipment.

OPTIONAL MANUAL TRANSMISSION: A special high-performance four-speed manual all-synchromesh close-ratio transmission with floor-mounted gear shifter was optional equipment.

OPTIONAL MANUAL TRANSMISSION: A special heavy-duty four-speed manual all-synchromesh close-ratio transmission with floor-mounted gear shifter was optional.

CHASSIS FEATURES

Wheelbase: 98 inches. Overall length: [Convertible] 175.2 inches. Overall height: [Coupe] 49.6 inches. Overall width: 69.6 inches. Front tread: 57.6 inches. Rear tread: 58.3 inches. Ground clearance: Five inches. Tires: 7.75 x 15 red sidewall or whitewall. Frame: Full-length steel ladder type with five cross members and separate body. Front suspension: Independent; unequal-length A-arms, coil springs; tubular shocks and anti-roll bar. Steering: Saginaw recirculating ball, 17.6:1 ratio; 2.9 turns lock-to-lock; turning circle 41.6 feet. Rear suspension: Independent; transverse leaf springs; transverse struts; half shafts with universal-joints; trailing arms and tubular shock absorbers. Rear axle type: Hypoid semi-floating. Brakes: Hydraulic, vented four-wheel discs; 11.75-inch diameter; single calipers; total swept area 461 sq. in. Six-inch wide pressed steel disc wheels. Standard rear axle ratio 3.55:1. Available rear axle gear ratios: 3.08:1; 3.36:1; 3.55:1; 3.70:1; 4.11:1; 4.56:1.

OPTIONS

RPO 898 Genuine leather seat trim ($79). RPO A01 Soft-Ray tinted glass, all windows ($15.80). RPO A02 Soft-Ray tinted glass, windshield ($10.55). RPO A31 Electric power windows ($57.95). RPO A82 Headrests ($42.15). RPO A85 Shoulder harness for coupe only ($26.35). RPO C07 Auxiliary hardtop for convertible ($231.75). RPO C48 Heater and defroster deletion ($97.85 credit). RPO C60 Air conditioning ($412.90). RPO F41 Special front and rear suspension ($36.90). RPO J50 Power brakes ($42.15). RPO J56 Special heavy-duty brakes ($342.30). RPO K66 Transistor ignition system ($73.75). RPO L36 427-cid 390-hp V-8 ($200.15). RPO L68 427-cid 400-hp V-8 ($305.50). RPO L71 427-cid 435-hp V-8 ($437.10). RPO L79 327-cid 350-hp V-8 ($105.35). RPO L88 427-cid 560-hp V-8 ($947.90). RPO L89 Aluminum cylinder heads for RPO L71 V-8 ($368.65). RPO M20 Four-speed manual transmission ($184.30). RPO M21 Four-speed close-ratio manual transmission ($184.30). RPO M22 Heavy-duty close-ratio four-speed manual transmission ($237.00). RPO M35 Powerglide automatic transmission ($194.85). RPO N03 36-gallon fuel tank for coupe only ($198.05). RPO N11 Off-road exhaust system ($36.90). RPO N14 Side mount exhaust system ($131.65). RPO N36 Telescopic steering wheel ($42.15). RPO N40 Power steering ($94.80). RPO P48 Special cast-aluminum knock-off wheels ($263.30). RPO P92 7.75 x 15, white sidewall tires ($31.35). RPO QB1 7.75 x 15 red sidewall tires ($46.65). RPO U15 Speed-warning indicator ($10.55). RPO U69 AM-FM radio ($199.10).

HISTORICAL FOOTNOTES

Eighty-eight percent of 1967 Corvettes came with a four-speed manual transmission; 10.1 percent had Powerglide automatic transmission; 20.8 percent had power brakes; 16.5 percent had air conditioning; 10.5 percent had a telescoping steering wheel and 25.1 percent came with power steering. A 327-cid 300 hp V-8-powered Corvette of this vintage would go from 0-to-60 mph in 7.8 seconds; from 0-to-100 mph in 23.1 seconds. The 1967 Corvette is considered the most refined of the original Sting Ray models of 1963-1967.

1967 CORVETTE

Model Number	Body/Style Number	Body Type & Seating	Factory Price	Shipping Weight	Production Total
194	37	2-dr FsBk Cpe-2P	$4,353	3,000 lbs.	8,504
194	67	2-dr Conv-2P	$4,141	3,020 lbs.	14,436

Nicky Wright

1967 Corvette coupe with 427-cid V-8.

The Sting Ray name was not used in 1968.

CORVETTE SERIES V-8) SERIES 9000

The Corvette's first major restyling since 1963 occurred in this year. As the sales brochure read, "Corvette '68 . . . all different all over." The fastback was replaced by a tunneled-roof coupe. It featured a removable back window and a two-piece detachable roof section or T-top. The convertible's optional hardtop had a glass rear window. The front end was more aerodynamic than those on previous Corvettes. As before, the headlights were hidden. Now they were vacuum-operated, rather than electrical. The wipers also disappeared when not in use. Except for the rocker panels, the sides were devoid of chrome. Conventional door handles were eliminated and in their place were push buttons. The blunt rear deck contained four round taillights with the word Corvette printed in chrome in the space between them. The wraparound, wing-like rear bumper and license plate holder treatment resembled that used on the 1967 models. Buyers had their choice of 10 exterior colors: Tuxedo Black, Polar White, Corvette Bronze, LeMans Blue, International Blue, Cordovan Maroon, Rally Red, Silverstone Silver, British Green and Safari Yellow. All convertibles came with a choice of Black, White or Beige soft tops. Interior colors were: Black, Red, Medium Blue, Dark Blue, Dark Orange, Tobacco, and Gunmetal.

I.D. NUMBERS

The Vehicle Identification Number (VIN) is stamped on a plate on the inner vertical surface of the left windshield pillar visible through the windshield. For 1968 the numbers were: [Convertibles] 194678S100001 to 194678S128566; [Coupes] 194378S100001 to 194378S128566. The first symbol (1) indicated Chevrolet. The second and third symbols identify the body series (94 = Corvette). The fourth and fifth symbols indicate the body style number (67 = convertible; 37 = coupe). The sixth symbol indicates the model year (8 = 1968). The seventh symbol identifies the assembly plant S = St. Louis. The last six symbols indicate the sequential production number. Engine code suffixes were: HE = 327-cid 300-hp V-8 with 10.0:1 compression; four-barrel carburetor and manual transmission. HO = 327-

1968 Chevrolet Corvette convertible, the exterior was completely redesigned for 1968.

1968 Corvette T-top coupe

cid 300-hp V-8 with 10.0:1 compression ratio, four-barrel carburetor and Turbo Hydra-Matic (THM) transmission. HP = 327-cid 300-hp V-8 with 10.0:1 compression ratio, four-barrel carburetor and manual transmission. HT = 327-cid 350-hp V-8 with 11.0:1 compression ratio, four-barrel carburetor and manual transmission. IL = 427-cid 390-hp V-8 with 10.25:1 compression ratio, four-barrel carburetor and manual transmission. IM = 427-cid 400-hp V-8 with 10.25:1 compression ratio, three two-barrel carburetors and manual transmission. IO = 427-cid 400-hp V-8 with 10.25:1 compression ratio, three two-barrel carburetors and THM automatic transmission. IQ = 427-cid 390-hp V-8 with 10.25:1 compression ratio, four-barrel carburetor and THM automatic transmission. IR = 427-cid 435-hp V-8 with 11.0:1 compression ratio, three two-barrel carburetors and manual transmission. IT = 427-cid 430-hp V-8 with 12.5:1 compression ratio, four-barrel carburetor and manual transmission. IU = 427-cid 435-hp V-8 with 11.0:1 compression ratio, three two-barrel carburetors and manual transmission. The beginning engine numbers were 0001001 and up at each assembly plant with F = Flint, Mich. and T = Tonawanda, N.Y. Corvette engines have the last six digits of the VIN stamped on the block next to the engine number. The body number plate was located on the engine side of the cowl. The Fisher Body Style Number 68-19467 identifies a Corvette convertible and the Fisher Body Style Number 68-19437 identifies a Corvette coupe. The Body Number is the production serial number of the body. The Trim Number indicates the interior trim color and material.

PAINT CODES

The Paint Number indicates the color combination. (900) Tuxedo Black; (972) Polar White; (974) Rally Red; (976) LeMans Blue; (978) International Blue; (983) British Green; (984) Safari Yellow; (986) Silverstone Silver; (988) Cordovan Maroon; and (992) Corvette Bronze.

VINYL UPHOLSTERY CODES: (STD) Black; (407) Red; (411) Blue; (414) Bright Blue; (425) Orange; (435) Tobacco; (442) Gunmetal.

LEATHER UPHOLSTERY CODES: (402) Black; (408) Red; (415) Blue; (426) Orange; (436) Tobacco.

ENGINES

BASE ENGINE: [RPO L75] V-8. Overhead valve. Cast-iron block. Displacement: 327 cid. Bore and stroke: 4.00 x 3.25 inches. Compression ratio: 10.25:1. Brake hp: 300. Five main bearings. Hydraulic valve lifters. Carburetor: Rochester Type 4MV four-barrel Model 7028207.

OPTIONAL ENGINE: [RPO L79] V-8. Overhead valve. Cast-iron block. Displacement: 327 cid. Bore and

Nicky Wright

1968 Corvette convertible with non-stock wheels and paint.

stroke: 4.00 x 3.25 inches. Compression ratio: 11.0:1. Brake hp: 350 at 5800 rpm. Torque: 360 lbs.-ft. at 3600 rpm. Five main bearings. Hydraulic valve lifters. High-performance camshaft. Carburetor: Holley four-barrel.

OPTIONAL ENGINE: [RPO L36] V-8. Overhead valve. Cast-iron block. Displacement: 427 cid. Bore and stroke: 4.251 x 3.76 inches. Compression ratio: 10:25:1. Brake hp: 390 at 5400 rpm. Torque: 460 lbs.-ft. at 3600 rpm. Five main bearings. Hydraulic valve lifters. High-performance camshaft. Carburetor: Holley four-barrel.

OPTIONAL ENGINE: [RPO L71] V-8. Overhead valve. Cast-iron block. Displacement: 427 cid. Bore and stroke: 4.251 x 3.76 inches. Compression ratio: 11.0:1. Brake hp: 435 at 5800 rpm. Torque: 460 lbs.-ft. at 4000 rpm. Five main bearings. Mechanical valve lifters. Special-performance camshaft. Carburetor: Three Holley two-barrels.

OPTIONAL ENGINE [RPO L71/L89] V-8. Overhead valve. Cast iron block. Bore and stroke: 4.251 x 3.76 inches. Displacement: 427 cid. Compression ratio: 11.0:1. Brake hp: 435 at 5800 rpm. Taxable hp: 57.80. Torque: 460 at 4000 rpm. Five main bearings. Mechanical valve lifters. Aluminum cylinder heads. Extra-large exhaust valves. Special-performance camshaft. Crankcase capacity: 5 qt. (Add 1 qt. for filter). Cooling system capacity: 21 qt. (Add 1 qt. for heater). Carburetor: Three Holley two-barrels. Sales code: L71/L89.

OPTIONAL ENGINE: [RPO L88] V-8. Overhead valve. Displacement: 427 cid. Bore and stroke: 4.251 x 3.76 inches. Compression ratio: 12.50:1. Brake hp: 560 at 6400 rpm. Five main bearings. Mechanical valve lifters. Special-ultra-high-performance camshaft with .5365-in. intakes. Carburetor: Single Holley 850CFM four-barrel.

TRANSMISSIONS

STANDARD MANUAL TRANSMISSION: A three-speed manual all-synchromesh transmission with floor-mounted gear shifter was standard equipment.

AUTOMATIC TRANSMISSION: An Turbo Hydra-Matic automatic transmission with floor-mounted gear shifter was optional equipment.

OPTIONAL MANUAL TRANSMISSION: A high-performance all-synchromesh four-speed manual transmission with floor-mounted gear shifter was optional equipment.

OPTIONAL MANUAL TRANSMISSION: A special high-performance four-speed manual all-synchromesh close-ratio transmission with floor-mounted gear shifter was optional equipment.

OPTIONAL MANUAL TRANSMISSION: A special heavy-duty four-speed manual all-synchromesh close-ratio transmission with floor-mounted gear shifter was optional.

CHASSIS FEATURES

Wheelbase: 98 inches. Overall length: 182.1 inches. Overall height: 48.6 inches. Overall width: 69.2 inches. Front tread: 58.3 inches. Rear tread: 59.0 inches. Tires:

Nicky Wright

1968 Corvette convertible,

F70-15. Frame: Full-length ladder type with five cross members. Steel box sections, welded. Front suspension: Unequal-length A-arms with coil springs; tube shocks and stabilizer bar. Steering: Saginaw recirculating ball. Turns lock-to-lock: 2.9. Turning radius: 39.9 feet. Rear suspension: Trailing arms, toe links, transverse chromium-carbon steel leaf spring, tube shocks and anti-roll bar. Rear axle type: Sprung differential, hypoid gear. Brakes: Four-wheel disc brakes. Vented discs front and rear. Optional power assist. Diameter: 11.8 inches front and 11.8 inches rear. Total swept area: 259 sq. in. per ton 461.2 in. total. Wheels: Slotted steel discs. Standard rear axle ratio: 3.36:1. Available rear axle gear ratios: 3.08:1; 3.36:1; 3.55:1; 3.70:1; 4.11:1; 4.56:1.

OPTIONS

RPO 898 Genuine leather seat trim ($79). RPO A01 Soft-Ray tinted glass, all windows ($15.80). RPO A31 Electric power windows ($57.95). RPO A82 Restraints ($42.15). RPO A85 Custom shoulder belts ($26.35). RPO C07 Auxiliary hardtop for convertible ($231.75). RPO C08 Vinyl cover for auxiliary hardtop ($52.70). RPO C50 Rear window defroster ($31.60). RPO C60 Air conditioning ($412.90). RPO F41 Special front and rear suspension ($36.90). RPO G81 Positraction rear axle, all ratios ($46.35). RPO J50 Power brakes ($42.15). RPO J56 Special heavy-duty brakes ($384.45). RPO K66 Transistor ignition system ($73.75). RPO L36 427-cid 390-hp V-8 ($200.15). RPO L68 427-cid 400-hp V-8 ($305.50). RPO L71/81 427-cid 435-hp ($437.10). RPO L79 327-cid 350-hp V-8 ($105.35). RPO L88 427-cid 560-hp V-8 ($947.90). RPO M20 Four-speed manual transmission ($184.30). RPO M21 Four-speed close-ratio manual transmission ($184.30). RPO M22 Heavy-duty close-ratio four-speed manual transmission ($263.30). RPO M35 Turbo Hydra-Matic automatic transmission ($226.45). RPO N11 Off-road exhaust system ($36.90). RPO N36 Telescopic steering wheel ($42.15). RPO N40 Power steering ($94.80). RPO P01 Bright metal wheel cover ($57.95). RPO PT6 Red stripe nylon tires F70 x 15 ($31.30). RPO PT7 F70 x 15 white stripe tires ($31.35). RPO UA6 Alarm system ($26.35). RPO U15 Speed-warning indicator ($10.55). RPO U69 AM-FM radio ($172.75). RPO U79 Stereo radio ($278.10).

HISTORICAL FOOTNOTES

Just over 80 percent of 1968 Corvettes were equipped with four-speed manual transmission; 81 percent had tinted glass; 36.3 percent had power steering; 19.8 percent had air conditioning and 33.7 percent had power brakes. The L79-powered Corvette of this year could go from 0-to-60 mph in 7.7 seconds and from 0-to-100 mph in 20.7 seconds. The L71-powered Corvette of this year could go from 0-to-30 in 3.0 seconds; from 0-to-50 in 5.3 seconds and from 0-to-60 in 6.5 seconds. It did the quarter mile in 13.41 seconds at 109.5 mph. Top speed (L71) was 142 mph.

1968 CORVETTE

Model Number	Body/Style Number	Body Type & Seating	Factory Price	Shipping Weight	Production Total
194	37	2-dr FsBk Cpe-2P	$4,663	3,055 lbs.	9,936
194	67	2-dr Conv-2P	$4,347	3,070 lbs.	18,630

Nicky Wright

1969 Corvette Stingray with deluxe wheel covers

CORVETTE STINGRAY SERIES (V-8) SERIES 9000

After a year's absence, the Stingray name (now spelled as one word) re-appeared on the front fenders. The back-up lights were integrated into the center taillights. The ignition was now on the steering column and the door depression button used in 1968 was eliminated. (A key lock was put in its place.) Front and rear disc brakes, headlight washers, center console, wheel trim rings, carpeting, and all-vinyl upholstery were standard. Buyers had their choice of 10 exterior colors: Tuxedo Black, Can-Am White, Monza Red, LeMans Blue, Monaco Orange, Fathom Green, Daytona Yellow, Cortez Silver, Burgundy and Riverside Gold. All convertibles came with a choice of Black, White or Beige soft tops. Interior colors were: Black, Bright Blue, Green, Red, Gunmetal, and Saddle.

I.D. NUMBERS

The Vehicle Identification Number (VIN) is stamped on a plate on the inner vertical surface of the left windshield pillar visible through the windshield. For 1969 the numbers were: [Convertibles] 194679S100001 to 194679S138762; [Coupes] 194379S100001 to 194379S138762. The first symbol (1) indicated Chevrolet. The second and third symbols identify the body series (94 = Corvette). The fourth and fifth symbols indicate the body style number (67 = convertible; 37 = coupe). The sixth symbol indicates the model year (9 = 1969). The seventh symbol identifies the assembly plant (S = St. Louis, Mo). The last six symbols indicate the sequential production number. Engine code suffixes were: HY = 350-cid 300-hp V-8 with 10.0:1 compression; four-barrel carburetor and manual transmission. HZ = 350-cid 300-hp V-8 with 10.0:1 compression ratio, four-barrel carburetor and Turbo Hydra-Matic (THM) automatic transmission. HW = 350-cid 350-hp V-8 with 11.0:1 compression ratio, four-barrel carburetor and manual transmission. HX = 350-cid 350-hp V-8 with 11.0:1 compression ratio, four-barrel carburetor and manual transmission. LM = 427-cid 390-hp V-8 with 10.25:1 compression ratio, four-barrel carburetor and manual transmission. LL = 427-cid 390-hp

Jerry Heasley

1969 Corvette L88 race car

Nicky Wright

The 1969 Corvette convertible featured headlight washers.

V-8 with 10.25:1 compression ratio, four-barrel carburetor and THM automatic transmission. LQ = 427-cid 400-hp V-8 with 10.25:1 compression ratio, three two-barrel carburetors and manual transmission. LQ = 427-cid 400-hp V-8 with 10.25:1 compression ratio, three two-barrel carburetors and THM automatic transmission. LO = 427-cid 430-hp V-8 with 12.0:1 compression ratio, four-barrel carburetor and manual transmission. LV = 427-cid 430-hp V-8 with 12.0:1 compression ratio, four-barrel carburetor and THM automatic transmission. LR = 427-cid 435-hp V-8 with 11.0:1 compression ratio, three two-barrel carburetors and manual transmission. LX = 427-cid 435-hp V-8 with 11.0:1 compression ratio, three two-barrel carburetors and THM automatic transmission. LP = 427-cid 435-hp V-8 with 11.0:1 compression ratio, three two-barrel carburetors and manual transmission. LW = 427-cid 435-hp V-8 with 11.0:1 compression ratio, three two-barrel carburetors and THM automatic transmission. LT = 427-cid 435-hp V-8 with 11.0:1 compression ratio, three two-barrel carburetors and manual transmission. LU = 427-cid 435-hp V-8 with 11.0:1 compression ratio, three two-barrel carburetors and manual transmission. The beginning engine numbers were 0001001 and up at each assembly plant with F = Flint, Mich. and T = Tonawanda, N.Y. Corvette engines have the last six digits of the VIN stamped on the block next to the engine number. The body number plate was located on the engine side of the cowl. The Fisher Body Style Number 69-19467 identifies a Corvette Stingray convertible and the Fisher Body Style Number 69-19437 identifies a Corvette Stingray coupe. The Body Number is the production serial number of the body. The Trim Number indicates the interior trim color and material.

Nicky Wright

1969 Corvette Stingray convertible

1969 Corvette Stingray convertible with side-mount exhaust system.

PAINT CODES

Tuxedo Black (900), Can-Am White (972), Monza Red (974), LeMans Blue (976), Hugger Orange (990) , Fathom Green (983), Daytona Yellow (984), Cortez Silver (986), Burgundy (988) and Riverside Gold (980). All convertibles came with a choice of Black, White or Beige soft tops. Interior colors were: Black, Bright Blue, Green, Red, Gunmetal, and Saddle.

VINYL UPHOLSTERY CODES: (STD/ZQ4) Black; (407) Red; (411) Blue; (416) Gunmetal; (420) Saddle; (427) Green.

LEATHER UPHOLSTERY CODES: (402) Black; (408) Red; (412) Blue; (417) Gunmetal; (421) Saddle; (428) Green.

ENGINES

BASE ENGINE: Overhead valve V-8. Cast-iron block. Displacement: 350 cid. Bore and stroke: 4.00 x 3.48 inches. Compression ratio: 10.25:1. Brake hp: 300 at 4800 rpm. Five main bearings. Hydraulic valve lifters. Carburetor: Rochester four-barrel Model 7029203.

OPTIONAL ENGINE: [RPO L46] V-8. Overhead valve. Cast-iron block. Displacement: 350 cid. Bore and stroke: 4.00 x 3.48 inches. Compression ratio: 11.0:1. Brake hp: 350. Five main bearings. Hydraulic valve lifters. Carburetor: Rochester four-barrel.

OPTIONAL ENGINE: [RPO L36] V-8. Overhead valve. Cast-iron block. Displacement: 427 cid. Bore and stroke: 4.251 x 3.76 inches. Compression ratio: 10:25:1. Brake hp: 390 at 5400 rpm. Torque: 460 lbs.-ft. at 3600 rpm. Five main bearings. Hydraulic valve lifters. High-performance camshaft. Carburetor: Holley four-barrel.

OPTIONAL ENGINE: [RPO L68] V-8. Overhead valve. Cast-iron block. Displacement: 427 cid. Bore and stroke: 4.251 x 3.76 inches. Compression ratio: 10.25:1. Brake hp: 400. Five main bearings. Three Holley two-barrel carburetors.

OPTIONAL ENGINE: [RPO L71] V-8. Overhead valve. Cast-iron block. Displacement: 427 cid. Bore and stroke: 4.251 x 3.76 inches. Compression ratio: 11.0:1. Brake hp: 435 @ 5800 rpm. Torque: 460 lbs.-ft. at 4000 rpm. Five main bearings. Mechanical valve lifters. Special-performance camshaft. Carburetor: Three Holley two-barrels.

OPTIONAL ENGINE: [RPO L88] V-8. Overhead valve. Displacement: 427 cid. Bore and stroke: 4.251 x 3.76 inches. Compression ratio: 12.0:1. Brake hp: 430 (actually about 560 @ 6400 rpm). Five main bearings. Mechanical valve lifters. Special-ultra-high-performance camshaft with .5365-inch intakes. Carburetor: Holley four-barrel.

OPTIONAL ENGINE: [RPO L89] V-8. Overhead valve. Displacement: 427 cid. Bore and stroke: 4.251 x 3.76 inches. Compression ratio: 12.0:1. Brake hp: 435. Five main bearings. Mechanical valve lifters. Carburetor: Holley four-barrel.

OPTIONAL ENGINE: [RPO ZL1] V-8. Overhead valve. Displacement: 427 cid. Bore and stroke: 4.251 x 3.76 inches. Compression ratio: 12.5:1. Brake hp: 430 at 5200 rpm (actually over 500). Torque: 450 lbs.-ft. at 4400 rpm. Aluminum block. Five main bearings. Mechanical valve lifters. Special-ultra-high-performance camshaft.

Nicky Wright

Backup lights were moved inside the taillights on the 1969 Corvette.

Carburetor: Single Holley 850CFM four-barrel on aluminum manifold.

TRANSMISSIONS

STANDARD MANUAL TRANSMISSION: A three-speed manual all-synchromesh transmission with floor-mounted gear shifter was standard equipment.

AUTOMATIC TRANSMISSION: A Turbo Hydra-Matic automatic transmission with floor-mounted gear shifter was optional equipment.

OPTIONAL MANUAL TRANSMISSION: A high-performance all-synchromesh four-speed manual transmission with floor-mounted gear shifter was optional equipment.

OPTIONAL MANUAL TRANSMISSION: A special high-performance four-speed manual all-synchromesh close-ratio transmission with floor-mounted gear shifter was optional equipment.

OPTIONAL MANUAL TRANSMISSION: A special heavy-duty four-speed manual all-synchromesh close-ratio transmission with floor-mounted gear shifter was optional.

CHASSIS FEATURES

Wheelbase: 98 inches. Overall length: 182.5 inches. Overall height: 47.9 inches. Overall width: 69.0 inches. Front tread: 58.7 inches. Rear tread: 59.4 inches. Tires: F70-15. Frame: Full-length welded-steel ladder type with five cross members. steel box sections, welded. Front suspension: Unequal-length A-arms with coil springs; tube shocks and stabilizer bar. Steering: Saginaw recirculating ball; ratio 17.6:1; turns lock-to-lock: 2.9; turning radius: 39.0 feet. Rear suspension: Trailing arms, toe links, transverse chromium-carbon steel leaf spring, tube shocks and anti-roll bar. Rear axle type: Sprung differential, hypoid gear. Brakes: Four-wheel disc brakes. Vented discs front and rear. optional power assist; diameter: 11.75 inches front and 11.75 inches rear; total swept area: 461 sq. in. 15 x 8-inch slotted steel disc wheels. Standard rear axle ratio 3.36:1. Available rear axle gear ratios: 3.08:1; 3.36:1; 3.55:1; 3.70:1; 4.11:1; 4.56:1.

OPTIONS

RPO 898 Genuine leather seat trim ($79). RPO A01

Nicky Wright

1969 Corvette engine

Soft-Ray tinted glass, all windows ($16.90). RPO A31 Electric power windows ($63.20). RPO A85 Custom shoulder belts ($42.15). RPO C07 Auxiliary hardtop for convertible ($252.80). RPO C08 Vinyl cover for auxiliary hardtop ($57.95). RPO C50 Rear window defroster ($32.65). RPO C60 Air conditioning ($428.70). RPO F41 Special front and rear suspension ($36.90). RPO G81 Positraction rear axle, all ratios ($46.35). RPO J50 Power brakes ($42.15). RPO K05 Engine block heater ($10.55). RPO K66 Transistor ignition system ($81.10). RPO L36 427-cid 390-hp V-8 ($221.20). RPO L46 350-cid 350-hp V-8 ($131.65). RPO L68 427-cid 400-hp V-8 ($326.55). RPO L71 427-cid 435-hp V-8 ($437.10). RPO L88 427-cid 435-hp V-8 ($1032.15). RPO L89 427-cid 435-hp V-8 ($832.05). RPO ZL1 Optional special 427-cid aluminum V-8 ($3,000). RPO M20 Four-speed manual transmission ($184.80). RPO M21 Four-speed close-ratio manual transmission ($184.80). RPO M22 Heavy-duty close-ratio four-speed manual transmission ($290.40). RPO M40 Turbo Hydra-Matic automatic transmission ($221.80). RPO N14 Side mount exhaust system ($147.45). RPO N37 Tilt-telescopic steering wheel ($84.30). RPO N40 Power steering ($105.35). RPO P02 Wheel covers ($57.95). RPO PT6 Red stripe nylon tires, F70 x 15 ($31.30). RPO PT7 F70 x 15, white stripe tires ($31.30). TJ2 Front fender louver trim ($21.10). RPO UA6 Alarm system ($26.35). RPO U15 Speed-warning indicator ($11.60). RPO U69 AM-FM radio ($172.45). RPO U79 Stereo radio ($278.10).

HISTORICAL FOOTNOTES

The majority of 1969 Corvettes, 59.2 percent, came with power steering; 78.4 percent had four-speed manual transmissions and one-in-four had power windows. A 350-cid 300-hp V-8 was available this season. Cars with this powerplant and automatic transmission were capable of 0-to-60 mph speeds in the 8.4 second bracket and could move from 0-to-100 mph in approximately 21.7 seconds.

1969 CORVETTE

Model Number	Body/Style Number	Body Type & Seating	Factory Price	Shipping Weight	Production Total
194	37	2-dr FsBk Cpe-2P	$4,763	3,091 lbs.	22,129
194	67	2-dr Conv-2P	$4,420	3,096 lbs.	16,633

Jerry Heasley

1969 Corvette Stingray L89 convertible

Jerry Heasley

1970 Corvette

CORVETTE STINGRAY SERIES (V-8) SERIES 9000

Refinements were made to the basic styling used since 1968. A new ice-cube-tray design grille and matching side fender louvers; rectangular, amber front signal lights; fender flares; and square exhaust exits were exterior changes. The bucket seats and safety belt retractor containers were also improved. Standard equipment included: Front and rear disc brakes; headlight washers; wheel trim rings; carpeting; center console and all-vinyl upholstery (in either Black; Blue; Green; Saddle; or Red). Buyers had their choice of 10 exterior colors: Mulsanne Blue; Bridgehampton Blue; Donnybrooke Green; Laguna Gray; Marlboro Maroon; Corvette Bronze; Monza Red; Cortez Silver; Classic White; and Daytona Yellow. All convertibles came with a choice of Black or White soft tops. Interior colors were: Black; Blue; Green; Red; Brown; and Saddle.

I.D. NUMBERS

The Vehicle Identification Number (VIN) is stamped on a plate on the inner vertical surface of the left windshield pillar visible through the windshield. For 1970 the numbers were: [Convertibles] 194670S100001 to 194670S117316; [Coupes] 194370S100001 to 194370S117316. The first symbol (1) indicated Chevrolet. The second symbol identified the body series (9 = Corvette). The third symbol indicated the type of engine with an even number like 4 indicating a V-8 engine. The fourth and fifth symbols indicate the body style number (67 = convertible; 37 = coupe). The sixth symbol indicates the model year (0 = 1970). The seventh symbol identifies the assembly plant (S = St. Louis, Mo). The last six symbols indicate the sequential production number. Engine code suffixes were: CTG = 350-cid 300-hp V-8 with 10.25:1 compression ratio, four-barrel carburetor, and THM-400 automatic transmission. CTM = 350-cid 300-hp V-8 with 10.25:1 compression ratio, four-barrel carburetor, and THM-400 automatic transmission. CTD = 350-cid 300-hp V-8 with 10.25:1 compression ratio, four-barrel carburetor, and manual transmission. CTL = 350-cid 300-hp V-8 with 10.25:1 compression ratio, four-barrel carburetor, and manual transmission. CTN = 350-cid 350-hp V-8 with 11.0:1 compression ratio, four-barrel carburetor, and manual transmission. CTO = 350-cid 350-hp V-8 with 11.0:1 compression ratio, four-barrel carburetor, and manual transmission. CTP = 350-cid 350-hp V-8 with 11.0:1 compression ratio, four-barrel carburetor, transistor ignition, and manual transmission. CTQ = 350-cid 350-hp V-8 with 11.0:1 compression ratio, four-barrel carburetor, transistor ignition, and manual transmission. CTR = 350-cid 370-hp V-8 with 11.0:1 compression ratio, four-barrel carburetor, transistor ignition, and M-22 transmission. CTU = 350-cid 370-hp V-8 with 11.0:1 compression ratio, four-barrel carburetor,

Nicky Wright

1970 Corvette Stingray LT1 with T-tops

transistor ignition, and M-22 transmission. CTV = 350-cid 370-hp V-8 with 11.0:1 compression ratio, four-barrel carburetor, transistor ignition, and M-22 transmission. CGW = 454-cid 390-hp V-8 with 10.25:1 compression ratio, four-barrel carburetor, and manual transmission. CZU = 454-cid 390-hp V-8 with 10.25:1 compression ratio, four-barrel carburetor, and manual transmission. CZL = 454-cid 465-hp V-8 with 11.25:1 compression ratio, four-barrel carburetor, aluminum heads, transistor ignition, and manual transmission. CZN = 454-cid 465-hp V-8 with 11.25:1 compression ratio, four-barrel carburetor, aluminum heads, transistor ignition and THM-400 automatic transmission. CRI = 454-cid 390-hp V-8 with 10.25:1 compression ratio, four-barrel carburetor, and manual transmission. CTH = 350-cid 350-hp V-8 with 11.0:1 compression ratio, four-barrel carburetor, and manual transmission. CTJ = 350-cid 350-hp V-8 with 11.0:1 compression ratio, four-barrel carburetor, and manual transmission. CTK = 350-cid 370-hp V-8 with 11.0:1 compression ratio, four-barrel carburetor, transistor ignition, and manual transmission. CRJ = 454-cid 390-hp V-8 with 10.25:1 compression ratio, four-barrel carburetor transistor ignition, and THM-400 automatic transmission. The beginning engine numbers were 0001001 and up at each assembly plant with F = Flint, Mich. and T = Tonawanda, N.Y. Corvette engines have the last six digits of the VIN stamped on the block next to the engine number. The body number plate was located on the engine side of the cowl. The Fisher Body Style Number 70-19467 identifies a Corvette Stingray convertible and the Fisher Body Style Number 70-19437 identifies a Corvette Stingray coupe. The Body Number is the production serial number of the body. The Trim Number indicates the interior trim color and material.

PAINT CODES: The Paint Number indicates the color combination: (972) Classic White; (974) Monza Red; (975) Marlboro Maroon; (976) Mulsanne Blue; (979) Bridgehampton Blue; (982) Donnybrooke Green; (984) Daytona Yellow; (986) Cortez Silver; (992) Laguna Gray; (993) Corvette Bronze.

VINYL UPHOLSTERY CODES: (400) Black; (407) Red; (411) Blue; (414) Brown; (418) Saddle; (422) Green.

LEATHER UPHOLSTERY CODES: (403) Black; (424) Saddle.

ENGINES

BASE ENGINE: [RPO ZQ3] Overhead valve. Cast-iron block. Displacement: 350 cid. Bore and stroke: 4.00 x 3.48 inches. Compression ratio: 10.25:1. Brake hp: 300 at 4800 rpm. Five main bearings. Hydraulic valve lifters. Carburetor: Rochester Type Quadra-Jet four-barrel Model 4MV.

OPTIONAL ENGINE: [RPO L46] V-8. Overhead valve V-8. Cast-iron block. Displacement: 350 cid. Bore and stroke: 4.00 x 3.48 inches. Compression ratio: 11.0:1. Brake hp: 350 at 5600 rpm. Torque: 380 lb.-ft. at 3800 rpm. Five main bearings. Hydraulic valve lifters. Carburetor: Rochester Quadra-Jet four-barrel.

OPTIONAL ENGINE: [RPO LS5] V-8. Overhead valve. Cast-iron block. Displacement: 454 cid. Bore and stroke: 4.251 x 4.00 inches. Compression ratio: 10.25:1. Brake hp: 390 at 4800 rpm. Torque: 500 lbs.-ft. at 3400

1970 Corvette Stingray LT1 coupe, fender louvers are now a single grate.

rpm. Five main bearings. Hydraulic valve lifters. High-performance camshaft. Carburetor: Rochester 750CFM Quadra-Jet four-barrel.

OPTIONAL ENGINE: [RPO LT1] V-8. Overhead valve. Cast-iron block. Displacement: 350 cid. Bore and stroke: 4.00 x 3.48 inches. Compression ratio: 11.0:1. Brake hp: 370 at 6000 rpm. Torque: 380 lbs.-ft. at 4000 rpm. Five main bearings. Solid valve lifters. High-performance camshaft. Carburetor: Holley four-barrel on aluminum intake manifold.

PROPOSED OPTIONAL ENGINE: [RPO LS7] V-8. Overhead valve. Cast-iron block. Displacement: 454 cid. Bore and stroke: 4.251 x 4.00 inches. Compression ratio: 11.25:1. Brake hp: 465 at 5200 rpm. Torque: 490 lbs.-ft. at 3400 rpm. Five main bearings. Solid valve lifters. High-performance camshaft. Carburetor: Holley 800CFM four-barrel.

*(**NOTE:** Only one car with the LS7 engine was built. Sports Car Graphic editor Paul Van Valkenburgh drove it 2,500 miles from a press conference at Riverside, Calif., to Detroit and raved about it. The car did the quarter mile in 13.8 seconds at 108 mph. However, GM's policies against ultra-high-performance cars at this time led to the option being stillborn. The LS7 option is listed in some early 1970 sales literature but none were ever sold.)*

TRANSMISSION

AUTOMATIC TRANSMISSION: A Turbo Hydra-Matic automatic transmission with floor-mounted gear shifter was standard equipment.

OPTIONAL MANUAL TRANSMISSION: A close-ratio four-speed manual transmission with floor-mounted gear shifter was a no-cost option.

OPTIONAL MANUAL TRANSMISSION: A heavy-duty close-ratio four-speed manual transmission with floor-mounted gear shifter was optional equipment.

CHASSIS FEATURES

Wheelbase: 98 inches. Overall length: 182.5 inches. Overall height: 47.4 inches. Overall width: 69.0 inches. Ground clearance: 4.5 inches. Front tread: 58.7 inches. Rear tread: 59.4 inches. Tires: F70-15. Frame: Full-length welded-steel ladder type with five cross members. Steel box sections, welded. Front suspension: Unequal-length A-arms with coil springs, tube shocks, and stabilizer bar. Steering: Saginaw recirculating ball; ratio 17.6:1; turns lock-to-lock 2.9; turning radius 39.0 feet. Rear suspension: Trailing arms; toe links; transverse chromium-carbon steel leaf springs; tube shocks; and anti-roll bar. Rear axle type: Sprung differential, hypoid gear. Brakes: Four-wheel disc brakes; vented discs front and rear; optional power assist; diameter 11.75 inches front and 11.75 inches rear; total swept area 461 sq. in.; 15 x 8-inch slotted steel disc wheels. Standard rear axle ratio: 3.36:1. Available rear axle gear ratios: 2.73:1; 3.08:1; 3.36:1; 3.55:1; 4.11:1; 4.56:1.

OPTIONS

RPO Custom interior trim ($158). RPO A31 Electric power windows ($63.20). RPO A85 Custom shoulder belts ($42.15). RPO C07 Auxiliary hardtop for convertible ($273.85). RPO C08 Vinyl cover for auxiliary hardtop ($63.20). RPO C50 Rear window defroster ($36.90). RPO C60 Air conditioning ($447.65). RPO G81 Positraction rear axle, all ratios ($12.65). RPO J50 Power brakes ($47.40). RPO L46 350-cid 350-hp V-8 ($158.). RPO LS5

1970 Corvette Stingray convertible.

Nicky Wright

1970 Corvette LT1 coupe

454-cid 390-hp V-8 ($289.65). RPO LT1 350-cid 370-hp V-8 ($447.60). RPO M21 Four-speed close-ratio manual transmission (no-cost option). RPO M22 Heavy-duty close-ratio four-speed manual transmission ($95.). RPO M40 Turbo Hydra-Matic automatic transmission (no cost option). RPO N37 Tilt-telescopic steering wheel ($84.30). RPO N40 Power steering ($105.35). RPO P01 Custom wheel covers ($57.95). RPO PT7 White stripe nylon tires, F70 x 15 ($31.30). RPO PU9 F70 x 15 raised-white-letter tires ($33.15). RPO T60 Heavy-duty battery ($15.80). RPO UA6 Alarm system ($31.60). RPO U69 AM-FM radio ($172.75). RPO U79 Stereo radio ($278.10). Beginning in April 1970, the LT1 engine was made available as part of a ZR1 option. The "Z" meant it was part of Chevrolet's "Special Items" group. The ZR1 package included the LT1 engine; M22 heavy-duty four-speed manual transmission; J50/J56 dual-pin brakes with heavy-duty front pads and power assist; and F41 suspension consisting of special 89 lb./in. ride rate front springs and 121 lb./in. ride rate rear springs, matching shock absorbers, and a 0.75-inch front stabilizer bar.

HISTORICAL FOOTNOTES

Most 1970 Corvettes, 70.5 percent, came with four-speed manual transmission; 33.5 percent had tilting steering wheels; 27.9 percent power windows; 38.5 percent air-conditioning; and 68.8 percent power steering. An L56-powered 1970 Corvette would do 0-to-60 mph in seven seconds and go from 0-to-100 mph in 14 seconds. An LT1-powered 1970 Corvette could do 0-30 mph in 2.5 seconds, 0-60 mph in 5.7 seconds and 0-to-100 mph in 13.5 seconds. The LT1 Corvette did the quarter mile in 14.17 seconds at 102.15 mph and had a top speed of 122 mph.

1970 CORVETTE

Model Number	Body/Style Number	Body Type & Seating	Factory Price	Shipping Weight	Production Total
194	37	2-dr FsBk Cpe-2P	$5,192	3,153 lbs.	10,668
194	67	2-dr Conv-2P	$4,849	3,167 lbs.	6,648

NOTE: A total of 1,287 buyers separately checked off the LT1 engine option in 1970. In addition, 25 ZR1 Corvettes carried the LT1 engine.

Jerry Healsey

1971 Corvette Stingray LT1 coupe in Mille Miglia Red

CORVETTE STINGRAY (SERIES V-8) SERIES 9000

If you liked the 1970 Corvette, you'd like the 1971 version. They were virtually the same car. A new resin process (that supposedly improved the body) and a different interior were the major changes. Under the hood, the compression ratios were dropped a bit to enable Corvette engines to run on lower octane fuel. Standard equipment included: All-vinyl upholstery; dual exhaust; outside rearview mirror; carpeting; center console; wheel trim rings; electric clock; tachometer; heavy-duty battery; front and rear disc brakes with warning light; and tinted glass. Buyers had their choice of 10 exterior colors: Mulsanne Blue; Bridgehampton Blue; Brands Hatch Green; Steel Cities Gray; Ontario Orange; Mille Miglia Red; Nevada Silver; Classic White; Sunflower Yellow; and War Bonnet Yellow. All convertibles came with a choice of Black or White soft tops. Interior colors were: Black; Dark Blue; Dark Green; Red; and Saddle.

I.D. NUMBERS

The Vehicle Identification Number (VIN) is stamped on a plate on the inner vertical surface of the left windshield pillar visible through the windshield. For 1971 the numbers were: [Convertibles] 194671S100001 to 194671S21801; [Coupes] 194371S100001 to 194371S121801. The first symbol (1) indicated Chevrolet. The second symbol identified the body series (9 = Corvette). The third symbol indicated the type of engine with an even number like 4 indicating a V-8 engine. The fourth and fifth symbols indicate the body style number (67 = convertible; 37 = coupe). The sixth symbol indicates the model year (1 = 1971). The seventh symbol identifies the assembly plant (S = St. Louis, Mo). The last six symbols indicate the sequential production number. Engine code suffixes were: CJL = 350-cid 270-hp V-8 with 8.5:1 compression ratio, four-barrel carburetor, and manual transmission. CGT = 350-cid 270-hp V-8 with 8.5:1 compression ratio, four-barrel carburetor, and THM-400 automatic transmission. CJK = 350-cid 270-hp V-8 with 8.5:1 compression ratio, four-barrel carburetor, and THM-400 automatic transmission. CGZ = 350-cid 330-hp V-8 with 9.0:1 compression ratio, four-barrel carburetor, and manual transmission. CGY = 350-cid 330-hp V-8 with 9.0:1 compression ratio, four-barrel carburetor, and manual transmission. CJK = 350-cid 330-hp V-8 with 9.0:1 compression ratio, four-barrel carburetor, and THM-400 automatic transmission. CPH = 454-cid 365-hp V-8 with 8.5:1 compression ratio, four-barrel carburetor, and manual transmission. CPJ = 454-cid 365-hp V-8 with 8.5:1 compression ratio, four-barrel carburetor, and THM-400 automatic transmission. CPW = 454-cid 425-hp V-8 with 9.0:1 compression ratio, four-

1971 Corvette Stingray LT1 with T-tops

barrel carburetor, and manual transmission. CPX = 454-cid 425-hp V-8 with 9.0:1 compression ratio, four-barrel carburetor, and THM-400 automatic transmission. The beginning engine numbers were 0001001 and up at each assembly plant with F = Flint, Mich. and T = Tonawanda, N.Y. Corvette engines have the last six digits of the VIN stamped on the block next to the engine number. The body number plate was located on the engine side of the cowl. The Fisher Body Style Number 71-19467 identifies a Corvette Stingray convertible and the Fisher Body Style Number 71-19437 identifies a Corvette Stingray coupe. The Body Number is the production serial number of the body. The Trim Number indicates the interior trim color and material.

PAINT CODES

(905) Nevada Silver; (912) Sunflower Yellow; (972) Classic White; (973) Mille Miglia Red; (976) Mulsanne Blue; (979) Bridgehampton Blue; (983) Brands Hatch Green; (987) Ontario Orange; (988) Steel Cities Gray; (989) War Bonnet Yellow.

VINYL UPHOLSTERY CODES: (400) Black; (407) Red; (412) Dark Blue; (414) Brown; (417) Saddle; (423) Dark Green.

LEATHER UPHOLSTERY CODES: (403) Black; (420) Saddle.

ENGINES

BASE ENGINE: [RPO ZQ3] V-8. Overhead valve. Cast-iron block. Bore and stroke: 4.00 x 3.48 inches. Displacement: 350 cid. Compression ratio: 10.25:1. Brake hp: 300 at 4800 rpm. Taxable hp: 51.20. Torque: 380 at 3200 rpm. Five main bearings. Hydraulic valve lifters. Crankcase capacity: 4 qt. (Add 1 qt. for filter). Cooling system capacity: 14 qt. (Add 1 qt. for heater). Carburetor: Rochester 7029203 four-barrel.

1971 Corvette Stingray LT1

1971 Corvette Stingray L86 coupe in Ontario Orange

OPTIONAL ENGINE: [RPO LT1] V-8. Overhead valve. Cast-iron block. Bore and stroke: 4.00 x 3.48 inches. Displacement: 350 cid. Compression ratio: 9.00:1. Brake hp: 330 at 5600 rpm. Net brake hp: 275 at 5600 rpm. Taxable hp: 51.20. Torque: 360 at 4000 rpm. Net torque: 300 at 4000 rpm. Five main bearings. Hydraulic valve lifters. Crankcase capacity: 4 qt. (Add 1 qt. for filter). Cooling system capacity: 14 qt. (Add 1 qt. for heater). Carburetor: Rochester Rochester Type Quadra-Jet four-barrel Model 4MV. .

OPTIONAL ENGINE: [RPO LT1/ZR1] V-8. Overhead valve. Cast-iron block. Bore and stroke: 4.00 x 3.48 inches. Displacement: 350 cid. Compression ratio: 9.00:1. Brake hp: 330 at unknown rpm. Net brake hp: unknown at unknown rpm. Taxable hp: 51.20. Torque: unknown at unknown rpm. Net torque: unknown at unknown rpm. Five main bearings. Hydraulic valve lifters. Crankcase capacity: 4 qt. (Add 1 qt. for filter). Cooling system capacity: 14 qt. (Add 1 qt. for heater). Carburetor: Rochester Rochester Type Quadra-Jet four-barrel Model 4MV.

NOTE: Competition engine; only eight assembled.

OPTIONAL ENGINE: [RPO LS5]. V-8. Overhead valve. Cast iron block. Bore and stroke: 4.251 x 4.00 inches. Displacement: 454 cid. Compression ratio: 8.50:1. Brake hp: 365 at 4800 rpm. Net brake hp: 285 at 4000 rpm. Torque: 465 at 3200 rpm. Net torque: 390 at 3200 rpm. Five main bearings. Hydraulic valve lifters. High-performance camshaft. Crankcase capacity: 5 qt. (Add 1 qt. for filter). Cooling system capacity: 21 qt. (Add 1 qt. for heater). Carburetor: Rochester 750CFM Quadra-Jet four-barrel.

OPTIONAL ENGINE: [RPO LS6] V-8. Overhead valve. Cast-iron block. Bore and stroke: 4.251 x 4.00 inches. Displacement: 454 cid. Compression ratio: 8.5:1. Brake hp: 425 at 5600 rpm. Net brake hp: 325 at 6500 rpm. Torque: 475 at 4000 rpm. Net torque: 390 at 3600 rpm. Five main bearings. Hydraulic valve lifters. High-performance camshaft. Crankcase capacity: 5 qt. (Add 1 qt. for filter). Cooling system capacity: 21 qt. (Add 1 qt. for heater). Carburetor: Holley 880CFM four-barrel.

TRANSMISSION

AUTOMATIC TRANSMISSION: A Turbo Hydra-Matic automatic transmission with floor-mounted gear shifter was standard equipment.

OPTIONAL MANUAL TRANSMISSION: A close-ratio four-speed manual transmission with floor-mounted gear shifter was a no-cost option.

OPTIONAL MANUAL TRANSMISSION: A heavy-duty close-ratio four-speed manual transmission with floor-mounted gear shifter was optional equipment.

CHASSIS FEATURES

Wheelbase: 98 inches. Overall length: 182.5 inches. Overall height: 47.4 inches. Overall width: 69.0 inches. Ground clearance: 4.5 inches. Front tread: 58.7 inches. Rear tread: 59.4 inches. Tires: F70-15. Frame: Full-length welded-steel ladder type with five cross members. Steel box sections, welded. Front suspension: Unequal-length A-arms with coil springs, tube shocks, and stabilizer bar. Steering: Saginaw recirculating ball; ratio 17.6:1; turns lock-to-lock 2.9; turning radius 39.0 feet. Rear suspension: Trailing arms; toe links; transverse chromium-carbon steel leaf springs; tube shocks; and anti-roll bar. Rear axle type: Sprung differential, hypoid gear. Brakes: Four-wheel disc brakes; vented discs front and rear; optional power

1971 Corvette Stingray ZR2 convertible with 454-cid 425-hp LS6 V-8 with four-speed manual transmission

assist; diameter: 11.75 inches front and 11.75 inches rear; total swept area: 461 sq. in.; 15 x 8-inch slotted steel disc wheels. Standard rear axle ratio 3.36:1. Available rear axle gear ratios: 2.73:1; 3.08:1; 3.36:1; 3.55:1; 4.11:1; 4.56:1.

OPTIONS

RPO Custom interior trim ($158). RPO A31 Electric power windows ($79). RPO A85 Custom shoulder belts ($42). RPO C07 Auxiliary hardtop for convertible ($274). RPO C08 Vinyl cover for auxiliary hardtop ($63). RPO C50 Rear window defroster ($42). RPO C60 Air conditioning ($459). RPO G81 Positraction rear axle, all ratios ($13). RPO J50 Power brakes ($47). RPO LS5 454-cid 365-hp V-8 ($295). RPO LS6 454-cid 425-hp V-8 ($1221). RPO LT1 350-cid 330-hp V-8 ($483). RPO ZR1 350-cid 330-hp V-8 ($1010). RPO ZR2 454-cid 425-hp V-8 ($1747). RPO M21 Four-speed close-ratio manual transmission (no-cost option). RPO M22 Heavy-duty close-ratio four-speed manual transmission ($100). RPO M40 Turbo Hydra-Matic automatic transmission (no-cost option). RPO N37 Tilt-Telescopic steering wheel ($84.30). RPO N40 Power steering ($115.90). RPO P02 Custom wheel covers ($63). RPO PT7 White stripe nylon tires, F70 x 15 ($28). RPO PU9 F70 x 15 raised-white-letter tires ($42). RPO T60 Heavy-duty battery ($15.80). RPO U69 AM-FM radio ($178). RPO U79 Stereo radio ($283). The LT1 engine was again available as part of the ZR1 option. The "Z" meant it was part of Chevrolet's "Special Items" group. The ZR1 package included the LT1 engine, M22 heavy-duty four-speed manual transmission, J50/J56 dual-pin brakes with heavy-duty front pads and power assist and F41 suspension consisting of special 89 lb./in. ride rate front springs and 121 lb./in. ride rate rear springs, matching shock absorbers and a 0.75-inch front stabilizer bar.

HISTORICAL FOOTNOTES

Slightly over one-third of 1971 Corvettes had a tilting steering wheel; 53.9 percent had a four-speed manual transmission; 82.1 percent had power steering; 52.7 percent had air conditioning; and 28.4 percent had power windows. A 1971 Corvette with the base L48 engine could go 0-to-60 mph in 7.1 seconds, 0-to-100 mph in 19.8 seconds and do the standing-start quarter mile in 15.5 seconds at 90.36 mph. A 1971 Corvette with the LS5 engine could go 0-to-60 mph in 5.7 seconds, 0-to-100 mph in 14.1 seconds and do the standing-start quarter mile in 14.2 seconds at 100.33 mph. A 1971 Corvette with the LS6 engine and 3.36:1 rear axle was tested by *Car and Driver* magazine in June 1971. It moved from 0-to-60 mph in 5.3 seconds, from 0-to-80 mph in 8.5 seconds and from 0-to-100 mph in 12.7 seconds. The same car did the quarter mile in 13.8 seconds at 104.65 mph. A 1971 Corvette with the LT1 engine, M-21 transmission, and 3.70:1 rear axle was tested by *Car and Driver* magazine in June 1971. It moved from 0-to-40 mph in 3.4 seconds, 0-to-60 mph in 6.0 seconds, and from 0-to-100 mph in 14.5 seconds. The same car did the quarter mile in 14.57 seconds at 100.55 mph and its speed was 137 mph.

1971 CORVETTE

Model Number	Body/Style Number	Body Type & Seating	Factory Price	Shipping Weight	Production Total
194	37	2-dr FsBk Cpe-2P	$5,536	3,153 lbs.	14,680
194	67	2-dr Conv-2P	$5,299	3,167 lbs.	7,121

NOTE: A total of 1,949 buyers separately checked off the LT1 engine option in 1971. In addition, eight ZR1 Corvettes carried the LT1 engine.

Nicky Wright

1972 Corvette Stingray LT1 convertible with 350-cid 225-hp V-8 engine

CORVETTE STINGRAY SERIES (V-8) SERIES 9000

The 1972 Corvette was basically the same as the 1971. Among the standard equipment was a Positraction rear axle; outside rearview mirror; tinted glass; flo-thru ventilation system; front and rear disc brakes; electric clock; carpeting; wheel trim rings; all-vinyl upholstery; and anti-theft alarm system. Buyers had their choice of 10 exterior colors: Sunflower Yellow; Pewter Silver; Bryar Blue; Elkhart Green; Classic White; Mille Miglia Red; Targa Blue; Ontario Orange; Steel Cities Gray and War Bonnet Yellow. All convertibles came with a choice of Black or White soft tops. Interior colors were: Black; Blue; Red; and Saddle.

I.D. NUMBERS

The Vehicle Identification Number (VIN) is stamped on a plate on the inner vertical surface of the left windshield pillar visible through the windshield. For 1972 the numbers were: [Convertibles] 1Z67K2S500001 to 1Z67K2S527004; [Coupes] 1Z37K2S500001 to 1Z37K2S527004. The first symbol (1) indicated Chevrolet. The second symbol identified the body series (Z = Corvette). The third and fourth symbols indicate the body style number (67 = convertible; 37 = coupe). The fifth symbol indicates engine: K = Base 350-cid V-8; W = LS5 454-cid V-8 with dual exhausts. The sixth symbol indicates the model year (2 = 1972). The seventh symbol identifies the assembly plant (S = St. Louis, Mo). The last six symbols indicate the sequential production number. Engine code suffixes were: CRS = 350-cid 200-hp V-8 with 8.5:1 compression ratio, four-barrel carburetor, and K-19 automatic transmission. CKW = 350-cid 200-hp V-8 with 8.5:1 compression ratio, four-barrel carburetor, and four-speed manual transmission. CDH = 350-cid 200-hp V-8 with 8.5:1 compression ratio, four-barrel carburetor, and NB2 four-speed manual transmission. CKX = 350-cid 200-hp V-8 with 8.5:1 compression ratio, four-barrel carburetor, and THM automatic transmission. CDJ = 350-cid 200-hp V-8 with 8.5:1 compression ratio, four-barrel carburetor, and NB2 (Calif.) THM automatic transmission. CKY = 350-cid 255-hp V-8 with 9.0:1 compression ratio, four-barrel carburetor, and four-speed manual transmission. CRT = 350-cid 255-hp V-8 with 9.0:1 compression ratio, four-barrel carburetor, and four-speed manual transmission with Air Injection Reactor (AIR) system. CKZ = 350-cid 255-hp V-8 with 9.0:1 compression ratio, four-barrel carburetor, and heavy-duty four-speed manual transmission. CPH = 454-cid 270-hp V-8 with 8.5:1 compression ratio, four-barrel carburetor, and four-speed manual transmission. CPJ = 454-cid 270-hp V-8 with 8.5:1 compression ratio, four-barrel carburetor, and THM automatic transmission. CPR = 454-cid 270-hp V-

1972 Corvette Stingray with T-tops.

8 with 8.5:1 compression ratio, four-barrel carburetor, and four-speed manual transmission with Air Injection Reactor (AIR) system. CPR = 454-cid 270-hp V-8 with 8.5:1 compression ratio, four-barrel carburetor, and THM automatic transmission with Air Injection Reactor (AIR) system. The beginning engine numbers were 0001001 and up at each assembly plant with F = Flint, Mich. and T = Tonawanda, N.Y. The body number plate was located on the engine side of the cowl. The Fisher Body Style Number 72-19467 identifies a Corvette Stingray convertible and the Fisher Body Style Number 72-19437 identifies a Corvette Stingray coupe. The Body Number is the production serial number of the body. The Trim Number indicates the interior trim color and material.

PAINT CODES

(912) Sunflower Yellow; (924) Pewter Silver; (945) Bryar Blue; (946) Elkhart Green; (972) Classic White; (973) Mille Miglia Red; (979) Targa Blue; (987) Ontario Orange; (988) Steel Cities Gray; (989) War Bonnet Yellow.

VINYL UPHOLSTERY CODES: (400) Black; (407) Red; (412) Blue; (417) Saddle.

1972 Corvette LT1 convertible

Nicky Wright

1972 was the last year for chrome bumpers.

LEATHER UPHOLSTERY CODES: (404) Black; (421) Saddle.

ENGINES

BASE ENGINE: [RPO ZQ3] V-8. Overhead valve. Cast iron block. Displacement: 350 cid. Bore and stroke: 4.00 x 3.48 inches. Compression ratio: 8.5:1. Brake hp: 200 at 4400 rpm. Torque: 300 lbs.-ft. at 2800 rpm. Five main bearings. Hydraulic valve lifters. Carburetor: Rochester Type Quadra-Jet four-barrel Model 4MV.

OPTIONAL ENGINE: [RPO LS5] V-8. Overhead valve. Cast iron block. Displacement: 454 cid. Bore and stroke: 4.251 x 4.00 inches. Compression ratio: 8.5:1. Brake hp: 270 at 4000 rpm. Torque: 390 lbs.-ft. at 3200 rpm. Five main bearings. Hydraulic valve lifters. High-performance camshaft. Carburetor: Rochester 750CFM Quadra-Jet four-barrel.

OPTIONAL ENGINE: [RPO LT1] V-8. Overhead valve. Cast iron block. Displacement: 350 cid. Bore and stroke: 4.00 x 3.48 inches. Compression ratio: 9.0:1. Brake hp: 255 at 5600 rpm. Torque: 280 lbs.-ft. at 4000 rpm. Five main bearings. Forged steel crankshaft. Solid valve lifters. High-performance camshaft. Carburetor: Holley four-barrel on aluminum intake manifold. 2.50-inch diameter dual exhaust system.

TRANSMISSION

AUTOMATIC TRANSMISSION: A Turbo Hydra-Matic automatic transmission with floor-mounted gear shifter was standard equipment.

OPTIONAL MANUAL TRANSMISSION: A close-ratio four-speed manual transmission with floor-mounted gear shifter was a no-cost option.

CHASSIS FEATURES

Wheelbase: 98 inches. Overall length: 182.5 inches. Overall height: 47.4 inches. Overall width: 69.0 inches. Ground clearance: 4.5 inches. Front tread: 58.7 inches. Rear tread: 59.4 inches. Tires: F70-15. Frame: Full-length welded-steel ladder type with five cross members; steel box sections; welded. Front suspension: Unequal-length A-arms with coil springs, tube shocks, and stabilizer bar. Steering: Saginaw recirculating ball; ratio 17.6:1; turns lock-to-lock 2.9; turning radius 39.0 feet. Rear suspension: Trailing arms, toe links, transverse chromium-carbon steel leaf springs; tube shocks; and anti-roll bar. Rear axle type: Sprung differential, hypoid gear. Brakes: Four-wheel disc brakes; vented discs front and rear; optional power assist; diameter: 11.75 inches front and 11.75 inches rear; total swept area: 461 sq. in.; 15 x 8-inch slotted steel disc wheels. Standard rear axle ratio 3.36:1. Available rear axle gear ratios: 3.70:1; 3.08:1; 3.36:1; 3.55:1; 4.11:1.

OPTIONS

RPO Custom interior trim ($158). RPO A31 Electric power windows ($85.35). RPO A85 Custom shoulder belts ($26.35). RPO C07 Auxiliary hardtop for convertible ($273.85). RPO C08 Vinyl roof covering for auxiliary hardtop ($158). RPO C50 Rear window defroster ($42.15). RPO C60 Air conditioning ($464.50). RPO G81 Positraction rear axle, all ratios ($12.65). RPO J50 Power brakes ($47.40). RPO LS5 454-cid 270-hp V-8 ($294.90).

1972 Corvette Stingray with T-tops and standard wheel covers.

RPO LT1 350-cid 255-hp V-8 ($483.45). RPO ZR1 350-cid 255-hp V-8 ($1,010.05). RPO M21 Four-speed close-ratio manual transmission (no-cost option). RPO M40 Turbo Hydra-Matic automatic transmission (no-cost option). RPO N37 Tilt-telescopic steering wheel ($84.30). RPO N40 Power steering ($115.90). RPO P02 Custom wheel covers ($63.20). RPO PT7 White stripe nylon tires F70 x 15 ($30.35). RPO PU9 F70 x 15, raised-white-letter tires ($43.65). RPO T60 Heavy-duty battery ($15.80). RPO U69 AM-FM radio ($178). RPO U79 Stereo radio ($283.35).

HISTORICAL FOOTNOTES

Over one-third, 35.1 percent, of 1972 Corvettes came with power windows; 35.1 percent had power windows; 88.2 percent had power steering; 63 percent had air conditioning; 48.1 percent had a tilting steering wheel; six percent had a close-ratio four-speed manual transmission; 7 percent had a heavy-duty four-speed manual transmission and 6.4 percent were powered by the LT1 engine. A 1972 Corvette with the base V-8 could do 0-to-30 mph in 3.1 seconds, 0-60 mph in 8.5 seconds and the quarter mile in 15.2 seconds at 83 mph. A 1972 Corvette with the optional LT1 V-8 could do 0-to-30 mph in 2.9 seconds, 0-60 mph in 6.9 seconds and the quarter mile in 14.3 seconds at 92 mph. A 1972 Corvette with the optional LS5 V-8 could do 0-to-30 mph in 3.8 seconds, 0-60 mph in 6.8 seconds and the quarter mile in 14.1 seconds at 93 mph. *Motor Trend* magazine tested a 1972 LT1 coupe with the M21 transmission and 3.70:1 axle in June 1972. The car did 0-to-30 mph in 2.9 seconds, 0-to-45 mph in 4.8 seconds, 0-to-60 mph in 6.9 seconds, 0-to-75 mph in 10.2 seconds and the quarter mile in 14.3 seconds at 92 mph. In its October/November 1971 edition, *Corvette News* said that "the engines in most cases still give about the same performance level in 1972 as they did in 1971."

1972 CORVETTE

Model Number	Body/Style Number	Body Type & Seating	Factory Price	Shipping Weight	Production Total
Z	37	2-dr FsBk Cpe-2P	$5,533	3,115 lbs.	20,496
Z	67	2-dr Conv-2P	$5,296	3,215 lbs.	6,508

NOTE: A total of 1,336 buyers separately checked off the LT1 engine option in 1972. In addition, 20 ZR1 Corvettes carried the LT1 engine.

Jerry Heasley

The 1973 Corvette from the movie **Corvette Summer**

CORVETTE STINGRAY SERIES (V-8) SERIES 9000

There were predictions in the automotive press that Chevrolet would introduce a mid-engine Corvette this year. However, nothing as radical as that came to be. Major changes for 1973 were a new domed hood, body-color urethane plastic front bumper, and a fixed rear window (which added a little extra trunk space). Corvettes also had a new coolant-recovery system, new chassis mounts, a non-removable rear window, and steel-guard-beam doors. The "egg-crate" front fender side vents of 1971-1972 models were replaced with non-trimmed air-duct types. Radial tires became standard and an effort was made to reduce noise. It was generally effective, but a *Road & Track* report found the 1973 to be louder than a 1971 in certain circumstances. Buyers who wanted a leather interior could select from Black; Medium Saddle; and Dark Saddle. Buyers had their choice of 10 exterior colors: Classic White; Silver; Medium Blue; Dark Blue; Blue-Green; Elkhart Green; Yellow; Yellow Metallic; Mille Miglia Red; and Orange. All convertibles came with a choice of Black or White soft tops. Interior colors were: Black; Midnight Blue; Dark Red; Dark Saddle; and Medium Saddle.

I.D. NUMBERS

The Vehicle Identification Number (VIN) is stamped on a plate on the inner vertical surface of the left windshield pillar visible through the windshield. For 1973 the numbers were: [Convertibles] 1Z67K3S400001 to 1Z67K3S434464; [Coupes] 1Z37K3S400001 to 1Z37K3S434464. The first symbol (1) indicated Chevrolet. The second symbol identified the body series (Z = Corvette). The third and fourth symbols indicate the body style number (67 = convertible; 37 = coupe). The fifth symbol indicates engine: K = Base 350-cid V-8; T = L82 350-cid V-8 with dual exhausts; X or W = LS4 454 V-8. The sixth symbol indicates the model year (3 = 1973). The seventh symbol identifies the assembly plant (S = St. Louis, Mo). The last six symbols indicate the sequential production number. Engine code suffixes were: CKZ = 350-cid 190-hp V-8 with 8.5:1 compression ratio, four-barrel carburetor, and manual transmission. CLB = 350-cid 190-hp V-8 with 8.5:1 compression ratio, four-barrel carburetor, and manual transmission with NB2. CLA = 350-cid 190-hp V-8 with 8.5:1 compression ratio, four-barrel carburetor, and THM automatic transmission. CLC = 350-cid 190-hp V-8 with 8.5:1 compression ratio, four-barrel carburetor, and THM automatic transmission with NB2. CLR = 350-cid 250-hp V-8 with 9.0:1 compression ratio, four-barrel carburetor, and manual transmission. CLS = 350-cid 250-hp V-8 with 9.0:1 compression ratio, four-barrel carburetor, and manual transmission with NB2. CLD = 350-cid 250-hp V-8 with 9.0:1 compression ratio, four-barrel carburetor, and THM automatic transmission. CLH = 350-cid 250-hp V-8 with 9.0:1 compression ratio, four-barrel carburetor, and THM automatic transmission with NB2. CWS = 454-cid 275-hp V-8 with 8.5:1 compression ratio, four-barrel carburetor, and THM automatic transmission with NB2. CWT = 454-cid 275-hp V-8 with 8.5:1 compression ratio, four-barrel carburetor, and manual transmission with NB2. CWM = 454-cid 275-hp V-8 with 8.5:1 compression ratio, four-barrel carburetor, and manual transmission. CWR = 454-cid 275-hp V-8 with 8.5:1 compression ratio, four-barrel carburetor, and THM automatic transmission. The beginning engine numbers were 0001001 and up at each assembly plant with F = Flint, Mich. and T = Tonawanda, N.Y. The body number plate was located on the engine side of the cowl. The Style Number 73-1YZ67 identifies a Corvette Stingray convertible and the Style Number 73-1YZ37 identifies a Corvette Stingray coupe. The Body Number is the production serial number of the body. The Trim Number indicates the interior trim color and material.

PAINT CODES

(910) Classic White; (914) Silver; (922) Medium Blue; (927) Dark Blue; (945) Blue-Green; (947) Elkhart Green; (952) Yellow; (953) Yellow Metallic; (976) Mille Miglia Red; (980) Orange.

VINYL UPHOLSTERY CODES: (400) Black; (413) Midnight Blue; (415) Medium Saddle; (418) Dark Saddle; (425) Dark Red.

LEATHER UPHOLSTERY CODES: (404) Black; (416) Medium Saddle; (422) Dark Saddle.

ENGINES

BASE ENGINE: [RPO ZQ3] V-8. Overhead valve. Cast-iron block. Displacement: 350 cid. Bore and stroke: 4.00 x 3.48 inches. Compression ratio: 8.5:1. Brake hp: 190 at 4400 rpm. Five main bearings. Hydraulic valve lifters. Carburetor: Rochester Type Quadra-Jet four-barrel Model 4MV.

OPTIONAL ENGINE: [RPO LS4] V-8. Overhead valve. Cast-iron block. Displacement: 454 cid. Bore and stroke: 4.251 x 4.00 inches. Compression ratio: 8.5:1. Brake hp: 275 at 4000 rpm. Five main bearings. Hydraulic valve lifters. High-performance camshaft. Carburetor: Rochester Quadra-Jet four-barrel.

OPTIONAL ENGINE: [RPO L82] V-8. Overhead valve. Cast-iron block. Displacement: 350 cid. Bore and stroke: 4.00 x 3.48 inches. Compression ratio: 9.0:1. Brake hp: 250 at 5200 rpm. Torque: 285 lbs.-ft. at 4000 rpm. Five main bearings. Forged steel crankshaft. Hydraulic valve lifters. High-performance camshaft. Carburetor: Rochester four-barrel. 2.50-inch diameter dual exhaust system.

TRANSMISSION

AUTOMATIC TRANSMISSION: A Turbo Hydra-Matic automatic transmission with floor-mounted gear shifter was standard equipment.

On the 1973 Corvette Stingray, the redesigned nose was a urethane plastic.

Nicky Wright

1973 Corvette Stingray coupe

OPTIONAL MANUAL TRANSMISSION: A close-ratio four-speed manual transmission with floor-mounted gear shifter was a no-cost option.

CHASSIS FEATURES

Wheelbase: 98 inches. Overall length: 182.5 inches. Overall height: 47.4 inches. Overall width: 69.0 inches. Ground clearance: 4.5 inches. Front tread: 58.7 inches. Rear tread: 59.4 inches. Tires: F70-15. Frame: Full-length welded-steel ladder type with five cross members; steel box sections, welded. Front suspension: Unequal-length A-arms with coil springs, tube shocks, and stabilizer bar. Steering: Saginaw recirculating ball; ratio 17.6:1; turns lock-to-lock 2.9; turning radius 39.0 feet. Rear suspension: Trailing arms, toe links, transverse chromium-carbon steel leaf springs; tube shocks; and anti-roll bar. Rear axle type: Sprung differential, hypoid gear. Brakes: Four-wheel disc brakes; vented discs front and rear; optional power assist; diameter: 11.75 inches front and 11.75 inches rear; total swept area: 461 sq. in.; 15 x 8-inch slotted steel disc wheels. Standard rear axle ratio 3.36:1. Available rear axle gear ratios: 3.70:1; 3.08:1; 3.36:1; 3.55:1; 4.11:1.

OPTIONS

RPO Custom interior trim ($154). RPO A31 Electric power windows ($83). RPO A85 Custom shoulder belts ($41). RPO C07 Auxiliary hardtop for convertible ($267). RPO C08 Vinyl roof covering for auxiliary hardtop ($62). RPO C50 Rear window defroster ($41). RPO C60 Air conditioning ($452). RPO G81 Positraction rear axle, all ratios ($12). RPO J50 Power brakes ($46). RPO L82 350-cid 250-hp

V-8 ($299). RPO LS4 454-cid 275-hp V-8 ($250). RPO M21 Four-speed close-ratio manual transmission (no-cost option). RPO M40 Turbo Hydra-Matic automatic transmission (no-cost option). RPO N37 Tilt-telescopic steering wheel ($82). RPO N40 Power steering ($113). RPO P02 Custom wheel covers ($62). RPO QRM White stripe nylon steel-belted radial tires GR70 x 15 ($32). RPO QRZ GR70 x 15 raised-white-letter steel-belted radial tires ($43.65). RPO T60 Heavy-duty battery ($15). RPO U58 AM-FM stereo radio ($276). RPO U69 AM-FM radio ($173). RPO UF1 Map light ($5). YJ8 Cast aluminum wheels ($175). RPO Z07 Off-road suspension and brake package ($369).

HISTORICAL FOOTNOTES

The majority of 1973 Corvettes, 70.8 percent, were sold with air conditioning; 41.2 percent had a four-speed manual transmission; 91.5 percent had power steering; 79.3 percent had power brakes and 46 percent had power windows. A 1973 L82-powered Corvette tested by *Road & Track* magazine went from 0-to-30 mph in 3.1 seconds, from 0-to-40 mph in 4.3 seconds, from 0-to-50 mph in 5.6 seconds, from 0-to-60 mph in 7.2 seconds, from 0-to-70 mph in 9.1 seconds, from 0-to-80 mph in 11.7 seconds, from 0-to-100 mph in 17.9 seconds and from 0-to-110 mph in 21.9 seconds. It did the standing-start quarter mile in 15.5 seconds at 94 mph and had a top speed of 124 mph. A 1973 L82-powered Corvette tested by *Car and Driver* magazine went from 0-to-40 mph in 3.5 seconds, from 0-to-60 mph in 6.7 seconds, from 0-to-80 mph in 10.8 seconds and from 0-to-100 mph in 17.1 seconds. It did the standing-start quarter mile in 15.1 seconds at 95.4 mph and had a top speed of 117 mph. The 1973 Corvette was the only one that combined the new soft body-color front end with chrome rear bumpers. The late Larry Shinoda once said that the 1973 model was his favorite Stingray model because its front and rear styling were the closest to what designers had originally hoped for in this series.

1973 CORVETTE

Model Number	Body/Style Number	Body Type & Seating	Factory Price	Shipping Weight	Production Total
Z	37	2-dr FsBk Cpe-2P	$5,921	3,407 lbs.	25,521
Z	67	2-dr Conv-2P	$5,685	3,407 lbs.	4,943

NOTE: 4,000 vehicle identification numbers were not asigned this year.

1974 Corvette Stingray coupe with standard wheel covers

CORVETTE STINGRAY SERIES (V-8) SERIES 9000

A restyled, sloping rear end and the elimination of the conventional rear bumper with a body-color urethane bumper substituted were two noticeable changes for 1974 Corvettes. The new rear end eliminated the last vestiges of the long-lived rear-deck-lid spoiler and replaced it with a smooth-surfaced rear deck and a body-colored resilient urethane extension covering the actual rear bumper and including the circular taillights. The new rear end met federal energy-absorbing standards. It added 30 pounds to the weight of the Corvette. The rear cap section was of a two-piece design for 1974, but was changed to a one-piece design with a pair of fake bumperettes molded in for 1975. The increased weight of the rear end cap necessitated minor suspension changes such as revised front and rear spring rates. A new optional "Gymkhana" suspension featured a 0.9375-inch diameter front stabilizer bar; heavier-duty front suspension bushings; front springs with a 550 lb./in. rating and rear springs with a 304 lbs./in. rating. The power steering, seat belts, and radiator were improved. The alarm system activator was relocated. Buyers once again had their choice of 10 exterior finishes: Classic White; Silver Mist; Corvette Gray; Corvette Medium Blue; Mille Miglia Red; Bright Yellow; Dark Green; Dark Brown; Medium Red; and Corvette Orange. All convertibles came with a choice of Black or White soft tops. Interior colors were: Black; Dark Blue; Neutral; Dark Red; Saddle; and Silver.

I.D. NUMBERS

The Vehicle Identification Number (VIN) is stamped on a plate on the inner vertical surface of the left windshield pillar visible through the windshield. For 1974 the numbers were: [Convertibles] 1Z67[ ]4S400001 to 1Z67[ ]4S437502; [Coupes] 1Z37[ ]4S400001 to 1Z37[ ]4S437502. The first symbol (1) indicated Chevrolet. The second symbol identified the body series (Z = Corvette). The third and fourth symbols indicate the body style number (67 = convertible; 37 = coupe). The fifth symbol [in blank] indicates engine: J = 350-cid 195-hp four-barrel V-8; T = 350-cid 250-hp four-barrel V-8; Z = LS4 454-cid 270-hp four-barrel V-8. The sixth symbol indicates the model year (4 = 1974). The seventh symbol identifies the assembly plant (S = St. Louis, Mo). The last six symbols indicate the sequential production number. Engine code suffixes were: CKZ = 350-cid 195-hp V-8 with 9.0:1 compression ratio, four-barrel carburetor, and manual transmission. CLB = 350-cid 195-hp V-8 with 9.0:1 compression ratio, four-barrel carburetor, and manual transmission with NB2. CLA = 350-cid 195-hp V-8 with 9.0:1 compression ratio, four-barrel carburetor, and THM automatic transmission. CLC

Jerry Heasley

The rear rack is designed to hold the T-top pieces on the 1974 Corvette.

= 350-cid 195-hp V-8 with 9.0:1 compression ratio, four-barrel carbureto,r and THM automatic transmission with NB2. CLR = 350-cid 250-hp V-8 with 9.0:1 compression ratio, four-barrel carburetor, and manual transmission. CLD = 350-cid 250-hp V-8 with 9.0:1 compression ratio, four-barrel carburetor, and THM automatic transmission. CWM = 454-cid 270-hp V-8 with 8.25:1 compression ratio, four-barrel carburetor, and manual transmission. CWR = 454-cid 270-hp V-8 with 8.25:1 compression ratio, four-barrel carburetor, and THM automatic transmission. CWS = 454-cid 270-hp V-8 with 8.25:1 compression ratio, four-barrel carburetor, and THM automatic transmission with NB2. The beginning engine numbers were 0001001 and up at each assembly plant with F = Flint, Mich. and T = Tonawanda, N.Y. The body number plate was located on the engine side of the cowl. The Style Number 74-1YZ67 identifies a Corvette Stingray convertible and the Style Number 74-1YZ37 identifies a Corvette Stingray coupe. The Body Number is the production serial number of the body. The Trim Number indicates the interior trim color and material.

PAINT CODES

(910) Classic White; (914) Silver Mist; (917) Corvette Gray; (922) Corvette Medium Blue; (946) Bright Yellow; (948) Dark Green; (968) Dark Brown; (974) Medium Red; (976) Mille Miglia Red; (980) Corvette Orange.

VINYL UPHOLSTERY CODES: (400) Black; (406) Silver; (408) Neutral; (413) Dark Blue; (415) Saddle; (425) Dark Red.

LEATHER UPHOLSTERY CODES: (404) Black; (407) Silver; (416) Saddle.

ENGINES

BASE ENGINE: [RPO ZQ3] V-8. Overhead valve. Cast iron block. Displacement: 350 cid. Bore and stroke: 4.00 x 3.48 inches. Compression ratio: 9.0:1. Brake hp: 195 at 4400 rpm. Torque: 275 lbs.-ft at 2800 rpm. Five main bearings. Hydraulic valve lifters. Carburetor: Rochester Type Quadra-Jet four-barrel Model 4MV.

OPTIONAL ENGINE: [RPO LS4] V-8. Overhead valve. Cast iron block. Displacement: 454 cid. Bore and stroke: 4.251 x 4.00 inches. Compression ratio: 8.25:1. Brake hp: 270 at 4400 rpm. Torque: 380 lbs.-ft. at 2800 rpm. Five main bearings. Hydraulic valve lifters. High-performance camshaft. Carburetor: Rochester Quadra-jet four-barrel.

OPTIONAL ENGINE: [RPO L82] V-8. Overhead valve. Cast iron block. Displacement: 350 cid. Bore and stroke: 4.00 x 3.48 inches. Compression ratio: 9.0:1. Brake hp: 250 at 5200 rpm. Torque: 285 lbs.-ft. at 4000 rpm. Five main bearings. Forged steel crankshaft. Hydraulic valve lifters. High-performance camshaft. Carburetor: Rochester four-barrel. 2.50-inch diameter dual exhaust system.

TRANSMISSION

AUTOMATIC TRANSMISSION: A Turbo Hydra-Matic automatic transmission with floor-mounted gear shifter was standard equipment.

OPTIONAL MANUAL TRANSMISSION: A close-ratio four-speed manual transmission with floor-mounted gear shifter was a no cost option.

CHASSIS FEATURES

Wheelbase: 98 inches. Overall length: 185.5 inches. Overall height: 47.4 inches. Overall width: 69.0 inches. Ground clearance: 4.5 inches. Front tread: 58.7 inches. Rear tread: 59.5 inches. Tires: F70-15. Frame: Full-length welded-steel ladder type with five cross members; steel

1974 Corvette Stingray convertible in Silver Mist

box sections, welded. Front suspension: Unequal-length A-arms with coil springs, tube shocks, and stabilizer bar. Steering: Saginaw recirculating ball; ratio 17.6:1; turns lock-to-lock 2.9; turning radius 39.0 feet. Rear suspension: Trailing arms, toe links, transverse chromium-carbon steel leaf springs, tube shocks, and anti-roll bar. Rear axle type: Sprung differential, hypoid gear. Brakes: Four-wheel disc brakes; vented discs front and rear; optional power assist; diameter: 11.75 inches front and 11.75 inches rear; total swept area: 461 sq. in.; 15 x 8-inch slotted steel disc wheels. Standard rear axle ratio 3.36:1. Available rear axle gear ratios: 3.70:1; 3.08:1; 3.36:1; 3.55:1; and 4.11:1.

OPTIONS

RPO Custom interior trim ($154). RPO A31 Electric power windows ($86). RPO A85 Custom shoulder belts ($41). RPO C07 Auxiliary hardtop for convertible ($267). RPO C08 Vinyl covered auxiliary hardtop ($329). RPO C50 Rear window defroster ($43). RPO C60 Air conditioning ($467). RPO FE7G81 Gymkhana suspension ($7). RPO Positraction rear axle, all ratios ($12). RPO J50 Power brakes ($49). RPO L82 350-cid 250-hp V-8 ($299). LS4 454-cid 270-hp V-8 ($250). RPO M21 Four-speed close-ratio manual transmission (no-cost option). RPO M40 Turbo Hydra-Matic automatic transmission (no-cost option). RPO N37 Tilt-Telescopic steering wheel ($82). RPO N40 Power steering ($117). RPO QRM White stripe nylon steel-belted radial tires GR70 x 15 ($32). RPO QRZ GR70 x 15 raised-white-letter steel-belted radial tires ($45). RPO U05 Dual horns ($4). RPO U58 AM-FM stereo radio ($276). RPO U69 AM-FM radio ($173). RPO UA1 Heavy-duty battery ($15). RPO UF1 Map light ($5). RPO Z07 Off-road suspension and brake package ($369).

HISTORICAL FOOTNOTES

Most 1974 Corvettes, 95.6 percent, had power steering; 88.3 percent had power brakes; 63.1 percent had power windows; 72.9 percent had tilting steering wheel; 77.7 percent had air conditioning and 33.7 percent had a four-speed manual transmission.

1974 CORVETTE Model Number	Body/Style Number	Body Type & Seating	Factory Price	Shipping Weight	Production Total
Z	37	2-dr FsBk Cpe-2P	$6,002	3,532 lbs.	32,028
Z	67	2-dr Conv-2P	$5,766	3,532 lbs.	5,474

1975 Corvette Stingray coupe in Orange Flame

CORVETTE STINGRAY SERIES (V-8) SERIES 9000

Most of the changes on the Corvette for 1975 were hidden. The bumpers were improved (but looked the same). Under the hood were a catalytic converter and a new High-Energy ignition. On the inside, the speedometer included kilometers-per-hour for the first time. This was the last year for the Corvette convertible. For awhile, buyers once again had their choice of 10 exterior finishes: Classic White; Silver; Bright Blue; Steel Blue; Bright Green; Bright Yellow; Medium Saddle; Orange Flame; Dark Red; and Mille Miglia Red. All convertibles came with a choice of Black or White soft tops. Interior colors were: Black; Dark Blue; Neutral; Dark Red; Medium Saddle; and Silver.

I.D. NUMBERS

The Vehicle Identification Number (VIN) is stamped on a plate on the inner vertical surface of the left windshield pillar visible through the windshield. For 1975 the numbers were: [Convertibles] 1Z67[ ]5S400001 to 1Z67[ ]5S438465; [Coupes] 1Z37[ ]5S400001 to 1Z37[ ]5S438465. The first symbol (1) indicated Chevrolet. The second symbol identified the body series (Z = Corvette). The third and fourth symbols indicate the body style number (67 = convertible; 37 = coupe). The fifth symbol [in blank] indicates engine: J = 350-cid 165-hp V-8; T = 350-cid 205-hp V-8. The sixth symbol indicates the model year (5 = 1975). The seventh symbol identifies the assembly plant (S = St. Louis, Mo). The last six symbols indicate the sequential production number. Engine code suffixes were: CUB = 350-cid 165-hp V-8 with 8.5:1 compression ratio, four-barrel carburetor, and manual transmission. CUD = 350-cid 205-hp V-8 with 9.0:1 compression ratio, four-barrel carburetor, and manual transmission. Other Corvette suffixes: CRJ = 350-cid V-8 with four-barrel carburetor, and manual transmission; CRK = 350-cid V-8 with four-barrel carburetor and automatic transmission; CRL = 350-cid V-8 with four-barrel carburetor, and manual transmission; CRM = 350-cid V-8 with four-barrel carburetor, and automatic transmission; CUT = 350-cid V-8 with four-barrel carburetor, and manual transmission; and CUA manual transmission. The beginning engine numbers were 0001001 and up at each assembly plant with F = Flint, Mich. and T = Tonawanda, N.Y. The body number plate was located on the engine side of the cowl. The Style Number 75-1YZ67 identifies a Corvette Stingray convertible and the Style Number 75-1YZ37 identifies a Corvette Stingray coupe. The Body Number is the production serial number of the body. The Trim Number indicates the interior trim color and material.

PAINT CODES

(10) Classic White; (13) Silver; (22) Bright Blue; (27) Steel Blue; (42) Bright Green; (56) Bright Yellow; (67) Medium Saddle; (70) Orange Flame; (74) Dark Red; and

Jerry Heasley

1975 Corvette Stingray coupe

(76) Mille Miglia Red.

VINYL UPHOLSTERY CODES: (400) Black; (406) Silver; (408) Neutral; (413) Dark Blue; (415) Saddle; (425) Dark Red.

LEATHER UPHOLSTERY CODES: (404) Black; (407) Silver; (416) Saddle.

ENGINES

BASE ENGINE: [RPO L48] V-8. Overhead valve. Cast iron block. Displacement: 350 cid. Bore and stroke: 4.00 x 3.48 inches. Compression ratio: 8.5:1. Brake hp: 165 at 3800 rpm. Torque: 255 lbs.-ft. at 2400 rpm. Five main bearings. Hydraulic valve lifters. Carburetor: Rochester Type Quadra-Jet four-barrel Model 4MV.

OPTIONAL ENGINE: [RPO L82] V-8. Overhead valve. Cast iron block. Displacement: 350 cid. Bore and stroke: 4.00 x 3.48 inches. Compression ratio: 9.0:1. Brake hp: 205 at 4800 rpm. Torque: 255 lbs.-ft. at 3600 rpm. Five main bearings. Forged steel crankshaft. Hydraulic valve lifters. High-performance camshaft. Carburetor: Rochester Quadra-Jet four-barrel.

TRANSMISSION

AUTOMATIC TRANSMISSION: A Turbo Hydra-Matic automatic transmission with floor-mounted gear shifter was standard equipment.

OPTIONAL MANUAL TRANSMISSION: A close-ratio four-speed manual transmission with floor-mounted gear shifter was a no-cost option.

CHASSIS FEATURES

Wheelbase: 98 inches. Overall length: 185.5 inches. Overall height: 47.4 inches. Overall width: 69.0 inches. Ground clearance: 4.5 inches. Front tread: 58.7 inches. Rear tread: 59.5 inches. Tires: F70-15. Frame: Full-length welded-steel ladder type with five cross members; steel box sections, welded. Front suspension: Unequal-length A-arms with coil springs, tube shocks, and stabilizer bar. Steering: Saginaw recirculating ball; ratio 17.6:1; turns lock-to-lock 2.9; turning radius 39 feet. Rear suspension: Trailing arms, toe links, transverse chromium-carbon steel leaf springs, tube shocks, and anti-roll bar. Rear axle type: Sprung differential, hypoid gear. Brakes: Four-wheel disc brakes; vented discs front and rear; optional power assist; diameter 11.75 inches front and 11.75 inches rear; total swept area 461 sq. in.; 15 x 8-inch slotted steel disc wheels. Standard rear axle ratio 3.36:1. Available rear axle gear ratios: 3.70:1; 3.08:1; 3.36:1; 3.55:1.

OPTIONS

RPO Custom interior trim ($154). RPO A31 Electric power windows ($93). RPO A85 Custom shoulder belts ($41). RPO C07 Auxiliary hardtop for convertible ($267). RPO C08 Vinyl-covered auxiliary hardtop ($350). RPO C50 Rear window defroster ($46). RPO C60 Air conditioning ($490). RPO FE7G81 Gymkhana suspension

Jerry Heasley

1975 Corvette convertible

($7). RPO Positraction rear axle, all ratios ($12). RPO J50 Power brakes ($50). RPO L82 350-cid 205-hp V-8 ($336). RPO M21 Four-speed close-ratio manual transmission (no-cost option). RPO M40 Turbo Hydra-Matic automatic transmission (no-cost option). RPO N37 Tilt-telescopic steering wheel ($82). RPO N40 Power steering ($129). RPO QRM White stripe nylon steel-belted radial tires GR70 x 15 ($35). RPO QRZ GR70 x 15 raised-white-letter steel-belted radial tires ($48). RPO U05 Dual horns ($4). RPO U58 AM-FM stereo radio ($284). RPO U69 AM-FM radio ($178). RPO UA1 Heavy-duty battery. ($15). RPO UF1 Map light ($5). RPO Z07 Off-road suspension and brake package ($400).

Jerry Heasley

1975 was the last year for the convertible option.

HISTORICAL FOOTNOTES

The 454-cid Corvette engine was dropped this year, as was the convertible style. Car and Driver tested a 1975 model and covered the quarter-mile in 16.1 seconds. The magazine timed the car at 0-to-60 mph in 7.7 seconds and found it to have a top speed of 129 mph. Robert D. Lund became Chevrolet general manager. Zora Arkus-Duntov retired as the division's chief engineer. He was replaced by David R. McLellan.

1975 CORVETTE Model Number	Body/Style Number	Body Type & Seating	Factory Price	Shipping Weight	Production Total
Z	37	2-dr FsBk Cpe-2P	$6,810	3,532 lbs.	33,836
Z	67	2-dr Conv-2P	$6,550	3,532 lbs.	4,629

1976 Chevrolet Corvette Stingray T-top coupe

CORVETTE STINGRAY SERIES (V-8) SERIES Z

Unlike some advertisers, Chevrolet was correct in billing the fiberglass-bodied Corvette as "America's only true production sports car." The big-block V-8 disappeared after 1974, leaving a 350-cid (5.7-liter) small-block as the power plant for all Corvettes in the next decade. Two V-8s were offered this year, both with a four-barrel carburetor. The base L48 version now developed 180 hp (15 more than in 1975). An optional L82 V-8 produced 210 hp. The L82 had special heads with larger valves, impact-extruded pistons and finned aluminum rocker covers. The standard V-8 drove a new, slightly lighter weight automatic transmission: the Turbo Hydra-Matic 350, which was supposed to improve shifting at wide-open throttle. Optional engines kept the prior Turbo Hydra-Matic 400, but with a revised torque converter. A wide-range four-speed manual gearbox (with 2.64:1 first gear ratio) was standard and a close-ratio version was available at no extra cost. A new Carburetor Outside Air Induction system moved intake from the cowl to above the radiator. The convertible was dropped this year, so only the Stingray coupe remained. It had twin removable roof panels. A partial steel underbody replaced the customary fiberglass, to add strength and improve shielding from exhaust system heat. A new one-piece bar Corvette nameplate was on the rear, between twin-unit tail lamps (which were inset in the bumper cover). Of the 10 body colors, eight were Corvette exclusives. This year's colors were Classic White; Silver; Bright Blue; Dark Green; Mahogany; Bright Yellow; Buckskin; Dark Brown; Orange Flame; and Red. Corvettes had side marker lights with reflectors, parking lamps that went on with the headlamps, lane-change turn signals and two-speed wiper/washers. Inside was a new, smaller-diameter four-spoke sport steering wheel with crossed-flags medallion, which actually came from the Chevrolet Vega subcompact. Not everyone appreciated its lowly origin, so it lasted only this year. A grained vinyl-trimmed instrument panel (with stitched seams) held a 160-mph speedometer with trip odometer and 7,000-rpm electronic tachometer. A key lock in the left front fender set the anti-theft alarm. Corvettes had fully-independent suspension and four-wheel disc brakes. Wide GR70 SBR tires rode 15 x 8-inch wheels. A total of 5,368 Corvettes had the FE7 Gymkhana suspension installed, 5,720 came with the L82 V-8 and 2,088 had the M21 four-speed close-ratio manual gearbox. Cast-aluminum wheels were a new option, and were installed on 6,253 cars. Standard equipment included bumper guards; flush retracting headlamps; Soft-Ray tinted glass; Hide-A-Way wipers; wide-view day/night mirror; and center console with lighter and ashtray. Behind the seatbacks were three carpeted storage compartments. Bucket seats had textured-vinyl or leather upholstery and deep-pleated saddle-stitching. Interior leather trim was now available in seven colors, while vinyl was available in four colors.

I.D. NUMBERS

The Vehicle Identification Number (VIN) is stamped on a plate on the inner vertical surface of the left windshield pillar visible through the windshield. For 1976 the numbers were: 1Z37[ ]6S400001 to 1Z37[ ]6S446558. The first symbol (1) indicated Chevrolet. The second symbol identified the body series (Z = Corvette). The third and fourth symbols indicate the body style number (37 = coupe). The fifth symbol [in blank] indicates engine: L = 350-cid 180-hp V-8; X = 350-cid 210-hp V-8. The sixth symbol indicates the model year (6 = 1976). The seventh symbol identifies the assembly plant (S = St. Louis, Mo). The last six symbols indicate the sequential production number. The sequential serial number is repeated on the engine block itself, stamped on a pad just ahead of the

Nicky Wright

1976 Corvette coupe

cylinder head on the right (passenger) side, combined with a three-letter engine code identification suffix. Cast into the top rear (right side) of the block is a date built code. The first letter of that four-symbol code shows the month the block was cast. The next number (or numbers) reveals the day of the month, while the final digit indicates year. Engine code suffixes for 1976 were: CHC = 350-cid 210-hp V-8 with four-barrel carburetor, and manual transmission. CKC = 350-cid 210-hp V-8 with four-barrel carburetor, and automatic transmission. CKW = 350-cid 180-hp V-8 with four-barrel carburetor, and manual transmission. CKX = 350-cid 180-hp V-8 with four-barrel carburetor, and automatic transmission. CLS = 350-cid 180-hp V-8 with four-barrel carburetor, and automatic transmission. The beginning engine numbers were 0001001 and up at each assembly plant. The body number plate was located on the engine side of the cowl. The Style Number 76-1YZ37 identifies a Corvette Stingray coupe. The Body Number is the production serial number of the body. The Trim Number indicates the interior trim color and material.

PAINT CODES

(10) Classic White; (13) Silver; (22) Bright Blue; (33*) Dark Green; (37) Mahogany; (56) Bright Yellow; (64) Buckskin; (69) Dark Brown; (70) Orange Flame; (72) Red. (*) Dark Green was originally supposed to be code 39.

VINYL UPHOLSTERY CODES: (19V) Black; (71V) Firethorn; (64V) Buckskin; (15V) White.

LEATHER UPHOLSTERY CODES: (192) Black; (712) Firethorn; (642) Buckskin; (152) Smoked Gray; (692) Dark Brown; (322) Blue-Green; (112) White.

ENGINES

BASE ENGINE: [RPO L48] V-8. 90-degree overhead valve. Cast iron block and head. Displacement: 350 cid (5.7 liters). Bore and stroke: 4.00 x 3.48 inches. Compression ratio: 8.5:1. Brake hp: 180 at 4000 rpm. Torque: 270 lbs.-ft. at 2400 rpm. Five main bearings. Hydraulic valve lifters. Carburetor: Rochester M4MC.

OPTIONAL ENGINE: [RPO L82] V-8. 90-degree overhead valve. Cast iron block and head. Displacement: 350 cid (5.7 liters). Bore and stroke: 4.00 x 3.48 inches. Compression ratio: 9.0:1. Brake hp: 210 at 5200 rpm. Torque: 255 lbs.-ft. at 3600 rpm. Five main bearings. Hydraulic valve lifters. Carburetor: Rochester M4MC.

TRANSMISSION

AUTOMATIC TRANSMISSION: A Turbo Hydra-Matic automatic transmission with floor-mounted gear shifter was standard equipment.

OPTIONAL MANUAL TRANSMISSION: A close-ratio four-speed manual transmission with floor-mounted gear shifter was a no-cost option.

CHASSIS FEATURES: Wheelbase: 98 inches.

Nicky Wright

1976 Chevrolet Corvette Stingray T-top coupe

Overall length: 185.2 inches. Height: 48 inches. Width: 69 inches. Front Tread: 58.7 inches. Rear Tread: 59.5 inches. Wheel size: 15 x 8 inches. Standard tires: GR70 x 15.

TECHNICAL FEATURES

Transmission: Four-speed fully-synchronized manual transmission (floor shift) standard. Gear ratios: (1st) 2.64:1; (2nd) 1.75:1; (3rd) 1.34:1; (4th) 1.00:1; (Rev) 2.55:1. Close-ratio four-speed fully-synchronized manual transmission optional: (1st) 2.43:1; (2nd) 1.61:1; (3rd) 1.23:1; (4th) 1.00:1; (Rev) 2.35:1. Three-speed automatic optional: (1st) 2.52:1; (2nd) 1.52:1; (3rd) 1.00:1; (Rev) 1.94:1. Three-speed automatic ratios with L82 engine: (1st) 2.48:1; (2nd) 1.48:1; (3rd) 1.00:1; (Rev) 2.08:1. Standard final drive ratio: 3.36:1 w/4-spd, 3.08:1 w/auto, except with optional L82 engine 3.55:1 w/4-spd, 3.55:1 or 3.70:1 with close-ratio four-speed, or 3.36:1 w/auto. Positraction standard. Steering: Recirculating ball. Front suspension: Unequal-length control arms with ball joints, coil springs, and stabilizer bar. Rear suspension: Independent with trailing-link, transverse semi-elliptic leaf springs. Brakes: Four-wheel disc (11.75 inch disc diameter). Ignition: HEI electronic. Body construction: Separate fiberglass body and box-type ladder frame with cross-members. Fuel tank: 18 gallons.

OPTIONS

RPO Custom interior trim ($164). RPO A31 Electric power windows ($107). RPO C49 Rear window defogger ($78). RPO C08 Vinyl covered auxiliary hardtop ($350). RPO C60 Air conditioning ($523). RPO FE7 Gymkhana suspension ($35). Positraction rear axle, all ratios ($13). RPO J50 Power brakes ($59). RPO L82 350-cid 210-hp V-8 ($481). RPO M21 Four-speed close-ratio manual transmission (no-cost option). RPO M40 Turbo Hydra-Matic automatic transmission (no-cost option). RPO N37 Tilt-telescopic steering wheel ($95). RPO N40 Power steering ($151). RPO QRM White stripe nylon steel-belted radial tires GR70 x 15 ($37). RPO QRZ GR70 x 15 raised-white-letter steel-belted radial tires ($51). RPO U58 AM-FM stereo radio ($281). RPO U69 AM-FM radio ($187). RPO UA1 Heavy-duty battery ($16). RPO UF1 Map light ($10). RPO YJ8 Aluminum wheels ($299).

HISTORICAL FOOTNOTES

Introduced October 2, 1975. Model-year production: 46,558. Calendar-year production: 47,425. Calendar-year sales by U.S. dealers: 41,673. Model-year sales by U.S. dealers: 41,027. Though largely a carry-over from 1975, Corvette set a new sales record. The basic design dated back to 1968. *Car and Driver* (March 1976) tested the L48 and L82 Corvettes. The L48 had the M21 transmission and a 3.36:1 rear axle. It went from 0-to-30 mph in 2.7 seconds, 0-to-60 mph in 6.8 seconds and 0-to-100 mph in 20.2 seconds. It did the standing start quarter mile in 15.4 seconds at 91.5 mph. It had a top speed of 121 mph. The L82 had the M40 transmission and a 3.70:1 rear axle. It went from 0-to-30 mph in 2.8 seconds, 0-to-60 mph in 6.8 seconds and 0-to-100 mph in 19.5 seconds. It did the standing start quarter mile in 15.3 seconds at 92.1 mph. It had a top speed of 121 mph. *Car and Driver* (April 1976) also tested an L82 Corvette with the M40 transmission and 3.36:1 rear axle. It went from 0-to-30 mph in 2.8 seconds, 0-to-60 mph in 7.1 seconds and 0-to-100 mph in 19.5 seconds. It did the standing start quarter mile in 15.3 seconds at 91.9 mph. It had a top speed of 124.5 mph.

1976 CORVETTE

Model Number	Body/Style Number	Body Type & Seating	Factory Price	Shipping Weight	Production Total
Z	Z37	2-dr Cpe-2P	$7,605	3,445 lbs.	46,558

Nicky Wright

1977 Chevrolet Corvette T-top coupe

1977

CORVETTE SERIES (V-8) SERIES Z

Since the Stingray front fender nameplate departed this year, Chevrolet's sports car technically no longer had a secondary title. Changes were fairly modest this year and mainly hidden (such as a steel hood reinforcement) or inside. New crossed-flags emblems stood between the headlamps and on the fuel filler door. A thinner blacked-out pillar gave the windshield and side glass a more integrated look. The Corvette's console was restyled in an aircraft-type cluster design, with individual-look gauges. A voltmeter replaced the former ampmeter. "Door ajar" and "headlamp up" warning lights were abandoned. New heater/air conditioning controls, an ashtray, and a lighter were on the horizontal surface. A recessed pocket was now seen behind the shift lever. Power window switches moved to the new console. The manual shift lever was almost an inch higher, with shorter travel. Automatic transmission levers added a pointer and both manual and automatic shifters added a new black leather boot. A shorter steering column held a multi-function control lever. This year's steering wheel had a leather-wrapped rim. This year's colors were Classic White; Silver; Black; Corvette Light Blue; Corvette Dark Blue; Corvette Chartreuse (used on one car); Corvette Yellow; Corvette Orange; Medium Red; Corvette Tan; and Corvette Dark Red. The Custom interior, formerly an extra-cost option, was now standard. "Dynasty" horizontal-ribbed cloth upholstery was framed with leather (the first cloth trim offered on a Corvette), or buyers could have the customary all-leather seat panels. Leather came in ten colors, cloth in six. Two new trim colors were available: Red and Blue. Door panel inserts were satin finish Black instead of the prior wood grain. Both the instrument panel and door trim panels lost their embossed stitch lines. New padded sunshades could swivel to side windows. Passenger-side roof pillars held a soft vinyl coat hook. Power trains were the same as in 1976, but power brakes and steering were now standard. A total of 6,148 Corvettes came with the special L82 V-8 engine under the hood, while 7,269 had the optional Gymkhana suspension. Only 5,743 Corvettes had the M20 four-speed manual gearbox and 2,060 used the M26 close-ratio four-speed. A mere 289 Corvettes came with trailering equipment. New options included an AM/FM stereo radio with tape player, cruise control (for cars with automatic transmission only,) and a luggage carrier that could hold the roof panels. Glass roof panels were announced, but delayed for another year.

I.D. NUMBERS

The Vehicle Identification Number (VIN) is stamped on a plate on the inner vertical surface of the left windshield pillar visible through the windshield. For 1977 the numbers were: [Coupes] 1Z37[ ]7S400001 to 1Z37[ ]7S449213. The first symbol (1) indicated Chevrolet. The second symbol

1977 Corvette T-top coupe

identified the body series (Z = Corvette). The third and fourth symbols indicate the body style number (37 = coupe). The fifth symbol [in blank] indicates engine: L = 350-cid 180-hp V-8; X = 350-cid 210-hp V-8. The sixth symbol indicates the model year (7 = 1977). The seventh symbol identifies the assembly plant (S = St. Louis, Mo). The last six symbols indicate the sequential production number. The sequential serial number is repeated on the engine block itself, stamped on a pad just ahead of the cylinder head on the right (passenger) side, combined with a three-letter engine code identification suffix. Cast into the top rear (right side) of the block is a date built code. The first letter of that four-symbol code shows the month the block was cast. The next number (or numbers) reveals the day of the month, while the final digit indicates year. Engine code suffixes for 1977 were: CHD = 350-cid 180-hp V-8 with four-barrel carburetor, automatic transmission, and California emissions system. CKD = 350-cid 180-hp V-8 with four-barrel carburetor, automatic transmission, and high-altitude emissions system. CKZ = 350-cid 180-hp V-8 with four-barrel carburetor, and manual transmission. CLA = 350-cid 180-hp V-8 with four-barrel carburetor and automatic transmission. CLB = 350-cid 180-hp V-8 with four-barrel carburetor, automatic transmission, and high-altitude emissions system. CLC = 350-cid 180-hp V-8 with four-barrel carburetor, automatic transmission, and California emissions system. CLD = 350-cid 210-hp V-8 with four-barrel carburetor and manual transmission. CLF = 350-cid 210-hp V-8 with four-barrel carburetor and automatic transmission. The beginning engine numbers were 0001001 and up at each assembly plant. The body number plate was located on the engine side of the cowl. The Style Number 77-1YZ37 identifies a Corvette coupe. The Body Number is the production serial number of the body. The Trim Number indicates the interior trim color and material.

PAINT CODES

(10) Classic White; (13) Silver; (19) Black; (26) Corvette Light Blue; (28) Corvette Dark Blue; (41) Corvette Chartreuse was used on one car; (52) Corvette Yellow; (66) Corvette Orange; (72) Medium Red; (80) Corvette Tan; (83) Corvette Dark Red.

CLOTH/LEATHER UPHOLSTERY CODES: (15C) Smoked Gray; (19C) Black; (27C) Blue; (69C) Brown; (72C) Red.

LEATHER UPHOLSTERY CODES: (192) Black; (722) Red; (642) Buckskin; (152) Smoked Gray; (692) Brown; (112) White.

ENGINES

BASE ENGINE: [RPO L48] V-8. 90-degree overhead valve. Cast iron block and head. Displacement: 350 cid (5.7 liters). Bore and stroke: 4.00 x 3.48 inches. Compression ratio: 8.5:1. Brake hp: 180 at 4000 rpm. Torque: 270 lbs.-ft. at 2400 rpm. Five main bearings. Hydraulic valve lifters. Carburetor: Rochester M4MC.

OPTIONAL ENGINE: [RPO L82] V-8. 90-degree overhead valve. Cast iron block and head. Displacement: 350 cid (5.7 liters). Bore and stroke: 4.00 x 3.48 inches. Compression ratio: 9.0:1. Brake hp: 210 at 5200 rpm. Torque: 255 lbs.-ft. at 3600 rpm. Five main bearings. Hydraulic valve lifters. Carburetor: Rochester M4MC.

1977 Corvette T-top coupe

TRANSMISSION

AUTOMATIC TRANSMISSION: A Turbo Hydra-Matic automatic transmission with floor-mounted gear shifter was standard equipment.

OPTIONAL MANUAL TRANSMISSION: A four-speed manual transmission with floor-mounted gear shifter was a no-cost option.

CHASSIS FEATURES

Wheelbase: 98 inches. Overall length: 185.2 inches. Height: 48 inches. Width: 69 inches. Front tread: 58.7 inches. Rear tread: 59.5 inches. Standard tires: GR70 x 15.

TECHNICAL FEATURES

Transmission: Four-speed manual transmission (floor shift) standard. Gear ratios: (1st) 2.64:1; (2nd) 1.75:1; (3rd) 1.34:1; (4th) 1.00:1; (Rev) 2.55:1. Close-ratio four-speed manual transmission optional: (1st) 2.43:1; (2nd) 1.61:1; (3rd) 1.23:1; (4th) 1.00:1; (Rev) 2.35:1. Three-speed automatic optional: (1st) 2.48:1; (2nd) 1.48:1; (3rd) 1.00:1; (Rev) 2.08:1. Standard final drive ratio: 3.36:1. Steering/Suspension/Body: Same as 1976. Brakes: Four-wheel disc. Ignition: Electronic. Fuel tank: 17 gallon.

OPTIONS

RPO A31 Electric power windows ($116). RPO B32 Color-keyed floor mats ($22). RPO C49 Rear window defogger ($84). RPO C60 Air conditioning ($553). RPO D35 Sport mirrors ($36). RPO FE7 Gymkhana suspension ($38). RPO L82 350-cid 210-hp V-8 ($495). RPO M21 Four-speed close-ratio manual transmission (no-cost option). RPO M40 Turbo Hydra-Matic automatic transmission (no-cost option). RPO N37 Tilt-telescopic steering column ($165). RPO N40 Power steering ($151). RPO QRZ White letter steel-belted radial tires GR70 x 15 ($57). RPO UA1 Heavy-duty battery ($17). RPO U58 AM-FM stereo radio ($281). RPO U69 AM-FM radio ($187). RPO UM2 AM-FM stereo radio with tape system ($414). RPO V54 Luggage rack and roof panel rack ($73). RPO YJ8 Aluminum wheels ($321). RPO ZN1 Trailering package ($83). RPO ZX2 Convenience group ($22).

HISTORICAL FOOTNOTES

Introduced: September 30, 1976. Model-year production: 49,213 (Chevrolet initially reported 49,034 units). Calendar-year production: 46,345. Calendar-year sales by U.S. dealers: 42,571. Model-year sales by U.S. dealers: 40,764.

1977 CORVETTE

Model Number	Body/Style Number	Body Type & Seating	Factory Price	Shipping Weight	Production Total
Z	Z37	2-dr Cpe-2P	$8,648	3,448 lbs.	49,213

1978 Indianapolis 500 Pace Car

1978

CORVETTE SERIES (V-8) SERIES Z

To mark Corvette's 25th anniversary, the 1978 model received a major aerodynamic restyling with large wraparound back window and a fastback roofline. This was the Corvette's first restyling since 1968. Two special editions were produced, one well known and the other little more than an optional paint job. New tinted glass lift-out roof panels were wired into the standard anti-theft system. A 24-gallon fuel cell replaced the former 17-gallon tank, filling space made available by a new temporary spare tire. Inside was a restyled, padded instrument panel with face-mounted round instruments and a new locking glove box that replaced the former map pocket. The restyled interior had more accessible rear storage area with a roll shade to hide luggage. The wiper-washer control was moved from the steering column back to the instrument panel, but turn signal and headlight-dimmer controls remained on the steering column. Door trim was now of a cut-and-sew design with soft expanded vinyl or cloth. As in 1977, the seats had leather side bolsters, with either leather or cloth seating areas in a fine rib pattern. Corvette's optional L82 high-performance 350-cid V-8 reached 220 hp as a result of a new dual-snorkel cold-air intake system, larger-diameter exhaust and tailpipes and lower-restriction mufflers. The automatic transmission used with the optional V-8 lost weight and had a low-inertia, high-stall torque converter. Base engines used a Muncie four-speed manual gear box with higher first-second gear ratios than before; the performance V-8 used a close-ratio Borg-Warner. The axle ratios used in cars sold in California and high-altitude counties were switched from 3.08:1 to 3.55:1. A total of 12,739 had the optional L82 engines, 3,385 Corvettes had the M21 four-speed close-ratio gearbox, and 38,614 had automatic transmission. Glass roof panels, which had been promised earlier, actually became available this year. What Chevrolet described as "aggressive" 60-series white-letter tires also joined the option list for the first time. An optional AM/FM-CB stereo radio used a tri-band power antenna on the rear deck. Each of this year's Corvettes could have Silver Anniversary emblems on the nose and rear deck. A total of 15,283 displayed the $399 special two-tone "Silver Anniversary" paint combination with silver metallic on top and charcoal silver on the lower body. Pinstripes accentuated the fender's upper profiles, wheel openings, front fender vents, hood, and rear license cavity. Interiors were also silver. Various other options were required, including aluminum wheels. For a considerably higher price, buyers could have the Limited Edition replica of the Indy Pace Car with distinctive black-over-silver paint and red accent striping. Equipment in this "Indy Package" (RPO code Z78) included a special silver interior with new lightweight high-back seats, special front and rear spoilers, P255/60R15 white-letter tires on alloy wheels and lift-off glass canopy roof panels. The Indy Pace Car package's content included nearly all Corvette options, plus special decals (unless the customer specified that they be omitted). Upholstery was silver leather or leather with smoke gray cloth inserts. The year's 11 Corvette colors were Classic White; Silver; Silver Anniversary; Black; Corvette Light Blue; Corvette Yellow; Corvette Light Beige; Corvette Red; Corvette Mahogany; Corvette Dark Blue; and Corvette Dark Brown.

I.D. NUMBERS

The Vehicle Identification Number (VIN) is stamped on a plate on the inner vertical surface of the left windshield pillar visible through the windshield. For 1978 the numbers were: [Coupe] 1Z87[ ]8S400001 to 1Z87[ ]8S440274; [Indy Pace Car] 1Z87[ ]8S900001 to 1Z87[ ]8S906502. The first symbol (1) indicated Chevrolet. The second symbol identified the body series (Z = Corvette). The third and fourth symbols indicate the body style number (87 = coupe). The fifth symbol [in blank] indicates engine: L = 350-cid 175-hp or 185-hp V-8; H = 350-cid 220-hp V-8. The sixth symbol indicates the model year (8 = 1978). The seventh symbol identifies the assembly plant (S = St. Louis, Mo). The last six symbols indicate the sequential production number. The sequential serial number is repeated on the engine block itself, stamped on a pad just ahead of the cylinder head on the right (passenger) side, combined with a three-letter engine code identification suffix. Cast into the top rear (right side) of the block is a date built code. The first letter of that four-symbol code shows the month the block was cast. The next number (or numbers) reveals the day of the month, while the final digit indicates year. Engine code suffixes for 1978 were: CHW = RPO L48 350-cid 185-hp V-8 with 8.2:1 compression ratio, four-barrel carburetor, and manual transmission. CLM = RPO L48 350-cid 185-hp V-8 with 8.2:1 compression ratio, four-barrel carburetor, and automatic transmission. CLR = RPO L48 350-cid 175-hp V-8 with 8.2:1 compression ratio, four-barrel carburetor, California emissions, and automatic transmission. CLS = RPO L48 350-cid 175-hp V-8 with 8.2:1 compression ratio, four-barrel carburetor, high-altitude county emissions, and automatic transmission. CMR = RPO L82 350-cid 220-hp V-8 with 8.9:1 compression ratio, four-barrel carburetor, and manual transmission. CMS = RPO L82 350-cid 220-hp V-8 with 8.9:1 compression ratio, four-barrel carburetor, and automatic transmission. CUT = RPO L48 350-cid 185-hp V-8 with 8.2:1 compression ratio, four-barrel carburetor, and automatic transmission. The beginning engine numbers were 0001001 and up at each assembly plant. The body number plate was located on the engine side of the cowl. The Style Number 78-1YZ37 identifies a Corvette coupe. The Body Number is the production serial number of the body. The Trim Number indicates the interior trim color and material.

PAINT CODES: (10) Classic White; (13) Silver; (13/07) Silver Anniversary; (19) Black; (26) Corvette Light Blue; (52) Corvette Yellow; (59) Corvette Light Beige; (72) Corvette Red; (82) Corvette Mahogany; (83) Corvette Dark Blue; (89) Corvette Dark Brown.

CLOTH UPHOLSTERY CODES: (12C) Oyster; (15C) Silver; (19C) Black; (29C) Dark Blue; (59C) Light Beige; (69C) Dark Brown; (72C) Red; (76C) Mahogany.

LEATHER UPHOLSTERY CODES: (122) Oyster; (152) Silver; (192) Black; (292) Dark Blue; (592) Light Beige; (692) Dark Brown; (722) Red; (762) Mahogany.

ENGINES

BASE ENGINE: [RPO L48] V-8. 90-degree overhead valve. Cast iron block and head. Displacement: 350 cid (5.7 liters). Bore and stroke: 4.00 x 3.48 inches. Compression ratio: 8.2:1. Brake hp: 185 at 4000 rpm. Torque: 280 lbs.-ft. at 2400 rpm. Five main bearings. Hydraulic valve lifters. Carburetor: Rochester M4MC.

BASE ENGINE: [RPO L48] V-8. 90-degree overhead valve. Cast iron block and head. Displacement: 350 cid (5.7 liters). Bore and stroke: 4.00 x 3.48 inches. Compression ratio: 8.2:1. Brake hp: 175 at 4000 rpm. Torque: 270 lbs.-ft. at 2400 rpm. Five main bearings. Hydraulic valve lifters. Carburetor: Rochester M4MC. California emissions and high-altitude emissions.

OPTIONAL ENGINE: [RPO L82] V-8. 90-degree overhead valve. Cast iron block and head. Displacement: 350 cid (5.7 liters). Bore and stroke: 4.00 x 3.48 inches. Compression ratio: 8.9:1. Brake hp: 220 at 5200 rpm. Torque: 260 lbs.-ft. at 3600 rpm. Five main bearings. Hydraulic valve lifters. Carburetor: Rochester M4MC.

TRANSMISSION

AUTOMATIC TRANSMISSION: A Turbo Hydra-Matic automatic transmission with floor-mounted gear shifter was standard equipment.

OPTIONAL MANUAL TRANSMISSION: A four-speed manual transmission with floor-mounted gear shifter was a no-cost option.

CHASSIS FEATURES

Wheelbase: 98 inches. Overall length: 185.2 inches. Height: 48 inches. Width: 69 inches. Front tread: 58.7 inches. Rear tread: 59.5 inches. Standard tires: P277/70R-15 steel-belted radial.

TECHNICAL FEATURES

Transmission: Four-speed manual transmission (floor shift) standard. Gear ratios: (1st) 2.85:1; (2nd) 2.02:1; (3rd) 1.35:1; (4th) 1.00:1; (Rev) 2.85:1. Close-ratio four-speed manual available at no extra charge: (1st) 2.43:1; (2nd) 1.61:1; (3rd) 1.23:1; (4th) 1.00:1; (Rev) 2.35:1. Three-speed automatic optional: (1st) 2.52:1; (2nd) 1.52:1; (3rd) 1.00:1; (Rev) 1.94:1. Standard final drive ratio: 3.36:1 with four-speed, 3.08:1 w/auto. except L82 V-8, 3.70:1 with four-speed and 3.55:1 w/auto. Steering/Suspension/Body: Same as 1976-77. Brakes: Four-wheel disc (11.75-inch disc diameter). Ignition: Electronic. Fuel tank: 24 gallons.

1978 Indianapolis 500 Pace Car

OPTIONS

RPO A31 Electric power windows ($130). RPO AU3 Power door locks ($120). RPO B2Z Silver Anniversary Paint ($399). RPO CC1 Removable glass roof panels ($349). RPO C60 Air conditioning ($605). RPO D35 Sport mirrors ($40). RPO FE7 Gymkhana suspension ($41). RPO G95 Positraction axle, optional highway ratio ($15). RPO K30 Cruise Control ($99). RPO L82 350-cid 210-hp V-8 ($525). RPO M21 Four-speed close-ratio manual transmission (no cost option). RPO MX1 Turbo Hydra-Matic automatic transmission (no cost option). RPO N37 Tilt-telescopic steering column ($175). RPO QBS P255/60R-15 White-letter steel-belted radial tires ($216.32). RPO QGR P255/70R-15 White-letter steel-belted radial tires ($51). RPO UA1 Heavy-duty battery ($18). RPO UM2 AM-FM stereo radio with tape system ($419). RPO UP6 AM-FM stereo radio with CB system ($638). RPO U58 AM-FM stereo radio ($286). RPO U69 AM-FM radio ($199). RPO U75 Power antenna ($49). RPO U81 Dual rear speakers ($49). RPO YJ8 Aluminum wheels ($340). RPO ZN1 Trailering package ($89). RPO ZX2 Convenience group ($84).

HISTORICAL FOOTNOTES

Introduced: October 6, 1977. Model-year production: 46,772 (but some industry sources have reported a total of 47,667). Calendar-year production: 48,522. Calendar-year sales by U.S. dealers: 42,247. Model year sales by U.S. dealers: 43,106. The limited-edition Indianapolis 500 Pace Car replica was created to commemorate the selection of Corvette as the pace car for the 62nd Indianapolis 500 race on May 28, 1978. A production run of 2,500 was planned, but so many potential buyers who saw it at the New York Auto Show in February wanted one that the goal quickly expanded to 6,500 or roughly one for every Chevrolet dealer. Buyers also had to endure a selection of "forced RPOs" (items installed at the factory whether wanted or not). The mandatory extras included power windows, air conditioning, sport mirrors, a tilt-telescope steering wheel, a rear defogger, an AM/FM stereo with either an 8-track tape player or CB radio, plus power door locks, and a heavy-duty battery. Before long, the original $13,653 list price meant little, as speculators eagerly paid double that amount and more. Later the price retreated to around the original list. Even though so many were built, the Indy Pace Car is still a desirable model. Dave McLellan became head of engineering for Corvettes and worked on the next-generation models.

1978 CORVETTE

Model Number	Body/Style Number	Body Type & Seating	Factory Price	Shipping Weight	Production Total
1Y	Z87	2-dr Cpe-2P	$9,446	3,401 lbs.	40,274

Nicky Wright

1979 Corvette with T-tops and the L48 195-hp V-8

CORVETTE SERIES (V-8) SERIES Z

"The Corvette evolution continues," declared the 1979 Corvette sales catalog. Not much of that evolution was visible, however, after the prior year's massive restyle. Under the hood, the base engine received the dual-snorkel air intake introduced in 1978 for the optional L82 V-8, which added 10 horsepower. The L82 V-8 had a higher-lift cam, special heads with larger valves and higher compression, impact-extruded pistons, a forged steel crankshaft, and finned aluminum rocker covers. The "Y" pipe exhaust system had new open-flow mufflers, while the automatic transmission received a higher numerical (3.55:1) rear axle ratio. All Corvettes now had the high-back bucket seats introduced on the 1978 limited-edition Indianapolis 500 Pace Car. A high pivot point let the seat backrest fold flat on the passenger side, level with the luggage area floor. An AM/FM radio was now standard. Corvettes had black roof panel and window moldings. Bolt-on front and rear spoilers (also from the Indianapolis 500 Pace Car) became available. Buyers who didn't want the full Gymkhana suspension could now order heavy-duty shocks alone. Standard equipment included the L48 V-8 with four-barrel carburetor, either automatic transmission or a four-speed manual gear box (close-ratio version available), power four-wheel disc brakes and limited-slip differential. Other standard items included tinted glass; a front stabilizer bar; concealed windshield wipers and washers; a day/night inside mirror; a wide outside mirror; an anti-theft alarm system; a four-spoke sport steering wheel; an electric clock; a trip odometer; a heater and defroster; bumper guards, and a luggage security shade. The standard tires were P225/70R15 steel-belted radial blackwalls on 15 x 8-inch wheels. Corvettes had a four-wheel independent suspension. The bucket seats came with cloth-and-leather or all-leather trim. The aircraft-type console held a 7,000-rpm tachometer, a voltmeter and oil-pressure, temperature and fuel gauges. Seat inserts could have either leather or cloth trim. The ten body colors were Classic White; Silver; Black; Corvette Light Blue; Corvette Yellow; Corvette Dark Green; Corvette Light Beige; Corvette Red; Corvette Dark Brown; and Corvette Dark Blue. Interiors came in Black; Dark Blue; Dark Brown; Light Beige; Red; Dark Green; and Oyster.

I.D. NUMBERS

The Vehicle Identification Number (VIN) is stamped on a plate on the inner vertical surface of the left windshield pillar visible through the windshield. For 1979 the numbers were: 1Z87[]9S400001 to 1Z87[]9S453807. The first symbol (1) indicated Chevrolet. The second symbol identified the body series (Z = Corvette). The third and fourth symbols indicate the body style number (87 = coupe). The fifth symbol [in blank] indicates engine: 8 = 350-cid 195-hp V-8; 4 = 350-cid 225-hp V-8 The sixth symbol indicates the model year (9 = 1979). The seventh symbol identifies the

1979 Corvette In Corvette Yellow

assembly plant (S = St. Louis, Mo). The last six symbols indicate the sequential production number. The sequential serial number is repeated on the engine block itself, stamped on a pad just ahead of the cylinder head on the right (passenger) side, combined with a three-letter engine code identification suffix. Cast into the top rear (right side) of the block is a date built code. The first letter of that four-symbol code shows the month the block was cast. The next number (or numbers) reveals the day of the month, while the final digit indicates year. Engine code suffixes for 1979 were: ZAA = RPO L48 early-production 350-cid 195-hp V-8 with 8.2:1 compression ratio, four-barrel carburetor, manual transmission. ZAB = RPO L48 early-production 350-cid 195-hp V-8 with 8.2:1 compression ratio, four-barrel carburetor, and automatic transmission. ZAC = RPO L48 early-production 350-cid 195-hp V-8 with 8.2:1 compression ratio, four-barrel carburetor, California emissions, and automatic transmission. ZAD = RPO L48 350-cid 195-hp V-8 with 8.2:1 compression ratio, four-barrel carburetor, high-altitude county emissions, and automatic transmission. ZAF = RPO L48 350-cid 195-hp V-8 with 8.2:1 compression ratio, four-barrel carburetor, and manual transmission. ZAH = RPO L48 350-cid 195-hp V-8 with with 8.2:1 compression ratio, four-barrel carburetor, and automatic transmission. ZAJ = RPO L48 350-cid 195-hp V-8 with 8.2:1 compression ratio, California emissions, four-barrel carburetor, and automatic transmission. ZAF = RPO L82 350-cid 225-hp V-8 with 8.9:1 compression ratio, four-barrel carburetor, and manual transmission. ZBB = RPO L82 350-cid 225-hp V-8 with 8.9:1 compression ratio, four-barrel carburetor, and automatic transmission. The beginning engine numbers were 0001001 and up at each assembly plant. The body number plate was located on the engine side of the cowl. The Style Number 79-1YZ37 identifies a Corvette coupe. The Body Number is the production serial number of the body. The Trim Number indicates the interior trim color and material.

PAINT CODES

(10) Classic White; (13) Silver; (19) Black; (28) Corvette Light Blue; (52) Corvette Yellow; (58) Corvette Dark Green; (59) Corvette Light Beige; (72) Corvette Red; (82) Corvette Dark Brown; (83) Corvette Dark Blue.

CLOTH UPHOLSTERY CODES: (12C) Oyster; (29C) Dark Blue; (49C) Dark Green; (59C) Light Beige.

LEATHER UPHOLSTERY CODES: (122) Oyster; (192) Black; (292) Dark Blue; (492) Dark Green; (592) Light Beige; (722) Red.

ENGINES

BASE ENGINE: [RPO L48] V-8. 90-degree overhead valve. Cast iron block and head. Displacement: 350 cid (5.7 liters). Bore and stroke: 4.00 x 3.48 inches. Compression ratio: 8.2:1. Brake hp: 195 at 4000 rpm. Torque: 285 lbs.-ft. at 3200 rpm. Five main bearings. Hydraulic valve lifters. Carburetor: Rochester M4MC.

OPTIONAL ENGINE: [RPO L82] V-8. 90-degree overhead valve. Cast iron block and head. Displacement: 350 cid (5.7 liters). Bore and stroke: 4.00 x 3.48 inches. Compression ratio: 8.9:1. Brake hp: 225 at 5200 rpm. Torque: 270 lbs.-ft. at 3600 rpm. Five main bearings. Hydraulic valve lifters. Carburetor: Rochester M4MC.

TRANSMISSION

AUTOMATIC TRANSMISSION: A Turbo Hydra-Matic automatic transmission with floor-mounted gear shifter was standard equipment.

OPTIONAL MANUAL TRANSMISSION: A four-speed manual transmission with floor-mounted gear shifter was a no-cost option.

CHASSIS FEATURES

Wheelbase: 98 inches. Overall length: 185.2 inches. Height: 48 inches. Width: 69 inches. Front tread: 58.7 inches. Rear tread: 59.5 inches. Wheel size: 15 x 8 inches. Standard tires: P225/70R-15 SBR.

TECHNICAL FEATURES

Transmission: Four-speed manual transmission (floor shift) standard. Gear ratios: (1st) 2.85:1; (2nd) 2.02:1; (3rd) 1.35:1; (4th) 1.00:1; (Rev) 2.85:1. Close-ratio four-speed manual transmission optional: (1st) 2.43:1; (2nd) 1.61:1; (3rd) 1.23:1; (4th) 1.00:1; (Rev) 2.35:1. Three-speed automatic optional: (1st) 2.52:1; (2nd) 1.52:1; (3rd) 1.00:1; (Rev) 1.93:1. Standard final drive ratio: 3.36:1 with four-speed manual transmission, 3.55:1 with automatic transmission. Steering: Recirculating ball. Front suspension: Control arms, coil springs and stabilizer bar. Rear suspension: Independent, with single transverse leaf spring and lateral struts. Brakes: Four-wheel disc (11.75-inch disc diameter). Ignition: Electronic. Body construction: Fiberglass, on separate frame. Fuel tank: 24 gallons.

OPTIONS

RPO A31 Electric power windows ($141). RPO CC1 Removable glass roof panels ($365). RPO C49 Rear window defogger ($102). RPO C60 Air conditioning ($635). RPO D35 Sport mirrors ($45). RPO FE7 Gymkhana suspension ($49). RPO F51 Heavy-duty shock absorbers ($33). RPO G95 Highway ratio rear axle ($19). RPO K30 Cruise Control ($113). RPO L82 350-cid 225-hp V-8 ($565). RPO MM4 Four-speed manual transmission (no-cost option). RPO M21 Four-speed manual close-ratio transmission (no-cost option). RPO MX1 Turbo Hydra-Matic automatic transmission (no-cost option). RPO N37 Tilt-telescopic steering column ($190). RPO QGR P255/70R-15 Raised-white-letter steel-belted radial tires ($54). RPO QBS P255/60R-15 White Aramid BR tires ($226.20). RPO U58 AM-FM stereo radio ($90). RPO UM2 AM-FM stereo radio with 8-track tape system ($228). RPO UN3 AM-FM stereo radio with cassette ($234). RPO UP6 AM-FM stereo radio with CB system and power antenna ($439). RPO U75 Power antenna ($52). RPO U81 Dual rear speakers ($52). RPO UA1 Heavy-duty battery ($21). RPO ZN1 Trailering package ($98). RPO ZQ2 Power windows and door locks ($272). RPO ZX2 Convenience group ($84).

HISTORICAL FOOTNOTES

Introduced: September 25, 1978. Model-year production: 53,807 (Chevrolet initially reported a total of 49,901 units). Calendar-year production: 48,568. Calendar-year sales by U.S. dealers: 38,631. Model-year sales by U.S. dealers: 39,816. For what it's worth, 7,949 Corvettes were painted this year in Classic White, while 6,960 carried Silver paint. Only 4,385 Corvettes had the MM4 four-speed manual gearbox, while 4,062 ran with the close-ratio M21 version.

1979 CORVETTE

Model Number	Body/Style Number	Body Type & Seating	Factory Price	Shipping Weight	Production Total
1Y	Z87	2-dr Cpe-2P	$10,220	3,372 lbs.	53,807

Nicky Wright

1980 Corvette with custom pinstripes and aluminum wheels

1980

CORVETTE SERIES (V-8) SERIES Z

The 1980 Corvette was more streamlined and lost close to 250 pounds. The hood and doors were lighter with thinner door glass. Corvette bodies held new fiberglass bumper structures. The lift-off roof panels were made of lightweight, low-density microscopic glass beads. The body panels were urethane-coated. Weight cuts also hit the power train. The differential housing and supports were made of aluminum. The 350-cid (5.7-liter) V-8 had a new aluminum intake manifold, while the 305-cid (5.0-liter)

V-8 used in cars sold in California had a stainless exhaust manifold. The Corvette hoods had a new low profile. The front bumper had an integrated lower air dam and the bumper cover now extended to the wheel openings. New two-piece front cornering lamps worked whenever the lights were switched on. A deep-recessed split grille held integral parking lamps. Front fender air vents contained functional black louvers. New front and rear spoilers were molded in and integrated with the bumper caps and were no longer of a bolt-on type. New emblems included an engine identifier for the optional L82 V-8. The dashboard carried a new 85-mph speedometer. Only two storage bins stood behind the seat, where three used to be. Turbo Hydra-Matic transmissions added a lock-up torque converter that engaged at about 30 mph, while the four-speed manual transmission got new gear ratios. In California, Corvette buyers could only get the 305-cid V-8 with automatic transmission this year. The base V-8 lost five horsepower, while the optional version gained five. New standard equipment this year included formerly-optional power windows, a tilt-telescopic steering wheel, and Four Season air conditioning. Rally wheels held P225/70R-15/B blackwall SBR tires with trim rings and center caps. Body colors were: White; Silver; Black; Dark Blue; Dark Brown; Yellow; Dark Green; Frost Beige; Dark Claret; and Red. Interiors came in Black; Claret; Dark Blue; Doeskin; Oyster; and Red.

I.D. NUMBERS

The Vehicle Identification Number (VIN) is stamped on a plate on the inner vertical surface of the left windshield pillar visible through the windshield. For 1980 the numbers were: [Coupe] 1Z87[ ]AS400001 to 1Z87[ ]AS440614. The first symbol (1) indicated Chevrolet. The second symbol identified the body series (Z = Corvette). The third and fourth symbols indicate the body style number (87 = coupe). The fifth symbol [in blank] indicates engine: 8 = L48 350-cid 190-hp V-8; H = California L48 350-cid 180-hp V-8; 6 = L82 350-cid 230-hp V-8. The sixth symbol indicates the model year A = 1980. The seventh symbol identifies the assembly plant (S = St. Louis, Mo). The last six symbols indicate the sequential production number. The sequential serial number is repeated on the engine block itself, stamped on a pad just ahead of the cylinder

Nicky Wright

1980 Corvette in Black

head on the right (passenger) side, combined with a three-letter engine code identification suffix. Cast into the top rear (right side) of the block is a date built code. The first letter of that four-symbol code shows the month the block was cast. The next number (or numbers) reveals the day of the month, while the final digit indicates the year. Engine code suffixes for 1980 were: ZCA = RPO LG4 350-cid 180-hp V-8 with 8.5:1 compression ratio, four-barrel carburetor, California emissions, and automatic transmission. ZAM = RPO L48 350-cid 190-hp V-8 with 8.2:1 compression ratio, four-barrel carburetor, and manual transmission. ZAK = RPO L48 350-cid 190-hp V-8 with 8.2:1 compression ratio, four-barrel carburetor, and automatic transmission. ZBC = RPO L82 350-cid 230-hp V-8 with 9.0:1 compression ratio and four-barrel carburetor. ZBC = RPO L82 350-cid 230-hp V-8 with 9.0:1 compression ratio, four-barrel carburetor, and automatic transmission. The beginning engine numbers were 0001001 and up at each assembly plant. The body number plate was located on the engine side of the cowl. The Style Number 80-1YZ37 identifies a Corvette coupe. The Body Number is the production serial number of the body. The Trim Number indicates the interior trim color and material.

PAINT CODES

(10) White; (13) Silver; (19) Black; (28) Dark Blue; (47) Dark Brown; (52) Yellow; (58) Dark Green; (59) Frost Beige; (76) Dark Claret; (83) Red.

CLOTH UPHOLSTERY CODES: (12C) Oyster; (29C) Dark Blue; (59C) Doeskin; (79C) Claret.

LEATHER UPHOLSTERY CODES: (122) Oyster; (192) Black; (292) Dark Blue; (592) Doeskin; (722) Red; (792) Claret.

ENGINES

BASE ENGINE: [RPO L48] V-8. 90-degree overhead valve. Cast-iron block and head. Displacement: 350 cid (5.7 liters). Bore and stroke: 4.00 x 3.48 inches. Compression ratio: 8.2:1. Brake hp: 190 at 4200 rpm. Torque: 280 lbs.-ft. at 2400 rpm. Five main bearings. Hydraulic valve lifters. Carburetor: Rochester Quadrajet.

Nicky Wright

The L48 350-cid V-8 produced 190 hp

The 1980 Corvette was more than 250 lbs. lighter than in 1979.

BASE CALIFORNIA ENGINE: [RPO LG4] V-8. 90-degree overhead valve. Cast-iron block and head. Displacement: 305 cid (5.0 liters). Bore and stroke: 3.74 x 3.48 inches. Compression ratio: 8.5:1. Brake hp: 180 at 4200 rpm. Torque: 255 lbs.-ft. at 2000 rpm. Five main bearings. Hydraulic valve lifters. Carburetor: Rochester Quadrajet.

OPTIONAL ENGINE: [RPO L82] V-8. 90-degree overhead valve. Cast-iron block and head. Displacement: 350 cid (5.7 liters). Bore and stroke: 4.00 x 3.48 inches. Compression ratio: 9.0:1. Brake hp: 230 at 5200 rpm. Torque: 275 lbs.-ft. at 3600 rpm. Five main bearings. Hydraulic valve lifters. Carburetor: Rochester Quadrajet.

TRANSMISSION

AUTOMATIC TRANSMISSION: A Turbo Hydra-Matic automatic transmission with floor-mounted gear shifter was standard equipment.

OPTIONAL MANUAL TRANSMISSION: A four-speed manual transmission with floor-mounted gear shifter was a no-cost option.

CHASSIS FEATURES

Wheelbase: 98 inches. Overall length: 185.3 inches. Height: 48.1 inches. Width: 69 inches. Front tread: 58.7 inches. Rear tread: 59.5 inches. Wheel size: 15 x 8 inches.

1980 Corvette Eckler Conversion

1980 Corvette L82

Standard tires: P225/70R-15/B SBR. Optional tires: P255/60R-15/B.

TECHNICAL FEATURES

Transmission: Four-speed manual transmission (floor shift) standard. Gear ratios: (1st) 2.88:1; (2nd) 1.91:1; (3rd) 1.33:1; (4th) 1.00:1; (Rev) 2.78:1. Three-speed Turbo Hydra-Matic optional: (1st) 2.52:1; (2nd) 1.52:1; (3rd) 1.00:1; (Rev) 1.93:1. Standard final drive ratio: 3.07:1 with four-speed manual transmission, 3.55:1 with automatic transmission. Steering: Recirculating ball. Front suspension: Control arms, coil springs and stabilizer bar. Rear suspension: Independent, with single transverse leaf spring and lateral struts. Brakes: Four-wheel disc (11.75-inch disc diameter). Ignition: Electronic. Body construction: Fiberglass, on separate frame. Fuel tank: 24 gallons.

OPTIONS

RPO AU3 Power door locks ($140). RPO CC1 Removable glass roof panels ($391). RPO C49 Rear window defogger ($109). RPO FE7 Gymkhana suspension ($55). RPO F51 Heavy-duty shock absorbers ($35). RPO K30 Cruise control ($123). RPO LG4 305-cid 180-hp V-8 mandatory in cars sold in California ($55 credit). RPO L82 350-cid 230-hp V-8 ($595). RPO MM4 Four-speed manual transmission (no-cost option). RPO MX1 Turbo Hydra-Matic automatic transmission (no-cost option). RPO N90 Four aluminum wheels ($407). RPO QGB P255/70R-15 Raised-white-letter steel-belted radial tires ($62). RPO QXH P255/60R-15 Raised white-letter steel-belted radial tires ($426.16). RPO UA1 Heavy-duty battery ($21). RPO U58 AM-FM stereo radio ($46). RPO UM2 AM-FM stereo radio with 8-track tape system ($155). RPO UN3 AM-FM stereo radio with cassette ($168). RPO UP6 AM-FM stereo radio with CB system and power antenna ($391). RPO U75 Power antenna ($56). RPO U81 Dual rear speakers ($52). RPO V54 Roof panel carrier ($125). RPO YF5 California emissions certification ($250). RPO ZN1 Trailering package ($105).

HISTORICAL FOOTNOTES

Introduced: October 25, 1979. Model-year production: 40,614 (but Chevrolet reported a total of 40,564 units). Calendar-year production: 44,190. Model-year sales by U.S. dealers: 37,471. Production continued at the St. Louis, Missouri, plant but a new GMAD operation at Bowling Green, Kentucky, was planned to begin production of the next-generation Corvettes. Chevrolet engineers released a TurboVette that used a Garrette AiResearch turbocharger and fuel injection, but press people who drove it discovered performance more sluggish than a regular L82 V-8 could dish out. Only 5,726 Corvettes had the MM4 four-speed manual gearbox. And only 5,069 carried the special L82 engine. A total of 9,907 had the Gymkhana suspension.

1980 CORVETTE

Model Number	Body/Style Number	Body Type & Seating	Factory Price	Shipping Weight	Production Total
1Y	Z87	2-dr Cpe-2P	$13,140	3,206 lbs.	40,614

More than 40,000 1980 Corvette coups were built.

CORVETTE SERIES — (V-8) — SERIES Y

Probably the most significant change this year was hidden from view. Corvettes with Turbo Hydra-Matic had a new fiberglass-reinforced monoleaf rear spring that weighed just eight pounds (33 pounds less than the multi-leaf steel spring it replaced). The new spring eliminated interleaf friction. Manual-shift models kept the old spring, as did those with optional Gymkhana suspension. Side door glass was made even thinner again, in a further attempt to cut overall car weight. A new L81 version of the 350-cid V-8 arrived this year. It was rated for 190 hp, with lightweight magnesium rocker arm covers. New stainless-steel free-flowing exhaust manifolds weighed 14 pounds less than the previous cast-iron manifolds. A new thermostatically-controlled auxiliary electric fan boosted cooling and allowed use of a smaller main fan. The engine air cleaner had a new chromed cover. A new Computer Command Control system controlled fuel metering, as well as the torque converter lock-up clutch that operated in second and third gears. Manual transmission was available in all 50 states. It was the first time in several years that buyers of Corvettes sold in California could order a stick shift. A quartz crystal clock was now standard. The Corvette's standard anti-theft alarm added a starter-interrupt device. Joining the option list was a six-way power seat. Electronic-tuning radios could have built-in cassette or 8-track tape players or a CB transceiver. The Corvette's ample standard equipment list included either four-speed manual or automatic transmission (same price); four-wheel power disc brakes; limited-slip differential; power steering; tinted glass; twin remote-control sport mirrors; and concealed two-speed wipers. Also standard were halogen high-beam retractable headlamps; air conditioning; power windows; a tilt-telescope leather-wrapped steering wheel; a tachometer; an AM/FM radio; a trip odometer; courtesy lights; and a luggage compartment security shade. Corvette buyers had a choice of cloth-and-vinyl or leather-and-vinyl upholstery. Corvettes rode on P225/70R-15 steel-belted radial blackwall tires on 15 x 8 inch wheels. The optional Gymkhana suspension (price $54) was also included with the trailer towing package. Body colors this year were Mahogany Metallic; White; Silver Metallic; Black; Bright Blue Metallic; Dark Blue Metallic; Yellow; Beige; Red; Maroon Metallic; and Charcoal Metallic. Four two-tone combinations were available: Silver and Dark Blue; Silver and Charcoal; Beige and Dark Bronze; and Autumn Red and Dark Claret. (All two-tone cars were painted at the new plant in Bowling Green, Kentucky). Interiors came in Silver Gray; Charcoal; Dark Blue; Camel; Dark Red; and Medium Red.

I.D. NUMBERS

The Vehicle Identification Number (VIN) is visible through the windshield on the driver's side. For 1981 the numbers were: [St. Louis Assembly Plant] 1G1AY87[ ]4BS400001 to 1G1AY87[ ]4BS431611. [Bowling Green Assembly Plant] 1G1AY87[ ]4B5100001 to 1G1AY87[ ]4B5108995. The first symbol (1) indicates U.S. built. The second symbol (G) indicates General Motors product. The third symbol (1) indicates Chevrolet Motor Division vehicle. The fourth symbol (A) indicates the type of non-passive passenger restraint system used. The fifth symbol (Y) indicates car line or series, in this case Corvette. The sixth and seventh symbols indicate the body style number (87 = two-door plainback special coupe). The eighth symbol [in blank] indicates engine: 6 = L82 350-cid (5.7-liter) 230-hp Chevrolet V-8. The ninth symbol is a check digit that varies. The 10th symbol indicates model year (B = 1981). The 11th symbol indicates the assembly plant (S = St. Louis, Mo. and 5 = Bowling Green, Ky). The last six symbols indicate the sequential production number starting with 100001 at each factory. The sequential serial number is repeated on the engine block itself, stamped on a pad just ahead of the cylinder head on the right (passenger) side, combined with a three-letter engine code identification suffix. Cast into the top rear (right side) of the block is a date built code. The first letter of that four-symbol code shows the month the block was cast. The next number (or numbers) reveals the day of the month, while the final digit indicates year. Engine code suffixes for 1981 were: ZDA = RPO L81 350-cid 190-hp V-8 with 8.2:1 compression ratio, four-barrel carburetor, and manual transmission. ZDB = RPO L81 350-cid 190-hp V-8 with 8.2:1 compression ratio, four-barrel carburetor, California emissions, and automatic transmission. ZDC = RPO L81 350-cid 190-hp V-8 with 8.2:1 compression ratio, four-barrel carburetor, California emissions, and manual transmission. ZDD = RPO L81 350-cid 190-hp V-8 with 8.2:1 compression ratio, four-barrel carburetor, and automatic transmission.

PAINT CODES

(06) Mahogany Metallic; (10) White; (13) Silver Metallic; (19) Black; (24) Bright Blue Metallic; (28) Dark Blue Metallic; (52) Yellow; (59) Beige; (75) Red; (79) Maroon Metallic; (84) Charcoal Metallic; (33/38) Silver and Dark Blue; (33/39) Silver and Charcoal; (50/74) Beige and Dark Bronze; (80/98) Autumn Red and Dark Claret.

1981 Corvette coupe factory illustrations

CLOTH UPHOLSTERY CODES: (19C) Charcoal; (29C) Dark Blue; (64C) Camel; (67C) Dark Red.

LEATHER UPHOLSTERY CODES: (152) Silver Gray; (192) Charcoal; (292) Dark Blue; (642) Camel; (672) Dark Red; (752) Medium Red.

ENGINE

BASE ENGINE: [RPO L81] V-8. 90-degree overhead valve. Cast-iron block and head. Displacement: 350 cid (5.7 liters). Bore and stroke: 4.00 x 3.48 inches. Compression ratio: 8.2:1. Brake hp: 190 at 4200 rpm. Torque: 280 lbs.-ft. at 1600 rpm. Five main bearings. Hydraulic valve lifters. Carburetor: Rochester Quadrajet.

TRANSMISSION

AUTOMATIC TRANSMISSION: A Turbo Hydra-Matic automatic transmission with floor-mounted gear shifter was standard equipment.

OPTIONAL MANUAL TRANSMISSION: A four-speed manual transmission with floor-mounted gear shifter was a no cost option.

CHASSIS FEATURES

Wheelbase: 98 inches. Overall length: 185.3 inches. Height: 48.1 inches. Width: 69 inches. Front tread: 58.7 inches. Rear tread: 59.5 inches. Wheel size: 15 x 8 inches. Standard tires: P225/70R-15/B SBR. Optional tires: P255/60R-15.

TECHNICAL FEATURES

Transmission: Four-speed manual transmission (floor shift) standard. Gear ratios: (1st) 2.88:1; (2nd) 1.91:1; (3rd) 1.33:1; (4th) 1.00:1; (Rev) 2.78:1. Three-speed Turbo Hydra-Matic optional: (1st) 2.52:1; (2nd) 1.52:1; (3rd) 1.00:1; (Rev) 1.93:1. Standard final drive ratio: 2.72:1 with four-speed manual transmission, 2.87:1 with automatic transmission. Steering: Recirculating ball. Front suspension: Control arms, coil springs and stabilizer bar. Rear suspension: Independent, with single transverse leaf spring and lateral struts. Brakes: Four-wheel disc (11.75-inch disc diameter). Ignition: Electronic. Body construction: Fiberglass, on separate frame. Fuel tank: 24 gallons.

OPTIONS

RPO AU3 Power door locks ($145). RPO A42 Power driver seat ($183). RPO CC1 Removable glass roof panels ($414). RPO C49 Rear window defogger ($119). RPO DG7 Electric sport mirrors ($117). RPO D84 Two-tone paint ($399). RPO FE7 Gymkhana suspension ($57). RPO F51 Heavy-duty shock absorbers ($37). RPO G92 Performance axle ratio ($20). RPO K35 Cruise control ($155). RPO MM4 Four-speed manual transmission (no cost option). RPO N90 Four aluminum wheels ($428). RPO QGR P255/70R-15 Raised-white-letter steel-belted radial tires ($72). RPO QXH P255/60R-15 Raised white-letter steel-belted radial tires ($491.92). RPO UL5 Radio delete ($118 credit). RPO UM4 AM-FM electronic tuning stereo radio with 8-track tape system ($386). RPO UM5 AM-FM electronic tuning stereo radio with 8-track tape and CB system ($712). RPO UM6 AM-FM electronic tuning stereo radio with cassette ($423). RPO UN5 AM-FM electronic tuning stereo radio with cassette and CB system ($750). RPO U58 AM-FM stereo radio ($95). RPO U75 Power antenna ($55). RPO V54 Roof panel carrier ($135). RPO YF5 California emissions certification ($46). RPO ZN1 Trailering package ($110).

HISTORICAL FOOTNOTES

Introduced: September 25, 1980. Model-year production: 40,606 (but Chevrolet first reported a total of 40,593 units). Calendar-year production: 27,990. Model-year sales by U.S. dealers: 33,414. Of the total output this model year, 8,995 Corvettes came out of the new plant at Bowling Green, Kentucky, which began production in June 1981. Despite some weak years in the industry, Corvette sales remained strong through this period.

1981 CORVETTE

Model Number	Body/Style Number	Body Type & Seating	Factory Price	Shipping Weight	Production Total
1Y	Z87	2-dr Cpe-2P	$15,248	3,179 lbs.	40606

1982 Corvette Collector Edition

CORVETTE SERIES (V-8) SERIES Y

For the first time since 1955, no stick shift Corvettes were produced. Every Corvette had a new type of four-speed automatic transmission with lock-up function in every gear except first. Under the hood was a new kind of 350-cid V-8 with Cross-Fire fuel injection. Twin throttle-body injectors with computerized metering helped boost horsepower to 200 (10 more than in 1981) and cut emissions at the same time. This was the first fuel-injected Corvette in nearly two decades. It had a much different type of fuel-injection system since mini-computerization had arrived. In the gas tank was a new electric fuel pump. Externally, the final version of the "big" (Stingray-style) Corvette changed little, but the Collector Edition model displayed quite a few special features, highlighted by a frameless glass lift-up hatch in place of the customary fixed backlight. Its unique Silver-Beige metallic paint was accented by pin stripes and a "fading shadow" treatment on hood, fenders and doors . . . plus distinctive cloisonné emblems. Special finned wheels were similar to the cast-aluminum wheels that dated back to 1967. The Collector Edition's removable glass roof panels had special bronze coloring and solar screening. The model's crossed-flags emblems read "Corvette Collector Edition" around the rim. Inside was a matching Silver-Beige metallic interior with multi-tone leather seats and door trim. Even the Collector Edition's hand-sewn leather-wrapped steering wheel kept the theme color and its leather-covered horn button had a cloisonné emblem. The tires were P255/60R-15 Goodyear SBR WLT Eagle GT. Standard equipment for other Corvettes included power brakes and steering, P225/70R-15/B SBR tires on steel wheels with center hub and trim rings, cornering lamps, front fender louvers, halogen high-beam retractable headlamps, dual remote sport mirrors, and tinted glass. The body-color front bumper had a built-in air dam. Also standard: Luggage security shade; air conditioning; push-button AM/FM radio; concealed wipers; power windows; time-delay dome/courtesy lamps; headlamp-on reminder; a lighted visor vanity mirror; a leather wrapped tilt/telescoping steering wheel; a 7,000-rpm tachometer; an analog clock with sweep second hand; a day/night mirror; a lighter; and a trip odometer. Bucket seats could be trimmed in all-cloth or leather options. Standard body colors were: White; Silver; Black; Silver Blue; Dark Blue; Bright Blue; Charcoal; Silver Green; Gold; Silver Beige; Red; and Dark Claret. Four two-tones were available: White and Silver; Silver and Charcoal; Silver and Dark Claret; and Silver Blue and Dark Blue. Interiors came in Charcoal; Camel; Dark Blue; Dark Red; Silver Beige; Silver Green; and Silver Gray.

I.D. NUMBERS

The Vehicle Identification Number (VIN) is visible through the windshield on the driver's side.

Jerry Heasley

1982 Corvette Collector Edition in Silver Beige paint unique to the model

The numbers were: [Coupes] 1G1AY8786C5100001 to 1G1AY8786C512408. The first symbol (1) indicates U.S. Built. The second symbol (G) indicates General Motors product. The third symbol (1) indicates Chevrolet Motor Division vehicle. The fourth symbol (A) indicates non-passive manual seat belts. The fifth symbol (Y) indicates car line or series: (Y = Chevrolet Corvette). The sixth and seventh symbols indicate the body style number (87 = two-door plainback special coupe; 07 = Collector Edition two-door hatchback coupe). The eighth symbol indicates engine: 8 = 5.7-liter Cross-Fire Injection (CFI) Chevrolet V-8. The ninth symbol is a check digit that varies. The 10th symbol indicates model year (C = 1982). The 11th symbol indicates the assembly plant: (5 = Bowling Green, Ky). The last six symbols indicate the sequential production number starting with 100001 at each factory. The sequential serial number is repeated on the engine block itself, stamped on a pad just ahead of the cylinder head on the right (passenger) side, combined with a three-letter engine code identification suffix. Cast into the top rear (right side) of the block is a date built code. The first letter of that four-symbol code shows the month the block was cast. The next number (or numbers) reveals the day of the month, while the final digit indicates year. Engine code suffixes for 1982 were: ZBA = RPO L83 350-cid 200-hp V-8 with 9.0:1 compression ratio, cross-fire fuel injection, and automatic transmission. ZBC = Early-production RPO L83 350-cid 200-hp V-8 with 9.0:1 compression ratio, cross-fire fuel injection, California emissions, and automatic transmission. ZBN = RPO L83 350-cid 200-hp V-8 with 9.0:1 compression ratio, cross-fire fuel injection, California emissions, and automatic transmission.

PAINT CODES

(10) White; (13) Silver; (19) Black; (24) Silver Blue; (26) Dark Blue; (31) Bright Blue; (39) Charcoal; (40) Silver Green; (56) Gold; (59) Silver Beige; (70) Red; (99) Dark Claret; (10/13) White and Silver; (13/39) Silver and Charcoal; (13/99) Silver and Dark Claret; (24/26) Silver Blue and Dark Blue.

CLOTH UPHOLSTERY CODES: (22C) Dark Blue; (64C) Camel; (74C) Dark Red.

LEATHER UPHOLSTERY CODES: (132) Silver Gray; (182) Charcoal; (222) Dark Blue; (402) Silver Green; (642) Camel; (742) Dark Red.

ENGINE

BASE ENGINE: [RPO L83] V-8. 90-degree overhead valve. Cast-iron block and head. Displacement: 350 cid (5.7 liters). Bore and stroke: 4.00 x 3.48 inches. Compression ratio: 9.0:1. Brake hp: 200 at 4200 rpm. Torque: 285 lbs.-ft. at 2800 rpm. Five main bearings. Hydraulic valve lifters. Induction: Cross-fire fuel injection (twin TBI).

TRANSMISSION

AUTOMATIC TRANSMISSION: A Turbo Hydra-Matic automatic transmission with floor-mounted gear shifter was standard equipment.

CHASSIS FEATURES

Wheelbase: 98 inches. Overall length: 185.3 inches. Height: 48.4 inches. Width: 69 inches. Front tread: 58.7 inches. Rear tread: 59.5 inches. Wheel size: 15 x 8 inches. Standard tires [Base Corvette]: P225/70R-15 SBR. Standard Tires [Collector Edition Corvette]: P255/60R-15.

TECHNICAL FEATURES

Transmission: THM 700-R4 four-speed overdrive automatic (floor shift). Gear ratios: (1st) 3.06:1; (2nd) 1.63:1; (3rd) 1.00:1; (4th) 0.70:1; (Rev) 2.29:1. Standard final drive ratio: 2.72:1 (except 2.87:1 with aluminum wheels). Steering: Recirculating ball (power assisted). Front suspension: Upper/lower A-arms, coil springs, stabilizer bar. Rear suspension: Fully independent with half-shafts, lateral struts, control arms, and transverse leaf springs. Brakes: Power four-wheel discs (11.75-inch disc diameter). Ignition: Electronic. Body construction: Separate fiberglass body and ladder-type steel frame. Fuel tank: 24 gallons.

OPTIONS

RPO AU3 Power door locks ($155). RPO A42 Power driver seat ($197). RPO CC1 Removable glass roof panels ($443). RPO C49 Rear window defogger ($129). RPO DG7 Electric sport mirrors ($125). RPO D84 Two-tone paint ($428). RPO FE7 Gymkhana suspension ($61). RPO K35

Chevrolet

1982 Corvette Collector Edition, one of 6,759 built

Cruise control ($165). RPO N90 Four aluminum wheels ($458). RPO QGR P255/70R-15 Raised-white-letter steel-belted radial tires ($80). RPO QXH P255/60R-15 Raised-white-letter steel-belted radial tires ($542.52). RPO UL5 Radio delete ($124 credit). RPO UM4 AM-FM electronic tuning stereo radio with 8-track tape system ($386). RPO UM6 AM-FM electronic tuning stereo radio with cassette ($423). RPO UN5 AM-FM electronic tuning stereo radio with cassette and CB system ($755). RPO U58 AM-FM stereo radio ($101). RPO U75 Power antenna ($60). RPO V08 Heavy-duty cooling ($57). RPO V54 Roof panel carrier ($144). RPO YF5 California emissions certification ($46).

HISTORICAL FOOTNOTES

Introduced: December 12, 1981. Model-year production: 25,407. Calendar-year production: 22,838. Model-year sales by U.S. dealers: 22,086. All Corvettes now came from the factory at Bowling Green, Kentucky. Production fell dramatically this year, reaching the lowest total since 1967. The 1982 model was the last Corvette to employ the same basic body introduced in 1968. Its chassis dated back to even five years before that. No doubt, some buyers preferred to wait for the next generation to arrive. Still, this was the end of the big 'Vette era: "An enthusiast's kind of Corvette. A most civilized one," according to the factory catalog. *Road & Track* called it "truly the last of its series," though one with an all-new drive train. The Collector Edition earned the dubious distinction of being the first Corvette to cost more than $20,000. The Collector Edition was built to order, rather than according to a predetermined schedule. It carried a special VIN code with a "0" in the sixth position (Body Code 07), but did not have a separate serial number sequence. The special VIN plates were used to prevent swindlers from turning an ordinary Corvette into a special edition (which had happened all too often with 1978 Indy Pace Car replicas).

Chevrolet

1982 Corvette interior

1982 CORVETTE Model Number	Body/Style Number	Body Type & Seating	Factory Price	Shipping Weight	Production Total
1Y	Z87	2-dr Cpe-2P	$18,290	3,213 lbs.	18,648
1982 CORVETTE COLLECTOR EDITION					
1Y	Y07	2-dr Hatch Cpe-2P	$22,538	3,222 lbs.	6,759

Jerry Heasley

A total of 51,547 1984 Corvettes coupes were built.

CORVETTE SERIES (V-8) SERIES Y

The eagerly-awaited sixth-generation Corvette for the '80s missed the 1983 model year completely, but arrived in spring 1983 in an all-new form. An aerodynamic exterior featuring an "acute" windshield rake (64 degrees) covered a series of engineering improvements. A one-piece, full-width fiberglass roof (no T-bar) was removable. It had a transparent, acrylic lift-off panel with a solar screen optional. At the rear was a frameless glass back window or hatch above four round tail lamps. Hidden headlamps were featured, along with clear, integrated halogen fog lamps and front cornering lamps. The dual sport mirrors were electrically remote controlled. The unit body (with partial front frame) used a front-hinged "clam shell" hood with integral twin-duct air intake. The sole 1984 V-8 was L83 350-cid (5.7-liter) V-8 with cross-fire fuel injection. Stainless steel headers led into its exhaust system. The air cleaner and the valve train had cast magnesium covers. After being unavailable in 1982, a four-speed manual gearbox returned as the standard Corvette transmission (although not until January 1984). A four-plus-three-speed automatic with computer-activated overdrive in every gear except first, was offered at no extra cost. It used a hydraulic clutch. Overdrive was locked out during rigorous acceleration above specified speeds and when a console switch was activated. Under the chassis were an aluminum drive shaft, forged-aluminum suspension arms, and a fiberglass transverse leaf spring. Power rack-and-pinion steering and power four-wheel disc brakes were standard. Optional Goodyear 50-series "uni-directional" tires were designed for mounting on a specific wheel. Inside, an electronic instrument panel featured both analog and digital LCD readouts in either English or metric measure. A Driver Information System between the speedometer and tachometer gave a selection of switch-chosen readings. At the driver's left was the parking brake. Corvette's ample standard equipment list included an advanced (and very necessary) theft-prevention system with starter-interrupt. Other standard equipment included: air conditioning; power windows; electronic-tuning seek/scan AM/FM stereo radio with digital clock; reclining bucket seats; leather-wrapped tilt/telescope steering wheel; luggage security shade; and side window defoggers. Body colors were White; Bright Silver Metallic; Medium Gray Metallic; Black; Light Blue Metallic; Medium Blue Metallic; Gold Metallic; Light Bronze Metallic; Dark Bronze Metallic; and Bright Red. Two-tone options were Silver and Medium Gray; Light Blue and Medium Blue; and Light Bronze and Dark Bronze. Interiors came in Carmine; Bronze; Graphite; Medium Blue; Medium Gray; and Saddle.

I.D. NUMBERS

The Vehicle Identification Number (VIN) is visible through the windshield on the driver's side. The numbers

The 1984 Corvette coupe in Bright Silver Metallic

were: 1G1AY0782E5100001 to 1G1AY0782E5151547. The first symbol (1) indicates U.S. built. The second symbol (G) indicates General Motors product. The third symbol (1) indicates Chevrolet Motor Division vehicle. The fourth symbol (A) indicates non-passive manual seat belts. The fifth symbol (Y) indicates car line or series: (Y = Chevrolet Corvette). The sixth and seventh symbols indicate the body style number (07 = two-door hatchback coupe). The eighth symbol indicates engine: 8 = 5.7-liter Cross-Fire Injection (CFI) Chevrolet V-8. The ninth symbol is a check digit that varies. The 10th symbol indicates model year (E = 1984). The 11th symbol indicates the assembly plant: (5 = Bowling Green, Ky). The last six symbols indicate the sequential production number starting with 100001 at each factory. The sequential serial number is repeated on the engine block itself, stamped on a pad just ahead of the cylinder head on the right (passenger) side, combined with a three-letter engine code identification suffix. Cast into the top rear (right side) of the block is a date built code. The first letter of that four-symbol code shows the month the block was cast. The next number (or numbers) reveals the day of the month, while the final digit indicates the year. Engine code suffixes for 1984 were: ZFC = RPO L83 350-cid 205-hp V-8 with 9.0:1 compression ratio, cross-fire fuel injection, and THM automatic transmission. ZFD = RPO L83 350-cid 205-hp V-8 with 9.0:1 compression ratio, cross-fire fuel injection, and manual transmission. ZFF = RPO L83 350-cid 205-hp V-8 with 9.0:1 compression ratio, cross-fire fuel injection, California emissions, and THM automatic transmission. ZFH = RPO L83 350-cid 205-hp V-8 with 9.0:1 compression ratio, cross-fire fuel injection, and THM automatic transmission for export. ZFJ = RPO L83 350-cid 205-hp V-8 with 9.0:1 compression ratio, cross-fire fuel injection, and manual transmission for export. ZFK = RPO L83 350-cid 205-hp V-8 with 9.0:1 compression ratio, cross-fire fuel injection, and THM automatic transmission. ZFM = RPO L83 350-cid 205-hp V-8 with 9.0:1 compression ratio, cross-fire fuel injection, California emissions, and automatic transmission. ZFN = RPO L83 350-cid 205-hp V-8 with 9.0:1 compression ratio, cross-fire fuel injection, California emissions, and automatic transmission. ZFR = RPO L83 350-cid 205-hp

Jerry Heasley

The 1984 Corvette had the 350-cid, 205-hp L83 V-8.

V-8 with 9.0:1 compression ratio, cross-fire fuel injection, California emissions, and automatic transmission.

PAINT CODES

(10) White; (16) Bright Silver Metallic; (18) Medium Gray Metallic; (19) Black; (20) Light Blue Metallic; (23) Medium Blue Metallic; (53) Gold Metallic; (63) Light Bronze Metallic; (66) Dark Bronze Metallic; (72) Bright Red; (16/18) Silver and Medium Gray; (20/23) Light Blue and Medium Blue; (83/66) Light Bronze and Dark Bronze.

CLOTH UPHOLSTERY CODES: (12C) Green; (15C) Medium Gray; (28C) Medium Blue; (62C) Saddle; (65C) Bronze.

SPORT CLOTH UPHOLSTERY CODES: (12V) Green; (15V) Medium Gray; (28V) Medium Blue; (62V) Saddle; (65V) Bronze.

LEATHER UPHOLSTERY CODES: (122) Graphite; (152) Medium Gray; (622) Saddle; (652) Bronze; (742) Carmine.

ENGINE

BASE ENGINE: [RPO L83] V-8. 90-degree overhead valve. Cast-iron block and head. Displacement: 350 cid (5.7 liters). Bore and stroke: 4.00 x 3.48 inches. Compression ratio: 9.0:1. Brake hp: 205 at 4200 rpm. Torque: 290 lbs.-ft. at 2800 rpm. Five main bearings. Hydraulic valve lifters. Induction: Cross-fire fuel injection (twin TBI).

TRANSMISSION

AUTOMATIC TRANSMISSION: A Turbo Hydra-Matic automatic transmission with floor-mounted gear shifter was standard equipment.

MANUAL TRANSMISSION: A four-speed manual transmission was available with overdrive capability to improve fuel efficiency.

CHASSIS FEATURES

Wheelbase: 96.2 inches. Overall length: 176.5 inches. Height: 46.7 inches. Width: 71 inches. Front tread: 59.6 inches. Rear tread: 60.4 inches. Wheel size: 15 x 7 inches. Standard tires: P215/65R-15. Optional tires: Eagle P255/50VR-16 on 16 x 8 inch wheels.

TECHNICAL FEATURES

Transmission: THM 700-R4 four-speed overdrive automatic (floor shift) standard. Gear ratios: (1st) 3.06:1; (2nd) 1.63:1; (3rd) 1.00:1; (4th) 0.70:1; (Rev) 2.29:1. Four-speed manual transmission optional: (1st) 2.88:1; (2nd) 1.91:1; (3rd) 1.33:1; (4th) 1.00:1; (overdrive) 0.67:1; (Rev) 2.78:1. Standard final drive ratio: 2.73:1 with automatic transmission, 3.07:1 with four-speed manual transmission; (3.31:1 optional). Steering: Rack and pinion (power-assisted). Front suspension: Single fiberglass composite monoleaf transverse spring with unequal-length aluminum control arms and stabilizer bar. Rear suspension: Fully independent five-link system with transverse fiberglass single-leaf springs, aluminum upper/lower trailing links and strut-rod tie-rod assembly. Brakes: Four-wheel power

The C4 was a complete redesign that emphasized handling.

disc. Body construction: Unibody with partial front frame. Fuel tank: 20 gallons.

OPTIONS

RPO AG9 Power driver seat ($210). RPO AQ9 Sports cloth seats ($210). RPO AR9 Base leather seats ($400). RPO AU3 Power door locks ($165). RPO CC3 Removable transparent roof panel ($595). RPO D84 Two-tone paint ($428). RPO FG3 Delco-Bilstein shock absorbers ($189). RPO G92 Performance axle ratio ($22). RPO KC4 Engine oil cooler ($158). RPO K34 Cruise control ($185). RPO MM4 Four-speed manual transmission (no-cost option). RPO QZD P255/50VR-16 tires and 16-inch wheels ($561.20). RPO UL5 Radio delete ($331 credit). RPO UM6 AM-FM stereo radio with cassette ($153). RPO UN8 AM-FM stereo with Citizens Band ($153). RPO UU8 Delco-Bose stereo system ($895). RPO V01 Heavy-duty radiator ($57). RPO YF5 California emissions certification ($75). RPO Z51 Performance handling package ($600.20). RPO Z6A Rear window and side mirror defoggers ($160).

HISTORICAL FOOTNOTES

Introduced: March 25, 1983. Model-year production: 51,547 (in extended model year). Calendar-year production: 35,661. Calendar-year sales by U.S. dealers: 30,424. Model-year sales by U.S. dealers: 53,877 (including 25,891 sold during the 1983 model year). Car and Driver called the new Corvette "the most advanced production car on the planet." *Motor Trend* described it as "the best-handling production car in the world, regardless of price." Heady praise indeed. During its year-and-a-half model run, orders poured in well ahead of schedule, even though the new edition cost over $5,000 more than the 1982 version. The body offered the lowest drag coefficient of any Corvette: just 0.341. Testing at GM's Proving Grounds revealed 0.95G lateral acceleration—the highest ever for a production car. Only 6,443 Corvettes had a four-speed manual transmission and only 410 came with a performance axle ratio, but 3,729 had Delco-Bilstein shock absorbers installed.

1984 CORVETTE

Model Number	Body/Style Number	Body Type & Seating	Factory Price	Shipping Weight	Production Total
1Y	Y07	2-dr Hatch Cpe-2P	$21,800	3,088 lbs.	51,547

NOTE: Of the total production, 240 Corvettes were modified for use with leaded gasoline *(for export)*.

The 1985 Corvette coupe had a top speed of 150 mph.

CORVETTE SERIES (V-8) SERIES Y

Two details marked the 1985 Corvette as being different from its newly-restyled 1984 predecessor. The first detail was a new Tuned Port Injection nameplate on fender molding and the second was the straight tailpipes at the rear. That nameplate identified a new 350-cid (5.7-liter) V-8 under the hood. It had a tuned-port-fuel-injection (TPI) system and 230 hp. City fuel economy ratings went up. Otherwise, the only evident change was a slight strengthening in the intensity of the Red and Silver body colors. The Corvette's smoothly-sloped nose, adorned by nothing other than a circular emblem, held retracting halogen headlamps. Wide parking and signal lamps nearly filled the space between license plate and outer body edge. Wide horizontal side marker lenses were just ahead of the front wheels. The large air cleaner of 1982 was replaced by an elongated plenum chamber with eight curved aluminum runners. Mounted ahead of the radiator, it ducted incoming air into the plenum through a Bosch hot-wire mass-airflow sensor. Those tuned runners were meant to boost power at low to medium rpms, following a principle similar to that used for the tall intake stacks in racing engines. Electronic Spark Control (ESC) sensed knocking and adjusted timing to fit fuel octane. Under the chassis, the 1985 Corvette carried a reworked suspension (both standard and optional Z51) to soften the ride without losing control. The Z51 handling package now included 9.5-inch wheels all around, along with Delco-Bilstein gas-charged shock absorbers and a heavy-duty cooling system. The stabilizer bars in the Z51 package were thicker. Spring rates on both suspensions were reduced. Cast aluminum wheels held P255/50VR-16 Eagle GT tires. Brake master cylinders used a new large-capacity plastic booster. Manual gearboxes drove rear axles with 8.5-inch ring gears. The Corvette's instrument-cluster graphics had a bolder look and its roof panels added more solar screening. An optional leather-trimmed sport seat arrived at midyear. Corvette standard equipment included an electronic information center; air conditioning; limited-slip differential; power four-wheel disc brakes; power steering; cornering lamps and a seek-and-scan AM/FM stereo radio with four speakers; and automatic power antenna. Also standard were a cigarette lighter; a digital clock; a tachometer; intermittent windshield wipers; halogen fog lamps; and side window defoggers. Corvettes had contour high-back cloth bucket seats; power windows; a trip odometer; a theft-deterrent system with starter interrupt; a compact spare tire; dual electric remote-control sport mirrors and tinted glass. Black belt, windshield, and body side moldings, plus color-keyed rocker panel moldings protected the bodies. A four-speed overdrive automatic transmission was standard, with a four-speed manual (with overdrive in three gears) available at no extra cost. Body colors were: Silver Metallic; Medium Gray Metallic; Light Blue Metallic; Medium Blue Metallic; White; Black; Gold

The 1985 Corvette coupe featured fuel injection as an option for the first time since 1965.

Metallic; Light Bronze Metallic; Dark Bronze Metallic and Bright Red. Two-tone options were Silver and Gray; Light Blue and Medium Blue; and Light Bronze and Dark Bronze. Interiors came in Carmine; Bronze; Graphite; Medium Blue; Medium Gray; and Saddle.

I.D. NUMBERS

The Vehicle Identification Number (VIN) is visible through the windshield on the driver's side. The numbers were: [Coupes] 1G1YY0787F5100001 to 1G1YY0787F5139729. The first symbol (1) indicates U.S. Built. The second symbol (G) indicates General Motors product. The third symbol (1) indicates Chevrolet Motor Division vehicle. The fourth symbol (Y) indicates type of restraint system. The fifth symbol (Y) indicates car line or series: (Y = Chevrolet Corvette). The sixth and seventh symbols indicate the body style number (07 = two-door hatchback coupe). The eighth symbol indicates engine: 8 = 5.7-liter Tuned Port Injection (TPI) Chevrolet V-8. The ninth symbol is a check digit that varies. The 10th symbol indicates model year (F = 1985). The 11th symbol indicates the assembly plant: (5 = Bowling Green, Ky). The last six symbols indicate the sequential production number starting with 100001 at each factory. The sequential serial number is repeated on the engine block itself, stamped on a pad just ahead of the cylinder head on the right (passenger) side, combined with a three-letter engine code identification suffix. Cast into the top rear (right side) of the block is a date built code. The first letter of that four-symbol code shows the month the block was cast. The next number (or numbers) reveals the day of the month, while the final digit indicates year. Engine code suffixes for 1985 were: ZDF = RPO L98 350-cid 230-hp V-8 with 9.0:1 compression ratio, tuned port injection, and THM automatic transmission. ZJB = RPO L98 350-cid 230-hp V-8 with 9.0:1 compression ratio, tuned port injection, and manual transmission. ZJC = RPO L98 export V-8. ZJJ = RPO L98 350-cid 230-hp V-8 with 9.0:1 compression ratio, tuned port injection, engine oil cooler, and THM automatic transmission. ZJK = RPO L98 350-cid 230-hp V-8 with 9.0:1 compression ratio, tuned port injection, engine oil cooler, and manual transmission.

PAINT CODES

(13) Silver Metallic; (18) Medium Gray Metallic; (20) Light Blue Metallic; (23) Medium Blue Metallic; (40) White; (41) Black; (53) Gold Metallic; (63) Light Bronze Metallic; (66) Dark Bronze Metallic; (81) Bright Red; (13/18) Silver and Gray; (20/23) Light Blue and Medium Blue; (63/66) Light Bronze and Dark Bronze.

CLOTH UPHOLSTERY CODES: (12C) Green; (15C) Medium Gray; (28C) Medium Blue; (62C) Saddle; (65C) Bronze.

SPORT CLOTH UPHOLSTERY CODES: (12V) Green; (15V) Medium Gray; (28V) Medium Blue; (62V) Saddle; (65V) Bronze.

LEATHER UPHOLSTERY CODES: (122) Graphite; (152) Medium Gray; (282) Medium Blue leather; (622) Saddle; (652) Bronze; (742) Carmine.

ENGINE

BASE ENGINE: [RPO L98] V-8. 90-degree overhead valve. Cast iron block and head. Displacement: 350 cid (5.7 liters). Bore and stroke: 4.00 x 3.48 inches. Compression ratio: 9.0:1. Brake hp: 230 at 4000 rpm. Torque: 330 lbs.-ft. at 3200 rpm. Five main bearings. Hydraulic valve lifters.

Chevrolet

The 1985 Corvette coupe interior featured improved instrument graphics.

Induction: Tuned-port-induction (TPI) system.

TRANSMISSION

AUTOMATIC TRANSMISSION: A Turbo Hydra-Matic automatic transmission with floor-mounted gear shifter was standard equipment.

MANUAL TRANSMISSION: A four-speed manual transmission with overdrive capability was optional.

CHASSIS FEATURES

Wheelbase: 96.2 inches. Overall length: 176.5 inches. Height: 46.4 inches. Width: 71 inches. Front Tread: 59.6 inches. Rear Tread: 60.4 inches. Wheel Size: 16 x 8.5 inches. Standard Tires: P255/50VR-16 SBR.

TECHNICAL FEATURES

Transmission: THM 700-R4 four-speed overdrive automatic (floor shift) standard. Gear ratios: (1st) 3.06:1; (2nd) 1.63:1; (3rd) 1.00:1; (4th) 0.70:1; (Rev) 2.29:1. Four-speed manual transmission optional: (1st) 2.88:1; (2nd) 1.91:1; (3rd) 1.33:1; (4th) 1.00:1; (overdrive) 0.67:1; (Rev) 2.78:1. Planetary overdrive ratios: (2nd) 1.28:1; (3rd) 0.89:1; (4th) 0.67:1. Standard final drive ratio: 2.73:1 with automatic transmission. Steering: Rack and pinion (power-assisted). Front suspension: Single fiberglass composite monoleaf transverse spring with unequal-length aluminum control arms and stabilizer bar. Rear suspension: Fully independent five-link system with transverse fiberglass single-leaf springs, aluminum upper/lower trailing links and strut-rod/tie-rod assembly. Brakes: Four-wheel power disc. Body construction: Unibody with partial front frame. Fuel tank: 20 gallons.

OPTIONS

RPO AG9 Power driver seat ($215). RPO AQ9 Sports leather seats ($1,025). RPO AR9 Base leather seats ($400). RPO Sports seats, cloth ($625). RPO AU3 Power door locks ($170). RPO CC3 Removable transparent roof panel ($595). RPO D84 Two-tone paint ($428). RPO FG3 Delco-Bilstein shock absorbers ($189). RPO G92 Performance axle ratio ($22). RPO K34 Cruise control ($185). RPO MM4 Four-speed manual transmission (no-cost option). RPO UL5 Radio delete ($256 credit). RPO UN8 AM-FM stereo with Citizens Band ($215). RPO UU8 Delco-Bose stereo system ($895). RPO V08 Heavy-duty cooling ($225). RPO Z51 Performance handling package ($470). RPO Z6A Rear window and side mirror defoggers ($160).

HISTORICAL FOOTNOTES

Chevrolet claimed a 17 percent reduction in 0-60 mph times with the TPI power plant. To save weight, Corvettes used not only the fiberglass leaf springs front and rear, but over 400 pounds of aluminum parts (including steering, suspension components and frame members). A total of 14,802 Corvettes had the Z51 performance handling package installed, 9,333 had Delco-Bilstein shocks were ordered separately and only 9,576 had a four-speed manual transmission. Only 16 Corvettes are listed as having a CB radio, and only 82 were sold with an economy rear axle ratio.

1985 CORVETTE

Model Number	Body/Style Number	Body Type & Seating	Factory Price	Shipping Weight	Production Total
1Y	Y07	2-dr Hatch Cpe-2P	$24,873	3,088 lbs.	39,729

The 1986 Corvette coupe in Dark Red Metallic

CORVETTE SERIES (V-8) SERIES Y

One new body style and an engineering development were the highlights of 1986. The Corvette line added a convertible during the model year, the first since 1975. A computerized anti-lock braking system (ABS) was made standard. It was based on a Bosch ABS II design. During hard braking, the system detected any wheel that was about to lock up, then altered braking pressure, in a pulsating action, to prevent lock up from happening. Drivers could feel the pulses in the pedal. This safety innovation helped the driver to maintain traction and keep the car under directional control without skidding, even on slick and slippery surfaces. Corvette's engine was the same 350-cid (5.7-liter) 230-hp tuned-port-injected V-8 as 1985, but with centrally-positioned copper-core spark plugs. New aluminum cylinder heads had sintered metal valve seats and increased intake port flow, plus a higher (9.5:1) compression ratio. The engine had an aluminum intake manifold with tuned runners, magnesium rocker covers and an outside-air induction system. Both four-plus-three manual and four-speed overdrive automatic transmissions were available, now with an upshift indicator light on the instrument cluster. Three monolith catalytic converters in a new dual-exhaust system kept emissions down during warm up. Cast alloy wheels gained a new raised hub emblem and a brushed-aluminum look. The instrument cluster was tilted to cut glare. The sport seat from 1985 was made standard, with leather optional. Electronic air conditioning, announced earlier, arrived as a late option. Otherwise, standard equipment was similar to 1985. A new electronic Vehicle Anti-Theft System (VATS) was also made standard. A small electrically-coded pellet was embedded in the ignition key, while a decoder was hidden in the car. When the key was placed in the ignition, its resistance code was "read." Unless that code was compatible, the starter relay wouldn't close and the Electronic Control Module wouldn't activate the fuel injectors. Corvette's back end held four round recessed lenses, with 'Corvette' block letters in the center. The license plate sat in a recessed housing. Cloth seats had lateral support and back-angle adjustments. The new convertible (a.k.a. "roadster") had a manual top with a velour inner liner. The yellow console button that ordinarily controlled Corvette's hatch release instead opened a fiberglass panel behind the seats to reveal the top storage area. Size 16 x 8-1/2 inch cast-alloy aluminum wheels held uni-directional P255/50VR-16 Goodyear Eagle GT SBR tires. Corvettes came in Silver Metallic; Medium Gray Metallic; Medium Blue Metallic; Yellow; White; Black; Gold Metallic; Silver Beige Metallic; Copper Metallic; Medium Brown Metallic; Dark Red Metallic; and Bright Red. Two-tone combinations were Silver and Gray; Gray and Black; White and Silver; Silver Beige and Medium Brown; and Silver Beige and Black. Interior trims came win Blue; Black; Bronze; Graphite; Medium Gray; Red; Saddle; and White.

I.D. NUMBERS

The Vehicle Identification Number (VIN) is visible through the windshield on the driver's side. The numbers were: [Coupes] 1G1YY0789G5100001 to 1G1YY0789G5127794; [Convertibles] 1G1YY6789G-5900001 to 1G1YY6789G5907315. The first symbol (1) indicates U.S. Built. The second symbol (G) indicates General Motors product. The third symbol (1) indicates Chevrolet Motor Division vehicle. The fourth and fifth symbols (YY) indicate car line and series: (YY = Corvette). The sixth and seventh symbols indicate the body style number (07 = two-door hatchback coupe; 67 = convertible). The eighth symbol indicates engine: 8 = 5.7-liter Tuned-Port-Injection (TPI) Chevrolet V-8. The ninth symbol is a check digit that varies. The 10th symbol indicates model year (G = 1986). The 11th symbol indicates the assembly plant: (5 = Bowling Green, Ky). The last six symbols indicate the sequential production number starting with 100001 at each factory for coupes; 900001 for convertibles. The sequential serial number is repeated on the engine block itself, stamped on a pad just ahead of the cylinder

Chevrolet

13,372 1986 Corvetttes featured leather interiors.

head on the right (passenger) side, combined with a three-letter engine code identification suffix. Cast into the top rear (right side) of the block is a date built code. The first letter of that four-symbol code shows the month the block was cast. The next number (or numbers) reveals the day of the month, while the final digit indicates the year. Engine code suffixes for 1986 were: DKF = 350-cid V-8 with 9.5:1 compression ratio and 230 hp, cast iron cylinder heads, engine oil cooler, and THM automatic transmission. DKC = 350-cid V-8 with 9.5:1 compression ratio and 230 hp, cast iron cylinder heads, and manual transmission. DKH = 350-cid export V-8 with 9.5:1 compression ratio and 230 hp, cast iron cylinder heads, engine oil cooler, and THM automatic transmission. DKD = 350-cid export V-8 with 9.5:1 compression ratio and 230 hp, cast iron cylinder heads, manual transmission, and engine oil cooler. DKB = 350-cid export V-8 with 9.5:1 compression ratio and 230 hp, cast iron cylinder heads, and manual transmission. ZJS = 350-cid export V-8 with 9.5:1 compression ratio and 235 hp, aluminum cylinder heads, engine oil cooler, and THM automatic transmission. ZJH = 350-cid export V-8 with 9.5:1 compression ratio and 235 hp, aluminum cylinder heads, and THM automatic transmission. ZKD = 350-cid export V-8 with 9.5:1 compression ratio and 235 hp, aluminum cylinder heads, and THM automatic transmission. ZJW = 350-cid export V-8 with 9.5:1 compression ratio and 235 hp, aluminum cylinder heads, engine oil cooler, and manual transmission. ZKA = 350-cid export V-8 with 9.5:1 compression ratio and 235 hp, aluminum cylinder heads, and manual transmission.

PAINT CODES

(13) Silver Metallic; (18) Medium Gray Metallic; (20) Medium Blue Metallic; (35) Yellow; (40) White; (41) Black; (53) Gold Metallic; (59) Silver Beige Metallic; (66) Copper Metallic; (69) Medium Brown Metallic; (74) Dark Red Metallic; (81) Bright Red; (13/18) Silver and Gray; (18/41) Gray and Black; (40/13) White and Silver; (59/69) Silver Beige and Medium Brown; (spec) Silver Beige and Black (Used on 50 "Commemorative Edition" Corvette made for Malcolm Konner Chevrolet of New Jersey).

CLOTH UPHOLSTERY CODES: (12C) Green; (15C) Medium Gray; (21C) Blue; (62C) Saddle; (65C) Bronze.

LEATHER UPHOLSTERY CODES: (122) Graphite; (152) Medium Gray; (212) Blue; (622) Saddle; (652) Bronze; (732) Red.

ENGINE

BASE ENGINE: [RPO L98] V-8. 90-degree overhead valve. Cast iron block and head. Displacement: 350 cid (5.7 liters). Bore and stroke: 4.00 x 3.48 inches. Compression ratio: 9.5:1. Brake hp: 230 at 4000 rpm. Torque: 330 lbs.-ft. at 3200 rpm. Five main bearings. Hydraulic valve lifters. Induction: Tuned-Port-Injection system.

TRANSMISSION

AUTOMATIC TRANSMISSION: A Turbo Hydra-Matic automatic transmission with floor-mounted gear shifter was standard equipment.

MANUAL TRANSMISSION: A four-speed manual transmission with overdrive was optional

CHASSIS FEATURES

Wheelbase: 96.2 inches. Overall length: 176.5 inches. Height: 46.4 inches. Width: 71 inches. Front tread: 59.6 inches. Rear tread: 60.4 inches. Wheel size: 16 x 8.5 inches. (9.5 inches. wide with optional Z51 suspension). Standard tires: P245/50VR-16 or P255/50VR-16 SBR.

TECHNICAL FEATURES

Transmission: THM 700-R4 four-speed overdrive automatic (floor shift) standard. Gear ratios: (1st) 3.06:1;

Chevrolet

The 1986 Corvette console with four-speed manual transmission

(2nd) 1.63:1; (3rd) 1.00:1; (4th) 0.70:1; (Rev) 2.29:1. Four-speed manual transmission optional: (1st) 2.88:1; (2nd) 1.91:1; (3rd) 1.33:1; (4th) 1.00:1; (overdrive) 0.67:1; (Rev) 2.78:1. Standard final drive ratio: 2.59:1 or 3.07:1 with automatic transmission, 3.07:1 with four-speed manual transmission; (3.31:1 optional). Steering: Rack and pinion (power-assisted). Front suspension: Single fiberglass composite monoleaf transverse spring with unequal-length aluminum control arms and stabilizer bar. Rear suspension: Fully independent five-link system with transverse fiberglass single-leaf springs, aluminum upper/lower trailing links and strut-rod/tie-rod assembly. Brakes: Four-wheel power disc. Body construction: Unibody with partial front frame. Fuel tank: 20 gallons.

OPTIONS

RPO AG9 Power driver seat ($225). RPO AQ9 Leather sports seats ($1,025). RPO AR9 Base leather seats ($400). RPO AU3 Power door locks ($175). RPO B4P Radiator boost fan ($75). RPO B4Z Custom feature package ($195). RPO C2L Dual removable roof panels for coupe ($895). RPO 24S Removable roof panels with blue tint for coupe ($595). RPO 64S Removable roof panels with bronze tint for coupe ($595). RPO C68 Electronic air conditioning control ($150). RPO D84 Two-tone paint ($428). RPO FG3 Delco-Bilstein shock absorbers ($189). RPO G92 Performance axle ratio 3.07:1 ($22). RPO KC4 Engine oil cooler ($110). RPO K34 Cruise control ($185). RPO MM4 Four-speed manual transmission (no-cost option). RPO NN5 California emissions requirements ($99). RPO UL5 Radio delete ($256 credit). RPO UM6 AM-FM stereo radio with cassette ($122). RPO UU8 Delco-Bose stereo system ($895). RPO V01 Heavy-duty radiator ($40). RPO Z51 Performance handling package for coupe ($470). RPO Z6A Rear window and side mirror defoggers for coupe ($165). RPO 4001ZA Malcolm Konner Chevrolet Special Edition paint option for coupe ($500).

HISTORICAL FOOTNOTES

Introduced: October 3, 1985. Model-year production: 35,109. Calendar-year production (U.S.): 28,410. Model-year sales by U.S. dealers: 35,969. Styled like the Corvette roadster that would serve as the 1986 Indianapolis 500 Pace Car, the new convertible went on sale late in the model year. The actual Indianapolis 500 Pace Car was Yellow, differing from showroom models only in its special track lights. Chevrolet considered its "Indy Pace Car" to be synonymous with "open top," so all convertibles were considered Indy Pace Car models. Special decals were packed in the car, but not installed. The Corvette was the only street-legal vehicle to pace the 500-mile race since the 1978 Corvette Indy Pace Car. Instead of a conversion by an outside company, as had become the practice for most 1980s ragtops, Corvette's roadster was built by Chevrolet right alongside the coupe. Problems with cracking of the new aluminum cylinder heads meant the first 1986 models had old cast-iron heads. The difficulties were soon remedied. It was estimated that the new anti-theft system would require half an hour's work to overcome, which would dissuade thieves who are typically in a hurry. A total of 6,242 Corvettes had removable roof panels installed and 12,821 came with the Z51 performance handling package. Only 6,835 Corvettes carried the MM4 four-speed manual transmission.

1986 CORVETTE

Model Number	Body/Style Number	Body Type & Seating	Factory Price	Shipping Weight	Production Total
1Y	Y07	2-dr Hatch Cpe-2P	27,072	3,086	27,794
1Y	Y67	2-dr Conv. Cpe-2P	32,032	N/A	7,315

Jerry Heasley

1987 Corvette convertible

CORVETTE SERIES (V-8) SERIES Y

Except for the addition of roller hydraulic lifters to the Corvette's 350-cid (5.7-liter) V-8, little changed this year. Horsepower got a boost to 240 thanks to new friction-cutting roller-type valve lifters. The 1987 Corvettes also had a higher fuel-economy rating. Joining the option list was an electronic tire-pressure monitor that signaled a dashboard light to warn of low pressure in any tire. Two four-speed transmissions were available: manual or automatic. Standard equipment included power steering; power four-wheel disc brakes (with anti-locking); air conditioning; a theft-deterrent system; tinted glass; twin remote-control mirrors; power windows; intermittent wipers; tilt/telescope steering column; and an AM/FM seek/scan radio. Both the centers and slots of the wheels (unpainted in 1986) were now finished in Argent Gray. Corvettes came in Silver Metallic; Medium Gray Metallic; Medium Blue Metallic; Yellow; White; Black; Gold Metallic; Silver Beige Metallic; Copper Metallic; Medium Brown Metallic; Dark Red Metallic; and Bright Red. Two-tone combinations were Silver and Gray; Gray and Black; White and Silver; and Silver Beige and Medium Brown. Interior trims came in Blue; Black; Bronze; Graphite; Medium Gray; Red; Saddle; and White. A removable body-colored roof panel for hatchbacks or body-colored convertible top were standard, along with cloth-upholstered seats.

I.D. NUMBERS

The Vehicle Identification Number (VIN) is visible through the windshield on the driver's side. The numbers were: [Coupes] 1G1YY[2/3]182H5100001 to 1G1YY[2/3]182H5130632 (On convertibles the sixth symbol was a 3 instead of a 2). The first symbol (1) indicates U.S. built. The second symbol (G) indicates General Motors product. The third symbol (1) indicates Chevrolet Motor Division vehicle. The fourth and fifth symbols (YY) indicate body type and series: (YY = Corvette). The sixth symbol indicates body style: (2 = Two-door hatchback GM styles 07, 08, 77, 87 and 3 = Two-door convertible GM style 67). The seventh symbol indicates the restraint code: (1 = Manual belts and 2 = Automatic belts). The eighth symbol indicates engine: 8 = 5.7-liter Tuned-Port-Injection (TPI) Chevrolet/GM of Canada V-8. The ninth symbol is a check digit that varies. The 10th symbol indicates model year (H = 1987). The 11th symbol indicates the assembly plant: (5 = Bowling Green, Ky). The last six symbols indicate the sequential production number starting with 100001 at each factory for coupes and convertibles. The sequential serial number is repeated on the engine block itself, stamped on a pad just ahead of the cylinder head on the right (passenger) side, combined with a three-letter engine code identification suffix. Cast into the top rear (right side) of the block is a date built code. The first letter of that four-symbol code shows the month the block was cast. The next

Tagtops were reintroduced in 1986 and were available again in 1987.

number (or numbers) reveals the day of the month, while the final digit indicates year. Engine code suffixes for 1987 were: ZJN = 350-cid 240-hp V-8 with 9.0:1 compression ratio and THM automatic transmission. ZLC = 350-cid 240-hp V-8 with 9.0:1 compression ratio, engine oil cooler, and manual transmission. ZLB = 350-cid export V-8. ZLA = 350-cid 240-hp V-8 with 9.0:1 compression ratio, engine oil cooler, and THM automatic transmission. For 1987 Callaway Twin-Turbo Corvettes a different engine-coding system was used. Callaway engines were stamped with the first two symbols indicating model year, followed by three symbols indicating order in the Callaway production sequence, followed by four symbols matching the last four digits of the Chevrolet VIN.

PAINT CODES

(13) Silver Metallic; (18) Medium Gray Metallic; (20) Medium Blue Metallic; (35) Yellow; (40) White; (41) Black; (53) Gold Metallic; (59) Silver Beige Metallic; (66) Copper Metallic; (69) Medium Brown Metallic; (74) Dark Red Metallic; (81) Bright Red; (13/18) Silver and Gray; (18/41) Gray and Black; (40/13) White and Silver; (59/69) Silver Beige and Medium Brown.

CLOTH UPHOLSTERY CODES: (12C) Green; (15C) Medium Gray; (21C) Blue; (62C) Saddle; (65C) Bronze.

LEATHER UPHOLSTERY CODES: (122) Graphite; (152) Medium Gray; (212) Blue; (622) Saddle; (652) Bronze; (732) Red.

ENGINE

BASE ENGINE: [RPO L98] V-8. 90-degree overhead valve. Cast iron block and head. Displacement: 350 cid (5.7 liters). Bore and stroke: 4.00 x 3.48 inches. Compression ratio: 9.5:1. Brake hp: 240 at 4000 rpm. Torque: 345 lbs.-ft. at 3200 rpm. Five main bearings. Aluminum cylinder head. Hydraulic valve lifters. Induction: Tuned-Port-Injection system.

TRANSMISSION

AUTOMATIC TRANSMISSION: A Turbo Hydra-Matic automatic transmission with floor-mounted gear shifter was standard equipment.

MANUAL TRANSMISSION: A four-speed manual transmission was optional.

CHASSIS FEATURE

Wheelbase: 96.2 inches. Overall length: 176.5 inches. Height: (hatchback) 46.7 inches.; (convertible) 46.4 inches. Width: 71 inches. Front Tread: 59.6 inches. Rear Tread: 60.4 inches. Standard Tires: P245/60VR-15 Goodyear Eagle GT.

TECHNICAL FEATURES

Transmission: automatic or optional four-speed manual. Standard final drive ratio: 3.07:1 with manual transmission, 2.59:1 or 3.07:1 with automatic transmission. Steering: rack and pinion (power assisted). Front suspension: unequal-length control arms, single-leaf transverse spring and stabilizer bar. Rear suspension: upper/lower control arms with five links, single-leaf transverse springs, stabilizer bar. Brakes: Anti-lock; power four-wheel disc. Body construction: fiberglass; separate ladder frame with cross-members. Fuel tank: 20 gallons.

OPTIONS

RPO AC1 Power passenger seat ($240). RPO AC3 Power driver seat ($240). RPO AQ9 Leather sports seats ($1,025). RPO AR9 Base leather seats ($400). RPO AU3 Power door locks ($190). RPO B2K Callaway Twin Turbo installed by Callaway Engineering ($19,995). RPO B4P Radiator boost fan ($75). RPO C2L Dual removable roof panels for coupe ($915). RPO 24S Removable roof panels with blue tint for coupe ($615). RPO 64S Removable roof panels with bronze tint for coupe ($615). RPO C68 Electronic air conditioning control ($150). RPO DL8 Twin remote heated mirrors for convertible ($35). RPO D74 Illuminated driver vanity mirror ($58). RPO D84 Two-tone paint on hatchback ($428). RPO FG3 Delco-Bilstein shock absorbers ($189). RPO G92 Performance axle ratio 3.07:1 ($22). RPO KC4 Engine oil cooler ($110). RPO K34 Cruise control ($185). RPO MM4 Four-speed manual transmission (no-cost option). RPO NN5 California emissions requirements ($99). RPO UL5 Radio delete ($256 credit). RPO UM6 AM-FM stereo radio with cassette ($132). RPO UU8 Delco-Bose stereo system ($905). RPO V01 Heavy-duty radiator ($40). RPO Z51 Performance handling package for hatchback ($795).

Thanks in part to a 240-hp V-8, Car & Driver *magazine picked the 1987 Corvette as one of the world's top 10 cars.*

RPO Z52 Sport handling package ($470). RPO Z6A Rear window and side mirror defoggers for coupe ($165).

HISTORICAL FOOTNOTES

Introduced: October 9, 1986. Model-Year Production: 30,632. Calendar-year production (U.S.): 28,514. Model-year sales by U.S. dealers: 25,266. A $19,995 Callaway Twin-Turbo engine package could be ordered through specific Chevrolet dealers as RPO B2K. Cars that received this package were sent from Bowling Green, Kentucky, to the Callaway factory in Old Lyme, Connecticut, to receive engine modifications and other upgrades. A total of 184 Callaway Twin-Turbos were built (21 coupes and 63 convertibles). The 1987 Callaways had 345 hp and 465 lbs.-ft. of torque. All had manual transmissions and were not certified for sale in the state of California.

1987 CORVETTE

Model Number	Body/Style Number	Body Type & Seating	Factory Price	Shipping Weight	Production Total
1Y	Y07	2-dr Hatch Cpe-2P	$27,999	3,216 lbs.	20,007
1Y	Y67	2-dr Conv. Cpe-2P	$33,172	3,279 lbs.	10,625

Cheverolet

1988 Corvette coupe

CORVETTE SERIES (V-8) SERIES Y

By 1988, Chevrolet produced approximately 900,000 Corvettes in the 35 years since America's sports car bowed in 1953. Little changed in Corvette's appearance this year, except for restyled six-slot wheels. Optional 17-inch wheels looked similar to the standard 16-inch wheels, but held massive P275/40ZR-17 Goodyear Eagle GT tires. Suspension modifications were intended to improve control during hard braking, while brake components were toughened, including the use of thicker rotors. Under the hood, the standard 350-cid (5.7-liter) V-8 could breathe more easily with a pair of modified aluminum cylinder heads. Performance also got a boost via a new camshaft, though horsepower only rose by five. Both a convertible and a hatchback coupe were offered. Corvettes came in Silver Metallic; Medium Blue Metallic; Dark Blue Metallic; Yellow; White; Black; Dark Red Metallic; Bright Red; Gray Metallic and Charcoal Metallic. The only standard two-tone combination was White and Black. Interior trims came in Blue; Black; Gray; Red; Saddle; and White. A removable body-color roof panel for hatchbacks or body-color convertible top was standard, along with cloth-upholstered seats.

I.D. NUMBERS

The Vehicle Identification Number (VIN) is visible through the windshield on the driver's side. The numbers were: [Coupes] 1G1YY[2/3]182J5100001 to 1G1YY[2/3]182J5122789 (On convertibles the sixth symbol was a 3 instead of a 2). The first symbol (1) indicates U.S. built. The second symbol (G) indicates General Motors product. The third symbol (1) indicates Chevrolet Motor Division vehicle. The fourth and fifth symbols (YY) indicate body type and series: (YY = Corvette). The sixth symbol indicates body style: (02 = Two-door hatchback GM styles 07, 08, 77, 87and 03 = Two-door convertible GM style 67). The seventh symbol indicates the restraint code: (1 = Manual belts and 2 = Automatic belts). The eighth symbol indicates engine: (8 = 5.7-liter Tuned-Port-Injection (TPI) Chevrolet/GM of Canada V-8). The ninth symbol is a check digit that varies. The 10th symbol indicates model year (J = 1988). The 11th symbol indicates the assembly plant: (5 = Bowling Green, Ky). The last six symbols indicate the sequential production number starting with 100001 at each factory for coupes and convertibles. The sequential serial number is repeated on the engine block itself, stamped on a pad just ahead of the cylinder head on the right (passenger) side, combined with a three-letter engine code identification suffix. Cast into the top rear (right side) of the block is a date built code. The first letter of that four-symbol code shows the month the block was cast. The next number (or numbers) reveals the day of the month, while the final digit indicates the year. Engine code suffixes for 1988 were: ZMA = 350-cid 240/245-hp V-8 with 9.5:1 compression ratio and THM automatic transmission. ZMD = 350-cid 240/245-hp V-8 with 9.5:1 compression ratio, engine oil cooler, and THM automatic transmission. ZMC = 350-cid 240/245-hp V-8 with 9.5:1 compression ratio, engine oil cooler, and manual transmission. For 1988 Callaway Twin-Turbo Corvettes a different engine-coding system was used. Callaway engines were stamped with the first two symbols indicating model

1988 Corvette coupe

year, followed by three symbols indicating order in the Callaway production sequence, followed by four symbols matching the last four digits of the Chevrolet VIN.

PAINT CODES

(13) Silver Metallic; (20) Medium Blue Metallic; (28) Dark Blue Metallic; (35) Yellow; (40) White; (41) Black; (74) Dark Red Metallic; (81) Bright Red; (90) Gray Metallic; (96) Charcoal Metallic; (40/41) Black and White.

CLOTH UPHOLSTERY CODES: (19C) Black; (60C) Saddle.

LEATHER UPHOLSTERY CODES: (113) White; (192) Black; (212) Blue; (602) Saddle; (732) Red; (902) Gray.

1988 ENGINE

BASE ENGINE: [RPO L98] V-8. 90-degree overhead valve. Cast iron block and head. Displacement: 350 cid (5.7 liters). Bore and stroke: 4.00 x 3.48 inches. Compression ratio: 9.5:1. Brake hp: 240/245 (*) at 4000 rpm. Torque: 345 lbs.-ft. at 3200 rpm. Five main bearings. Aluminum cylinder head. Hydraulic valve lifters. Induction: Tuned-Port-Injection system.

(*) Engine rating is 245-hp for hatchbacks using 3.07:1 rear axle due to use of low-restriction mufflers with this option combination only.

TRANSMISSION

AUTOMATIC TRANSMISSION: A Turbo Hydra-Matic automatic transmission with floor-mounted gear shifter was standard equipment.

MANUAL TRANSMISSION: A four-speed manual transmission with overdrive was optional.

CHASSIS FEATURES

Wheelbase: 96.2 inches. Overall length: 176.5 inches. Height: (Hatchback) 46.7 inches; (Convertible) 46.4 inches. Width: 71.0 inches. Front tread: 59.6 inches. Rear tread: 60.4 inches. Standard tires: P255/50ZR-I6 Goodyear Eagle GT (Z-rated).

TECHNICAL FEATURES

Transmission: Automatic or optional four-speed manual. Steering: Rack and pinion (power assisted). Front suspension: Unequal-length control arms, single-leaf transverse springs and stabilizer bar. Rear suspension: Upper/lower control arms with five links, single-leaf transverse springs, stabilizer bar. Brakes: Anti-lock; power four-wheel disc. Body construction: Fiberglass; separate ladder frame with cross-members. Fuel tank: 20 gallons.

OPTIONS

RPO AC1 Power passenger seat ($240). RPO AC3 Power driver seat ($240). RPO AQ9 Leather sports seats ($1,025). RPO AR9 Base leather seats ($400). RPO B2K Callaway Twin Turbo installed by Callaway Engineering ($25,895). RPO B4P Radiator boost fan ($75). RPO C2L Dual removable roof panels for coupe ($915). RPO 24S Removable roof panels with blue tint for coupe ($615). RPO 64S Removable roof panels with bronze tint for coupe ($615). RPO C68 Electronic air conditioning control ($150). RPO DL8 Twin remote heated mirrors for convertible ($35). RPO D74 Illuminated driver vanity mirror ($58). RPO FG3 Delco-Bilstein shock absorbers ($189). RPO G92 Performance axle ratio 3.07:1 ($22). RPO KC4 Engine oil cooler ($110). RPO MM4 Four-speed manual transmission (no-cost option). RPO NN5 California emissions requirements ($99). RPO UL5 Radio delete ($297 credit). RPO UU8 Delco-Bose stereo system

The 1988 Corvette convertible listed at $34,820.

The1988 Corvette convertible with the ragtop up

($773). RPO V01 Heavy-duty radiator ($40). RPO Z01 35th Anniversary Special Edition package for hatchback ($4,795). RPO Z51 Performance handling package for hatchback ($1,295). RPO Z52 Sport handling package ($970). RPO Z6A Rear window and side mirror defoggers for coupe ($165).

HISTORICAL FOOTNOTES

Introduced: October 1, 1987. Model-year production: 22,789. Calendar-year production: 22,878. Model-year sales by U.S. dealers: 25,425. A $25,895 Callaway Twin-Turbo engine package could be ordered through specific Chevrolet dealers as RPO B2K. Cars that received this package were sent from Bowling Green, Kentucky, to the Callaway factory in Old Lyme, Connecticut, to receive engine modifications and other upgrades. The 1988 Callaways had 382 hp and 562 lbs.-ft. of torque. Callaway modified a Chevrolet truck-type Turbo Hydra-Matic transmission as a $6,500 option for Callaways. Chevrolet also built 56 Corvette race cars for use in the Sports Car Club of America's (SCCA) Corvette Challenge racing series. These "street-legal" track cars all had stock engines specially built at the Flint, Michigan, engine plant. They were matched for power and sealed to insure that all of the cars were as identical as possible in a technical sense. Protofab, an aftermarket race-car builder in Wixom, Michigan, installed race-car modifications and roll bars.

1988 CORVETTE

Model Number	Body/Style Number	Body Type & Seating	Factory Price	Shipping Weight	Production Total
1Y	Y07	2-dr Hatch Cpe-2P	$39,480	3,229 lbs.	15,382
1Y	Y67	2-dr Conv. Cpe-2P	$34,820	3,299 lbs.	7,407

NOTE: The above production figures include a total of 2,050 special 35th Anniversary Edition Corvette hatchback coupes, each with a specific build sequence number and special badges. This option listed for $4,795. The 35th Anniversary Edition Corvettes featured a custom two-tone paint scheme consisting of a White body color, painted White wheels and Black roof bow with transparent black roof panels. The white scheme was carried out through the interior trim, which included 35th Anniversary badges embroidered on the seat backs.

Jerry Heasley

This 1989 Corvette ZR-1 was one of only 84 released.

CORVETTE SERIES (V-8) SERIES Y

Most of the Corvette publicity this year centered on the eagerly-awaited ZR-1 which was claimed to be the world's fastest production automobile. After several announcements proved premature, the ZR-1's introduction was delayed until the 1990 model year. Meanwhile, the "ordinary" Corvette added a new ZF six-speed manual gearbox with two overdrive ratios. To meet fuel-economy standards, the ingenious transmission was designed with a computer that sent a signal to prevent shifts from first to second gear unless the gas pedal hit the floor. Instead, a blocking pin forced the shifter directly into fourth gear for improved fuel economy during light-throttle operation. Joining the option list was a new FX3 Delco-Bilstein Selective Ride Control system with a switch to select the desired degree of shock absorber damping for touring, sport, or competition driving. Only hatchbacks with a manual transmission and the Z51 Performance Handling package could get the ride-control option. For the first time since 1975, a removable fiberglass hardtop became available for the convertible, but not until late in the model year. Corvettes came in White; Medium Blue Metallic; Dark Blue Metallic; Black; Dark Red Metallic; Bright Red; Gray Metallic; and Charcoal Metallic. Chevrolet also painted 33 cars in two non-standard colors. Six were done in Yellow and 27 were done in Arctic Pearl. Interior trims came in Blue; Black; Gray; Red; Saddle; and White. A removable body-color roof panel for hatchbacks or body-color convertible top were standard, along with cloth upholstery.

I.D. NUMBERS

The Vehicle Identification Number (VIN) is visible through the windshield on the driver's side. The numbers were: [Coupes] 1G1YY[2/3]186K5100001 to 1G1YY[2/3]186K5126328. (On coupes the sixth symbol was a 2; on convertible a 3). The first symbol (1) indicates U.S. Built. The second symbol (G) indicates General Motors product. The third symbol (1) indicates Chevrolet Motor Division vehicle. The fourth and fifth symbols (YY) indicate body type and series: (YY = Corvette). (Note: Code YZ was planned for use on ZR-1s and appears on GM passenger-car VIN system cards.) The sixth symbol indicates body style: (2 = Two-door hatchback or liftback GM styles 07, 08, 77, 87 and 3 = Two-door convertible GM style 67). The

Engine difficulties ultimately held back the ZR-1 in 1989.

seventh symbol indicates the restraint code: (1 = Manual belts, 3 = Manual belts with driver-inflatable restraint system and 4 = Automatic belts). The eighth symbol indicates engine: (8 = 5.7-liter Tuned-Port-Injection (TPI) Chevrolet/GM of Canada V-8). The ninth symbol is a check digit that varies. The 10th symbol indicates model year (K = 1989). The 11th symbol indicates the assembly plant: (5 = Bowling Green, Ky). The last six symbols indicate the sequential production number starting with 100001 at each factory for coupes and convertibles. The sequential serial number is repeated on the engine block itself, stamped on a pad just ahead of the cylinder head on the right (passenger) side, combined with a three-letter engine code identification suffix. Cast into the top rear (right side) of the block is a date built code. The first letter of that four-symbol code shows the month the block was cast. The next number (or numbers) reveals the day of the month, while the final digit indicates the year. Engine code suffixes for 1989 were: ZRA = 350-cid 240/245-hp V-8 with 9.5:1 compression ratio, engine oil cooler, and manual transmission. ZRC = 350-cid 240/245-hp V-8 with 9.5:1 compression ratio, engine oil cooler, and THM automatic transmission. ZRB = 350-cid 240/245-hp V-8 with 9.5:1 compression ratio and THM automatic transmission. For 1989 Callaway Twin-Turbo Corvettes a different engine-coding system was used. Callaway engines were stamped with the first two symbols indicating model year, followed by three symbols indicating order in the Callaway production sequence, followed by four symbols matching the last four digits of the Chevrolet VIN.

PAINT CODES

(10) White; (20) Medium Blue Metallic; (28) Dark Blue Metallic; (41) Black; (68) Dark Red Metallic; (81) Bright Red; (90) Gray Metallic; (96) Charcoal Metallic. Chevrolet also painted 33 cars in two non-standard colors. Six were done in (35) Yellow and 27 were done in (31) Arctic Pearl.

CLOTH UPHOLSTERY CODES: (19C) Black; (60C) Saddle.

LEATHER UPHOLSTERY CODES: (192) Black; (212) Blue; (602) Saddle; (732) Red; (902) Gray.

ENGINE

BASE ENGINE: [RPO L98] V-8. 90-degree overhead valve. Cast iron block and head. Displacement: 350 cid (5.7 liters). Bore and stroke: 4.00 x 3.48 inches. Compression ratio: 9.5:1. Brake hp: 240/245 (*) at 4300 rpm. Torque: 340 lbs.-ft. at 3200 rpm. Five main bearings. Aluminum cylinder head. Hydraulic valve lifters. Induction: Tuned-Port-Injection system.

(*) Engine rating is 245-hp for hatchbacks using 3.07:1 rear axle due to use of low-restriction mufflers with this option combination only.

TRANSMISSION

AUTOMATIC TRANSMISSION: A Turbo Hydra-Matic automatic transmission with floor-mounted gear shifter was standard equipment.

MANUAL TRANSMISSION: A six-speed manual transmission was optional.

CHASSIS FEATURES

Wheelbase: 96.2 inches. Overall length: 176.5 inches. Height: (Hatchback) 46.7 inches.; (Convertible) 46.4 inches. Width: 71 inches. Front tread: 59.6 inches. Rear tread: 60:4 inches. Standard tires: P275/40VR-17 Goodyear Eagle GT (Z-rated).

TECHNICAL FEATURES

Transmission: Automatic or six-speed manual. Steering: Rack and pinion (power assisted). Front suspension: Unequal-length control arms, single-leaf transverse springs and stabilizer bar. Rear suspension: Upper/lower control arms with five links, single-leaf transverse springs, stabilizer bar. Brakes: Anti-lock; power four-wheel disc. Body construction: fiberglass; separate ladder frame with cross-members. Fuel tank: 20 gallons.

OPTIONS

RPO AC1 Power passenger seat ($240). RPO AC3 Power driver seat ($240). RPO AQ9 Leather sports seats ($1,025). RPO AR9 Base leather seats ($400). RPO B2K Callaway Twin Turbo installed by Callaway Engineering ($25,895). RPO B4P Radiator boost fan ($75). RPO CC2 Auxiliary hardtop for convertible ($1,995). RPO C2L Dual removable roof panels for coupe ($915). RPO 24S Removable roof panels with blue tint for coupe ($615). RPO 64S Removable roof panels with bronze tint for coupe ($615). RPO C68 Electronic air conditioning control ($150). RPO D74 Illuminated driver vanity mirror ($58). RPO FX3 Selective electronic Ride & Handling ($1,695). RPO G92 Performance axle ratio 3.07:1 ($22). RPO KO5 Engine block heater ($20). RPO KC4 Engine oil cooler ($110). RPO MN6 Six-speed manual transmission (no-cost option). RPO NN5 California emissions requirements ($100). RPO UJ6 Low tire pressure warning indicator ($325). RPO UU8 Delco-Bose stereo system ($773). RPO V01 Heavy-duty radiator ($40). RPO V56 Luggage rack for convertible ($140). RPO Z51 Performance handling package for hatchback ($575).

HISTORICAL FOOTNOTES

Model-year production: 26,412. Calendar-year production: 25,279. Model-year sales by U.S. dealers: 23,928. The $25,895 Callaway Twin-Turbo engine package could again be ordered through specific Chevrolet dealers as RPO B2K. Cars that received this package were sent from Bowling Green, Kentucky, to the Callaway factory in Old Lyme, Connecticut, to receive engine modifications and other upgrades. The 1989 Callaways had 382 hp and 562 lbs.-ft. of torque. Chevrolet built 60 Corvette Challenge cars with standard engines. Of these, 30 were shipped to Powell Development of America to receive race-modified engines and other competition modifications for the 1989 Sports Car Club of America (SCCA) Corvette Challenge racing series. At the end of the year, these cars had their original factory-numbered engines re-installed. Chevrolet built 84 ZR-1 type 1989 Corvettes for testing, but then said on April 19 that the ZR-1's introduction would be delayed until 1990.

1989 CORVETTE Model Number	Body/Style Number	Body Type & Seating	Factory Price	Shipping Weight	Production Total
1Y	Y07	2-dr Hatch Cpe-2P	$31,545	3,229 lbs.-	16,663
1Y	Y67	2-dr Conv. Cpe-2P	$36,785	3,269 lbs.	9,749

Jery Heasley

The 1990 Corvette ZR-1 was a hit with buyers.

CORVETTE SERIES (V-8) SERIES YY/YZ

Finally, after months of hoopla and a few false starts, the super-performance ZR-1 Corvette arrived in 1990. Intended for production in limited quantity, with a price tag higher than any General Motors product, the ZR-1 became a collectible long before anyone ever saw one "in the flesh." Customers seemed eager to pay far above the suggested retail price for the few examples that became available. Under the ZR-1's hood was a Lotus-designed 32-valve, dual-overhead-cam, 350-cid (5.7-liter) V-8, built by Mercury Marine in Oklahoma. Although the displacement was identical to the standard Corvette V-8, this was an all-new power plant with different bore-and-stroke dimensions. Wider at the rear than a standard model, partly to contain huge 315/35ZR-17 rear tires, the ZR-1 was easy to spot because of its convex rear end and rectangular tail lamps. Ordinary Corvettes continued to display a concave rear end with round tail lamps. Standard ZR-1 equipment included an FX3 Selective Ride adjustable suspension, which was also available on standard Corvettes with the six-speed manual gearbox. Four-speed overdrive automatic was available (at no cost) only on the regular Corvette. New standard equipment included an engine oil cooler, 17-inch alloy wheels, and improved ABS II-S anti-lock braking. The convertible added a new backlight made of flexible "Ultrashield" for improved scratch resistance and visibility. An air bag was installed in the new steering wheel on all Corvettes and a revised dashboard mixed digital and analog instruments. Corvettes came in White; Steel Blue Metallic; Black; Turquoise Metallic; Competition Yellow; Dark Red Metallic; Quasar Blue Metallic; Bright Red; Polo Green Metallic; and Charcoal Metallic. Interiors came in Blue; Black; Gray; Red; Saddle; and White. Standard features included a removable body-color roof panel for hatchbacks or a convertible top (Black, Saddle, or White top colors were available, but the choices you could order were determined by paint color). Cloth upholstery was also standard.

I.D. NUMBERS

The Vehicle Identification Number (VIN) is visible through the windshield on the driver's side. The numbers were: [Base] 1G1YY[2/3]380L5100001 to 1G1YY[2/3]380L5120597; [ZR1] 1G1YZ2]3J6L5800001 to 1G1YZ23J6L5803049. The first symbol (1) indicates U.S. built. The second symbol (G) indicates General Motors product. The third symbol (1) indicates Chevrolet Motor Division vehicle. The fourth and fifth symbols were (YY) for the Base Corvette or (YZ) for the Corvette ZR-1. The sixth symbol indicates body style: (2 = two-door hatchback or liftback GM styles 07, 08, 77, 87 and 3 = two-door convertible GM style 67). The seventh symbol indicates the restraint code: (1 = Manual belts, 3 = Manual belts with driver-inflatable restraint system and 4 = Automatic belts).

A total of 3,049 ZR-1 Corvettes were built for 1990.

The eighth symbol indicates engine: 8 = RPO L98 5.7-liter Tuned-Port-Injection (TPI) Chevrolet/GM of Canada V-8; J = RPO LT5 5.7-liter TPI V-8. The ninth symbol is a check digit that varies. The 10th symbol indicates model year (L = 1990). The 11th symbol indicates the assembly plant: (5 = Bowling Green, Ky). The last six symbols indicate the sequential production number starting with 100001 at each factory for base coupes and convertibles and 800001 for ZR-1s. The sequential serial number is repeated on the engine block itself, stamped on a pad just ahead of the cylinder head on the right (passenger) side, combined with a three-letter engine code identification suffix. Cast into the top rear (right side) of the block is a date built code. The first letter of that four-symbol code shows the month the block was cast. The next number (or numbers) reveals the day of the month, while the final digit indicates year. Engine code suffixes for 1990 were: ZSA = 350-cid 245/250-hp RPO L98 V-8 with 9.5:1 compression ratio and THM automatic transmission. ZSB = 350-cid 245/250-hp RPO L98 V-8 with 9.5:1 compression ratio, engine oil cooler, and manual transmission. ZSC = 350-cid 245/250-hp RPO L98 V-8 with 9.5:1 compression ratio, engine oil cooler, and THM automatic transmission. ZSD = 350-cid 375-hp RPO LT5 V-8 (ZR-1 model only) with air conditioning. ZSH = 350-cid 375-hp RPO LT5 V-8 (ZR-1 model only) with electronic air conditioning. For 1990 Callaway Twin-Turbo Corvettes a different engine-coding system was used. Callaway engines were stamped with the first two symbols indicating model year, followed by three symbols indicating order in the Callaway production sequence, followed by four symbols matching the last four digits of the Chevrolet VIN.

PAINT CODES

(10) White; (25) Steel Blue Metallic; (41) Black; (42) Turquoise Metallic; (53) Competition Yellow; (68) Dark Red Metallic; (80) Quasar Blue Metallic; (81) Bright Red; (91) Polo Green Metallic; (96) Charcoal Metallic.

CLOTH UPHOLSTERY CODES: (19C) Black; (60C) Saddle.

LEATHER UPHOLSTERY CODES: (193) Black; (223) Blue; (603) Saddle; (733) Red; (903) Gray.

ENGINES

BASE ENGINE: [RPO L98] V-8. 90-degree overhead valve. Cast iron block and head. Displacement: 350 cid (5.7 liters). Bore and stroke: 4.00 x 3.48 inches. Compression ratio: 9.5:1. Brake hp: 240/245 (*) at 4300 rpm. Torque: 340 lbs.-ft. at 3200 rpm. Five main bearings. Aluminum cylinder head. Hydraulic valve lifters. Induction: Tuned-Port-Injection system.

(*) Engine rating is 245-hp for hatchbacks using 3.07:1 rear axle due to use of low-restriction mufflers with this option combination only.

ZR-1 ENGINE: [RPO LT5] V-8. 90-degree overhead valve with four valves per cylinder. Four overhead

1990 Corvette ZR-1 in Bright Red

camshafts. Cast iron block and head. Displacement: 350 cid (5.7 liters). Bore and stroke: 4.00 x 3.48 inches. Compression ratio: 11.0:1. Brake hp: 375 at 5800 rpm. Torque: 370 lbs.-ft. at 5600 rpm. Five main bearings. Aluminum cylinder head. Hydraulic valve lifters. Induction: Tuned-Port-Injection system. LT5 engines were manufactured and assembled by Mercury Marine Corporation in Stillwater, Oklahoma, and shipped to the Corvette factory for installation in ZR-1 Corvettes.

TRANSMISSION

AUTOMATIC TRANSMISSION: An automatic transmission with floor-mounted gear shifter was standard equipment.

MANUAL TRANSMISSION: A six-speed manual transmission was optional.

CHASSIS FEATURES

Wheelbase: 96.2 inches. Overall length: (Base) 176.5 inches.; (ZR-1) 177.4 inches. Height: (Hatchback) 46.7 inches.; (Convertible) 46.4 inches. Width: (Base) 71 inches.; (ZR-1) 74 inches. Front tread: (All) 59.6 inches. Rear tread: (Base) 60:4 inches.; (ZR-1) 61.9 inches. Standard tires: P275/40ZR-17 Goodyear Eagle GT (ZR-1 uses P315/35ZR-17 at rear).

TECHNICAL FEATURES

Transmission: Automatic or six-speed manual. Steering: Rack and pinion (power assisted). Front suspension: Unequal-length control arms, single-leaf transverse springs and stabilizer bar. Rear suspension: Upper/lower control arms with five links, single-leaf transverse springs, stabilizer bar. Brakes: Anti-lock; power four-wheel disc. Body construction: Fiberglass; separate ladder frame with cross-members. Fuel tank: 20 gallons.

OPTIONS

RPO AC1 Power passenger seat ($270). RPO AC3 Power driver seat ($270). RPO AQ9 Leather sports seats ($1,050). RPO AR9 Base leather seats ($425). RPO B2K Callaway Twin Turbo installed by Callaway Engineering ($26,895). RPO CC2 Auxiliary hardtop for convertible ($1,995). RPO C2L Dual removable roof panels for coupe ($915). RPO 24S Removable roof panels with blue tint for coupe ($615). RPO 64S Removable roof panels with bronze tint for coupe ($615). RPO C68 Electronic air conditioning control ($180). RPO FX3 Electronic Selective Ride & Handling system ($1,695). RPO G92 Performance axle ratio 3.07:1 ($22). RPO KO5 Engine block heater ($20). RPO KC4 Engine oil cooler ($110). RPO MN6 Six-speed manual transmission (no-cost option). RPO NN5 California emissions requirements ($100). RPO UJ6 Low tire pressure warning indicator ($325). RPO UU8 Delco-Bose stereo system ($823). RPO U1F Delco-Bose stereo system with compact disc changer ($1,219). RPO V56 Luggage rack for convertible ($140). RPO Z51 Performance handling package for hatchback ($460). RPO ZR-1 Special performance package for coupe ($27,016).

HISTORICAL FOOTNOTES

Model-year production: 23,646. Calendar-year production: 22,154. Model-year sales by U.S. dealers:

The LT5 engine in the 1990 Corvette was assembled by Mercury Marine in Stillwater, Oklahoma.

22,690. The $26,895 Callaway Twin-Turbo engine package could again be ordered through specific Chevrolet dealers as RPO B2K. Cars that received this package were sent from Bowling Green, Kentucky, to the Callaway factory in Old Lyme, Connecticut, to receive engine modifications and other upgrades. For a limited time an RPO R9G option was offered through Chevrolet dealers for competition-minded Corvette buyers who wanted to participate in the new World Challenge racing series. Only 23 such cars were built. In 1990, Corvette chief engineer Dave McLellan was the annual recipient of the Society of Automotive Engineers' Edward N. Cole Award for automotive engineering innovation. McLellan was specifically recognized for his work on the ZR-1 package.

1990 CORVETTE Model Number	Body/Style Number	Body Type & Seating	Factory Price	Shipping Weight	Production Total
1YY	Y07	2-dr Hatch Cpe-2P	$31,979	3,223 lbs.	16,016
1YY	Y67	2-dr Conv. Cpe-2P	$37,264	3,263 lbs.	7,630
1990 CORVETTE ZR-1					
1YZ	Z07	2-dr Hatch Cpe-2P	$58,995	3,465 lbs.	3,049*

(*) ZR-1 option quantity included in hatchback coupe production of 16,016 and total model-year production of 23,646 Corvettes.

1990 Corvette ZR-1 with the LT5 375-hp V-8.

Nicky Wirght

Famed designer Larry Shinoda produced a special 1990 Corvette that featured superior aerodynamics.

Jerry Heasley

The body kit was easy to spot from all sides on the 1990 Corvettes designed by Larry Shinoda.

Jerry Heasley

The 1991 Corvette ZR-1 featured four horizontal fender louvers.

1991

CORVETTE SERIES V-8) SERIES YY/YZ

Not a year of great change after the launch of the ZR-1 the previous year. Standard Corvettes were restyled at the rear to more closely resemble the ZR-1 with a convex rear fascia and two rectangular tail lamps on either side of the car. A new front end with wrap-around parking lamps was used on both models, along with new side-panel louvers and wider body-color body side moldings. Although more alike the standard Corvette in a visual sense, the ZR-1 again had different doors and a wider rear to accommodate its 11-inch wide rear wheels. Also the high-mounted stop lamp went on the roof of the ZR-1, instead of on the rear fascia, as on the YY Corvette. All models were again equipped with ABS II-S anti-lock braking and driver's side airbag as well as an anti-theft system. The ZR-1 was again powered by the 32-valve DOHC 5.7-liter V-8 matched with a six-speed transaxle. Corvette models used the 5.7-liter TPI V-8 fitted with the four-speed overdrive automatic or optional six-speed manual transmission. Corvettes came in White; Steel Blue Metallic; Yellow; Black; Turquoise Metallic; Dark Red Metallic; Quasar Blue Metallic; Bright Red; Polo Green Metallic; and Charcoal Metallic. Interiors came in Blue; Black; Gray; Red; Saddle; and White. Standard features included a removable body-color roof panel for hatchbacks or a convertible top. Black, Saddle, Red, White, and (late in the year) Blue top colors were available, but the choices were determined by body paint color. Cloth upholstery was also standard.

I.D. NUMBERS

The Vehicle Identification Number (VIN) is visible through the windshield on the driver's side. The numbers were: [Base] 1G1YY[2/3]386M5100001 to 1G1YY[2/3]386M5118595; [ZR1] 1G1YZ23J6M5800001 to 1G1YZ23J6M5802044. The first symbol (1) indicates U.S. built. The second symbol (G) indicates General Motors product. The third symbol (1) indicates Chevrolet Motor Division vehicle. The fourth and fifth symbols were (YY) for the Base Corvette or (YZ) for the Corvette ZR-1. The sixth symbol indicates body style: (2 = two-door hatchback or liftback GM styles 07, 08, 77, 87 and 3 = two-door convertible GM style 67). The seventh symbol indicates the restraint code: (1 = Active manual belts, 3 = Active manual belts with driver-inflatable restraint system and 4 = Passive automatic belts). The eighth symbol indicates engine: 8 = RPO L98 5.7-liter Tuned-Port-Injection (TPI) Chevrolet/GM of Canada V-8; J = RPO LT5 5.7-liter TPI V-8. The ninth symbol is a check digit that varies. The 10th symbol indicates model year (M = 1991). The 11th symbol indicates the assembly plant: (5 = Bowling Green, K.Y.). The last six symbols indicate the sequential production number starting with 100001 at each factory for base coupes and convertibles and 800001 for ZR-1s. The sequential serial number is repeated on the engine block itself, stamped on a pad just ahead of the cylinder head on the right (passenger) side, combined with a three-letter engine code identification suffix. Cast into the top rear (right side) of the block is a date built code. The first letter of that four-symbol code shows the month the block was cast. The next number (or numbers) reveals the day of the month, while the final digit indicates the year. Engine code suffixes for 1991 were: ZTA = 350-cid 245/250-hp RPO L98 V-8 with 10.0:1 compression ratio and automatic transmission. ZTB = 350-cid 245/250-hp RPO L98 V-8 with 10.0:1 compression ratio, engine oil cooler, and manual transmission. ZTC = 350-cid 245/250-hp RPO L98 V-8 with 10.0:1 compression ratio, engine oil cooler, and automatic transmission. ZTK = 350-cid 375-hp RPO LT5 V-8 (ZR-1 model only). For 1991 Callaway Twin-Turbo Corvettes a different engine-coding system was used. Callaway engines were stamped with the first two symbols indicating model year, followed by three symbols indicating order in the Callaway production sequence, followed by four symbols matching the last four digits of the Chevrolet VIN.

PAINT CODES

(10) White; (25) Steel Blue Metallic; (35) Yellow; (41) Black; (42) Turquoise Metallic; (75) Dark Red Metallic; (80) Quasar Blue Metallic; (81) Bright Red; (91) Polo Green Metallic; (96) Charcoal Metallic.

CLOTH UPHOLSTERY CODES: (19C) Black; (60C) Saddle.

LEATHER UPHOLSTERY CODES: (193) Black; (223) Blue; (603) Saddle; (733) Red; (903) Gray.

ENGINES

BASE ENGINE: [RPO L98] V-8. 90-degree overhead valve. Cast iron block and head. Displacement: 350 cid (5.7 liters). Bore and stroke: 4.00 x 3.48 inches. Compression ratio: 10.0:1. Brake hp: 245/250(*) at 4000 rpm. Torque: 340 lbs.-ft. at 3200 rpm. Five main bearings. Aluminum cylinder head. Hydraulic valve lifters. Induction: Tuned-Port-Injection system.

(*) Engine rating is 250-hp for hatchbacks using 3.07:1 rear axle due to use of low-restriction mufflers with this option combination only.

ZR-1 ENGINE: [RPO LT5] V-8. 90-degree overhead valve with four valves per cylinder. Four overhead camshafts. Cast iron block and head. Displacement: 350 cid (5.7 liters). Bore and stroke: 4.00 x 3.48 inches. Compression ratio: 11.0:1. Brake hp: 375 at 5800 rpm. Torque: 370 lbs.-ft. at 5600 rpm. Five main bearings. Aluminum cylinder head. Hydraulic valve lifters. Induction: Tuned-Port-Injection system.

TRANSMISSION

AUTOMATIC TRANSMISSION: An automatic transmission with floor-mounted gear shifter was standard equipment.

MANUAL TRANSMISSION: A six-speed manual transmission was optional.

CHASSIS FEATURES

Wheelbase: 96.2 inches. Overall length: (Base) 178.6 inches.; (ZR-1) 178.5 inches. Height: (Hatchback) 46.7 inches.; (Convertible) 46.4 inches. Width: (Base) 71 inches.; (ZR-1) 73.2 inches. Front tread: (All) 59.6 inches. Rear tread: (Base) 60:4 inches.; (ZR-1) 61.9 inches. Standard tires: P275/40ZR-17 Goodyear Eagle GT (ZR-1 uses P315/35ZR-17 at rear).

TECHNICAL FEATURES

Transmission: Automatic or six-speed manual. Steering: Rack and pinion (power assisted). Front suspension: Unequal-length control arms, single-leaf transverse springs and stabilizer bar. Rear suspension: Upper/lower control arms with five links, single-leaf transverse springs, and stabilizer bar. Brakes: Anti-lock; power four-wheel disc. Body construction: Fiberglass; separate ladder frame with cross-members. Fuel tank: 20 gallons.

OPTIONS

RPO AC1 Power passenger seat ($290). RPO AC3 Power driver seat ($290). RPO AQ9 Leather sports seats ($1,050). RPO AR9 Base leather seats ($425). RPO B2K Callaway Twin Turbo installed by Callaway Engineering ($33,000). RPO CC2 Auxiliary hardtop for convertible ($1,995). RPO C2L Dual removable roof panels for coupe ($915). RPO 24S Removable roof panels with blue tint for coupe ($615). RPO 64S Removable roof panels with bronze tint for coupe ($615). RPO C68 Electronic air conditioning control ($180). RPO FX3 Electronic Selective Ride & Handling system ($1,695). RPO G92 Performance axle ratio 3.07:1 ($22). RPO KC4 Engine oil cooler ($110). RPO MN6 Six-speed manual transmission (no-cost option). RPO NN5 California emissions requirements ($100). RPO UJ6 Low tire pressure warning indicator ($325). RPO UU8 Delco-Bose stereo system ($823). RPO U1F Delco-Bose stereo system with compact disc changer ($1,219). RPO V56 Luggage rack for convertible ($140). RPO ZR1 Special performance package for coupe ($31,683).

HISTORICAL FOOTNOTES

Model-year production: 20,639. Calendar-year sales: 17,472. The $33,000 Callaway Twin-Turbo engine package could again be ordered through specific Chevrolet dealers as RPO B2K. The 62 Cars that received this package were sent from Bowling Green, Kentucky to the Callaway factory in Old Lyme, Connecticut, to receive engine modifications and other upgrades. Callaway built its 500th conversion on September 26, 1991. Twin Turbos made after that were "Callway 500" editions with special features and a $600 higher price tag. Corvette buyers who wanted to participate in World Challenge Series racing had to buy a stock Corvette from Chevrolet and handle race-prep work themselves.

1991 CORVETTE

Model Number	Body/Style Number	Body Type & Seating	Factory Price	Shipping Weight	Production Total
1YY	Y07	2-dr Hatch Cpe-2P	$32,455	3,223 lbs.	14,967
1YY	Y67	2-dr Conv. Cpe-2P	$38,770	3,263 lbs.	5,672
1991 CORVETTE ZR-1					
1YZ	Z07	2-dr Hatch Cpe-2P	$64,138	3,465	20,044

(*) ZR-1 option quantity included in hatchback coupe production of 14,967 and total model-year production of 20,639 Corvettes.

1992 Corvette Callaway Speedster

1992

CORVETTE SERIES (V-8) SERIES YY/YZ

Another year of little change in the makeup of the Corvette line. The ZR-1 was basically a carry-over from the year previous with new model badges above the rear fender vents. Standard Corvette models received an upgraded 300-hp 5.7-liter V-8 as well as Acceleration Slip Regulation. The ZR-1 was again powered by the 32-valve DOHC 5.7-liter V-8 matched with a six-speed transaxle. Corvette models used the aforementioned more powerful 5.7-liter V-8 fitted with the four-speed overdrive automatic or optional six-speed manual transmission. Both models had new rectangular exhausts. A new all-black dash treatment, relocated digital speedometer and improved instrument graphics were adopted. A Traction Control system became standard equipment along with new Goodyear GS-C tires. Corvettes came in White; Yellow; Black; Bright Aqua Metallic; Polo Green II Metallic; Black Rose Metallic; Dark Red Metallic; Quasar Blue Metallic; and Bright Red. Interiors came in Blue; Beige; Black; Light Beige; Light Gray; Red; and White. Standard features included a removable body-color roof panel for hatchbacks or a convertible top. All Corvette convertible buyers had a choice of Beige, Black, and White top colors and a Blue top was available with White Corvettes only. Also standard was Black cloth upholstery.

I.D. NUMBERS

The Vehicle Identification Number (VIN) is visible through the windshield on the driver's side. The numbers were: [Base] 1G1YY[2/3]3P6N5100001 to 1G1YY[2/3]3P6N5119977; [ZR1] 1G1YZ23J6N5800001 to 1G1YZ23J6N5800501. The first symbol (1) indicates U.S. built. The second symbol (G) indicates General Motors product. The third symbol (1) indicates Chevrolet Motor Division vehicle. The fourth and fifth symbols were (YY) for the Base Corvette or (YZ) for the Corvette ZR-1. The sixth symbol indicates body style: (2 = Two-door hatchback or liftback GM styles 07, 08, 77, 87 and 3 = Two-door convertible GM style 67). The seventh symbol indicates the restraint code: (1 = Active manual belts, 2 = Active manual belts with driver and passenger inflatable restraint system, 3 = Active manual belts with driver-inflatable restraint system, 4 = Passive automatic belts and 5 = Passive automatic belts with driver inflatable restraint system). The eighth symbol indicates engine: P = RPO LT1 5.7-liter Multiport-Fuel-Injection (MFI) Chevrolet/GM of Canada V-8; J = RPO LT5 5.7-liter MFI V-8. The ninth symbol is a check digit that varies. The 10th symbol indicates model year (N = 1992). The 11th symbol indicates the assembly plant: (5 = Bowling Green, Ky). The last six symbols indicate the sequential production number starting with 100001 at each factory for base coupes and convertibles and 800001 for ZR-1s. The sequential serial number is repeated on the engine block itself, stamped on a pad just ahead of the cylinder head on the right (passenger) side, combined with a three-letter engine code identification suffix. Cast into the top rear (right side) of the block is a date built code. The first letter of that four-symbol code shows the month the block was cast. The next number (or numbers) reveals the day of the month, while the final digit indicates the year. Engine code suffixes for 1992 were: ZAC = 350-cid 300-hp RPO LT1 V-8 with 10.3:1 compression ratio and automatic transmission. ZUB = 350-cid 300-hp RPO LT1 V-8 with 10.3:1 compression ratio and manual transmission. ZAA = 350-cid 375-hp RPO LT5 V-8 (ZR-1 model only).

PAINT CODES

(10) White; (35) Yellow; (41) Black; (43) Bright Aqua Metallic; (45) Polo Green II Metallic; (73) Black Rose Metallic; (75) Dark Red Metallic; (80) Quasar Blue Metallic; (81) Bright Red.

CLOTH UPHOLSTERY CODES: (19C) Black.

LEATHER UPHOLSTERY CODES: (103) White; (143) Light Gray; (193) Black; (643) Light Beige; (733) Red.

ENGINES

BASE ENGINE: [RPO LT1] V-8. 90-degree overhead valve. Cast iron block and head. Displacement: 350 cid (5.7 liters). Bore and stroke: 4.00 x 3.48 inches. Compression ratio: 10.3:1. Brake hp: 300 at 5000 rpm. Torque: 330 lbs.-ft. at 4000 rpm. Five main bearings. Aluminum cylinder head. Hydraulic valve lifters. Induction: Multiport Fuel Injection system.

ZR-1 ENGINE: [RPO LT5] V-8. 90-degree overhead valve with four valves per cylinder. Four overhead camshafts. Cast iron block and head. Displacement: 350 cid (5.7 liters). Bore and stroke: 4.00 x 3.48 inches. Compression ratio: 11.0:1. Brake hp: 375 at 5800 rpm. Torque: 370 lbs.-ft. at 5600 rpm. Five main bearings. Aluminum cylinder head. Hydraulic valve lifters. Induction: Multiport Fuel Injection system.

TRANSMISSION

AUTOMATIC TRANSMISSION: An automatic transmission with floor-mounted gear shifter was standard equipment.

MANUAL TRANSMISSION: A six-speed manual transmission was optional.

CHASSIS FEATURES

Wheelbase: 96.2 inches. Overall length: (Base) 178.6 inches.; (ZR-1) 178.5 inches. Height: (Hatchback) 46.3 inches.; (Convertible) 47.3 inches. Width: (Base) 71.1 inches.; (ZR-1) 73.1 inches. Front tread: (All) 57.7 inches. Rear tread: (Base) 59 inches.; (ZR-1) 60.6 inches. Standard tires: P275/40ZR-17 Goodyear Eagle GT (ZR-1 uses P315/35ZR-17 at rear).

TECHNICAL FEATURES

Transmission: Automatic or six-speed manual. Steering: Rack and pinion (power assisted). Front suspension: Unequal-length control arms, single-leaf transverse springs and stabilizer bar. Rear suspension: Upper/lower control arms with five links, single-leaf transverse springs, and stabilizer bar. Brakes: Anti-lock; power four-wheel disc. Body construction: Fiberglass; separate ladder frame with cross-members. Fuel tank: 20 gallons.

OPTIONS

RPO AC1 Power passenger seat ($305). RPO AC3 Power driver seat ($305). RPO AQ9 Leather sports seats ($1,100). RPO AQ9 White leather sports seats ($1,180). RPO AR9 Base leather seats ($425). RPO AR9 Base White leather seats ($555). RPO CC2 Auxiliary hardtop for convertible ($1,995). RPO C2L Dual removable roof panels for coupe ($950). RPO 24S Removable roof panels with blue tint for coupe ($650). RPO 64S Removable roof panels with bronze tint for coupe ($650). RPO C68 Electronic air conditioning control ($205). RPO FX3 Electronic Selective Ride & Handling system ($1,695). RPO G92 Performance axle ratio 3.07:1 ($50). RPO MN6 Six-speed manual transmission (no-cost option). RPO NN5 California emissions requirements ($100). RPO UJ6 Low tire pressure warning indicator ($325). RPO UU8 Delco-Bose stereo system ($823). RPO U1F Delco-Bose stereo system with compact disc changer ($1,219). RPO V56 Luggage rack for convertible ($140). RPO Z07 Adjustable suspension package for hatchback coupe ($2,045). RPO ZR-1 Special performance package for hatchback coupe ($31,683).

HISTORICAL FOOTNOTES

Model-year production: 20,479. Calendar-year sales: 19,819. The 1,000,000th Corvette was produced on July 2, 1992. It was a 1992 Corvette convertible and was posed for a factory publicity photograph alongside a first-year 1953 Corvette. With the introduction of the base LT1 V-8, the introduction of an Acceleration Slip Regulation (ASR) traction-control system as standard equipment and the standard use of Goodyear Eagle GS-C high-performance tires with directional and asymmetrical tread design, Chevrolet Motor Division could advertise that "The all-around performance of the Corvette has been raised to the highest point in the car's 39-year history." Eight major factors contributed to the increased power of the LT1 engine: 1) A reverse-flow cooling system; 2) Computer-controlled ignition timing; 3) A low-restriction exhaust system incorporating a two-piece converter and exhaust-runner assembly for easier service access; 4) The use of high-compression-ratio pistons; 5) The use of a new camshaft profile; 6) The use of new free-flowing cylinder heads; 7) The use of four-bolt main bearing caps on the three center bearings and 8) The use of new synthetic 5W-30 engine oil (also eliminating the need for a separate engine-oil cooler). An LT1-powered Corvette with automatic transmission was tested for 0-to-60 mph in 5.26

seconds and did the quarter mile in 13.9 seconds at 102.2 mph. An LT1-powered Corvette with the six-speed manual transmission was tested for 0-to-60 mph in 4.92 seconds and did the quarter mile in 13.7 seconds at 103.5 mph. A 1992 Corvette ZR-1 with standard manual transmission was tested for 0-to-60 mph in 4.3 seconds and did the quarter mile in 12.9 seconds. This proved that the LT1 engine had dramatically narrowed the performance gap between the base Corvette and the much more expensive ZR-1 Corvette.

On August 28, 1992, Chevrolet Motor Division announced that David McLellan would be retiring as Corvette chief engineer. McLellan had taken over the Corvette program after the retirement of Zora Arkus-Duntov in 1975. Chevy's assistant manager of public relations Tom Hoxie said in 1992, "During McLellan's 18-year tenure he transformed the Corvette from an American muscle car into an internationally-acclaimed, high-performance sports car that runs rings around a host of more expensive European and Japanese models." Said McLellan, "I can't think of a better time for me to be leaving. No manufacturer has ever built one million sports cars and at the age of 40 the Corvette is stronger than it's ever been. Our all-new car is a few years old and it's time to let someone else put their stamp on it."

1992 CORVETTE

Model Number	Body/Style Number	Body Type & Seating	Factory Price	Shipping Weight	Production Total
1YY	Y07	2-dr Hatch Cpe-2P	$33,635	3,223 lbs.	14,604
1YY	Y67	2-dr Conv. Cpe-2P	$40,145	3,269 lbs.	5,875
1992 CORVETTE ZR-1					
1YZ	Z07	2-dr Hatch Cpe-2P	$65,318	3,465 lbs.	502*

(*) ZR-1 option quantity included in hatchback coupe production of 14,604 and total model-year production of 20,479 Corvettes.

Jerry Heasley

The 350-cid V-8 produced 375 horses in the 1992 ZR-1.

1,719 1993 Corvettes featured Black ragtops.

CORVETTE SERIES (V-8) SERIES YY/YZ

Corvette for 1993 marked its 40th Anniversary with a special appearance package that included an exclusive "Ruby Red" exterior and interior with color-keyed wheel centers, headrest embroidery and bright emblems on the hood, deck and side-gills. This anniversary package was optional equipment on all models. The ZR-1's 5.7-liter LT5 V-8 was upgraded this year and featured significant power and torque increases. Improved air flow from cylinder head and valve train refinements boosted its rating from 375 hp to 405 hp! The 1993 Corvette also introduced GM's first Passive Keyless Entry system whereby simply leaving or approaching the Corvette automatically unlocked or locked the appropriate doors. The 1993 Corvette was also the first North American automobile to use recycled sheet-molded-compound body panels. The ZR-1 again used a six-speed transaxle. Standard Corvette models were again powered by the 5.7-liter LT1 V-8 connected to a four-speed overdrive automatic or optional six-speed manual transmission. Corvettes came in Arctic White; Black; Bright Aqua Metallic; Polo Green II Metallic; Competition Yellow; Ruby Red; Torch Red; Black Rose Metallic; Dark Red Metallic and Quasar Blue Metallic. Interiors came in Black; Light Beige; Light Gray; Red; Ruby Red; and White. Standard features included a removable body-color roof panel for hatchbacks or a convertible top. All Corvette convertibles except those with the Z25 40th Anniversary Package could be ordered with a Beige, Black, or White cloth top. The 40th Anniversary ragtops came only with an exclusive Ruby Red cloth top. Black cloth upholstery was also standard.

I.D. NUMBERS

The Vehicle Identification Number (VIN) is visible through the windshield on the driver's side. The numbers were: [Base] 1G1YY[2/3]3PXP5100001 to 1G1YY[2/3]3PXP5121142; [ZR-1] 1G1YZ23J3P5800001 to 1G1YZ23J3P5800448. The first symbol (1) indicates U.S. built. The second symbol (G) indicates General Motors product. The third symbol (1) indicates Chevrolet Motor Division vehicle. The fourth and fifth symbols were (YY) for the Base Corvette or (YZ) for the Corvette ZR-1. The sixth symbol indicates body style: (2 = Two-door hatchback or liftback GM styles 07, 08, 77, 87 and 3 = Two-door convertible GM style 67). The seventh symbol indicates the restraint code: (1 = Active manual belts, 2 = Active manual belts with driver and passenger inflatable restraint system, 3 = Active manual belts with driver-inflatable restraint system, 4 = Passive automatic belts and 5 = Passive automatic belts with driver inflatable restraint system). The eighth symbol indicates engine: P = RPO LT1 5.7-liter Multiport-Fuel-Injection (MFI) Chevrolet/GM of Canada V-8; J = RPO LT5 5.7-liter MFI V-8. The ninth symbol is a check digit that varies. The 10th symbol indicates model year (P = 1993). The

Jerry Heasley

1993 40th anniversary Corvette

11th symbol indicates the assembly plant: (5 = Bowling Green, Ky). The last six symbols indicate the sequential production number starting with 100001 at each factory for base coupes and convertibles and 800001 for ZR-1s. The sequential serial number is repeated on the engine block itself, stamped on a pad just ahead of the cylinder head on the right (passenger) side, combined with a three-letter engine code identification suffix. Cast into the top rear (right side) of the block is a date built code. The first letter of that four-symbol code shows the month the block was cast. The next number (or numbers) reveals the day of the month, while the final digit indicates the year. Engine code suffixes for 1993 were: ZVA = 350-cid 300-hp RPO LT1 V-8 with 10.5:1 compression ratio and automatic transmission. ZVB = 350-cid 300-hp RPO LT1 V-8 with 10.5:1 compression ratio and manual transmission. ZVC = 350-cid 405-hp RPO LT5 V-8 (ZR-1 model only).

PAINT CODES

(10) Artic White; (41) Black; (43) Bright Aqua Metallic; (45) Polo Green II Metallic; (53) Competition Yellow; (68) Ruby Red; (70) Torch Red; (73) Black Rose Metallic; (75) Dark Red Metallic; (80) Quasar Blue Metallic.

CLOTH UPHOLSTERY CODES: (19C) Black.

LEATHER UPHOLSTERY CODES: (103) White; (143) Light Gray; (193) Black; (643) Light Beige; (703) Red; (793) Ruby Red.

ENGINES

BASE ENGINE: [RPO LT1] V-8. 90-degree overhead valve. Cast iron block and head. Displacement: 350 cid (5.7 liters). Bore and stroke: 4.00 x 3.48 inches. Compression ratio: 10.5:1. Brake hp: 300 at 5000 rpm. Torque: 340 lbs.-ft. at 3600 rpm. Five main bearings. Aluminum cylinder head. Hydraulic valve lifters. Induction: Multiport-Fuel-Injection system.

ZR-1 ENGINE: [RPO LT5] V-8. 90-degree overhead valve with four valves per cylinder. Four overhead camshafts. Cast iron block and head. Displacement: 350 cid (5.7 liters). Bore and stroke: 4.00 x 3.48 inches. Compression ratio: 11.0:1. Brake hp: 405 at 5800 rpm. Torque: 385 lbs.-ft. at 5200 rpm. Five main bearings. Aluminum cylinder head. Hydraulic valve lifters. Induction: Multiport-Fuel-Injection system.

TRANSMISSION

AUTOMATIC TRANSMISSION: An automatic transmission with floor-mounted gear shifter was standard equipment.

MANUAL TRANSMISSION: A six-speed manual transmission was optional.

CHASSIS FEATURES

Wheelbase: 96.2 inches. Overall length: (Base) 178.5

Jerry Heasley

1993 Corvette convertible

inches.; (ZR-1) 178.5 inches. Height: (hatchback) 46.3 inches.; (convertible) 47.3 inches. Width: (Base) 70.1 inches.; (ZR-1) 73.1 inches. Front Tread: (All) 57.7 inches. Rear Tread: (Base) 59.1 inches.; (ZR-1) 60.6 inches. Standard Tires: (front) P255/45ZR-17 Goodyear Eagle GT/(rear) P285/40ZR-17 Goodyear Eagle GT; (ZR-1) P315/35ZR-17 inches rear.

TECHNICAL FEATURES

Transmission: automatic or six-speed manual. Steering: rack and pinion (power assisted). Front suspension: Unequal-length control arms, single-leaf transverse springs and stabilizer bar. Rear suspension: Upper/lower control arms with five links, single-leaf transverse springs, and stabilizer bar. Brakes: Anti-lock; power four-wheel disc. Body construction: fiberglass; separate ladder frame with cross-members. Fuel tank: 20 gallons.

OPTIONS

RPO AC1 Power passenger seat ($305). RPO AC3 Power driver seat ($305). RPO AQ9 Leather sports seats ($1,100). RPO AQ9 White leather sports seats ($1,180). RPO AR9 Base leather seats ($475). RPO AR9 Base White leather seats ($555). RPO CC2 Auxiliary hardtop for convertible ($1,995). RPO C2L Dual removable roof panels for coupe ($950). RPO 24S Removable roof panels with blue tint for coupe ($650). RPO 64S Removable roof panels with bronze tint for coupe ($650). RPO C68 Electronic air conditioning control ($205). RPO FX3 Electronic Selective Ride & Handling system ($1,695). RPO G92 Performance axle ratio 3.07:1 ($50). RPO MN6 Six-speed manual transmission (no-cost option). RPO NN5 California emissions requirements ($100). RPO UJ6 Low tire pressure warning indicator ($325). RPO UU8 Delco-Bose stereo system ($823). RPO U1F Delco-Bose stereo system with compact disc changer ($1,219). RPO V56 Luggage rack for convertible ($140). RPO Z07 Adjustable suspension package for hatchback coupe ($2,045). RPO Z25 40th Anniversary package ($1,455). RPO ZR1 Special performance package for hatchback coupe ($31,683).

HISTORICAL FOOTNOTES

Calendar-year sales totaled 20,487 Corvettes. Model-year production totaled 21,590. Even Corvettes without the optional RPO Z25 40th Anniversary package had the special anniversary-style embroided headrests. For the 1993 model year improvements in the LT5 engine's cylinder head and valve train included "blending" the valve heads and creating three-angle valve inserts, plus the use of a sleeve spacer to help maintain port alignment of the injector manifold. These added up to a 30-hp increase and higher torque rating. In addition, the LT5 was now equipped with four-bolt main bearings, platinum-tipped spark plugs and an electrical linear exhaust gas recirculating (EGR) system.

1993 CORVETTE

Model Number	Body/Style Number	Body Type & Seating	Factory Price	Shipping Weight	Production Total
1YY	Y07	2-dr Hatch Cpe-2P	$34,595	3,333 lbs.	15,898
1YY	Y67	2-dr Conv. Cpe-2P	$41,195	3,383 lbs.	5,692
1993 CORVETTE ZR-1					
1YY	N/A	2-dr Hatch Cpe-2P	$66,278	3,503 lbs.	448*

(*): ZR-1 option quantity is included in the production total of 14,604 hatchback coupes and in the total model-year production of 20,479.
NOTE: The RPO Z25 40th Anniversary Package was added to 6,749 cars with no body style breakout available.

Jerry Heasley

1993 40th anniversary Corvette

Chevrolet

1994 Corvette coupe

CORVETTE SERIES (V-8) SERIES YY/YZ

Several refinements that focused on safety and smoother operation were the order for 1994 Corvettes. A passenger-side airbag was added and all Corvettes now offered dual airbags. In addition, other interior changes included new carpeting, new door-trim panels, new seats, a new steering wheel, a redesigned instrument panel and a restyled console. Other new equipment included an optional rear-axle ratio, revised spring rates, a convertible backlight with heated glass and new exterior colors. The ZR-1 also received new non-directional wheels for 1994. The 5.7-liter V-8 powering the standard Corvettes now used sequential fuel injection, which provided a smoother idle, better drivability and lower emissions. That engine was mated to a refined 4L60-E electronic four-speed automatic overdrive transmission that provided a more consistent shift feel. A brake-transmission shift interlock safety feature was also new for 1994. The ZR-1 again used the LT5 5.7-liter V-8. It was fitted with a six-speed manual transmission, which was again a no-cost option for LT1-powered Corvette models. Corvettes came in Arctic White; Admiral Blue; Black; Bright Aqua Metallic; Polo Green Metallic; Competition Yellow; Copper Metallic; Torch Red; Black Rose Metallic; and Dark Red Metallic. Interiors came in Black; Light Beige; Light Gray; and Red. Standard features included a removable body-color roof panel for hatchbacks or a convertible top. All Corvette convertibles except those with Polo Green Metallic finish could be ordered with one of three top colors: Beige, Black, or White cloth. The White convertible top was not available for Polo Green Metallic cars. Leather seats became standard upholstery.

I.D. NUMBERS

The Vehicle Identification Number (VIN) is visible through the windshield on the driver's side.

1994 Corvette ZR-1 with five-spoke wheels

The numbers were: [Base] 1G1YY[2/3]2P9R5100001 to 1G1YY[2/3]2P9R5122882; [ZR1] 1G1YZ22J9R5800001 to 1G1YZ22J9R5800448. The first symbol (1) indicates U.S. built. The second symbol (G) indicates General Motors product. The third symbol (1) indicates Chevrolet Motor Division vehicle. The fourth and fifth symbols were (YY) for the Base Corvette or (YZ) for the Corvette ZR-1. The sixth symbol indicates body style: (2 = Two-door hatchback or liftback GM styles 07, 08, 77, 87 and 3 = Two-door convertible GM style 67). The seventh symbol indicates the restraint code: (1 = Active manual belts, 2 = Active manual belts with driver and passenger inflatable restraint system, 3 = Active manual belts with driver-inflatable restraint system, 4 = Passive automatic belts, 5 = Passive automatic belts with driver inflatable restraint system and 6 = Passive automatic belts with driver and passenger inflatable restraint system). The eighth symbol indicates engine: P = RPO LT1 5.7-liter Multiport-Fuel-Injection (MFI) Chevrolet/GM of Canada V-8; J = RPO LT5 5.7-liter MFI V-8. The ninth symbol is a check digit that varies. The 10th symbol indicates model year (R = 1994). The 11th symbol indicates the assembly plant: (5 = Bowling Green, Ky). The last six symbols indicate the sequential production number starting with 100001 at each factory for base coupes and convertibles and 800001 for ZR-1s. The sequential serial number is repeated on the engine block itself, stamped on a pad just ahead of the cylinder head on the right (passenger) side, combined with a three-letter engine code identification suffix. Cast into the top rear (right side) of the block is a date built code. The first letter of that four-symbol code shows the month the block was cast. The next number (or numbers) reveals the day of the month, while the final digit indicates the year. Engine code suffixes for 1994 were: ZWA = 350-cid 300-hp RPO LT1 V-8 with 10.5:1 compression ratio and automatic transmission. ZWB = 350-cid 300-hp RPO LT1 V-8 with 10.5:1 compression ratio and manual transmission. ZWC = 350-cid 405-hp RPO LT5 V-8 with 11.0:1 compression and manual transmission (ZR-1 model only).

PAINT CODES

(10) Arctic White; (28) Admiral Blue; (41) Black; (43) Bright Aqua Metallic; (45) Polo Green Metallic; (53) Competition Yellow; (66) Copper Metallic; (70) Torch Red; (73) Black Rose Metallic; (75) Dark Red Metallic.

LEATHER UPHOLSTERY CODES: (143) Light Gray; (193) Black; (643) Light Blue; (703) Red.

ENGINES

BASE ENGINE: [RPO LT1] V-8. 90-degree overhead valve. Cast iron block and head. Displacement: 350 cid (5.7 liters). Bore and stroke: 4.00 x 3.48 inches. Compression ratio: 10.5:1. Brake hp: 300 at 5000 rpm. Torque: 340 lbs.-ft. at 3600 rpm. Five main bearings. Aluminum cylinder head. Hydraulic valve lifters. Induction: Sequential multiport-fuel injection.

ZR-1 ENGINE: [RPO LT5] V-8. 90-degree overhead valve with four valves per cylinder. Four overhead camshafts. Cast iron block and head. Displacement: 350 cid (5.7 liters). Bore and stroke: 4.00 x 3.48 inches. Compression ratio: 11.0:1. Brake hp: 405 at 5800 rpm. Torque: 385 lbs.-ft. at 5200 rpm. Five main bearings. Aluminum cylinder head. Hydraulic valve lifters. Induction: Sequential multiport-fuel-injection system.

TRANSMISSION

AUTOMATIC TRANSMISSION: An automatic transmission with floor-mounted gear shifter was standard

Chevrolet

1994 Corvette convertible with standard leather seats

equipment.

MANUAL TRANSMISSION: A six-speed manual transmission was optional.

CHASSIS FEATURES

Wheelbase: 96.2 inches. Overall length: (Base) 178.5 inches.; (ZR-1) 178.5 inches. Height: (Hatchback) 46.3 inches.; (Convertible) 47.3 inches. Width: (Base) 70.7 inches.; (ZR-1) 73.1 inches. Front tread: (All) 57.7 inches. Rear tread: (Base) 59.1 inches.; (ZR-1) 60.6 inches. Standard tires: (front) P255/45ZR-17 Goodyear Eagle GT/(rear) P285/40ZR-17 Goodyear Eagle GT; (ZR-1) P315/35ZR-17 inches rear.

TECHNICAL FEATURES

Transmission: Automatic or six-speed manual.. Steering: Rack and pinion (power assisted). Front suspension: unequal-length control arms, single-leaf transverse springs and stabilizer bar. Rear suspension: upper/lower control arms with five links, single-leaf transverse springs, stabilizer bar. Brakes: Anti-lock; power four-wheel disc. Body construction: fiberglass; separate ladder frame with cross-members. Fuel tank: 20 gallons.

OPTIONS

RPO AC1 Power passenger seat ($305). RPO AC3 Power driver seat ($305). RPO AQ9 Sports seats ($625). RPO CC2 Auxiliary hardtop for convertible ($1,995). RPO C2L Dual removable roof panels for coupe ($950). RPO 24S Removable roof panels with blue tint for coupe ($650). RPO 64S Removable roof panels with bronze tint for coupe ($650). RPO FX3 Electronic Selective Ride & Handling system ($1,695). RPO G92 Performance axle ratio 3.07:1 ($50). RPO MN6 Six-speed manual transmission (no-cost option). RPO NG1 New York emission requirements ($100). RPO UJ6 Low tire pressure warning indicator ($325). RPO U1F Delco-Bose stereo system with compact disc changer ($396). RPO WY5 Extended-mobility run-flat tires ($70). RPO YF5 California emissions requirements ($100). RPO Z07 Adjustable suspension package for hatchback coupe ($2,045). RPO ZR1 Special performance package for hatchback coupe ($31,258).

HISTORICAL FOOTNOTES

Calendar-year sales totaled 21,839 Corvettes. Model-year production totaled 23,330.

1994 CORVETTE Model Number	Body/Style Number	Body Type & Seating	Factory Price	Shipping Weight	Production Total
1YY	Y07	2-dr Hatch Cpe-2P	$36,185	3,317 lbs.	17,984
1YY	Y67	2-dr Conv. Cpe-2P	$42,960	3,358 lbs.	5,346
1994 CORVETTE ZR-1					
1YZ	Z07	2-dr Hatch Cpe-2P	$67,443	3,503 lbs.	448*

(*): ZR-1 option quantity is included in the production total of 17,984 hatchback coupes and in the total model-year production of 23,330.

Jerry Heasley

1995 Corvette ZR-1

CORVETTE SERIES (V-8) SERIES YY/YZ

The big news of 1995 was the final appearance of the ZR-1 performance coupe after several years of availability. The ZR-1 was first announced in 1989, but not actually offered until 1990. Changes on the Corvette included the addition of heavy-duty brakes with larger front rotors as standard equipment, along with new low-rate springs (except ZR-1). DeCarbon gas-charged shock absorbers were used for improved ride quality. In addition to exterior color changes, Corvettes featured a new "gill" panel behind the front wheel openings to help quickly distinguish the 1995 models from predecessors. Other improvements included reinforced interior stitching and a quieter-running cooling fan. Engine and transmission offerings remained unchanged from the year previous. Corvettes came in Dark Purple Metallic; Dark Purple Metallic and Arctic White; Arctic White; Admiral Blue; Black; Bright Aqua Metallic; Polo Green Metallic; Competition Yellow; Torch Red; and Dark Red Metallic. Interiors came in Black; Light Beige; Light Gray; Red; and White. Standard features included a removable body-color roof panel for hatchbacks or a convertible top. All Corvette convertibles except those with Dark Purple Metallic, Arctic White, or Polo Green Metallic finish could be ordered with one of three top colors: Beige, Black, or White cloth top. The Dark Purple Metallic and Arctic White combination was available only with a White convertible top, which was again not available for Polo Green Metallic cars. Leather seats were standard equipment.

I.D. NUMBERS

The Vehicle Identification Number (VIN) is visible through the windshield on the driver's side. The numbers were: [Base] 1G1YY[2/3]P7S5100001 to 1G1YY[2/3]P7S5120294; [ZR1] 1G1YZ22JOS5800001 to 1G1YZ22JOS5800448. The first symbol (1) indicates U.S. built. The second symbol (G) indicates General Motors product. The third symbol (1) indicates Chevrolet Motor Division vehicle. The fourth and fifth symbols were (YY) for the Base Corvette or (YZ) for the Corvette ZR-1. The sixth symbol indicates body style: (2 = Two-door hatchback or liftback GM styles 07, 08, 77, 87 and 3 = Two-door convertible GM style 67). The seventh symbol indicates the restraint code: (1 = Active manual belts, 2 = Active manual belts with driver and passenger inflatable

Jerry Heasley

1995 was the last year for the ZR-1.

restraint system, 3 = Active manual belts with driver-inflatable restraint system, 4 = Passive automatic belts, 5 = Passive automatic belts with driver inflatable restraint system and 6 = Passive automatic belts with driver and passenger inflatable restraint system). The eighth symbol indicates engine: P = RPO LT1 5.7-liter Multiport-Fuel-Injection (MFI) Chevrolet/GM of Canada V-8; J = RPO LT5 5.7-liter MFI V-8. The ninth symbol is a check digit that varies. The 10th symbol indicates model year (S = 1995). The 11th symbol indicates the assembly plant: (5 =

Jerry Heasley

1995 Corvette ZR-1

Jerry Heasley

The 1995 Corvette had square taillights and a rectangular exhaust.

Bowling Green, K.Y.). The last six symbols indicate the sequential production number starting with 100001 at each factory for base coupes and convertibles and 800001 for ZR-1s. The sequential serial number is repeated on the engine block itself, stamped on a pad just ahead of the cylinder head on the right (passenger) side, combined with a three-letter engine code identification suffix. Cast into the top rear (right side) of the block is a date built code. The first letter of that four-symbol code shows the month the block was cast. The next number (or numbers) reveals the day of the month, while the final digit indicates year. Engine code suffixes for 1995 were: ZUC = 350-cid 300-hp RPO LT1 V-8 with 10.5:1 compression ratio and automatic transmission. ZUD = 350-cid 300-hp RPO LT1 V-8 with 10.5:1 compression ratio and manual transmission. ZUF = 350-cid 405-hp RPO LT5 V-8 with 11.0:1 compression and manual transmission (ZR-1 model only).

PAINT CODES

(05) Dark Purple Metallic; (05/10) Dark Purple Metallic and Arctic White; (10) Arctic White; (28) Admiral Blue; (41) Black; (43) Bright Aqua Metallic; (45) Polo Green Metallic; (53) Competition Yellow; (70) Torch Red; (75) Dark Red Metallic.

LEATHER UPHOLSTERY CODES: (143) Light Gray; (193) Black; (194) Pace Car Black; (643) Light Blue; (703) Red.

ENGINES

BASE ENGINE: [RPO LT1] V-8. 90-degree overhead valve. Cast iron block and head. Displacement: 350 cid (5.7 liters). Bore and stroke: 4.00 x 3.48 inches. Compression ratio: 10.5:1. Brake hp: 300 at 5000 rpm. Torque: 340 lbs.-ft. at 3600 rpm. Five main bearings. Aluminum cylinder head. Hydraulic valve lifters. Induction: Sequential multiport-fuel injection.

ZR-1 ENGINE: [RPO LT5] V-8. 90-degree overhead valve with four valves per cylinder. Four overhead camshafts. Cast iron block and head. Displacement: 350 cid (5.7 liters). Bore and stroke: 4.00 x 3.48 inches. Compression ratio: 11.0:1. Brake hp: 405 at 5800 rpm. Torque: 385 lbs.-ft. at 5200 rpm. Five main bearings. Aluminum cylinder head. Hydraulic valve lifters. Induction: Sequential multiport-fuel-injection system.

TRANSMISSION

AUTOMATIC TRANSMISSION: An automatic transmission with floor-mounted gear shifter was standard equipment.

MANUAL TRANSMISSION: A six-speed manual transmission was optional.

CHASSIS FEATURES

Wheelbase: 96.2 inches. Overall length: (Base) 178.5 inches.; (ZR-1) 178.5 inches. Height: (Hatchback) 46.3 inches.; (Convertible) 47.3 inches. Width: (Base) 70.7 inches.; (ZR-1) 73.1 inches. Front tread: (All) 57.7 inches. Rear tread: (Base) 59.1 inches.; (ZR-1) 60.6 inches. Standard tires: (front) P255/45ZR-17 Goodyear Eagle GT/(rear) P285/40ZR-17 Goodyear Eagle GT; (ZR-1) P275/40ZR-17 inches front.

TECHNICAL FEATURES

Transmission: Automatic or six-speed manual. Steering: Rack and pinion (power assisted). Front suspension: Unequal-length control arms, single-leaf transverse springs and stabilizer bar. Rear suspension: Upper/lower control arms with five links, single-leaf transverse springs, stabilizer bar. Brakes: Anti-lock; power four-wheel disc. Body construction: Fiberglass; separate ladder frame with cross-members. Fuel tank: 20 gallons.

OPTIONS

RPO AG1 Power driver seat ($305). RPO AG2 Power passenger seat ($305). RPO AQ9 Sports seats ($625). RPO CC2 Auxiliary hardtop for convertible ($1,995). RPO C2L Dual removable roof panels for coupe ($950). RPO 24S Removable roof panels with blue tint for coupe ($650). RPO 64S Removable roof panels with bronze tint for coupe ($650). RPO FX3 Electronic Selective Ride & Handling system ($1,695). RPO G92 Performance axle ratio 3.07:1 ($50). RPO MN6 Six-speed manual transmission (no-cost option). RPO NG1 New York emission requirements ($100). RPO UJ6 Low tire pressure warning indicator ($325). RPO U1F Delco-Bose stereo system with compact disc changer ($396). RPO WY5 Extended-mobility tires ($100). RPO YF5 California emissions requirements ($100). RPO Z07 Adjustable suspension package for hatchback coupe ($2,045). RPO Z4Z Indy 500 Pace Car Replica for convertibles only ($2,816). RPO ZR-1 Special Performance package for hatchback coupe ($31,258).

HISTORICAL FOOTNOTES

Calendar-year sales totaled 18,966 Corvettes. Model-year production totaled 20,742. For the third time in its existence (also 1978 and 1986), Corvette was selected as the official pace car for the Indianapolis 500. The 1995 Dark Purple Metallic over Arctic White Corvette was driven by 1960 Indy 500 winner Jim Rathmann. Chevy built a total of 527 cars equipped with the RPO Z4Z Indy 500 Pace Car Replica package that sold for $2,816 over the price of a standard LT1-powered Corvette convertible.

1995 CORVETTE Model Number	Body/Style Number	Body Type & Seating	Factory Price	Shipping Weight	Production Total
1Y	Y07	2-dr Hatch Cpe-2P	$36,785	3,203 lbs.	15,771
1Y	Y67	2-dr Conv. Cpe-2P	$43,665	3,360 lbs.	4,971
1995 CORVETTE ZR-1					
1Y	Z07	2-dr Hatch Cpe-2P	$68,043	3,512 lbs.	448*

(*): ZR-1 option quantity included in production of 15,771 hatchback coupes and in total model-year production of 20,742.

Jerry Heasley

This is the 1996 Corvette Collector Edition. All convertible tops were black.

CORVETTE SERIES (V-8) SERIES YY/YZ

Nineteen ninety-six was a landmark year for Corvette enthusiasts. With the demise of the ZR-1, Chevrolet offset the void by introducing two new special edition Corvettes, the Grand Sport and Collector Edition models. The Grand Sport evoked memories of its 1962-63 racing predecessors, sporting Admiral Blue Metallic Paint, a white stripe, red "hash" marks on the left front fender and black five-spoke aluminum wheels. Powering the Grand Sport and optional in all other Corvettes was a 330-hp 5.7-liter LT4 V-8 featuring a specially-prepared crankshaft, steel camshaft, and water pump gears driven by a roller chain. The LT4 was available only with the six-speed manual transmission. The Collector Edition Corvette was produced as a tribute to the final year of production of the fourth-generation Corvette (the fifth-generation model was to debut the following year). The 1996 Collector Edition Corvette featured exclusive Sebring Silver paint, Collector Edition emblems, silver five-spoke aluminum wheels and a 5.7-liter LT1 V-8. On all Corvettes, 1996 marked the introduction of the optional Selective Real Time Damping system that employed sensors at each wheel to measure movement. Data retrieved from each wheel and the Powertrain Control Module was processed by an electronic controller that calculated the damping mode to provide optimum control. Also optional was a Z51 Performance Handling Package available on the Corvette coupe, and tuned for autocross and Gymkhana competition. Standard Corvette models again used the 5.7-liter V-8 with sequential fuel injection and four-speed automatic transmission. Corvettes came in Dark Purple Metallic; Arctic White; Sebring Silver Metallic; Admiral Blue; Black; Bright Aqua Metallic; Polo Green Metallic; Competition Yellow; and Torch Red. Interiors came in Black; Light Beige; Light Gray; Red; and Red and Black. Standard features included a removable body-color roof panel for hatchbacks or a convertible top. All Corvette convertibles except those with code 13, 28, or 45 paint colors could be ordered with one of three cloth top colors: Beige, Black, or White. Sebring Silver Metallic (code 13) cars came only with Black cloth tops. Admiral Blue (code 28) Grand Sports came only with White cloth tops. Polo Green Metallic (code 45) cars came with Beige or Black cloth tops, but not White. Leather seats were standard equipment.

Jerry Heasley

1996 Corvette Collector Edition

I.D. NUMBERS

The Vehicle Identification Number (VIN) is visible through the windshield on the driver's side. The numbers were: [Base] 1G1YY[2/3]257T5100001 to 1G1YY[2/3]257T5120536; [Grand Sport] 1G1YY2251T5600001 to 1G1YY2251T5601000. The first symbol (1) indicates U.S. built. The second symbol (G) indicates General Motors product. The third symbol (1) indicates Chevrolet Motor Division vehicle. The fourth and fifth symbols were (YY) Corvette. The sixth symbol indicates body style: (2 = Two-door hatchback or liftback GM styles 07, 08, 77, 87 and 3 = Two-door convertible GM style 67). The seventh symbol indicates the restraint code: (1 = Active manual belts, 2 = Active manual belts with driver and passenger inflatable restraint system, 3 = Active manual belts with driver-inflatable restraint system, 4 = Passive automatic belts, 5 = Passive automatic belts with driver inflatable restraint system, 6 = Passive automatic belts with driver and passenger inflatable restraint system and 7 = Active manual driver's belt and passive automatic passenger's belt with driver and passenger inflatable restraint system). The eighth symbol indicates engine: P = RPO LT1 5.7-liter Sequential multiport-fuel-injection (MFI) Chevrolet/Pontiac/Buick/Cadillac V-8; 5 = RPO LT4 5.7-liter sequential multiport-fuel-injection (MFI) Chevrolet only. The ninth symbol is a check digit that varies. The 10th symbol indicates model year (T = 1996). The 11th symbol indicates the assembly plant: (5 = Bowling Green, Ky). The last six symbols indicate the sequential production number starting with 100001 at each factory for base coupes and convertibles and 800001 for ZR-1s. The sequential serial number is repeated on the engine block itself, stamped on a pad just ahead of the cylinder head on the right (passenger) side, combined with a three-letter engine code identification suffix. Cast into the top rear (right side) of the block is a date built code. The first letter of that four-symbol code shows the month the block was cast. The next number (or numbers) reveals the day of the month, while the final digit indicates the year. Engine code suffixes for 1996 were: ZXA = 350-cid 300-hp RPO LT1 V-8 with 10.4:1 compression ratio and automatic transmission. ZXD = 350-cid 330-hp RPO LT4 V-8 with 10.8:1 compression ratio and manual transmission.

PAINT CODES

(05) Dark Purple Metallic; (10) Arctic White; (13) Sebring Silver Metallic; (28) Admiral Blue; (41) Black; (43) Bright Aqua Metallic; (45) Polo Green Metallic; (53) Competition Yellow; (70) Torch Red

LEATHER UPHOLSTERY CODES: (143) Light Gray; (144) Light Gray Collector Edition; (193) Black; (194) Black Collector Edition; (195) Black Grand Sport; (643) Light Beige; (703) Red; (704) Red Collector Edition and (705) Red; Black Grand Sport.

ENGINES

BASE ENGINE: [RPO LT1] V-8. 90-degree overhead valve. Cast iron block and head. Displacement: 350 cid (5.7 liters). Bore and stroke: 4.00 x 3.48 inches. Compression ratio: 10.4:1. Brake hp: 300 at 5000 rpm. Torque: 335 lbs.-ft. at 4000 rpm. Five main bearings. Aluminum cylinder head. Hydraulic valve lifters. Induction: Sequential multiport-fuel injection.

OPTIONAL ENGINE: [RPO LT4] V-8. 90-degree overhead valve with four valves per cylinder. Four overhead camshafts. Cast iron block and head. Displacement: 350 cid (5.7 liters). Bore and stroke: 4.00 x 3.48 inches. Compression ratio: 10.8:1. Brake hp: 330 at 5800 rpm. Torque: 340 lbs.-ft. at 4500 rpm. Five main bearings. Aluminum cylinder head. Hydraulic valve lifters. Induction: Sequential multiport-fuel-injection system.

TRANSMISSION

AUTOMATIC TRANSMISSION: An automatic transmission with floor-mounted gear shifter was standard equipment for the LT1.

MANUAL TRANSMISSION: A six-speed manual transmission was mandatory with the optional V-8.

CHASSIS FEATURES

Wheelbase: 96.2 inches. Overall length: (Base) 178.5 inches. Height: (hatchback) 46.3 inches.; (convertible) 47.3 inches. Width: (Hatchback) 70.7 inches.; (Convertible) 73.1 inches. Front tread: (All) 57.7 inches. Rear tread: (All) 59.1 inches. Standard tires: (front) P255/45ZR-17/(rear) P285/40ZR-17; (Grand Sport coupe) (front) P275/40ZR-17/(rear) P315/35ZR-17; (Grand Sport convertible) (front) P255/45ZR-17/(rear) P285/40ZR-17.

TECHNICAL FEATURES

Transmission: Four-speed automatic. Steering: Rack and pinion (power assisted). Front Suspension: Independent SLA forged-aluminum upper and lower control arms and steering knuckle, transverse monoleaf springs, steel stabilizer bar, and spindle offset. Rear suspension: Independent five-link design with tow and camber adjustment, forged-aluminum control links and steering knuckle, transverse monoleaf springs, steel tie rods, stabilizer bar, and tubular U-joint aluminum driveshaft. Brakes: Anti-lock: power four-wheel disc. Body construction: fiberglass; separate ladder frame with cross-members. Fuel tank: 20 gallons.

OPTIONS

RPO AG1 Power driver seat ($305). RPO AG2 Power

Jerry Heasley

The 1996 Corvette Grand Sport in Admiral Blue with a white stripe

1996 Corvette Convertible Collector Edition

passenger seat ($305). RPO AQ9 Sports seats ($625). RPO CC2 Auxiliary hardtop for convertible ($1,995). RPO C2L Dual removable roof panels for coupe ($950). RPO 24S Removable roof panels with blue tint for coupe ($650). RPO 64S Removable roof panels with bronze tint for coupe ($650). RPO F45 Electronic Selective Real Time Damping ($1,695). RPO G92 Performance axle ratio 3.07:1 ($50). RPO LT4 350-cid 330-hp V-8 ($1,450). RPO MN6 Six-speed manual transmission (no-cost option). RPO N84 Spare tire delete ($100 credit). RPO UJ6 Low tire pressure warning indicator ($325). RPO U1F Delco-Bose stereo system with compact disc changer ($396). RPO WY5 Extended-mobility tires ($70). RPO Z15 Collector Edition ($1,250). RPO Z16 Grand Sport package ($2,880 with convertible or $3,250). RPO Z51 Performance Handling package ($350).

HISTORICAL FOOTNOTES

Calendar-year sales totaled 17,805 Corvettes. Model-year production totaled 21,536.

1996 CORVETTE

Model Number	Body/Style Number	Body Type & Seating	Factory Price	Shipping Weight	Production Total
1Y	Y07	2-dr Hatch Cpe-2P	37225	3298	17167
1Y	Y67	2-dr Conv. Cpe-2P	45060	3360	4369

NOTE 1: The Z15 Collector Edition option was installed on 5,412 cars.
NOTE 2: The Z16 Grand Sport Package option was installed on 1,000 cars.

1996 Corvette Grand Sport, a total of 1,000 Corvettes had this option

Jerry Heasley

1997 Corvette in Torch Red

C5 CORVETTE (V-8) SERIES YY

It was another landmark year for Corvette in that the 1997 C5 model was the first all-new Corvette in 13 years and only the fifth or sixth (depending upon your viewpoint) major change in the car's 44-year history. The "fifth-generation" Corvette was offered only as a coupe in its debut year. Among the equipment featured for the C5 was a new, more compact 5.7-liter LS1 V-8 that produced 350 hp and 345 lbs.-ft. of torque. A rear-mounted transaxle opened up more interior space and helped maintain a near 50/50 front-to-rear weight distribution. An Electronic Throttle Control system allowed engineers a limitless range of throttle progression. The 1997 Corvette's underbody structure was the stiffest in the car's history and consisted of two full-length, hydro-formed perimeter frame rails coupled to a backbone tunnel. The rails consisted of a single piece of tubular steel, replacing the 14 parts used previously. The cockpit of the all-new Corvette featured a twin-pod design reminiscent of the original 1953 Corvette. The instrument panel contained traditional backlit analog gauges and a digital Driver Information Center that comprised a display of 12 individual readouts in four languages. The new-design blunt tail section allowed for smoother airflow and resulting 0.29 coefficient of drag. The C5 Corvette was offered with a 4L60-E electronic four-speed overdrive automatic as the base transmission and an optional six-speed manual transmission. Corvettes came in Arctic White; Sebring Silver Metallic; Nassau Blue; Black; Light Carmine Red Metallic; Torch Red; and Fairway Green Metallic. Interiors came in Black; Light Gray; and Firethorn Red. Standard features included a removable body-color roof panel. Leather seats were standard equipment.

I.D. NUMBERS

The Vehicle Identification Number (VIN) is visible through the windshield on the driver's side. The numbers were: [Base] 1G1YY22G1V5100001 to 1G1YY22G1V5109093. The first symbol (1) indicates U.S. built. The second symbol (G) indicates General Motors product. The third symbol (1) indicates Chevrolet Motor Division vehicle. The fourth and fifth symbols (YY) indicate a Corvette. The sixth symbol incates body style (2 = two-door coupe GM styles 27, 37, 47 or 57). The seventh symbol indicates restraint code: (2 = Active

The all-new 1997 C5

manual belts with driver and front passenger inflatable restraint system, 4 = Active manual belts with frontal and side-impact driver and front passenger inflatable restraint system). The eighth symbol indicates engine: G = RPO LS1 5.7-liter sequential multiport-fuel-injection (MFI) Chevrolet V-8. The ninth symbol is a check digit that varies. The 10th symbol indicates model year (V = 1997). The 11th symbol indicates the assembly plant: (5 = Bowling Green, Ky). The last six symbols indicate the sequential production number starting with 100001 at each factory. The sequential serial number is repeated on the engine block itself, stamped on a pad just ahead of the cylinder head on the right (passenger) side, combined with a three-letter engine code identification suffix. Cast into the top rear (right side) of the block is a date built code. The first letter of that four-symbol code shows the month the block was cast. The next number (or numbers) reveals the day of the month, while the final digit indicates year. Engine code suffixes for 1997 were: ZYD = 350-cid 345-hp RPO LS1 V-8 with 10.1:1 compression ratio and automatic transmission. ZYC = 350-cid 345-hp RPO LS1 V-8 with 10.1:1 compression ratio and manual transmission.

PAINT CODES

(10) Arctic White; (13) Sebring Silver Metallic; (23) Nassau Blue Metallic; (41) Black; (53) Light Carmine Red Metallic; (70) Torch Red; (87) Fairway Green Metallic.

LEATHER UPHOLSTERY CODES: (193) Black; (923) Light Gray; (943) Red.

ENGINE

BASE V-8: [RPO LS1] Overhead valve V-8. Cast aluminum block and head. Displacement: 346 cu. in. (5.7 liters). Bore & stroke: 3.90 x 3.62 in. Compression ratio: 10.1:1. Brake horsepower: 345 at 5600 RPM. Torque: 350 lb.-ft. at 4400 RPM. Hydraulic valve lifters. Sequential fuel injection.

TRANSMISSION

AUTOMATIC TRANSMISSION: A 4L60-E electronic overdrive transmission with floor-mounted gear shifter was standard equipment.

MANUAL TRANSMISSION: A six-speed manual transmission was optional.

CHASSIS FEATURES

Wheelbase: 104.5 in. Overall length: 179.7 in. Height: 47.7 in. Width: 73.6 in. Front tread: 62.0 in. Rear tread: 62.1 in. Standard tires: (front) P245/45ZR-17, (rear) P275/40ZR-18.

TECHNICAL FEATURES

Transmission: AL60-E electronic four-speed automatic. Steering: Rack and pinion (power assisted). Front suspension: Independent SLA forged-aluminum upper and lower control arms and steering knuckle, transverse monoleaf springs, steel stabilizer bar, and spindle offset. Rear suspension: Independent five-link design with tow and camber adjustment, cast-aluminum upper and lower control arms and knuckle, transverse monoleaf springs, steel tie rods and stabilizer bar, and tubular U-jointed metal matrix composite driveshaft. Brakes: Anti-lock: power four-wheel disc. Body construction: Fiberglass; integral perimeter frame with center backbone/all-welded steel body frame construction. Fuel tank: 19.1 gallons.

CORVETTE OPTIONS

RPO CJ2 Dual-zone air conditioning ($365). RPO AQ9 Adjustable leather bucket seats, requires six-way power passenger seat ($625). RPO G92 Performance axle ratio, not available with six-speed manual transmission ($100). RPO CYF California emission system ($170). RPO JL4 Active-handling System ($500). RPO Z51 Performance handling Package with Bilstein adjustable Ride-Control system ($350). RPO F45 Continuously Variable Real Time Damping, not available with RPO Z51 Pkg ($1,695). RPO AAB Memory package to recall settings for outside rearview mirrors, radio, power seats, and heating-ventilation and air-conditioning controls ($150). RPO U1S Remote CD changer ($600). RPO UN0 Delco/Bose music system ($100). RPO V49 Front license plate frame ($15). RPO T96 Fog lamps ($65). RPO D42 Luggage shade and cargo net ($50). RPO B34 Front floor mats ($25). RPO B84 Body side moldings ($75). RPO C2L Dual body color-keyed roof panel and blue transparent roof panel ($950). RPO CC3 Roof panel with blue tint ($650). RPO AG2 Power six-way passenger seat ($305).

HISTORY

The all-new C5 Corvette was designed under the direction of John Cafaro. *American Woman Motorscene* magazine named the 1997 Corvette its "Most likely to be immortalized" car. The C5 Corvette could do five second 0-to-60-mph runs and cover the quarter mile in 13.28 seconds at 107.6 mph according to *Vette* magazine.

1997 CORVETTE Model Number	Body/Style Number	Body Type & Seating	Factory Price	Shipping Weight	Production Total
1Y	Y07	2-dr Hatch Cpe-2P	$37,795	3,229 lbs.	9,752

Jerry Heasley

1997 Corvette

Jerry Heasley

1998 Corvette convertible in Black

C5 CORVETTE (V-8) SERIES YY

In its 45th year, the Corvette returned to offering convertible and coupe models with the debut of a "topless" version of the C5 Corvette. The convertible's glass rear window was heated and the top had an "express-down" feature that released the tonneau cover and automatically lowered the windows part way at the touch of a button. New-for-1998 was a magnesium wheel option featuring lightweight wheels with a unique bronze tone. Standard features included stainless steel exhaust system; Extended Mobility Tires capable of running for 200 miles with no air pressure; dual heated electric remote breakaway outside rearview mirrors; daytime running lamps; and five-mph front and rear bumpers. The LS1 V-8 and four-speed automatic transmission were again the standard offering, with the T56 six-speed manual transmission optional. Corvettes were available in Arctic White; Light Pewter Metallic; Sebring Silver Metallic; Radar Blue (Pace Car only); Nassau Blue Metallic; Navy Blue; Black; Light Carmine Red Metallic; Aztec Gold; Torch Red; and Fairway Green Metallic. Leather seats were standard and came in Black; Medium Pearl Purple Metallic; Light Oak; Light Gray; and Firethorn Red. Convertible tops came in Black, Light Oak, and White.

I.D. NUMBERS

The Vehicle Identification Number (VIN) is visible through the windshield on the driver's side. The numbers were: 1G1YY[2/3]2G1W5100001 to 1G1YY[2/3]2G1W5131069. The first symbol (1) indicates U.S. built. The second symbol (G) indicates General Motors product. The third symbol (1) indicates Chevrolet Motor Division vehicle. The fourth and fifth symbols (YY) indicate a Corvette coupe or convertible. The sixth symbol incates body style (2 = two-door coupe GM styles 27, 37, 47 or 57 or 3 = two-door convertible GM body style 67). The seventh symbol indicates restraint code: (2 = Active manual belts with driver and front passenger inflatable restraint system, 4 = Active manual belts with frontal and side-impact driver and front passenger inflatable restraint system). The eighth symbol indicates engine: G = RPO LS1 5.7-liter Sequential multiport-fuel-injection (MFI) Chevrolet V-8. The ninth symbol is a check digit that varies. The 10th symbol indicates model year (W = 1998). The 11th symbol indicates the assembly plant: (5

= Bowling Green, Ky). The last six symbols indicate the sequential production number starting with 100001 at each factory.

PAINT CODES

(10) Arctic White; (11) Light Pewter Metallic; (13) Sebring Silver Metallic; (21) Radar Blue (Pace Car only); (23) Nassau Blue Metallic; (28) Navy Blue; (41) Black (53) Light Carmine Red Metallic; (58) Aztec Gold; (70) Torch Red; (87) Fairway Green Metallic; (95) Medium Pearl Purple Metallic.

LEATHER UPHOLSTERY CODES: (193) Black; (673) Light Oak; (923) Light Gray; (943) Firethorn Red.

ENGINES

BASE V-8: [RPO LS1] V-8 Overhead valve. Cast aluminum block and head. Displacement: 346 cid. (5.7 liters). Bore and stroke: 3.90 x 3.62 inches. Compression ratio: 10.1:1. Brake horsepower: 345 at 5600 rpm. Torque: 350 lbs.-ft. at 4400 rpm. Cast aluminum block and heads. Hydraulic valve lifters, two valves per cylinder. Induction: Sequential fuel injection.

TRANSMISSION

AUTOMATIC TRANSMISSION: A Turbo Hydera-Matc automatic transmission with floor-mounted gear shifter was standard equipment..

MANUAL TRANSMISSION: A four-speed manual transmission was optional.

CHASSIS FEATURES

Wheelbase: 104.5 in. Overall length: 179.7 in. Height: 47.7 in. Width: 73.6 in. Front tread: 62.0 in. Rear tread: 62.1 in. Standard tires: (front) P245/45ZR-17, (rear) P275/40ZR-18.

TECHNICAL FEATURES

Transmission: Automatic or optional four-speed manual. Steering: Rack and pinion (power assisted). Front suspension: independent SLA forged-aluminum upper and lower control arms and steering knuckle, transverse

Chevrolet

1998 Corvette Indianapolis 500 Pace Car

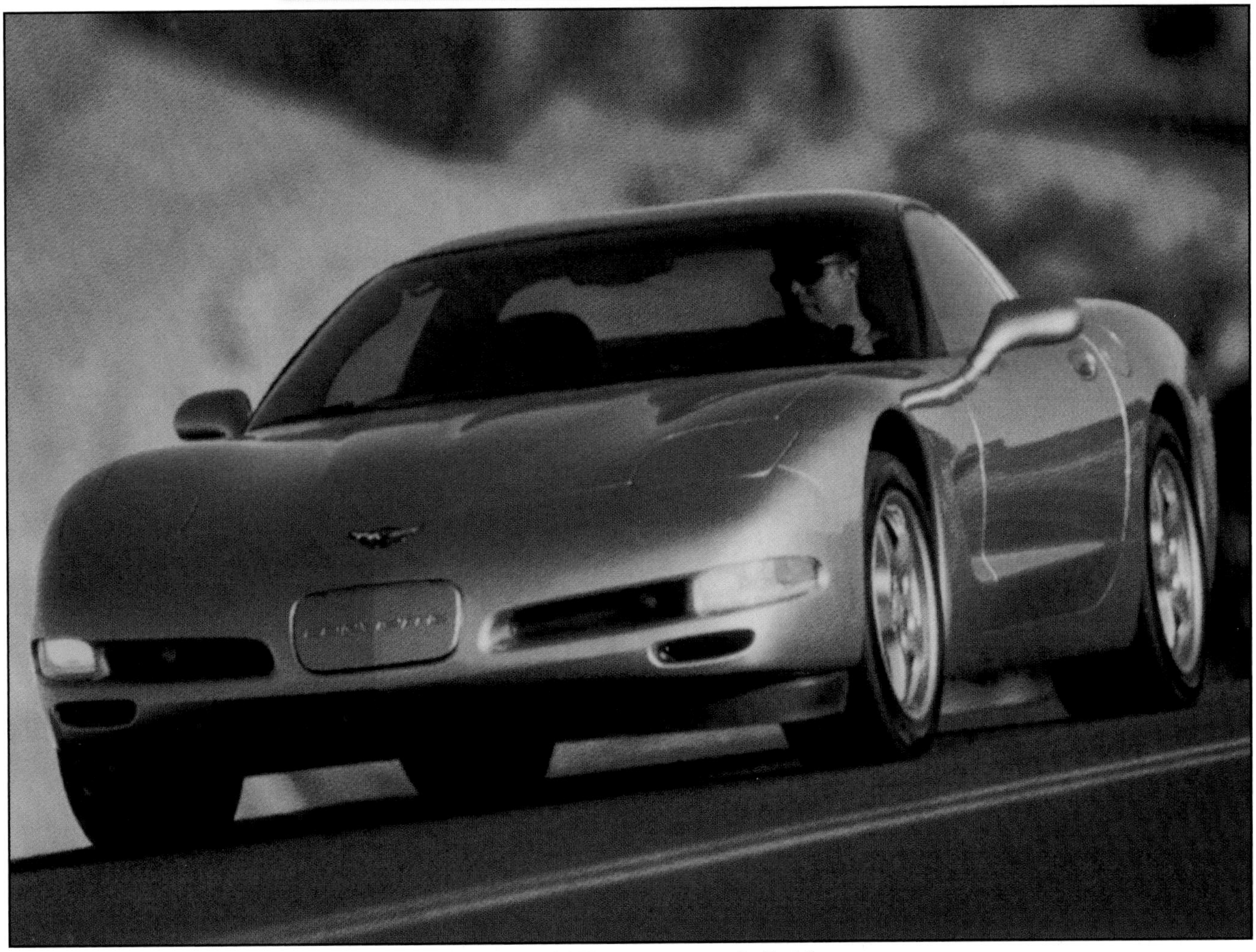
Chevrolet

1998 Corvette, 19,235 coupes were built this year

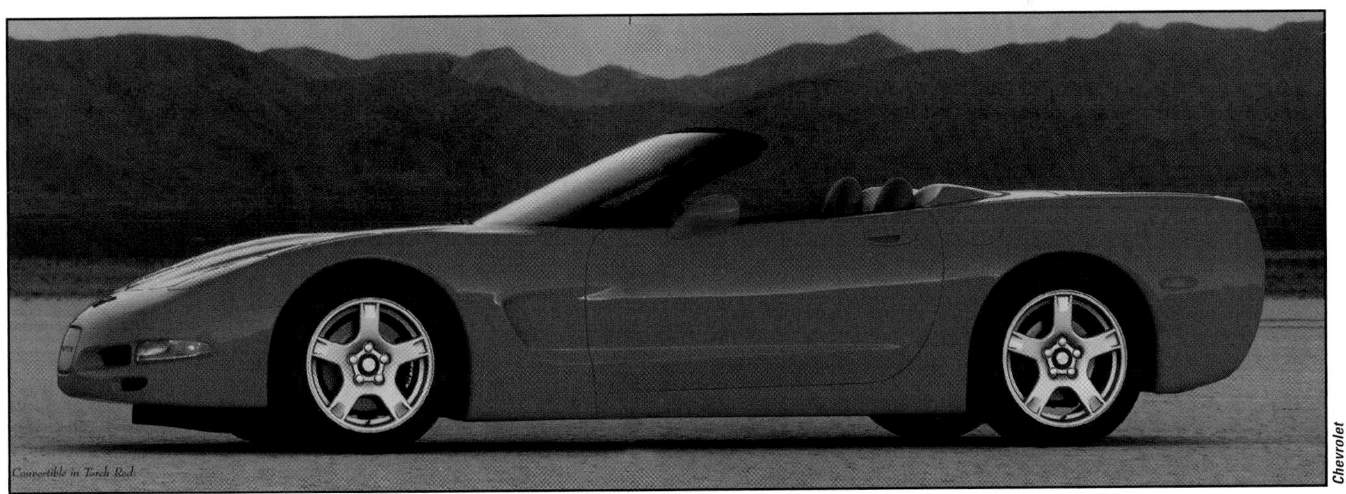

Convertible in Torch Red
Chevrolet

11,849 ragtops were built for 1998.

monoleaf springs, steel stabilizer bar, and spindle offset. Rear suspension: Independent five-link design with tow and camber adjustment, cast-aluminum upper and lower control arms and knuckle, transverse monoleaf springs, steel tie rods and stabilizer bar, and tubular U-jointed metal matrix composite driveshaft. Brakes: Anti-lock; power four-wheel disc. Body construction: fiberglass; integral perimeter frame with center backbone. All-welded steel body frame construction. Fuel tank: 19.1 gallons.

OPTIONS

RPO AAB Memory package to recall settings for outside rearview mirrors, radio, power seats and heating-ventilation and air-conditioning controls ($150). RPO

1998 Corvette Indianapolis 500 Pace Car in Pace Car Purple.

AG2 Power six-way passenger seat ($305). RPO AQ9 Sport seats ($625). RPO B34 Front floor mats ($25). RPO B84 Body side moldings ($75). RPO CC3 Roof panel with blue tint ($650). RPO C2L Dual body color-keyed roof panel and blue transparent roof panel ($950). RPO CJ2 Dual-zone air conditioning ($365). RPO D42 Luggage shade and cargo net ($50). RPO F45 Continuously Variable Real Time Damping, not available with RPO Z51 package ($1,695). RPO G92 Performance axle ratio, not available with six-speed manual transmission ($100). RPO JL4 Active-handling system ($500). RPO MN6 Six-speed manual transmission ($815). RPO NG1 Massachusetts/New York emissions requirements ($170). RPO N73 Custom magnesium wheels ($3,000). RPO T96 Fog lamps ($65). RPO UN0 Delco-Bose music system ($100). RPO U1S Remote CD changer ($600). RPO V49 Front license plate frame ($15). RPO CYF California emissions system ($170). RPO Z4Z Indy Pace Car package ($5,039 with automatic transmission or $5,804 with manual transmission). RPO Z51 Performance handling package with Bilstein adjustable Ride-Control system ($350).

HISTORICAL FOOTNOTES

Model-year production was 31,084 units. For the fourth time (1978, 1986, 1995, 1998), a Corvette was selected to pace the Indianapolis 500 with Indy 500 veteran Parnelli Jones driving the purple and yellow pace car. Corvette made its long-awaited return to Trans-Am racing successful by placing first in the 1998 season-opening event on the street circuit at Long Beach, California, in the No. 8 AutoLink Corvette driven by veteran road racer Paul Gentilozzi.

1998 CORVETTE

Model Number	Body/Style Number	Body Type & Seating	Factory Price	Shipping Weight	Production Total
1Y	Y07	2-dr Hatch Cpe-2P	$37,495	3,245 lbs.	19,235
1Y	Y67	2-dr Conv. Cpe-2P	$44,425	3,246 lbs.	11,849

NOTE 1: A total of 1,163 Corvettes had the Indy Pace Car package.

Jerry Heasley

1999 Corvette convertible

C5 CORVETTE (V-8) SERIES YY

The fifth-generation Corvette, in its third model year, added a fixed-roof hardtop to the lineup that already consisted of coupe and convertible body styles. The fixed-roof Corvette was the first offered since the legendary second-generation Sting Rays of 1963-1967. The new hardtop Corvette featured body lines unique to that model and they subtly set it apart from the coupe and convertible. Its standard equipment included the six-speed manual transmission (an automatic transmission was not available), limited-slip rear axle with 3.42:1 ratio and Z51 suspension with stiff springs, large stabilizer bars and large mono-tube shock absorbers. The Z51 suspension was also optional on coupes and convertibles. All 1999 Corvettes were powered by the 345-hp 5.7-liter LS1 V-8. The coupe and convertible used the 4L60-E electronically-controlled four-speed automatic overdrive transmission, with the six-speed manual unit optional. New optional features for 1999 Corvette coupe and convertible models included a Heads-Up Display (HUD) system which projected key instrumentation readouts onto the windshield to allow drivers to view vehicle vitals without taking their eyes off the road; Twilight Sentinel, with delayed shutoff of headlamps, allowed for exterior illumination after the ignition was turned off; and they also featured a power telescoping steering column that allowed drivers to more accurately tailor the position of the steering wheel to their specific needs. Optional again on all 1999 Corvettes was the Active-Handling System (AHS). AHS operated in harmony with the anti-lock braking and traction-control systems to selectively apply any of the four brakes in an effort to help the driver counteract and diffuse dangerous handling characteristics such as oversteer and understeer. The Corvette's standard equipment list included next-generation dual airbags; air conditioning; leather seating; power door locks and windows; a PassKey II theft-deterrent system; electronic speed control; an electronic Driver Information Center; and Remote Function Actuation with Remote Keyless Entry. Colors for 1999 C5 Corvette coupes and convertibles were: Arctic White; Light Pewter Metallic; Sebring Silver Metallic; Nassau Blue Metallic; Navy Blue; Black; Torch Red; and Magnetic Red II Clearcoat. The fixed-roof hardtop came only in five colors: Artic White; Light Pewter Metallic; Nassau Blue; Black; and Torch Red. Leather interiors were standard and came in Black; Light Oak; Light Gray; and Red. Convertible tops were available in White, Black, and Light Oak.

I.D. NUMBERS

The Vehicle Identification Number (VIN) is visible through the windshield on the driver's side. The numbers were: 1G1YY[1/2/3]2G5X5100000 to 1G1YY[1/2/3]2G5X5133283. The first symbol (1) indicates U.S. built. The second symbol (G) indicates General Motors product. The third symbol (1) indicates Chevrolet Motor Division vehicle. The fourth and fifth symbols (YY) indicate a Corvette. The sixth symbol incates body style: (1 = Fixed-roof hardtop, 2 = Two-door coupe GM styles 27, 37, 47 or 57 and 3 = Two-door convertible GM body style 67). The seventh symbol indicates restraint code: (2 = Active manual belts with driver and front passenger inflatable restraint system, 4 = Active manual belts with frontal and side-impact driver and front passenger inflatable restraint system). The eighth symbol indicates engine: G = RPO LS1 5.7-liter Sequential multiport-fuel-injection (MFI) Chevrolet V-8. The ninth symbol is a check digit that varies. The 10th symbol indicates model year (X = 1999). The 11th symbol indicates the assembly plant: (5 = Bowling Green, Ky). The last six symbols indicate the sequential production number starting with 100001 at each factory.

PAINT CODES: (10) Arctic White; (11) Light Pewter Metallic; (13) Sebring Silver Metallic; (23) Nassau Blue Metallic; (28) Navy Blue Metallic; (41) Black; (70) Torch Red; (86) Magnetic Red II Clear Coat

LEATHER UPHOLSTERY CODES: (191) Black; (671) Light Oak; (921) Pewter; (941) Firethorn Red.

ENGINE

BASE ENGINE: [LS6] V-8 Overhead valve. Cast aluminum block and head. Displacement: 346 cid. (5.7 liters). Bore and stroke: 3.90 x 3.62 in. Compression ratio: 10.1:1. Brake horsepower: 345 at 5600 rpm. Torque: 350 lbs.-ft. at 4400 rpm. Hydraulic valve lifters. Induction: Sequential multiport fuel injection.

TRANSMISSION

AUTOMATIC TRANSMISSION: A Turbo Hydera-Matc automatic transmission with floor-mounted gear shifter was standard equipment..

MANUAL TRANSMISSION: A four-speed manual transmission was optional.

CHASSIS FEATURES

Wheelbase: 104.5 inches. Overall length: 179.7 inches. Height: 47.9 inches. Width: 73.6 inches. Front tread: 62 inches. Rear tread: 62.1 inches. Standard tires: (front) P245/45ZR-17, (rear) P275/40ZR-18.

TECHNICAL FEATURES

Transmission: [Coupe and Convertible] four-speed overdrive automatic; [Hardtop] six-speed manual. Steering: Rack and pinion (power assisted). Front suspension: Independent SLA forged-aluminum upper and pressure-cast aluminum lower control arms, forged aluminum steering knuckle, transverse monoleaf springs, steel stabilizer bar, and spindle offset. Rear suspension: Independent five-link design with toe and camber adjustment, cast-aluminum upper and lower control arms and knuckle, transverse monoleaf springs, steel tie rods and stabilizer bar, and tubular U-jointed metal matrix composite driveshafts. Brakes: Anti-lock; power four-wheel disc. Body construction: Fiberglass; integral perimeter frame with center backbone/all-welded steel body frame construction. Fuel tank: 19.1 gallons.

OPTIONS

RPO AAB Memory package to recall settings for outside rearview mirrors, radio, power seats and heating/ventilation and air-conditioning controls for coupe and convertible ($150). RPO AG1 Power six-way passenger seat, hardtop only ($305). RPO AP9 Parcel net, hardtop only ($15). RPO AQ9 Sport seats, coupe and convertible ($625). RPO B34 Front floor mats ($25). RPO B84 Body side moldings ($75). RPO CC3 Roof panel with blue tint ($650). RPO C2L Dual body color-keyed roof panel and blue transparent roof panel ($950). RPO CJ2 Dual-zone air conditioning ($365). RPO D42 Luggage shade and cargo net ($50). RPO F45 Continuously Variable Real Time Damping, not available with RPO Z51 package or hard top ($1,695). RPO G92 Performance 3.15:1 axle ratio

Jerry Heasley

1999 Corvette

Jerry Heasley

1999 Corvette with 345-hp LS1 V-8 and Black leather interior

with automatic transmission, not available with six-speed manual transmission ($100). RPO JL4 Active-handling System ($500). RPO LS1 5.7-liter sequential fuel-injection aluminum V-8 (no-cost option). RPO MN6 Six-speed manual transmission, no charge in hardtop, in other models ($825). RPO N37 Tilt-telescope power steering column in coupe and convertible ($350). RPO N73 Custom magnesium wheels ($3,000). RPO R8C National Corvette Museum factory delivery option ($490). RPO T82 Twilight Sentinel for coupe or convertible ($60). RPO T96 Fog lamps ($69). RPO TR6 Lighting package, hardtop only ($95). RPO UN0 Delco-Bose music system ($100). RPO U1S Remote CD changer ($600). RPO UV6 Heads-up display ($375). RPO UZ6 Bose speaker and amplifier, hardtop only ($820). RPO V49 Front license plate frame ($15). RPO CYF California emission system ($170). RPO Z51 Performance handling Package ($350). RPO 86U Magnetic Red Metallic paint, coupe and convertible only ($500).

HISTORICAL FOOTNOTES

A fifth-generation Corvette C5 was the official pace car of the 67th running of the 24 Hours of LeMans in France. Additionally, Chevrolet introduced the Corvette C5-R, a General Motors-engineered and factory-backed GT2-classed sports car that competed in select U.S. and international sports car races.

1999 CORVETTE Model Number	Body/Style Number	Body Type & Seating	Factory Price	Shipping Weight	Production Total
1Y	Y07	2-dr Cpe-2P	$39,171	3,245 lbs.	18,078
1Y	Y37	2-dr Hdtp. Cpe-2P	$38,777	3,153 lbs.	4,031
1Y	Y67	2-dr Conv. Cpe-2P	$45,579	3,246 lbs.	11,161

Chevrolet

1999 Corvette interior

Chevrolet

2000 Corvette family: hardtop, coupe, and convertible

C5 CORVETTE (V-8) SERIES YY

"Still eliciting the passion of bargain-minded speed fiends, the Chevrolet Corvette delivers power, handling and style at a relatively reasonable price," said *Motor Trend* in its October 1999 "Complete Buyer's Guide 2000 & 2001 New Cars" issue. As in 1999, the hardtop was the "loss leader" model from a pricing and marketing standpoint, but the stripped-for-high-performance model from the enthusiast's view. The Goodyear Eagle F1 tires and an upgraded version of the Z51 Performance Handling suspension package were offered with this model. A coupe and a convertible remained available. New exterior and interior color options were the main changes for 2000. A new five-spoke aluminum wheel design with an optional high-polish version was made available. The Corvette's standard equipment list again included next-generation dual airbags; air conditioning; leather seating; power door locks and windows; a PassKey II theft-deterrent system; electronic speed control; an electronic Driver Information Center; and Remote Function Actuation with Remote Keyless Entry. Colors for 2000 Corvette C5 Coupes and Convertibles were: Arctic White; Light Pewter Metallic; Sebring Silver Metallic; Nassau Blue Metallic; Navy Blue Metallic; Black; Torch Red; Millennium Yellow Clear Coat; Magnetic Red II Clear Coat and Dark Bowling Green Metallic. Leather interiors were standard and came in Black; Light Oak; Torch Red; and Light Gray. Convertible tops were available in White, Black, and Light Oak.

I.D. NUMBERS

The Vehicle Identification Number (VIN) is visible through the windshield on the driver's side. The numbers were: 1G1YY[1/2/3]2G5Y5100000 to 1G1YY[1/2/3]2G5Y5133682. The first symbol (1) indicates U.S. built. The second symbol (G) indicates General Motors product. The third symbol (1) indicates Chevrolet Motor Division vehicle. The fourth and fifth symbols (YY) indicate a Corvette. The sixth symbol indicates body style: (1 = fixed-roof hardtop, 2 = two-door coupe GM styles 27, 37, 47 or 57 and 3 = two-door convertible GM body style 67). The seventh symbol indicates restraint code: (2 = Active manual belts with driver and front passenger inflatable restraint system). The eighth symbol indicates engine: G = RPO LS1 5.7-liter Sequential multiport-fuel-injection (MFI) Chevrolet V-8. The ninth symbol is a check digit that varies. The 10th symbol indicates model year (Y =

2000 Corvette coupe

2000). The 11th symbol indicates the assembly plant: (5 = Bowling Green, Ky). The last six symbols indicate the sequential production number.

PAINT CODES

(10U) Arctic White, (11U) Light Pewter Metallic, (13U) Sebring Silver Metallic, (23U) Nassau Blue Metallic, (28U) Navy Blue Metallic, (41U) Black, (70U) Torch Red, (79U) Millennium Yellow Clear Coat, (86U) Magnetic Red II Clear Coat, (91U) Dark Bowling Green Metallic.

LEATHER UPHOLSTERY CODES: (193) Black, (673) Light Oak, (703) Torch Red, (923) Light Gray.

ENGINE

BASE ENGINE: [LS6] V-8: Overhead valve V-8. Cast aluminum block and head. Displacement: 346 cid. (5.7 liters). Bore and stroke: 3.90 x 3.62 inches. Compression ratio: 10.1:1. Brake horsepower: 345 at 5600 rpm. Torque: 350 lbs.-ft. at 4400 rpm. Hydraulic valve lifters. Sequential multiport fuel injection.

TRANSMISSION

AUTOMATIC TRANSMISSION: A Turbo Hydera-Matc automatic transmission with floor-mounted gear shifter was standard equipment..

MANUAL TRANSMISSION: A four-speed manual transmission was optional.

CHASSIS FEATURES

Wheelbase: 104.5 inches. Overall length: 179.7 inches. Height: [Coupe and Hardtop] 47.7 inches.; [Convertible] 47.8 inches. Width: 73.6 inches. Front tread: 62 inches. Rear tread: 62.1 inches. Standard tires: (front) P245/45ZR-17, (rear) P275/40ZR-18.

TECHNICAL FEATURES

Transmission: [Coupe and Convertible] four-speed overdrive automatic; [Hardtop] six-speed manual. Steering: Rack and pinion (power assisted). Front suspension: Independent SLA forged-aluminum upper and pressure-cast aluminum lower control arms, forged aluminum steering knuckle, transverse monoleaf springs, steel stabilizer bar, and spindle offset. Rear suspension: Independent five-link design with toe and camber adjustment, cast-aluminum upper and lower control arms and knuckle, transverse monoleaf springs, steel tie rods and stabilizer bar, and tubular U-jointed metal matrix composite driveshafts. Brakes: Anti-lock; power four-wheel disc. Body construction: Fiberglass; integral perimeter frame with center backbone; all-welded steel body frame construction. Fuel tank: 19.1 gallons.

OPTIONS

RPO 1SA coupe and convertible base equipment group (no-cost option). RPO AAB Memory package to recall settings for outside rearview mirrors, radio, power seats and heating/ventilation and air-conditioning controls for coupe and convertible ($150). RPO AG1 Power six-way passenger seat, hardtop only ($305). RPO AP9 Parcel net, hardtop only ($15). RPO AQ9 Sport seats, coupe and convertible, requires AG2 ($625). RPO B34 Front floor mats ($25). RPO B84 Body side moldings ($75). RPO CC3 Roof panel with blue tint ($650). RPO C2L Dual body color-keyed roof panel and blue transparent roof panel ($1,100). RPO CJ2 Dual-zone air conditioning ($365). RPO CV3 Mexico export (no-cost option). RPO D42 Luggage shade and cargo net for coupe ($50). RPO DD0 Electronic monochromatic mirrors (N/A). RPO EXP Export option (N/A). RPO FE1 Base suspension (N/A). RPO FE3 Sport

Chevrolet

2000 Corvette coupe in Torch Red

suspension, included with Z51 (N/A). RPO FE9 Federal emissions (no-cost option). RPO F45 Selective Real Time Damping, not available with RPO Z06 package ($1,695). RPO G92 Performance 3.15:1 axle ratio, for automatic transmission only ($300). RPO GU2 2.73:1 standard axle ratio with M30 automatic transmission (N/A). RPO GU6 3.42:1 standard rear axle ratio with manual transmission (N/A). RPO JL4 Active-handling System ($500). RPO LS1 5.7-liter sequential fuel-injection aluminum V-8 (no-cost option). RPO MN6 Six-speed manual transmission, no charge in hardtop, in other models ($815). RPO MX0 M30 automatic transmission, included in G92 performance axle (no-cost option). RPO NB8 California and Northeast emissions requirements (no-cost option). RPO NC7 Emissions override. RPO NG1 Massachusetts and New York emissions requirements (no-cost option). RPO N37 Tilt-telescope power steering column in coupe and convertible ($350). RPO N73 Custom magnesium wheels ($2,000). RPO R8C National Corvette Museum factory delivery option ($490). RPO T82 Twilight Sentinel for coupe or convertible ($100). RPO T96 Fog lamps for coupe or convertible only ($69). RPO TR6 Lighting package, hardtop only ($95). RPO UN0 Delco-Bose music system with compact disc changer ($100). RPO U1S Remote 12-disc CD changer ($600). RPO UV6 Heads-up display ($375). RPO UZ6 Bose speaker and amplifier, hardtop only ($820). RPO V49 Front license plate frame ($15). RPO XGG Front tires P245/45ZR-17 (no-cost option). RPO CYF California emission system (no-cost option). RPO Z15 Gymkhana-Autocross package for hardtop, includes MN6, Z51, XGG, YGH, and GUG (no-cost option). RPO Z49 Canadian options (no-cost option). RPO Z51 Performance handling package ($350). RPO 79U Millennium Yellow paint with tint ($500). RPO 86U Magnetic Red Metallic Clear Coat paint, coupe and convertible only ($500).

HISTORICAL FOOTNOTES

Model-year production was 33,682 cars. A total of 3,578 of them left the factory with optional Millennium Yellow paint in honor of the Y2K year.

2000 CORVETTE Model Number	Body/Style Number	Body Type & Seating	Factory Price	Shipping Weight	Production Total
1Y	Y07	2-dr Cpe-2P	$39,475	3,245 lbs.	18,113
1Y	Y37	2-dr Hdtp. Cpe-2P	$38,900	3,173 lbs.	2,090
1Y	Y67	2-dr Conv. Cpe-2P	$45,900	3,248 lbs.	13,479

Jerry Heasley

2001 Z06 Corvette

C5 CORVETTE — (V-8) — SERIES YY

The 2001 Corvette continued as a two-door, two-passenger performance sports car available in three trims ranging from a base coupe to a convertible to an all-new Z06 higher-performance edition. At new-model-introduction time the coupe was equipped with a standard 350-cid 350-hp Chevrolet LS1 V-8 and four-speed automatic transmission. A six-speed manual transmission was optional. The Corvette Z06 included a 350-cid 385-hp Chevrolet LS6 V-8 and a unique six-speed manual transmission with overdrive. This transmission featured more aggressive gearing for quicker acceleration and more usable torque at various speeds. A built-in temperature-sensing unit was designed to alert the driver when transmission oil temperature got too high. The Goodyear tires on the Z06 were made especially for it and were an inch wider than standard tires front and rear, but 23 pounds lighter. The Z06 also featured a windshield and backlight made of thinner glass and a titanium exhaust system to reduce its weight by nearly 40 pounds. Standard on the C5 coupe was air conditioning; driver airbag; passenger airbag; alloy wheels; anti-lock brakes; anti-theft system; cruise control; rear defogger; keyless entry; power locks; power mirrors; heated side mirrors; power steering; power windows; AM/FM anti-theft radio with cassette; leather-trimmed power driver's seat; tachometer; tilt steering; automatic transmission; and Traction Control system. The C5 convertible came with all of the same standard equipment, plus a power antenna. The Z06 was basically equipped like the coupe, but with AM/FM cassette and radio optional and the automatic transmission was not available. Colors for 2001 Corvette Z06 Hardtops were: Quicksilver; Speedway White; Black; Torch Red; and Millennium Yellow Clear Coat. The standard Z06 Hardtop leather interiors came in Black; and Black with Torch Red inserts. Colors for 2001 Corvette C5 coupes and convertibles were: Light Pewter Metallic; Quicksilver Metallic; Navy Blue Metallic; Speedway White; Black; Torch Red; Millennium Yellow Clear Coat; Magnetic Red-II Clear Coat; and Dark Bowling Green Metallic. Leather interiors for Coupes and Convertibles came in Black; Light Oak; Firethorn Red; and Light Gray. Convertible Tops came in White, Black, and Light Oak.

Jerry Heasley

2001 Corvette interior

I.D. NUMBERS

The Vehicle Identification Number (VIN) is visible through the windshield on the driver's side. The numbers were: 1G1YY[1/2/3]2[G/S]515100000 and up. The first symbol (1) indicates U.S. built. The second symbol (G) indicates General Motors product. The third symbol (1) indicates Chevrolet Motor Division vehicle. The fourth and fifth symbols (YY) = Corvette Coupe or Convertible; (YZ) = Corvette Z06 Hardtop. The sixth symbol indicates body style: (1 = Z06 hardtop, 2 = two-door coupe GM styles 27, 37, 47 or 57 and 3 = two-door convertible GM body style 67). The seventh symbol indicates restraint code: (2 = Active manual belts with driver and front passenger inflatable restraint system). The eighth symbol indicates engine: G = RPO LS1 5.7-liter Sequential multiport-fuel-injection (MFI) Chevrolet V-8. S = RPO LS6 5.7-liter sequential multiport-fuel-injection (MFI) Chevrolet V-8. The ninth symbol is a check digit that varies. The 10th symbol indicates model year (1 = 2001). The 11th symbol indicates the assembly plant: (5 = Bowling Green, K.Y.). The last six symbols indicate the sequential production number.Z06

PAINT CODES

(12U) Quicksilver; (40U) Speedway White; (41U) Black; (70U) Torch Red; (79U) Millennium Clear Coat.

COUPE AND CONVERTIBLE PAINT CODES: (11U) Light Pewter Metallic; (12U) Quicksilver Metallic; (13U) Sebring Silver Metallic; (28U) Navy Blue Metallic; (40U) Speedway White; (41U) Black; (70U) Torch Red; (79U) Millennium Yellow Clear Coat; (86U) Magnetic Red-II Clear Coat.

LEATHER UPHOLSTERY CODES: (193) Black; (706) Black and Torch Red; (673) Light Oak; (703) Torch Red; (903) Light Gray.

ENGINES

BASE ENGINE: [LS1] V-8: Overhead valve V-8. Cast aluminum block and head. Displacement: 346 cid. (5.7 liters). Bore and stroke: 3.90 x 3.62 inches. Compression ratio: 10.1:1. Brake horsepower: 350 at 5600 rpm. Torque: 360 lbs.-ft. at 4000 rpm. Hydraulic valve lifters. Induction: Sequential multiport fuel injection.

OPTIONAL ENGINE: [LS6] V-8 Overhead valve. Cast aluminum block and head. Displacement: 346 cid. (5.7 liters). Bore and stroke: 3.90 x 3.62 inches. Compression ratio: 10.5:1. Brake horsepower: 385 at 6000 rpm. Torque: 385 lbs.-ft. at 4800 rpm. Hydraulic valve lifters. Induction: Sequential multiport fuel injection.

TRANSMISSION

AUTOMATIC TRANSMISSION: A four-speed automatic transmission with floor-mounted gear shifter

Jerry Heasley

2001 Corvette coupe

was standard equipment in coupes and convertibles.

MANUAL TRANSMISSION: A unique six-speed manual transmission with floor-mounted gear shifter was standard equipment in Z06. The MNG six-speed manual transmission was optional in coupes and convertibles.

CHASSIS FEATURES

Wheelbase: 104.5 inches. Overall length: 179.7 inches. Height: (coupe and hardtop) 47.7 inches.; (convertible) 47.8 inches. Width: 73.6 inches. Front tread: 62 inches. Rear tread: 62.1 inches. Standard tires coupe and convertible: (front) P245/45ZR-17, (rear) P275/40ZR-18. Standard tires Z06: (front) P265/40ZR-17, (rear) P295/35ZR-18.

TECHNICAL FEATURES

Transmission: (Coupe and Convertible) Four-speed overdrive automatic; (Hardtop) Six-speed manual. Steering: Rack and pinion (power assisted). Front suspension: Independent SLA forged-aluminum upper and pressure-cast aluminum lower control arms, forged aluminum steering knuckle, transverse monoleaf springs, steel stabilizer bar, and spindle offset. Rear suspension: Independent five-link design with toe and camber adjustment, cast-aluminum upper and lower control arms and knuckle, transverse monoleaf springs, steel tie rods and stabilizer bar, and tubular U-jointed metal matrix composite driveshafts. Brakes: Anti-lock; power four-wheel disc. Body construction: Fiberglass; integral perimeter frame with center backbone/all-welded steel body frame construction. Fuel tank: 19.1 gallons.

CORVETTE Z06 OPTIONS

RPO AAB Memory package to recall settings for outside rearview mirrors, radio, power seats, heating-ventilation, and air-conditioning controls for coupe and convertible ($150). RPO AG1 Power six-way driver seat, hardtop only ($305). RPO B34 Front floor mats ($25). RPO B84 Body side moldings ($75). RPO CJ2 Dual-zone air conditioning ($365). RPO CV3 Mexico export (no-cost option). RPO DD0 Electronic monochromatic mirrors ($120). RPO EXP Export option (N/A). RPO FE4 suspension, includes RPO M12 six-speed manual transmission unique to Z06 (N/A). RPO GU6 3.42:1 standard rear axle ratio with manual transmission (no-cost option). RPO NB8 California and Northeast emissions requirements (no-cost option). RPO NC7 Federal emissions override (no-cost option). RPO NG1 Massachusetts and New York emissions requirements (no-cost option). RPO N37 Tilt-telescope power steering column in coupe and convertible ($350). RPO R6M New Jersey surcharge, mandatory in New Jersey ($252). RPO R8C National Corvette Museum factory delivery option ($490). RPO V49 Front license plate frame ($15). RPO YF5 California emission system (no-cost option). RPO Z49 Canadian options (no-cost option). RPO 79U Millennium Yellow paint with tint ($500).

CORVETTE COUPE AND CONVERTIBLE OPTIONS

RPO 1SA Option package coupe and convertible base equipment group (no-cost option). RPO 1SB Option Package includes RPO 1SA ($1,700 on coupe and $1,800 for convertible). RPO 1SC Option Package includes RPO 1SB ($2,700 on coupe and $2,600 on convertible). RPO AAB Memory package to recall settings for outside rearview mirrors, radio, power seats, heating-ventilation, and air-conditioning controls, requires CJ2 ($150). RPO AG1 Power six-way driver seat, standard on Z06 ($305). RPO AN4 Child seat tether (N/A). RPO AP9 Luggage shade and parcel net ($50). RPO B34 Front floor mats ($25). RPO B84 Body side moldings ($75). RPO CC3 Transparent roof panel with blue tint ($750). RPO C2L Dual body color-keyed roof panel and blue transparent roof panel ($1,200). RPO CV3 Mexico export (no-cost option). RPO DD0 Electronic monochromatic mirrors ($120). RPO EXP Export option (N/A). RPO FE1 Base suspension (N/A). RPO FE3 Sport suspension, included with Z51 (N/A). RPO FE9 Federal emissions (no-cost option). RPO F45 Selective Real Time Damping, not available with Z06 ($1,695). RPO 79U Millennium Yellow paint with tint ($600). RPO G92 Performance 3.15:1 axle ratio, for automatic transmission only ($300). RPO GU2 2.73:1 standard axle ratio with M30 automatic transmission (N/A). RPO GU6 3.42:1 standard rear axle ratio with manual transmission (N/A). RPO LS1 5.7-liter sequential fuel-injection alumium V-8 (no-cost option). RPO MN6 Six-speed manual transmission, no charge in hardtop, in other models ($815). RPO MX0 M30 automatic transmission, included in G92 performance axle (no-cost option). RPO NB8 California and Northeast emissions requirements (no-cost option). RPO NC7 Emissions override (no-cost option). RPO NG1 Massachusetts and New York emissions requirements (no-cost option). RPO N37 Tilt-telescope power steering column ($350). RPO N73 Sport magnesium wheels ($2,000). RPO QD4 Domestic standard five-spoke wheels (no-cost option). RPO QF5 Deluxe high-polish wheels ($1,250). RPO R6M New Jersey surcharge, mandatory in New Jersey ($252). RPO R8C National Corvette Museum factory delivery option ($490). RPO UN0 Delco-Bose music system with compact disc changer ($100). RPO U1S Remote 12-disc CD changer ($600). RPO V49 Front license plate frame ($15). RPO XGG Front tires P245/45ZR-17 (no-cost option). RPO YGH Rear tire P275/40ZR-18 (no-cost option). RPO YF5 California emission system (no-cost option). RPO Z49 Canadian options (no-cost option). RPO Z51 Performance handling package ($350). RPO 86U Magnetic Red Metallic Clear Coat paint ($600).

HISTORICAL FOOTNOTES

Automobile Magazine awarded the 2001 Corvette Z06 "Automobile of the Year" honors. In its August 2000 issue, *Road and Track* said of the Z06 "The Empire has struck back in big numbers." That same month, a *Motor Trend* test driver tested a Z06 and reported, "I did things in the Corvette I wouldn't consider in the Cobra R, things that would result in an off-track excursion and maybe a big crash in the Dodge RT/10." The Automobile Journalists Association of Canada gave the Corvette Z06 its 2001 "Car of the Year Award" for best new sports and performance car.

2001 CORVETTE Model Number	Body/Style Number	Body Type & Seating	Factory Price	Shipping Weight	Production Total
1Y	Y07	2-dr Cpe-2P	$40,475	3,214 lbs.	15,681
1Y	Y67	2-dr Conv. Cpe-2P	$47,000	3,110 lbs.	14,173
2001 CORVETTE Z06					
1Y	Z07	2-dr Hdtp-2P	$47,500	3,115 lb.	5,773

Five generations of Corvettes

Wieck Media

The 2002 Z06 Indy Pace Car

C5 CORVETTE (V-8) SERIES YY

In 2002, Chevrolet was looking forward to celebrating the Corvette's 50th anniversary. All 2002 Corvettes had a second-generation Active Handling system as standard equipment. This system featured dynamic rear brake proportioning to prevent rear wheel lockup, plus rear brake stability control to assist drivers in maintaining control under light braking and high-acceleration conditions. It also had integral traction control calibrated to allow better power and handling, while controlling excessive wheel spin. The system's on/off switch and "Competitive Mode" enabled drivers to disengage the traction control feature without giving up Active Handling's other benefits. The 2002 automatic transmission cooler case was constructed of lightweight cast aluminum, replacing stainless steel. Corvette coupes and convertibles received an AM/FM/ in-dash CD system as their new standard entertainment system. An AM/FM/cassette system was available when buyers ordered the remote 12-disc CD changer. The 12-disc CD changer is also available with a CD radio. Corvette's exterior color palette added Electron Blue, replacing Navy Blue Metallic for coupes and convertibles. Standard on the C5 coupe was air conditioning, a driver airbag, a passenger airbag, alloy wheels, anti-lock brakes, an anti-theft system, cruise control, a rear defogger, remote keyless entry, power locks, power mirrors, heated side mirrors, power steering, power windows, an AM/FM anti-theft radio with cassette, a leather-trimmed power driver's seat, a tachometer, tilt steering, an automatic transmission, and the Traction Control system. The C5 convertible came with all of the same standard equipment, plus a power antenna.

Z06 CORVETTE (V-8) SERIES YY + Z06

The Z06 Corvette, first introduced in 2001, was based on the former hardtop model and inspired by the legendary Z06 option of the '60s. It was aimed at true performance enthusiasts at the upper end of the high-performance market. For 2002, a 20-hp boost made the Z06 the quickest production Corvette ever. This improvement was the result of new hollow-stem valves, a higher-lift camshaft, a low-restriction mass air flow (MAF) sensor and a new low-restriction air cleaner. Eliminating the PUP converter from the exhaust system enabled better flow of spent gasses and reduced vehicle weight without compromising the car's NLEV (National Low Emission Vehicle) status. The Z06-specific FE4 high-performance suspension system featured a larger front stabilizer bar, revised shock valving, a stiffer rear leaf spring and specific camber settings—all calibrated for maximum control during high-speed operation. The Z06 also had new rear shock valving for a more controlled ride. Although retaining the 2001 design and color, the unique aluminum Z06 wheels were now produced using a casting, rather than a forging, process. The magnesium wheel option for coupes and

Wieck Media

A Speedway White 2002 C5 Corvette

convertibles was no longer available. Hydroformed frame rails and a four-wheel independent front suspension with cast-aluminum upper and lower A-arms were other Z06 features. The Z06 (and C-5 Corvettes equipped with the Z51 package) now had aluminum front stabilizer bar links and reduced weight. The rear suspension had a transverse leaf spring system. Now standard on Z06s, the Head-Up Display (HUD) system projected the speedometer and many other gauges digitally on the windshield, ahead of the steering wheel, enabling the driver to keep his or her eyes on the road ahead. New high-performance front brake pads on the Z06 provided improved lining durability and fade resistance in high-performance situations. Electron Blue took the place of Speedway White as one of five choices on the Z06. As in 2001, an AM/FM cassette/radio was optional in the Z06 and no automatic transmission was offered.

I.D. NUMBERS

The Vehicle Identification Number (VIN) is visible through the windshield on the driver's side. The numbers were: 1G1YY[1/2/3]2[G/S]515100000 and up. The first symbol 1 indicates U.S. built. The second symbol G indicates General Motors product. The third symbol 1 indicates Chevrolet Motor Division vehicle. The fourth and fifth symbols YY = Corvette coupe or convertible; YZ = Corvette Z06 hardtop. The sixth symbol indicates body style: 1 = Z06 hardtop, 2 = two-door coupe GM styles 27, 37, 47 or 57 and 3 = two-door convertible GM body style 67. The seventh symbol indicates restraint code: 2 = Active manual belts with driver and front passenger inflatable restraint system. The eighth symbol indicates engine: G = RPO LS1 5.7-liter sequential multiport-fuel-injection (MFI) Chevrolet V-8. S = RPO LS6 5.7-liter sequential multiport-fuel-injection (MFI) Chevrolet V-8. The ninth symbol is a check digit that varies. The 10th symbol indicates model year 2 = 2002. The 11th symbol indicates the assembly plant: 5 = Bowling Green, Kentucky. The last six symbols indicate the sequential production number.

COUPE AND CONVERTIBLE PAINT CODES

(11U) Light Pewter Metallic, (12U) Quicksilver Metallic, (21U) Electron Blue Metallic, (40U) Speedway White, (41U) Black, (70U) Torch Red, (79U) Millennium Yellow Clear Coat and (86U) Magnetic Red-II Clear Coat.

Z06 PAINT CODES

(12U) Quicksilver; (21U) electron Blue; (41U) Black; (70U) Torch Red, (79U) Millennium Clear Coat.

COUPE AND CONVERTIBLE TRIM CODES: [Leather upholstery] (19I) Black, (67I) Light Oak, (70I) Firethorn Red and (92I) Light Gray. Convertible tops: (10T) White, (41T) Black and (67T) Light Oak.

Z06 TRIM CODES: [Leather upholstery] (19I) Black, (70I) Firethorn Red.

ENGINES

BASE ENGINE: [LS1] V-8: Overhead-valve V-8. Cast-aluminum block and head. Displacement: 346 cu. in. (5.7 liters). Bore & stroke: 3.90 x 3.62 in. Compression ratio: 10.1:1. Brake hp: 350 at 5600 rpm. Torque: (six-speed

Wieck Media

The Z06 was lean and mean from all angles in 2002.

manual) 375 lbs.-ft. at 4400 rpm; (automatic) 360 lbs.-ft. at 4000 rpm. Hydraulic valve lifters. Sequential multiport fuel injection.

OPTIONAL ENGINE: [LS6] V-8: Overhead-valve V-8. Cast-aluminum block and head. Displacement: 346 cu. in. (5.7 liters). Bore & stroke: 3.90 x 3.62 in. Compression ratio: 10.5:1. Brake hp: 405 at 6000 rpm. Torque: 400 lbs.-ft. at 4800 rpm. Hydraulic valve lifters. Sequential multiport fuel injection.

TRANSMISSION

AUTOMATIC TRANSMISSION: A 4L60-E four-speed automatic transmission with floor-mounted gear shifter was standard equipment in coupes and convertibles.

MANUAL TRANSMISSION: A unique six-speed manual transmission with floor-mounted gear shifter was standard equipment in the Z06. A six-speed manual transmission was optional in coupes and convertibles.

CHASSIS DATA

Wheelbase: 104.5 in. Overall length: 179.7 in. Height: (coupe and hardtop) 47.7 in.; (convertible) 47.8 in. Width: 73.6 in. Front tread: 62.0 in. Rear tread: 62.1 in. Standard tires for coupe and convertible: (front) P245/45ZR17, (rear) P275/40ZR18. Standard tires for Z06: (front) P265/40ZR-17, (rear) P295/35ZR-18.

TECHNICAL

Transmission: (coupe and convertible) four-speed overdrive automatic; (hardtop) six-speed manual. Steering: speed sensitive power-assisted rack-and-pinion. Suspension (front): short/long arm (SLA) double wishbone, cast aluminum upper & lower control arms, transverse-mounted composite leaf spring, monotube shock absorber. Suspension (rear): short/long arm (SLA) double wishbone, cast aluminum upper & lower control arms, transverse-mounted composite leaf spring, monotube shock absorber. Brakes: Anti-lock: power four-wheel disc. Body construction: fiberglass; integral perimeter frame with center backbone/all-welded steel body frame construction. Fuel tank: 19.1 gallons.

CORVETTE COUPE AND CONVERTIBLE OPTIONS

RPO 1SA Option Package coupe and convertible base equipment group (N/A). RPO 1SB Option Package includes RPO 1SA ($1,750 on coupe and $1,850 for convertible). RPO AAB Memory Package to recall settings for outside rearview mirrors, radio, power seats and heating-ventilation and air-conditioning controls, requires CJ2 ($175). RPO AG1 Power six-way driver seat, standard on Z06 ($305). RPO AG2 Power passenger seat (N/A). RPO AN4 Child seat tether (N/A). RPO AP9 parcel net, coupe only ($15). RPO AQ9 Driver and passenger reclining bucket seats (N/A). AR9 Driver and passenger European bucket seats (N/A). RPO B34 Front floor mats ($25). RPO B84 Body side moldings ($150). RPO C2L dual roof package ($1,200). RPO C60 Basic climate control system (N/A). RPO CC3 Transparent roof panel with blue tint ($750). RPO CF7 Non-transparent roof panel (N/A). RPO CJ2 Auto Climate Control air conditioning (N/A). RPO CV3 Mexico export (N/A). RPO DD0 Electronic

The 2002 Corvette Z06 in Electron Blue

monochromatic mirrors ($120). RPO EXP Export option (N/A). RPO F45 Selective Real Time Damping, not available with Z06 ($1,695). RPO FE1 Base suspension (N/A). RPO FE3 Sport suspension, included with Z51 (N/A). RPO FE9 Federal emissions certificate (N/A). RPO G92 Performance axle ratio, 3.15:1 for automatic transmission only (N/A). RPO GU2 2.73:1 standard axle ratio with M30 automatic transmission (N/A). RPO GU6 3.42:1 standard rear axle ratio with manual transmission (N/A). RPO LS1 5.7-liter sequential fuel-injection aluminum V-8 (N/A). RPO M30 four-speed automatic transmission (N/A). RPO MM6 Six-speed manual transmission, no charge in hardtop, in other models ($915). RPO N37 Tilt-telescope power steering column ($350). RPO N73 Sport Magnesium Wheels (N/A). RPO NB8 California and Northeast emissions requirements (N/A). RPO NG1 Massachusetts and New York emissions requirements (N/A). RPO QD4 Domestic standard five-spoke wheels (N/A). RPO QF5 Deluxe high-polish wheels ($1,295). RPO R6M New Jersey surcharge, mandatory in New Jersey (N/A). RPO R8C National Corvette Museum factory delivery option ($490). RPO T96 fog lamps (N/A). RPO U1S Remote 12-disc CD changer ($600). RPO UL0 AM/FM cassette stereo ($600). RPO UN0 Delco/Bose music system with compact disc changer (N/A). RPO UV6 heads-up display (N/A). RPO V49 Front license plate frame ($15). RPO XGG Front tires P245/45ZR17 (N/A). RPO YGH Rear tire P275/40ZR18 (N/A). RPO Z49 Canadian options (N/A). RPO Z51 Performance handling Package ($395). NOTE: N/A = not applicable.

CORVETTE Z06 OPTIONS

RPO 1SA Option Package coupe and convertible base equipment group (N/A). RPO AAB Memory Package to recall settings for outside rearview mirrors, radio, power seats and heating-ventilation and air-conditioning controls, requires CJ2 ($175). RPO AG1 Power six-way driver seat, standard on Z06 ($305). RPO AN4 Child seat tether (N/A). AR9 Driver and passenger European bucket seats (N/A). RPO B34 Front floor mats ($25). RPO B84 Body side moldings ($150). RPO CJ2 Auto Climate Control air conditioning (N/A). RPO CV3 Mexico export (N/A). RPO DD0 Electronic monochromatic mirrors ($120). RPO EXP Export option (N/A). RPO FE9 Federal emissions certificate (N/A). RPO GU6 3.42:1 Standard rear axle ratio with manual transmission (N/A). RPO LS1 5.7-liter sequential fuel-injection alumium V-8 (N/A). RPO NB8 California and Northeast emissions requirements (N/A). RPO NG1 Massachusetts and New York emissions requirements (N/A). RPO QD4 Domestic standard five-spoke wheels (N/A). RPO R6M New Jersey surcharge, mandatory in New Jersey (N/A). RPO R8C National Corvette Museum factory delivery option ($490). RPO UN0 Delco/Bose music system with compact disc changer (N/A). RPO V49 Front license plate frame ($15). RPO XGG Front tires P245/45ZR17 (N/A). RPO YGH Rear tire P275/40ZR18 (N/A). RPO Z49 Canadian options (N/A). RPO Z51 Performance handling Package ($395). NOTE: N/A = not applicable.

HISTORICAL FOOTNOTES

American Le Mans Series Road Racing returned to the downtown streets of Miami after a seven-year absence in October 2002. A pair of Chevrolet Corvette C5-Rs went up against a total of eight Ferrari 550 Maranello, Saleen S7 and Dodge Vipers to finish one-two in the production-based GTS class and ninth and 10th overall. Co-Drivers Ron Fellows and Johnny O'Connell, in the No. 3 GM Goodwrench car, scored its sixth win out of nine 2002 ALMS races. Corvette teammates Andy Pilgrim and Kelly Collins, with two wins in the No. 4 car, finished second. Corvette won its second consecutive J.D. Power IQS award. In the same study, the car's Bowling Green Assembly Plant earned the Silver Award as the industry's second-highest quality plant in North America.

2003 CORVETTE Model Number	Body/Style Number	Body Type & Seating	Factory Price	Shipping Weight	Production Total
1Y	Y07	2-dr Cpe-2P	$41,855	3,212 lbs.	14,760
1Y	Y67	2-dr Conv.-2P	$48,380	3,207 lbs.	12,710
2003 CORVETTE Z06					
1Y	Y37	2-dr Hdtp-2P	$50,555	3,130 lbs.	8,297

Wieck Media

2002 Corvette instrument Panel

Wieck Media

The 2002 Corvette Z06 in Electron Blue

Wieck Media

The 50th Anniversary convertible was only slightly more popular than the coupe.

C5 CORVETTE (V-8) SERIES YY

For 50 years, the Chevrolet Corvette has been carefully crafted from a precise blend of power, performance, style and comfort. For 2003, Chevrolet's image machine continued to reign as one of GM's technology and style bellwethers. Model-year highlights included a 50th Anniversary Edition package, more standard equipment on the coupe and convertible models and the availability of Magnetic Selective Ride Control. This feature used a revolutionary damper design that controlled wheel and body motion with Magneto-Rheological fluid in the shock absorbers. By controlling the current to an electromagnetic coil inside the piston of the damper, the MR fluid's consistency could be changed, resulting in continuously variable real time damping. Magnetic Selective Ride Control was optional on 2003 coupe and convertible models. New standard equipment for coupe and convertible models included fog lamps, sport seats, a power passenger seat, dual-zone auto HVAC and a parcel net (and a luggage shade for the coupe). Also standard on the C5 coupe was air conditioning, a driver airbag, a passenger airbag, alloy wheels, anti-lock brakes, an anti-theft system, cruise control, a rear defogger, remote keyless entry, power locks, power mirrors, heated side mirrors, power steering, power windows, an AM/FM anti-theft radio with cassette, a leather-trimmed power driver's seat, a tachometer, tilt steering, an automatic transmission and the Traction Control system. The C5 convertible added a power antenna. The 2003 Corvette included Child Restraint Attachment System (CRAS) child seat hooks on the passenger seat to allow easier child seat connection. The air bag-"off" switch was used to disable the passenger-side air bag when a child seat was installed. All 2003 Corvettes featured a special 50th anniversary emblem on the front and rear. The emblem wass Silver and featured the number "50" with the signature cross-flag design. In addition, Medium Spiral Gray Metallic exterior paint replaces Pewter for 2003.

C5 CORVETTE 50th ANNIVERSARY (V-8) SERIES YY

The 50th Anniversary Edition package was available only during the 2003 model year on coupes and convertibles. It included special 50th Anniversary Red exterior paint, specific badging, a unique Shale interior (including color coordinated instrument panel and console) and champagne-painted anniversary wheels with special emblems. It also featured embroidered badges on the seats and floor mats, padded door armrests and grips and a Shale convertible top. The Anniversary Edition came with the standard Corvette LS1 engine, as well as Magnetic Selective Ride Control. A special 50th Anniversary Edition of the 2003 Corvette was the Official Pace Car of the Indianapolis 500 in May of 2003, marking the fifth time that a Corvette has paced the race.

C5 CORVETTE 50th ANNIVERSARY INDY PACE CAR (V-8) SERIES YY

At the time of the Indianapolis 500, the three 2003 Corvettes provided to the Speedway for Pace Car duties were the only 2003 models in existence. Motion picture star Jim Caviezel lead the field of Indy racing cars to the green flag as the Pace Car driver for "The Greatest Spectacle in Racing" on May 26, 2002. Caviezel played the lead role in "High Crimes," a 20th Century Fox film that told the story of an alleged military deserter charged with participating in a mass killing in El Salvador. Corvette brand manager Rick Baldick noted that the race signaled "the start of a year-long celebration leading up to Corvette's 50th anniversary in 2003." The Pace Car was virtually identical to the 50th Anniversary Edition Coupe made available at Chevrolet dealerships in the summer of 2002. It was equipped with a 350-hp 5.7-liter LS1 V-8. A few modifications were made to the 2003 Corvette 50th Anniversary Edition Pace Car to prepare it for pacing duties. They included special exterior graphics wrapped over the "Anniversary Red" exterior and a lower-restriction muffler system. A four-point racing-type safety belt setup and a safety strobe-light system were also required by the Indy Racing League. A special heavy-duty transmission and a power steering cooler were also added to the three pace cars.

Z06 CORVETTE (V-8) SERIES YY + Z06

The Z06 Corvette included a special engine, a unique six-speed manual gearbox, hollow-stem valves, a high-lift camshaft, a low-restriction mass air flow (MAF) sensor, a low-restriction air cleaner, a high-performance exhaust system, a Z06-specific FE4 high-performance suspension system, a fat front stabilizer, revised shock absorber valving, a stiffer rear leaf spring, specific camber settings, hydroformed frame rails, a four-wheel independent front suspension with cast-aluminum upper and lower A-arms, aluminum front stabilizer bar links, a transverse leaf spring system, the Head-Up Display (HUD) system and high-performance front brake pads. An AM/FM cassette/radio was optional in the Z06 and no automatic transmission was offered.

I.D. NUMBERS

The Vehicle Identification Number (VIN) is visible through the windshield on the driver's side. The numbers were: 1G1YY[1/2/3]2[G/S]515100000 and up. The first

Wieck Media

Special badging celebrated a half century of Corvettes.

A Torch Red 50th Anniversary Corvette

symbol 1 indicates U.S. built. The second symbol G indicates General Motors product. The third symbol 1 indicates Chevrolet Motor Division vehicle. The fourth and fifth symbols YY = Corvette coupe or convertible; YZ = Corvette Z06 Hardtop. The sixth symbol indicates body style: 1 = Z06 hardtop, 2 = two-door coupe GM styles 27, 37, 47 or 57 and 3 = two-door convertible GM body style 67. The seventh symbol indicates restraint code: 2 = Active manual belts with driver and front passenger inflatable restraint system, 4 = Driver and passenger air bags front and side with manual belts, 5 = Driver and passenger front and driver side air bags with manual belts. The eighth symbol indicates engine: G = RPO LS1 5.7-liter sequential multiport-fuel-injection (MFI) Chevrolet V-8. S = RPO LS6 5.7-liter sequential multiport-fuel-injection (MFI) Chevrolet V-8. The ninth symbol is a check digit that varies. The 10th symbol indicates model year 3 = 2003. The 11th symbol indicates the assembly plant: 5 = Bowling Green, Kentucky. The last six symbols indicate the sequential production number.

COUPE AND CONVERTIBLE PAINT CODES

(12U) Quicksilver Metallic, (21U) Electron Blue Metallic, (40U) Speedway White, (41U) Black, (70U) Torch Red, (79U) Millennium Yellow Clear Coat, (88U) Spiral Gray Metallic and (94U) Anniversary Red Metallic.

Z06 PAINT CODES: (12U) Quicksilver Metallic, (21U) Electron Blue Metallic, (41U) Black, (70U) Torch Red and (79U) Millennium Yellow Clear Coat.

COUPE AND CONVERTIBLE TRIM CODES

[Leather upholstery] (19I) Black, (67I) Light Oak, (70I) Red/Black, (92I) Light Gray. Convertible tops: (16T) White, (41T) Black, (54T) Shale and (67T) Light Oak.

Z06 TRIM CODES: [Leather upholstery] (19I) Black, (70I) Red/Black.

ENGINES

BASE ENGINE: [LS1] V-8: Overhead-valve V-8. Cast-aluminum block and head. Displacement: 346 cid. (5.7 liters). Bore & stroke: 3.90 x 3.62 in. Compression ratio: 10.1:1. Brake hp: 350 at 5600 rpm. Torque: (Six-speed manual) 375 lb.-ft. at 4400 rpm; (automatic) 360 lb.-ft. at 4000 rpm. Hydraulic valve lifters. Sequential multiport fuel injection.

OPTIONAL ENGINE: [LS6] V-8: Overhead-valve V-8. Cast-aluminum block and head. Displacement: 346 cu. in. (5.7 liters). Bore & stroke: 3.90 x 3.62 in. Compression ratio: 10.5:1. Brake hp: 405 at 6000 rpm. Torque: 400 lbs.-ft. at 4800 rpm. Hydraulic valve lifters. Sequential multiport fuel injection.

TRANSMISSION

AUTOMATIC TRANSMISSION: A 4L60-E four-speed automatic transmission with floor-mounted gear shifter was standard equipment in coupes and convertibles.

MANUAL TRANSMISSION: A unique six-speed manual transmission with floor-mounted gear shifter was standard equipment in Z06. A six-speed manual transmission was optional in coupes and convertibles.

CHASSIS DATA

Wheelbase: 104.5 in. Overall length: 179.7 in. Height: (coupe and hardtop) 47.7 in.; (convertible) 47.8 in. Width: 73.6 in. Front tread: 62 in. Rear tread: 62.1 in. Standard tires coupe and convertible: (front) P245/45ZR17, (rear) P275/40ZR18. Standard tires Z06: (front) P265/40ZR-17, (rear) P295/35ZR-18.

TECHNICAL

Transmission: (coupe and convertible) four-speed overdrive automatic; (hardtop) six-speed manual.

Wieck Media

The base LS1 gave the 2003 'Vette 350 hp.

Steering: rack and pinion (power assisted). Suspension (front): independent SLA forged-aluminum upper and pressure-cast aluminum lower control arms, forged aluminum steering knuckle, transverse monoleaf spring, steel stabilizer bar, spindle offset. Suspension (rear): independent five-link design with toe and camber adjustment, cast-aluminum upper and lower control arms and knuckle, transverse monoleaf spring, steel tie rods and stabilizer bar, tubular U-jointed metal matrix composite driveshafts. Brakes: Anti-lock: power four-wheel disc. Body construction: fiberglass; integral perimeter frame with center backbone/all-welded steel body frame construction. Fuel tank: 18.0 gallons.

CORVETTE COUPE AND CONVERTIBLE OPTIONS

RPO 1SA Option Package coupe and convertible base equipment group (N/A). RPO 1SB Option Package includes RPO 1SA ($1,200). RPO 1SC 50th Anniversary Option Package ($5,000). 79U Millennium Yellow Paint ($750). RPO AAB Memory Package to recall settings for outside rearview mirrors, radio, power seats and heating-ventilation and air-conditioning controls, requires CJ2 ($175). RPO AG1 Power six-way driver seat, standard on Z06 ($305). RPO AN4 Child seat tether (N/A). RPO AP9 Luggage shade and parcel net ($50). RPO AQ9 Driver and passenger reclining bucket seats (N/A). AR9 Driver and passenger European bucket seats (N/A). RPO B34 Front floor mats ($25). RPO B84 Body side moldings ($150). RPO C2L Dual roof package ($1,200). RPO CC3 Transparent roof panel with blue tint ($750). RPO CF7 Non-transparent roof panel (N/A). RPO CJ2 Auto Climate Control air conditioning (N/A). RPO CV3 Mexico export (N/A). RPO DD0 Electronic monochromatic mirrors ($120). RPO EXP Export option (N/A). RPO F55 Magnetic Selective Ride Control, not available with Z06 ($1,695). RPO FE1 Base suspension (N/A). RPO FE3 Sport suspension, included with Z51 (N/A). RPO FE9 Federal emissions certificate (N/A). RPO G92 Performance axle ratio, 3.15:1 for automatic transmission only (N/A). RPO GU2 2.73:1 standard axle ratio with M30 automatic transmission (N/A). RPO GU6 3.42:1 standard rear axle ratio with manual transmission (N/A). RPO LS1 5.7-liter sequential fuel-injection aluminum V-8 (N/A). RPO LS6 5.7-liter sequential fuel-injection aluminum 405-hp V-8 (N/A). RPO M30 Four-speed automatic transmission (N/A). RPO MM6 Six-speed manual transmission, no charge in hardtop, in other models ($915). RPO N37 Tilt-telescope power steering column ($350). RPO N73 Sport Magnesium Wheels

Wieck Media

Corvette's interior creature comforts had come a long way in 50 years.

(N/A). RPO NB8 California and Northeast emissions requirements (N/A). RPO NC7 Federal emissions override (N/A). RPO NG1 Massachusetts and New York emissions requirements (N/A). RPO QD4 Domestic standard five-spoke wheels (N/A). RPO QF5 Deluxe high-polish wheels ($1,295). RPO R6M New Jersey surcharge, mandatory in New Jersey (N/A). RPO R8C National Corvette Museum factory delivery option ($490). RPO U1S Remote 12-disc CD changer ($600). RPO UL0 AM/FM cassette stereo (N/A). RPO UN0 Delco/Bose music system with compact disc changer ($100). RPO UV6 heads-up display (N/A). RPO V49 Front license plate frame ($15). RPO XGG Front tires P245/45ZR17 (N/A). RPO YGH Rear tire P275/40ZR18 (N/A). RPO Z49 Canadian options (N/A). RPO Z51 Performance handling Package ($395). NOTE: N/A = not applicable.

CORVETTE Z06 OPTIONS

RPO 1SA Option package coupe and convertible base equipment group (N/A). 79U Millennium Yellow Paint ($750). RPO AAB Memory package to recall settings for outside rearview mirrors, radio, power seats and heating-ventilation and air-conditioning controls, requires CJ2 ($175). RPO AG1 Power six-way driver seat, standard on Z06 ($305). RPO AN4 Child seat tether (N/A). RPO AP9 Luggage shade and parcel net ($50). AR9 Driver and passenger European bucket seats (N/A). RPO B34 Front floor mats ($25). RPO B84 Body side moldings ($150). RPO CJ2 Auto Climate Control air conditioning (N/A). RPO CV3 Mexico export (N/A). RPO DD0 Electronic monochromatic mirrors ($120). RPO EXP Export option (N/A). RPO FE3 Sport suspension, included with Z51 (N/A). RPO FE9 Federal emissions certificate (N/A). RPO GU6 3.42:1 standard rear axle ratio with manual transmission (N/A). RPO LS6 5.7-liter sequential fuel-injection aluminum 405-hp V-8 (N/A). RPO NB8 California and Northeast emissions requirements (N/A). RPO NC7 Federal emissions override (N/A). RPO NG1 Massachusetts and New York emissions requirements (N/A). RPO QD4 Domestic standard five-spoke wheels (N/A). RPO QF5 Deluxe high-polish wheels ($1,295). RPO R6M New Jersey surcharge, mandatory in New Jersey (N/A). RPO R8C National Corvette Museum factory delivery option ($490). RPO UN0 Delco/Bose music system with compact disc changer ($100). RPO UV6 heads-up display (N/A). RPO V49 Front license plate frame ($15). RPO XGG Front tires P245/45ZR17 (N/A). RPO YGH Rear tire P275/40ZR18 (N/A). RPO Z49 Canadian options (N/A). NOTE: N/A = not applicable.

HISTORICAL FOOTNOTES

Chevrolet Motor Division announced updated plans for a Corvette 50th Anniversary Celebration on January 16, 2003, at a media briefing prior to the start of the Nashville International Auto and Truck Show Media Preview Luncheon. The 50th Anniversary Special Edition 2003 Corvette was unveiled April 10, 2002 along with the news that it would be the Official Pace Car of the 86th Indianapolis 500. On April 24, Chevy announced a special Commemorative Edition 2004 Corvette to celebrate Corvette Racing's historic Le Mans victories and 2001-2002 GTS class championships at the famed Le Mans 24 Hours. The 2004 Commemorative Edition Z06 featured a new hood using carbon fiber material, new exterior graphics and unique Le Mans Blue paint. A Silver and Red center graphic designed for the 2003 Le Mans race car was also to be used on a limited number of 2004 Commemorative Edition Z06s.

2003 CORVETTE					
Model Number	Body/Style Number	Body Type & Seating	Factory Price	Shipping Weight	Production Total
1Y	Y07	2-dr Cpe-2P	$43,475	3,246	12,812
1Y	Y67	2-dr Conv.-2P	$50,375	3,248	14,022
2003 CORVETTE Z06					
1Y	Y37	2-dr Hdtp-2P	$51,275	3,118	8,635

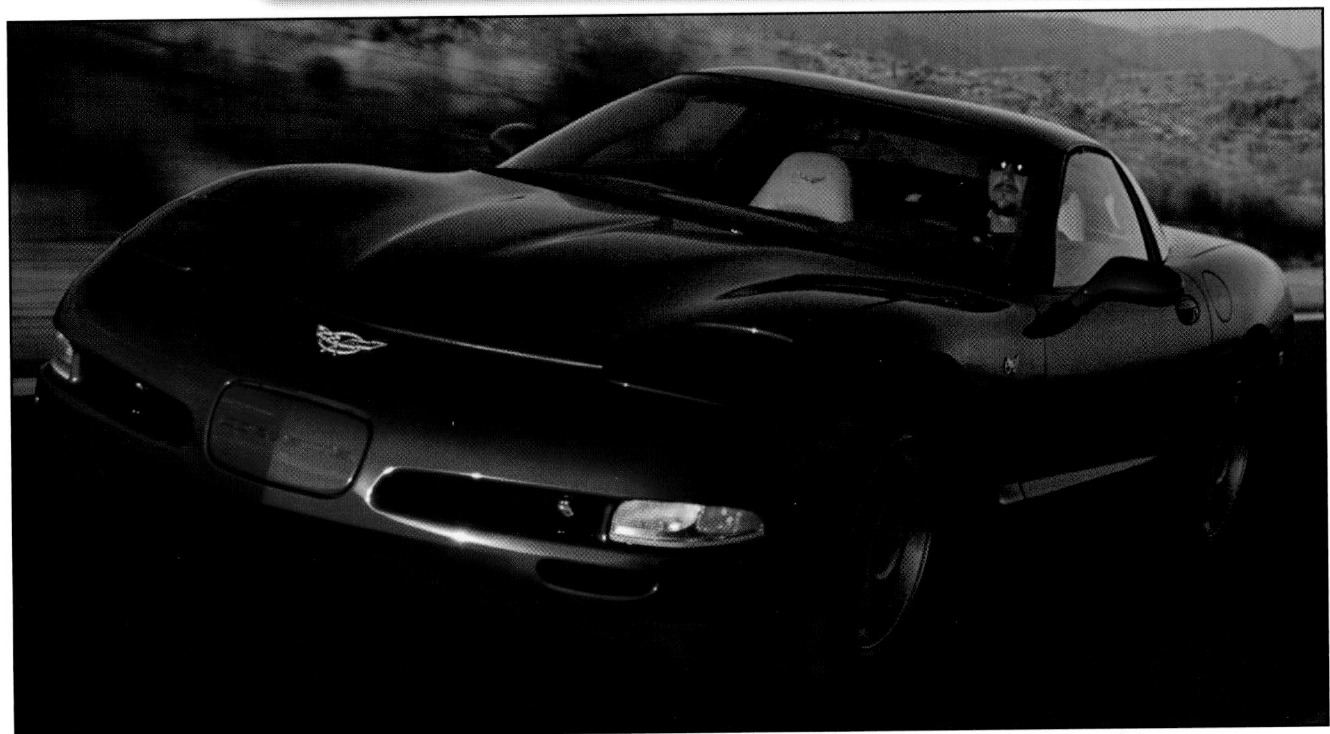

Wieck Media

2003 Corvette 50th Anniversary Edition

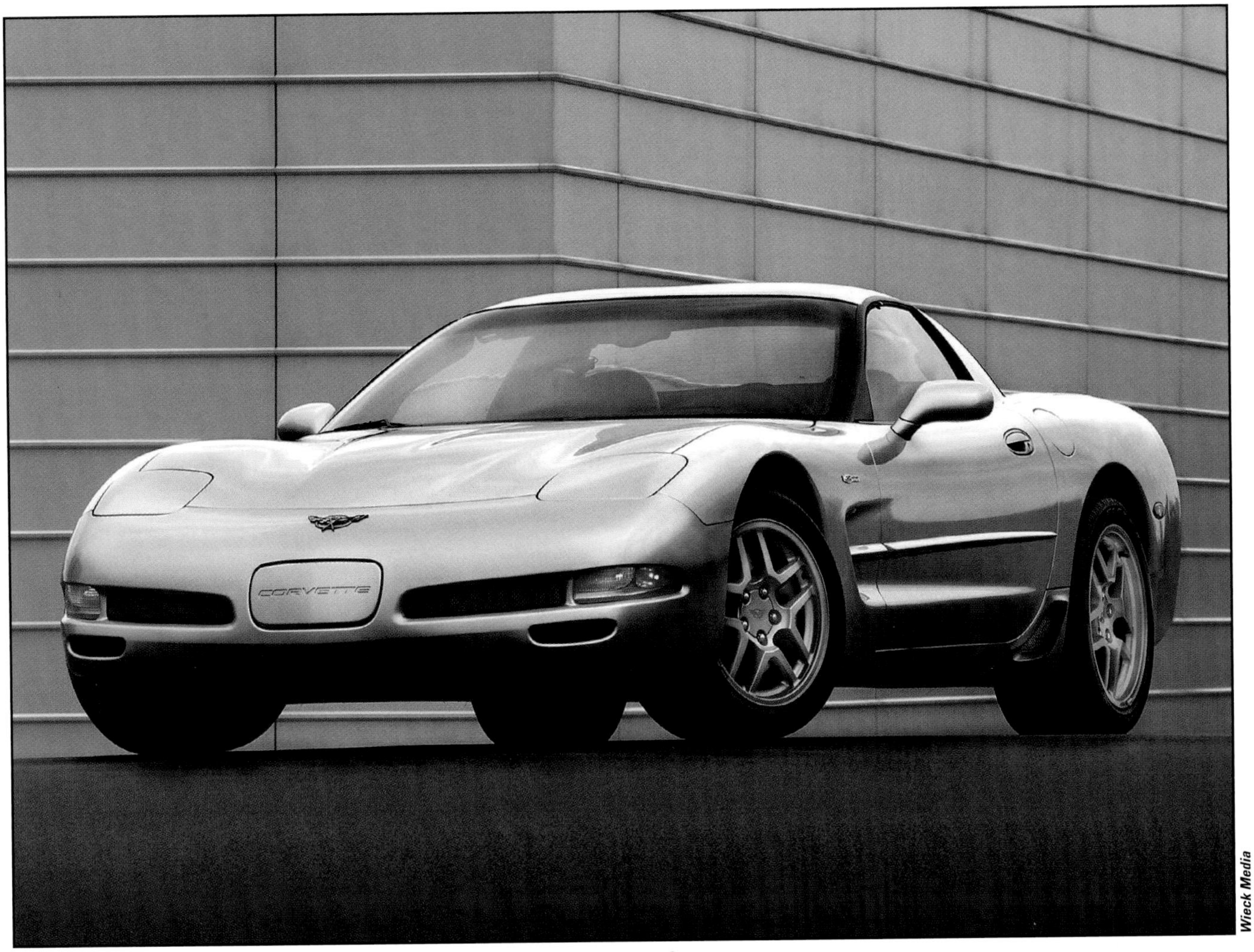
CORVETTE
Wieck Media

2003 Chevrolet Corvette

Wieck Media

Thousands of Corvette enthusiasts lined the streets of downtown Nashville to watch the parade of Corvettes from 1953 to 2003 to celebrate the 50th anniversary of the legendary vehicle.

Wieck Media

The Commemorative Edition Z06 was dressed to go fast.

C5 CORVETTE COUPE AND CONVERTIBLE (V-8) SERIES YY

The C5 Corvette maintained its well-earned status as an American sports car icon that had been admired and sought after for a generation. Coming off two consecutive quality awards from J.D. Power and Associates, the C5 continued to earn accolades, in its final season, for providing surprising interior room, cargo space, comfort and fuel economy in a high-performance sports car. Only a handful of cars rivaled the Corvette's ability to capture the fancy of so many consumers and hold it for so long. Chevrolet continued to celebrate the nameplate's golden anniversary in 2004, with efforts to keep the car fresh and "cutting edge" with new designs and technologies such as those featured on the current line: Magnetic Selective Ride Control, Goodyear EMT "run-flat" tires (coupe and convertible), active handling and a rear transaxle. Standard equipment included a 5.7-liter V-8, a four-speed automatic transmission, rear-wheel drive with a limited-slip rear axle, 17 x 8.5-in. front and 18 x 9.5-in. rear alloy wheel rims, Goodyear Eagle F1 GS Extended Mobility run-flat tires, four-wheel independent suspension, front and rear stabilizer bars, front and rear ventilated disc ABS brakes, a passenger airbag de-activation switch, daytime running lights, dusk-sensing headlights, automatic-delay on/off headlights, front fog lights, variable intermittent windshield wipers, a rear window defogger, two-passenger seating with leather bucket seats, a 6-Way power height-adjustable driver's seat with adjustable lumbar support, remote power door locks, one-touch power windows, heated power mirrors, an AM/FM stereo cassette, four Bose premium radio speakers, an element antenna, speed-proportional power steering, air conditioning, front reading lights, dual illuminating visor-vanity mirrors, a leather-wrapped steering wheel, front floor mats, a cargo area light, a tachometer, a trip computer, a clock, and a low-fuel indicator. In addition to or in place of the above, the convertible featured a folding manual roof, a glass convertible rear window, a remote trunk release, and a trunk light.

C5 CORVETTE COUPE AND CONVERTIBLE COMMEMORATIVE EDITION (V-8) SERIES YY + Z15/Z167/Z18

The 2004 Corvettes Commemorative Edition packages recognized the success of the C5-R competition coupes campaigned by the Corvette Racing Team. The Commemorative Edition Coupe and Convertible included new Le Mans Blue paint with Shale interior, special badges, and polished wheels. The convertible's top also was Shale to match the interior. The Commemorative Edition package contents included a Code 19U LeMans Blue exterior, a

Wieck Media

The Corvette paced the field for the sixth time at Indy in 2004.

Shale interior, special badges, special seat embroidery and RPO QF5 high-polished, five-spoke aluminum wheels with specific center caps. (The Commemorative Edition package was included with (and only available with) the 1SC package, which was a $3,700 option. It included a Shale convertible top with the convertible. The Z18 version of the Commemorative Edition package was for European market cars.

CORVETTE INDY PACE CAR (V-8) SERIES YY

A 2004 Corvette convertible was selected to serve as the Official Pace Car at the 2004 Indianapolis 500. Very few modifications were made to the Corvette to prepare it for this role. They included a heavy-duty transmission, power steering coolers, a lower-restriction muffler system, four-point racing-type safety belts and a safety strobe light system. A two-tone white-and-blue Indy Pace Car paint treatment incorporated Americana-themed graphics to tie into Chevrolet's new "An American Revolution" marketing theme. The theme highlighted Chevrolet's pride and passion for innovation and its success in motorsports,

Z06 CORVETTE (V-8) SERIES YY + Z06

The Z06 Corvette was a Corvette for the extreme performance enthusiast. All 2004 model Z06 Corvettes featured revised chassis tuning for quicker, smoother response in challenging environments. The chassis enhancements were subtle in terms of physical parts, but significant in terms of the car's performance and feel. GM engineers refined the Z06's shock-damping characteristics to provide improved handling in the most challenging conditions, while maintaining good ride control for the demands of daily driving. Continual analysis, development, and refinement of the shock valves in particular resulted in more damping control and force, delivered more smoothly. The new tuning was aimed at diminishing the impact of yaw and roll on the car, particularly in quick, transient maneuvers such as "S-turns" or a series of tight corners. The refinements were the result of extensive testing and development, including several high-speed test sessions at Germany's famed Nurburgring circuit. The Corvette Z06 was one of a handful of cars to break the 8-minute barrier for lap times at Nurburgring. The Corvette testing at Nurburgring wasn't just about raw speed, since the engineers gathered important data on tuning the chassis to the severe demands of a 14-mile course with some 170 turns and virtually constant elevation changes. The Z06 Corvette also included a special engine, a unique six-speed manual gearbox, hollow-stem valves, a high-lift camshaft, a low-restriction mass air flow (MAF) sensor, a low-restriction air cleaner, a high-performance exhaust system, a Z06-specific FE4 high-performance suspension system, a fat front stabilizer, revised shock absorber valving, a stiffer rear leaf spring, specific camber settings, hydroformed frame rails, a four-wheel independent front suspension with cast-aluminum upper and lower A-arms, aluminum front stabilizer bar links, a transverse leaf spring system, the Head-Up Display (HUD) system, and high-performance front brake pads. An AM/FM cassette/radio

Wieck Media

As usual, even the base Corvette interior was loaded for 2004.

was optional in the Z06 and no automatic transmission was offered.

Z06 CORVETTE COMMEMORATIVE EDITION (V-8) SERIES YY + Z06

The Commemorative Edition Z06 also is Le Mans Blue and also includes a C5-R Le Mans stripe scheme, special badges, polished Z06 wheels and a lightweight carbon fiber hood. For 2004, the regular Z06 was given two performance-enhancing upgrades. A lightweight, race-inspired carbon fiber hood was used on Z06s with the Commemorative Edition option and all Z06s had The carbon fiber hood (Commemorative Edition only) weighed 20.5 lbs. This was 10.6 lbs. less than the standard hood weighed and provided another means of saving weight on a car that already enjoyed a potent power-to-weight ratio. Previously reserved for racing and exotic sports cars, the carbon fiber hood combined extremely high strength and low weight. The inside hood panel was a hybrid of carbon fiber and Sheet Molded Compound (SMC). Specifically developed for the Corvette, the Commemorative Edition Z06 hood achieved a higher level of exterior finish quality than previous automotive applications of carbon fiber. On most carbon fiber parts, the woven pattern of the material was easily seen beneath the exterior finish. To diminish that effect and preserve the rich LeMans Blue paint finish, on the Commemorative Edition Z06 the carbon fibers were aligned in a single direction. The only visual cue that the hood was made from carbon fiber was in the red border surrounding the silver graphic on the car, which was arranged in a woven pattern signifying the material that lies underneath.

I.D. NUMBERS

The Vehicle Identification Number (VIN) was visible through the windshield on the driver's side. The first symbol 1 indicates U.S. built. The second symbol G indicates General Motors product. The third symbol 1 indicates Chevrolet Motor Division vehicle. The fourth and fifth symbols YY = Corvette coupe or convertible; YZ = Corvette Z06 hardtop. The sixth symbol indicates body style: 1 = Z06 hardtop, 2 = Two-door coupe GM styles 27, 37, 47 or 57 and 3 = Two-door convertible GM body style 67. The seventh symbol indicates restraint code: 2 = Active manual belts with driver and front passenger inflatable restraint system, 4 = Driver and passenger air bags front and side with manual belts, 5 = Driver and passenger front and driver side air bags with manual belts. The eighth symbol indicates engine: G = RPO LS1 5.7-liter sequential multiport-fuel-injection (MFI) Chevrolet V-8. S = RPO LS6 5.7-liter sequential multiport-fuel-injection

Wieck Media

Racy power seats were only part of the 2004 interior package.

(MFI) Chevrolet V-8. The ninth symbol is a check digit that varies. The 10th symbol indicates model year 4 = 2004. The 11th symbol indicates the assembly plant: 5 = Bowling Green, Kentucky. The last six symbols indicate the sequential production number.

CORVETTE PAINT CODES

(10U) Artic White, (19U) LeMans Blue (Commemorative Edition only), (41U) Black, (67U) Machine Silver, (70U) Torch Red, (79U) Millennium Yellow Clear Coat, (86U) Magnetic Red Metallic and (88U) Medium Spiral Gray Metallic.

CORVETTE TRIM CODES: [Leather upholstery] (193) Black, (673) Light Oak, (703) Torch Red, (704) Black and Torch Red, (923) Light Gray.

CONVERTIBLE TOP CODES: (16T) White, (41T) Black, (54T) Shale, (67T) Light Oak.

ENGINES

BASE ENGINE: [LS1] V-8: Overhead-valve V-8. Cast-aluminum block and head. Displacement: 346 cid. (5.7 liters). Bore & stroke: 3.90 x 3.62 in. Compression ratio: 10.1:1. Brake hp: 350 at 5200 rpm. Torque: (six-speed manual) 375 lbs.-ft. at 4000 rpm; (automatic) 360 lbs.-ft. at 4000 rpm. Hydraulic valve lifters. Sequential multiport fuel injection.

OPTIONAL ENGINE: [LS6] V-8: Overhead-valve V-8. Cast-aluminum block and head. Displacement: 346 cid. (5.7 liters). Bore & stroke: 3.90 x 3.62 in. Compression ratio: 10.5:1. Brake hp: 405 at 6000 rpm. Torque: 400 lbs.-ft. at 4800 rpm. Hydraulic valve lifters. Sequential multiport fuel injection.

TRANSMISSION

AUTOMATIC TRANSMISSION: A 4L60-E four-speed automatic transmission with floor-mounted gear shifter was standard equipment in coupes and convertibles.

MANUAL TRANSMISSION: A unique Tremec T56 (M12) six-speed manual transmission with floor-mounted gear shifter was standard equipment in Z06. A Tremec T56 (MM6) six-speed manual transmission was optional in coupes and convertibles.

CHASSIS DATA

Wheelbase: 104.5 in. Overall length: 179.7 in. Height: (all) 47.7 in. Width: 73.6 in. Front tread: (coupe and convertible) 61.9 in.; (Z06) 62.4 in. Rear tread: (Ccoupe and convertible) 62.0 in.; (Z06) 62.6 in. Standard tires coupe and convertible: (front) P245/45ZR17 Goodyear Eagle F1 GS Extended Mobility, (rear) P275/40ZR18 Goodyear Eagle F1 SC Extended Mobility. Standard

LeMans Blue was reserved for the Commemorative Edition 2004 'Vette.

tires Z06: (front) P265/40ZR-17 Goodyear Eagle F1 SC Asymmetric Tread, (rear) P295/35ZR-18 Goodyear Eagle F1 SC Asymmetric Tread.

TECHNICAL

Steering: rack and pinion (power assisted). Suspension (front): short/long arm (SLA) double wishbone, cast aluminum upper and lower control arms, transverse-mounted composite leaf spring, monotube shock absorber. Suspension (rear): short/long arm (SLA) double wishbone, cast aluminum upper and lower control arms, transverse-mounted composite leaf spring, monotube shock absorber Brakes: anti-lock: power four-wheel disc. Body construction: fiberglass; integral perimeter frame with center backbone/all-welded steel body frame construction. Fuel tank: 18.0 gallons.

OPTIONS

RPO 1SA Base Equipment Group includes fog lamps, Sport seats, power passenger seat, dual zone auto HVAC (N/A). RPO 1SB Option Package for coupe and convertible including 1SA above, Head Up Display, electrochromic mirrors, driver's memory package, Twilight Sentinel headlights, power telescoping steering column ($1,200). RPO 1SB option package for Z06 including 1SA above, Z16 Commemorative Edition, AAB memory package, DDO electrochromic mirrors, P36Z16 specific five-spoke aluminum polished wheels with specific center caps and special logo ($4,500). RPO 1SC 50th Commemorative Edition package including 1SB ($3,700). 79U Millennium Yellow paint ($750). RPO AAB Memory package to recall settings for outside rearview mirrors, radio, power seats and heating-ventilation and air-conditioning controls, requires CJ2 ($175). RPO AG1 6-Way power driver's seat, standard on Z06 (N/A). RPO AK5 Front and right front passenger air bags (N/A). RPO AQ9 Driver and passenger reclining bucket seats (N/A). AR9 Driver and passenger European bucket seats in Z06 (N/A). RPO AU0 remote keyless entry (N/A). RPO B34 Front floor mats ($25). RPO B84 Body side moldings ($150). RPO C05 Folding convertible top (N/A). RPO C2L Dual roof package ($1,200). RPO C88 Front passenger air bag shut-off switch (N/A). RPO CC3 Transparent roof panel with blue tint ($750). RPO CF7 Non-transparent roof panel (N/A). RPO CJ2 Auto Climate Control air conditioning (N/A). RPO CV3 Mexico export (N/A). RPO DDO Electronic monochromatic mirrors including inside rearview mirror and driver's side light-sensitive, auto-dimming outside rearview mirror ($120). RPO DL8 Power, heated, body-color outside rearview mirrors (N/A). RPO EXP Export option (N/A). RPO F55 Magnetic Selective Ride Control, not available with Z06 ($1,695). RPO FE1 Base suspension (N/A). RPO FE3 Sport suspension, included with Z51 (N/A). RPO FE4 Z06 Performance handling package (N/A). RPO FE9 Federal emissions certificate (N/A). RPO G92 automatic transmission 3.15:1 performance axle ratio ($395). RPO GU2 Standard 2.73:1 axle ratio with M30 automatic transmission (N/A). RPO GU6 Standard 3.42:1 rear axle ratio with manual transmission (N/A). RPO JL9 Four-wheel antilock disc brakes (N/A). RPO LS1 5.7-liter sequential fuel-injection aluminum V-8 (N/A). RPO LS6 5.7-liter sequential fuel-injection aluminum 405-hp V-8 (N/A). MM6 Six-speed manual transmission, no charge in hardtop, in other models ($915). RPO M30 Electronic four-speed automatic transmission (N/A). RPO MXO Including M30 electronic four-speed automatic transmission and G92 performance axle ratio (N/A). RPO N37 Power telescopic steering column, including manual tilt-wheel (N/A). RPO N73 Sport Magnesium Wheels (N/A). RPO NB8 California and Northeast emissions requirements

(N/A). RPO NC7 Federal emissions override (N/A). RPO NE1 Massachusetts, Maine, New York, Vermont emissions requirements (N/A). NK4 Leather-wrapped steering wheel (N/A). NW9 Traction control (N/A). RPO P12 Corvette Z06-specific wheels (N/A). RPO P36 Corvette Z06-specific five-spoke polished aluminum wheels ($1,295). RPO QF5 Deluxe high-polish wheels ($1,295). RPO QG1 deluxe five-spoke aluminum wheels (N/A). RPO R6M New Jersey surcharge, mandatory in New Jersey (N/A). RPO R8C National Corvette Museum factory delivery option ($490). T82 Twilight Sentinel (N/A). RPO T96 Front fog lamps (N/A). RPO U1S Remote 12-disc CD changer ($600). RPO U52 Analog instrumentation (N/A). RPO U73 Fixed-mast antenna (N/A). RPO U75 Power antenna (N/A). RPO UL0 AM/FM cassette Bose stereo (N/A). RPO UV6 Heads Up Display including digital readouts for vehicle speed, engine rpm, a performance up-shift guide for the six-speed manual transmission and readings from key gauges including water temperature, oil pressure and fuel level (N/A). RPO UV7 Integral front and rear antenna (N/A). RPO UZ6 Bose speaker and amplifier sound system feature (N/A). RPO V49 Front license plate frame ($15). RPO XFW Non-EMT P265/40ZR18 rear tires (N/A). RPO XGG Front tires P245/45ZR17 (N/A). YF5 California emissions (N/A). RPO YFU Non-EMT P295/35ZR17 front tires (N/A). RPO YGH Non-EMT P275/40ZR18 rear tire (N/A). RPO Z15 including a Code 19U LeMans Blue exterior, a Shale interior, special badges, special seat embroidery and RPO QF5 high-polished, five-spoke aluminum wheels with specific center caps. The Commemorative Edition package was included with—and only available with—the 1SC package. It included a Shale convertible top with the convertible (N/A). RPO Z16 Commemorative Edition package (N/A). The Z18 version of the Commemorative Edition package was for European market cars (N/A). RPO Z49 Canadian options (N/A). Z51 Performance Handling package including larger-diameter sway bars than previous years, (included with FE3 Sports suspension, includes power steering fluid cooler), not available with RPOs F55 and Z06 (N/A). NOTE: N/A = not applicable.

HISTORICAL FOOTNOTES

The Corvette performed Indy 500 pace car duties for a record sixth time. This also marked the third consecutive year and 15th time overall that a Chevrolet product had served as the official pace vehicle—the most appearances by any brand. "We're proud that this year's Memorial Day classic will showcase America's favorite sports car at the greatest spectacle in racing," said Brent Dewar, Chevrolet general manager. "As the 2004 model year is the last of Corvette's current design, pacing the Indy 500 acknowledges the significance the vehicle has played in American culture."

2004 CORVETTE Model Number	Body/Style Number	Body Type & Seating	Factory Price	Shipping Weight	Production Total
1Y	Y07	2-dr Cpe-2P	$43,735	3,246 lbs.	N/A
1Y	Y67	2-dr Conv.-2P	$50,735	3,248 lbs.	N/A
2004 CORVETTE Z06					
1Y	Y37	2-dr Hdtp-2P	$51,585	3,118 lbs.	N/A

Wieck Media

The low-slung 2005 C6 Corvette is a more compact dynamo, measuring 5.1 inches shorter and 1.1 inches narrower than the previous generation.

C6 CORVETTE

On the outside, the all-new 2005 'Vette is a modern blend of form, function and emotion. The C6 has a new size that makes it a more agile machine, even though it is more powerful than its C5 predecessor. The C6 is 5.1 inches shorter and 1.1 inches narrower than the C5, but has a 1.1-inch-longer wheelbase, allowing it to maintain the same interior room and cargo space. The C6's overall dimensions produce a "tighter" package that is similar to a Porsche 911. "Designing the next Corvette was every designer's dream and a tremendous challenge," says Tom Peters, chief designer of the C6. "Everybody had their personal vision of what a Corvette should look like." Peters said that the concept behind the exterior design was to keep it as fresh as possible, while reflecting the looks of the classic '63-'67 "midyear" Corvettes. Peter and his team wanted the new car to have an expressive "face," a tense, flexed look, powerful and dramatic arching fender forms, side extractors, round taillights and performance-oriented exhaust tips. "We wanted the C6 to say 'Corvette' at 100 yards," explains chief engineer Dave Hill." The 2005 Corvette's 6.0-liter LS2 V-8 is a fourth-generation Chevy small-block. GM Powertrain engineer Dave Muscaro describes it as "a state-of-the-art engine that draws on a rich heritage of performance."

EXTERIOR

Reworking two areas of the C6's front-end architecture enables the overall shortening of the car: The front sections of the hydro-formed rails have been shortened by 2.4 inches (60 mm). The fore-and-aft dimension of the front bumper beam has been shortened by .63-inch (16 mm). The new bumper beam is made from two high-strength-steel C-channels that are seam-welded together. At the rear, the body length is reduced via more effective positioning of energy-absorbing foam and the shortening the rear fascia and bumper structure. The new, traditional-looking center-mounted egg-crate grille is traditional, as well as functional, because the C6 has switched from the C5's "bottom breathing" design to one that takes air in 60 percent from the front and 40 percent from the bottom. The C6 also uses the first exposed headlights seen on a 'Vette since 1962. Peters says designers settled on exposed headlights because they fit the theme for the new Corvette—lean, purposeful and performance oriented. The use of fixed headlights saves weight, reduces complexity, and provides better lighting. HID Xenon low-beam projector-beam lenses and tungsten-halogen high-beam projector lenses are used. The projectors are housed in a polycarbonate enclosure that integrates the parking lights, sidemarker-and-turn lights and daytime running lights. Both lenses have chrome rings, but the

Wieck Media

Rated at 400 hp, the C6 Corvette is a modern muscle car with few peers.

bottom of the headlight assembly is body-colored for an integrated, upscale look. The center-bulge hood on the 400-hp C6 implies "muscle power" and radiates outward into the front fenders. The hood opening line falls in the valley where the fender meets the hood. The front fenders are more rounded and more sharply defined. They're a tad higher than the C5 fenders and feature a new beltline crease. The fenders carry down tight against the wheels and retain more definition as they blend into the central fuselage. Combined with the shortened front overhang, the fenders contribute to a tauter, more purposeful front-end design.

The Corvette's traditional "fighter jet" side-profile is continued in the C6. Viewed from above, the "cockpit" styling has been extended to the roof, with more defined dual blisters. "We looked to inspiration from modern jet fighters," said Peters. A new Keyless Access system eliminates exposed door handles and locks. The wheels used on the C6 are one-inch larger than C5 wheels, measuring 18.0 x 8.5 inches at the front and 19.0 x 10.0 inches at the rear. The rear wheels are also 0.5 inches wider than C5's. The five-spoke flangeless wheels are painted silver, but polished aluminum wheels are optional. The rear end appearance of the car, while emphasizing the shortened rear overhang, was kept bold and simple. Four round taillights follow a Corvette tradition dating from 1961. The taillight-license plate relationship was taken as an important styling cue for C6 designers. Reflector optics give the illuminated taillights a glow reminiscent of jet afterburners. On C6 coupes, the fender shapes emphasize crisper transitions and creases that run all the way to the back of the deck lid, drawing your eyes to the taut body form. A center high-mounted stoplight is integrated into the molded black spoiler located on the rear deck lid. The CHMSL is lit using light emitting diodes. A diffuser has been to the bottom of the C6's rear fascia to enhance airflow and add visual interest to the rear of the car. Four circular exhaust tips are integrated into the rear diffuser. The tips exit from the center of the diffuser and repeat the circular theme of the taillights. These design elements "frame" the rear of the C6, producing a narrower body cross section and making the car look and measure smaller at the rear.

The C6 kept the removable roof panel, but it is slightly larger.

Eight exterior colors are offered for the C6. Precision Red and Daytona Sunset Orange are new colors. Carryover hues include Le Mans Blue, Millennium Yellow, Magnetic Red, Machine Silver, Artic White and Black. The C6 uses a forward-hinged hood that is 15 percent smaller, 35 percent lighter and 40 percent stiffer. It closes more easily and securely and eliminates the need for driver checking. At the rear, revisions to the hatchback's hinges, gas struts and bumper stops ensure that the power-operated hatch seals securely every time. A handhold has been designed into the hatch's inside bottom edge to make closing it more convenient. The removable-roof panel used on C6s is 15 percent larger, but has the same stiffness as the C5 type and weighs just one pound more. The roof panel comes standard in body color. It is optionally available in tinted clear or with a dual-roof package. With new indexing side glass and redesigned seals, the roof panel contributes to a quieter interior. A simple three-lever release system makes the panel easier to remove and it snaps in place for easier storage. Small items, bags or briefcases can now be stored underneath the stowed pane. Thanks to more than 400 hours in the wind tunnel, the C6 has a low .28 drag coefficient. This was an important aspect of the designing the new body, since the car had a targeted top speed of 180 mph.

INTERIOR

The overall theme inside the C6 uses the 'Vette's dual-cockpit heritage as its inspiration. Major interior design elements include a flowing, wraparound upper feature line and a two-tone split between upper and lower instrument panel sections. The dual-cockpit uses high-quality materials and precision execution. The interior materials have been upgraded for better comfort and aesthetics. The instrument panel and doors are covered with soft-to-the-touch cast-skin foam-in-place trim with glare-reducing low-gloss finish. It looks like a leather-wrapped, padded panel and its feel is warm and inviting. The new material has double the life of conventional automotive paneling, resists fading and sun damage and minimizes the "fogging" caused by plasticizer migration. Aluminum trim plates with a woven tactile surface add richness and emphasize features. The flush-fitting radio and climate controls, the surrounding trim plates and the instrument panel-to-door closure illustrate the precision fit of interior components. The C6 offers a high-powered audio system, optional onboard navigation system and head-up display. An AM/FM radio with CD player and MP3 capability is standard. A new-technology in-the-windshield antenna enhances radio reception. An improved optional Bose audio system with an in-dash six-disc changer and XM Satellite Radio (U.S. only) is available. A full-function OnStar system provides Virtual Advisor, Personal Calling, emergency notification, stolen vehicle tracking, routing assistance and automatic unlocking. Onboard navigation is optional for the first time. Using a 6.5-inch color touch-screen display, the DVD-based system contains map data for the U.S. and Canada on one disc. The navigation system's voice-

Wieck Media

Wieck Media

Wieck Media

recognition software supports multiple languages.

The C6's instrument panel, gauges and driver information center are designed for maximum illumination and legibility. The easy-to-read analog gauges feature white-on-black numerals giving straightforward display of speed, rpms, oil pressure, water temperature, voltage and fuel level. To reduce visual clutter, major telltales are relocated to the area between the tachometer and speedometer, which are larger, more legible and housed in satin-finished aluminum bezels. While the analog gauges are traditional, the system used to illuminate them features cutting-edge white LED technology. The dials are backlit day and night for better contrast, even in direct-sun conditions. In addition, the inks used for the graphics and the method of the layers and application are also new. The driver information center utilizes organic light-emitting diode (OLED) technology for full-color, full-motion flat-panel displays with a higher level

Wieck Media

of brightness and sharpness. OLEDs are self-luminous and do not require backlighting, eliminating bulky and environmentally undesirable mercury lamps. The driver information center expands to a two-line display that gives more information, including trip computer functions, fuel economy, driving range, tire pressure and oil life remaining. A menu-selectable head-up display with street and track settings that appear on the windshield is optional. The display is focused so that it aligns with the driver's line of sight on the road ahead. The "Street" mode offers several configurations that show the speedometer and turn indicators and add information such as audio system data, gear position and high-beam indicator. "Track" mode shows a larger tach, a speedometer, engine condition gauges and a real-time lateral accelerometer displaying the maximum "g-force" experienced during a turn. The head-up display uses LCD pixels to construct the alpha-numeric characters and graphics, allowing different size and shape graphics.

The C6 seats are more supportive, more comfortable and lighter in weight. A two-layer composite seat frame supported by an aluminum base gives outstanding structural support and especially stiff seat backs. The standard 6-Way power seat includes a manual recliner. The optional 6-Way Sport seat includes power lower-lumbar adjustment and lateral side bolsters. The sport seat has head and torso side impact air bags that deploy through the side faces of the bolsters. Seat belt pre-tensioners are standard. Heated seats are a Corvette first. There is room in the C6 console for a cell phone, sunglasses and six CD cases. The lid is easier to open with more durable hinges and better lock placement. Both doors have storage pockets. The high-retention cupholders are improved. The glove box is larger and its hinges are damped to allow the door to open slowly. In the rear cargo area, the pocket doors are integrated into the floor for a cleaner look. The doors are hinged, to stay open for ease of access and to stay closed during spirited driving. Thanks to the extended mobility tires, the lack of a spare tire gives the storage area more room and a neater appearance.

ENGINE

The new 6.0-liter LS2 V-8 motor is rated for 400 hp at 6000 rpm and 400 lb.-ft. of torque at 4400 rpm. That's 50 horses and 40 lbs.-ft. of torque over the previous LS1. Several significant changes help improve performance, reliability, and serviceability. The aluminum block casting incorporates provisions for external knock sensors and revised oil galleries. The external sensors improve serviceability. A bore increase to 4.00 inches brings displacement to 6.0 liters. The LS2 has a higher-lift cam to take advantage of increased cylinder head flow. The camshaft sensor has been relocated to the front of the block giving room for new oil galleries. A new flat-top piston design with lower ring tension reduces friction and floating wrist pins help quiet the engine. A new "wingless" oil pan with cast baffling reduces mass and provides superior oil control under high-performance driving maneuvers. The new 'Vette engine also features revised 33 percent lighter exhaust manifolds, more efficient coil banks, a higher 10.9:1 compression ratio, a larger 90-mm single-blade throttle body, a better-sealing reduced-mass water pump, a more powerful engine controller incorporating all ETC functions. Mass has been cut to 7 kilos on the automatic V-8 and a higher 6,500 rev limit is provided. Chevy says the LS2 heads are derived from Z06 technology and include raised intake ports and an unshrouded-valve combustion chamber that helps produce a more efficient swirl of the air/fuel mixture, allowing higher compression. The LS2 utilizes 2-inch intake and 1.55-inch exhaust valves with upgraded valve springs. The new oil pan ensures better oil control during high-rpm/high-g-force driving maneuvers and reduces engine oil capacity 5.5 quarts with a dry filter. A gerotor-style oil pump fits in the shallow oil pan and offers superior pumping capability. Wall thickness of the exhaust manifolds is reduced from 4 mm to 3 mm, eliminating weight and helping enhance airflow by approximately four percent. The LS2 features long-life, iridium-tip spark plugs, pistons with full floating wrist pins, a redesigned water pump that significantly reduces the probability of a leak, and a stronger, long-life timing chain. The LS2 features the familiar 90-degree cylinder bank arrangement and 4.40-inch-bore centers. The lightweight deep-skirt block is cast from 319-T5 aluminum with cast-in-place iron cylinder bore liners. A die-cast aluminum valley cover and upper deck rails tie together the cylinder banks, increasing torsional and bending stiffness. Two horizontal cross bolts join with four vertical main cap bolts to make the LS2 smooth and strong and contribute additional strength and smoothness to the engine's rotating assembly. A separate ignition coil pack and short spark plug wire for each cylinder maximize the efficiency of the delivered coil energy, enhancing fuel efficiency and power. The ETC (electronic throttle control) system eliminates conventional mechanical items, such as the idle air control motor, cruise control module and throttle relaxer (traction control) to improve driveability. LS6-type improvements to the engine's crankcase breathing and ventilation include moving the PCV valve away from the rocker covers and into the block valley. Catalyst substrates improvements make the LS2's catalytic converters more effective and less restrictive at the same time. The new converters are mounted closer to the exhaust manifold for quicker lightoff and reduced cold-start emissions. Use of a restrictive quad catalyst was not necessary to meet emissions requirements. An additional benefit of the exhaust system's is the elimination of the LS1-style air injection reaction system. The exhaust system also has more gradual bends and an inline muffler that flows more efficiently. These changes, coupled with the use of just one converter per exhaust bank, reduce backpressure in the system and contribute to the LS6's

Wieck Media

high horsepower and torque ratings.

TRANSMISSION

Buyers of new-generation 2005 Corvettes will have the choice of do-it-yourself gear shifting or leaving gear selections up to the transmission. A Tremec T56 six-speed manual gearbox is standard in this new car, but a Hydra-Matic 4L65-E four-speed automatic is optional. The T56 unit also features revised gearing when it is teamed with the Z51 performance option. In this case, the Tremec gearbox is job-tailored, with numerically higher gears added to improve acceleration. In addition, a lower fifth gear is used to give the Z51-equipped 'Vette better fuel efficiency and a higher top speed than base models. To increase their durability in sustained high-speed situations, the Z51—as well as the Corvette's base European-style manual-transmission—come with a transmission cooler. The shift lever is an inch shorter than on C5s. This means shorter "throws" of the selector, since the travel for all synchronizers is reduced by 10 percent. An all-new shift linkage and new shift-rail bearings contribute to the gearbox's more positive, confident feel. Computer Aided Gear Selection (CAGS) has also been continued to raise the fuel economy of manual-transmission Corvettes. The automatic transmission used in the C6 is the new Hydra-Matic 4L65-E, which is an upgraded version of the C5's 4L60-E. The "L65" four-speed automatic is strengthened and revised to accommodate the LS2 V-8's impressive torque output of 400 lbs.-ft. A five-pinion planetary gear set has been engineered into the new automatic to replace the old four-pinion gear set. The extra gear reduces friction and loads carried by all of the gears. The washers between the gear sets are made of Teflon, a change that promotes optimal operation at high speeds. High vehicle speeds mean high temperatures, but the new automatic uses a four-plate oil cooler to keep things cool. When the temperature of the transmission fluid reaches 127 degrees Celsius (approximately 260 F), the torque converter lock does not disengage, except briefly during shifts. This prevents "fluid shear" inside the torque converter from making the transmission hotter. A highly advanced electronic controller, specifically calibrated for Performance Algorithm Shifting, is used inside the 4L65-E. It automatically selects the optimal gear for current driving conditions, allowing hot laps and hard cornering. The 4L65-E transmission shifts at higher rpm than the old 4L60-E, allowing it to take advantage of the LS2 V-8's higher horsepower and rev range.

CHASSIS

The C6 combines a real-world-tested backbone structure with a new suspension. "Backbone" construction creates a lightweight, high-strength chassis with hydro-formed steel frame rails, cored composite floors, an enclosed center tunnel, a rear-mounted transmission and an aluminum cockpit. The front rails, front bumpers, and hood hinges are stronger than C5 counterparts, resulting in a chassis that is more robust— yet shorter and lighter— than its predecessor. The short-long-arm and transverse-leaf-spring independent suspension remains, but the control arms, springs, dampers, bushings, stabilizer bars and steering gear are all redesigned. Extended Mobility tires that use the latest rubber compounds for run-flat capability help in tuning the suspension for greater lateral acceleration, more body control, a more relaxing ride, less road noise and better traction and stability in corners. Suspension and steering geometry are optimized for better handling and ride. New "directional" control arm bushings are used. With greater clearance in the hub knuckles and dampers, increased suspension travel has been achieved. The front and rear spring rates have also been tuned to take advantage of the greater travel of the suspension.

Three options allow C6 buyers to choose a setup that suits their driving style. Corvette Standard is tuned for a balance of ride comfort and precise handling. Magnetic Selective Ride Control (RPO F55) adds dampers that "read" road surfaces and instantly adjust the damping rates for optimal ride and body control. The Performance Package (RPO Z51) is a competition-ready system with more aggressive dampers and springs, larger stabilizer bars, asymmetrical-tread Goodyear Supercar tires, and larger cross-drilled brake rotors. Goodyear is supplying two different tires. For the Standard and F55 Magnetic Selective Ride Control suspensions, a standard directional-tread tire is offered for a balance between handling and ride.

The Z51 Performance Package features an asymmetrical-tread tire offering maximum handling performance. The wheel and tire sizes are the same for the Z51 option. The brake systems have been re-engineered to give improved heat dissipation and durability. Cars with Standard and F55 suspensions use redesigned 12.8-inch front and 12-inch rear rotors. The front rotors weigh 2 lbs. more than the similar-sized C5 type and are more durable. They generate less heat against the brake pads, reducing wear and fade. All C6 front calipers utilize dual pistons, while the rears use single pistons. The Z51 Performance Package includes larger-diameter 13.4-inch front and 13-inch rear cross-drilled rotors. In the C6, three standard dynamic chassis control systems—anti-lock braking, traction control and Active Handling—operate together. The anti-lock braking system detects and intervenes to prevent wheel lockup during braking. It features four channels, plus a steering sensor. ABS is tied into the Active Handling stability system and shares sensors for steering angle, wheel speed, and acceleration/deceleration in all directions. Traction control initiates individual wheel braking and/or engine torque reduction after sensing excessive wheelspin. Active Handling stability control influences the attitude of the car by applying braking to individual wheels. The optional Magnetic Selective Ride system integrates with these systems to enhance handling and body control by optimizing damping rates based on input from changing road surfaces.

Preliminary Specifications

Overview

Models

Body style / driveline: two-door hatchback coupe,rear-drive, front-engine

Construction: composite body panels, hydroformed steel frame with aluminum & magnesium structural and chassis components

Manufacturing location: Bowling Green, Kentucky

Engine: 6.0L LS2 V-8

Displacement (liters/cu in/cc): 6.0/364 /5970

Bore & stroke (in / mm): 4 x 3.62 / 101.6 x 92

Block material: cast aluminum

Cylinder head material: cast aluminum

Valvetrain: OHV, 2 valves per cylinder

Fuel delivery: SFI (sequential fuel injection)

Compression ratio: 10.9:1

Horsepower (hp / kw @ rpm): 400 / 298 @ 6000

Torque (lbs.-ft @ rpm): 400 @ 4400

Recommended fuel: 93 octane recommended, not required

Maximum engine speed (rpm): 6500

Estimated fuel economy (mpg city / hwy / combined): 19 / 28 / 23 (man) & 18 / 25 / 21 (auto)

Transmissions

Hydra-Matic 4L65-E . . . Tremec T56

6-speed manual . . . . Tremec T56 6-speed manual, w/ optional Z51 Sport Package

Type: . . . . four-speed automatic, with Performance Algorithm Shifting6-speed manual 6-speed manual

Gear ratios (:1):

First:	3.06	2.66	2.97
Second:	1.63	1.78	2.07
Third:	1.00	1.30	1.43
Fourth:	0.70	1.00	1.00
Fifth:	—	0.74	0.71
Sixth:	—	0.50	0.57
Reverse:	2.29	2.90	3.28
Final drive ratio:	std: 2.73; opt: 3.15	3.42	3.42

Chassis/Suspension

Front: short/long arm (SLA) double wishbone, cast aluminum upper & lower control arms, transverse-mounted composite leaf spring, monotube shock absorber

Rear: short/long arm (SLA) double wishbone, cast aluminum upper & lower control arms, transverse-mounted composite leaf spring, monotube shock absorber

Wieck Media

Traction control: electronic traction control, active handling
Steering type: speed sensitive, magnetic power-assisted rack-and-pinion
Steering ratio: 16.1:1 Steering wheel turns, Turning circle, **curb-to-curb (ft/m):** 39/12

Brakes

Type: . . . . .power-assisted disc with ABS, front and rear
Rotor diameter x thickness (in / mm):. . . .front: 12.8 x 1.26/325 x 32; rear: 12.0 x 1/305 x 26

Z51 Performance Suspension:

front: 13.4 x 1.26 / 340 x 32
rear: 13.0 x 1 / 330 x 26

Wheels/Tires

Std & Magnetic Selective Ride Control Z51 Sport Package
Wheel size:
front: 18 x 8.5; rear: 19 x 10
front: 18 x 8.5; rear: 19 x 10
Tires: Goodyear Eagle F1 GS
Extended Mobility
front: P245/40ZR-18
rear: P285/35ZR-19 Goodyear Eagle F1 SC
Extended Mobility
Asymmetric Tread
front: P245/40ZR-18
rear: P285/35ZR-19

Dimensions

Exterior
Wheelbase (in / mm): .105.7 / 2686
Overall length (in/mm): . . . . .174.6 / 4435
Overall width (in/mm):. . . . . 72.6 / 1844
Overall height (in/mm): 49.1/ 1246
Track (in/mm): . . . . front: 62.1 / 1577 rear: 60.7 / 1542
Curb weight (lb./kg):. . .est. 3245 / 1470 Weight distribution
(% front / rear):. . . . . .51 / 49

Interior

Seating capacity
(front / rear):. . . . . .2 / 0
Interior volume (cu ft/L): . . . . .52.1 / 1475
Head room (in/mm):. . . . . .37.9 / 962
Leg room (in/mm): . . . . 43 / 1093
Shoulder room (in/mm): . . . . .55.2 / 1403
Hip room (in/mm): . . . . .53.7 / 1363

Capacities

Cargo volume (hatchback area)
(cu ft/L): . . . . .22.4 / 634
Fuel tank (gal/L): . . . . .18.0 / 68.1
Engine oil (qt/L): . . . . .5.5 / 5.2

Wieck Media

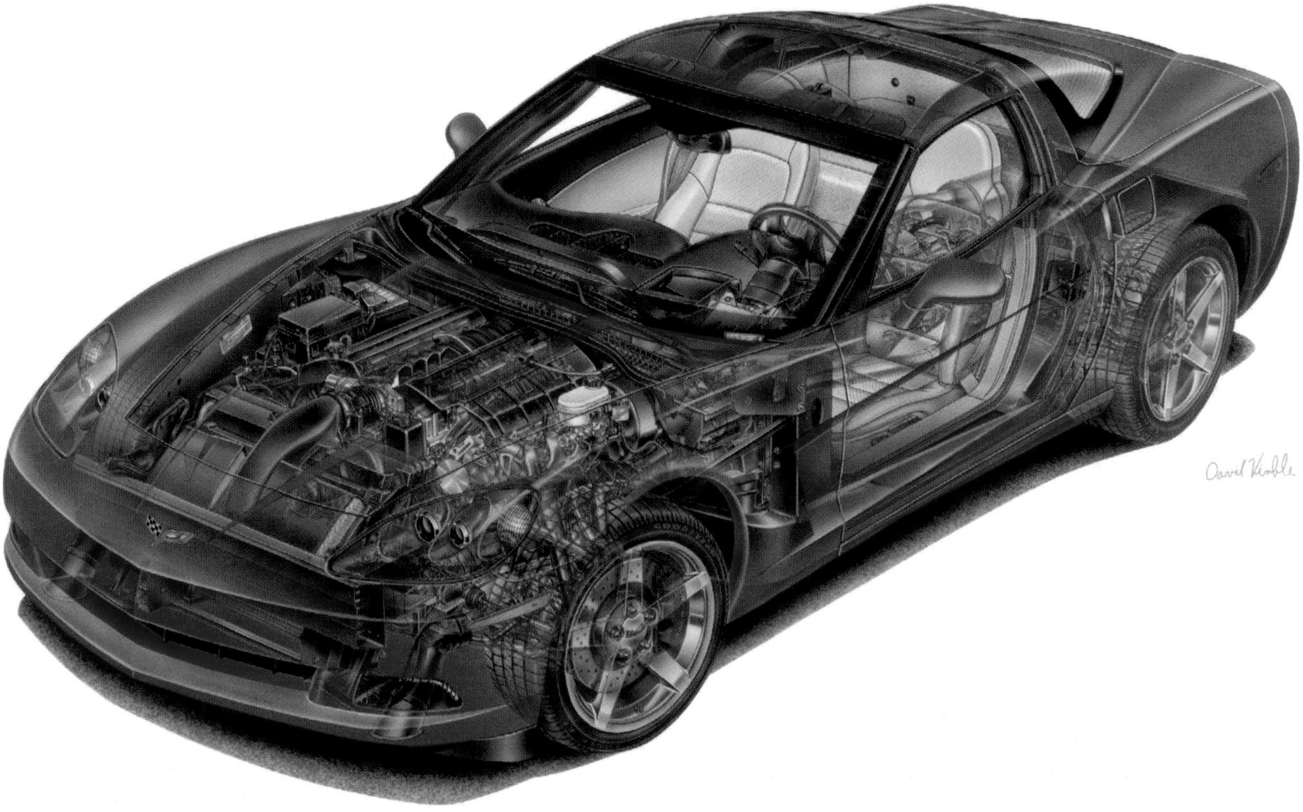

Wieck Media

2005 Corvette coupe cutaway

Wieck Media

2005 Corvette

A Brief History of CORVETTES IN COMPETITION

1956 Corvette race car

There's no doubt that someone would have taken a Corvette racing even if Zora Arkus-Duntov hadn't joined Chevrolet in 1953. However, Duntov's mark was stamped on every aspect of Corvette racing history as it unfolded in the '50s, '60s, '70s and even into the '80s and '90s, when Dave McLellan and Dave Hill expanded on his motor sports enthusiasm.

Duntov was a Russian-born engineer who developed the famed Ardun overhead-valve cylinder head for Ford flathead V-8s. Ardun conversions made Fords competitive on the street and in racing. They were a favorite of early American hot rodders.

Duntov was also a racing enthusiast. In 1946, he drove a Talbot racing car in the Indy 500 time trials. He failed to qualify, but returned in 1947 and tried again with a Martin racecar. This attempt to get into the big race also failed in one sense, but failures would be a part of the early Corvette racing program, too. In another sense, we must appreciate the fact that Zora never gave up after one or two failures. The Corvette's racing history prospered from his stubbornness.

After seeing a prototype of the first six-cylinder, automatic transmission Corvette at the 1952 GM Motorama in New York City, Duntov wrote to Chevrolet's chief engineer Ed Cole to give him his criticisms of the car. Cole liked what Zora had written and eventually hired him to come to work at Chevrolet in 1953. The timing was perfect. Chevrolet had been thinking of dropping the expensive-to-make fiberglass-bodied Corvette until Ford brought out the Thunderbird. The new two-seat rival from Dearborn sparked Ed Cole's competitive spirit. When Cole showed Duntov the 265-cid overhead-valve V-8 that Chevrolet was planning to introduce in 1955, Zora immediately realized its competition potential. With Cole's approval, he adapted the V-8 to the 1955 Corvette, which was otherwise nearly identical to 1953 and1954 models.

By 1955, ads began to appear that hinted at the Corvette's genuine sports-car potential. "For experts

Ron Mcqueeney

1957 Corvette SS Roadster

only!" said an ad in the March issue of Motor Trend. Another entitled, "Child of the magnificent ghost," compared the Corvette to early American sports cars like the Stutz Bearcat. However, there was no actual Corvette racing results until the summer of 1955, when one of the cars set a record time in its class at the Pikes Peak Hill Climb in Colorado.

By 1956, Duntov was well along on the design of a new high-lift camshaft that he hoped to use to take a Corvette to 150 mph at Daytona Beach. During NASCAR's 1956 Daytona Speedweek, Smokey Yunick (who passed away while The Standard Guide to Corvettes 1953-2001 was being compiled) was hired by Chevrolet to prepare three Corvettes for acceleration runs. The cars were good for 265 hp or one horsepower per cubic inch. Zora drove one, John Fitch drove the second, and Betty Skelton drove the

1957 Corvette SS race car

1957 Corvette race car

third. Duntov's car set a new two-way speed record for the flying mile, achieving precisely his desired goal of 150 mph!

Early in 1956, Duntov started work on the Sebring SS, a special tube-framed racecar with a magnesium body and a competition-style windscreen and headrest. He had hoped to race it in March at Sebring in the 12-hour sports car endurance race. The original driver was the legendary Juan Manuel Fangio, but he asked to be released from his contract because it was unclear if the car would be ready in time. The SS wasn't quite finished, but Duntov had a "mule" chassis without the magnesium body ready to go. Fangio drove it in practice and unofficially broke the track record. Duntov's SS lasted 23 racing laps before a bushing failed. John Fitch and Walt Hangsen finished ninth in another Corvette. A third one came in 15th.

Corvette ads of 1956 reflected the model's quick-changing image. "Bring on the hay bales!" was the challenge issued in a June 1956 Motor Trend advertisement. A July advertisement showed a Corvette on the starting grid at Sebring under the headline "The Real McCoy," suggesting that it was a real racing car. "Pebble Beach: 1st in Class C—Corvette; 2nd over-all—Corvette," said an ad printed in August that showed a hard-topped 'Vette crossing the finish line at Pebble Beach. By the fall, a third ad boasted, "The 1956 Corvette is proving, in open competition, that it is America's only true genuine production sports car."

To support the racing efforts, Chevrolet began producing special "heavy-duty" parts to make Corvettes go faster and handle better. Zora Arkus-Duntov was behind the release of many of these components, such as fuel injection, heavy-duty brakes, and heavy-duty steering. As the parts became available to racers, the wins started to come. A Corvette took a first in Class C at Pebble Beach and a first in Class B at Nassau, the Bahamas, with Ray Crawford behind the wheel. By the end of 1956, Dr. Dick Thompson, a Washington, D.C. dentist, drove his Corvette to the Sports Car Club of America's Class C-Production national championship.

In 1957, the Corvette team returned to Sebring with John Fitch and Piero Taruffi teaming up to drive a car to a first in class in the 12-hour race. That effort firmly established the Corvette as a world champion sports car. The same season, Dr. Thompson took the SCCA B-Production championship and J.R. Rose captured the SCCA B-Sports/Racing championship.

At least four big Corvette victories were registered in 1958. Drivers Jim Rathmann and Dick Doane came in first in the GT Class at the 12 Hours of Sebring. Ak Miller captured honors in the Sports Car Division at Pikes Peak,

1957 Corvette race car

Jim Jefford's "Purple People Eater" Corvette SR-2 took the SCCA B-Production title and Andy Porterfield was Pacific Coast B-Production Road Racing champion. Jeffords repeated his SCCA Class B-Production championship in 1959.

Over the next few years, Corvettes started to "rule the roost" in production-class road racing. They racked up checkered flags in all of the major events, as well as numerous regional and national championships. Dr. Thompson once said, "When I began racing my production

1960 CORV1 experimental racing Corvette

1963 Grand Sport replica

Corvette in 1956, nobody else was racing them. By 1962, when I won my fifth national title driving a Corvette, they were completely dominant."

Another well-known racecar driver who piloted Corvettes during the later 1950s was Roger Penske. Corvettes also began to show up at drag racing events across the country. Their lightweight fiberglass bodies combined with their powerful V-8s and Zora's racing hardware made them strong competitors in quarter-mile competition.

Having the Corvette name in racing headlines was also leading to increased sales of the production cars. Chevrolet knew it needed 10,000 sales per year to keep the Corvette alive, but sold only 300 in 1953; 3,640 in 1954; 700

1963 Corvette race car

1963 Corvette (left) race car

in 1955; 3,467 in 1956 and 6,339 in 1957. When the Corvette registered 9,168 deliveries in 1958, it was clear that racing had improved not only the breed, but also the breed's acceptance by sports-car lovers.

Factory-backed Corvette racing had actually ceased by 1958. Chevrolet pulled out of motor sports competition after the Automobile Manufacturer's Assoc. issued a resolution, on June 7, 1957, calling for its members to halt factory support of racing. Duntov frequently said that the AMA resolution and Chevrolet's acceptance of it was a personal blow to him. Of course, the ban didn't stop privately sponsored teams from racing and competitors like Dr. Thompson, Jim Jeffords, John Fitch, and Briggs Cunningham continued taking victory laps in Corvettes.

In 1960, a Corvette took another first in class at Sebring with Chuck Hall and Bill Fritts driving. Then, millionaire sportsman Briggs Cunningham entered three Corvettes in the French Grand Prix at LeMans. John

1963 Corvette Grand Sport race car

1964 Stingray at the 1987 "La Carrera Classic" Mexican road race

Fitch and Bob Grossman drove Cunningham's No. 3 car to an eighth place overall finish in the world-famous 24-hour endurance race, which gave the Corvette name some much-needed international recognition. Also in 1960, Dr. Thompson drove a unique Corvette called the Sting Ray Special to the SCCA's Class C-Sports/Racing title and Bob Johnson earned the SCCA B-Production championship.

As might be expected, private drivers could not achieve a string of victories such as this unless they had some support and Duntov was usually there to help them from behind the scenes. In addition to leaking special parts and technical advice to the car builders and drivers on an under-the-counter basis, Duntov created the SR-2 racing car—which Jim Jeffords drove to the SCCA

1964 Grand Sport prototype

1964 Corvette race car

championship—as part of his 1956 assault on Sebring.

GM styling chief Bill Mitchell was another behind-the-scenes supporter of racing. He found Zora's Corvette SS Sebring mule sitting in a General Motors' warehouse, where it had been gathering dust. He purchased the car for $1 and refurbished it as a sports-racing car at his own expense. Dr. Thompson used it in his 1960 SCCA championship drive. This car also inspired Mitchell's design of the production Sting Ray, which bowed a few years later in 1963.

1966 Corvette race car

1966 L88 Corvette race car

A Corvette first in class at the 12 Hours of Sebring seemed like a given by 1961, when Delmo Johnson and Dale Morgan garnered the honor. Ak Miller also repeated his first-in-class win at Pikes Peak in a Corvette. Meanwhile, Dr. Thompson was racking up enough points for his second-in-a-row SCCA Class B-Production title. To follow up in 1962, a Corvette took a first in class at the Daytona Continental; Dr. Thompson took the SCCA Class A-Production title and Pennsylvania driver Don Yenko became SCCA B-Production champ in his Corvette.

The all-new 1963 Sting Ray options list included the RPO Z06 special performance package for the coupe only. The $1,818 package included power brakes with sintered-metallic linings; heavy-duty shocks; stabilizers; knock-off type aluminum wheels; a positraction rear axle; a four-speed manual gearbox; and a 360-hp fuel-injected V-8. Also available for a short while was the incredible Corvette Grand Sport, which was built under a special just-for-racing program designed to insure the Corvette's dominance in road racing after Carroll Shelby's Cobras started beating the Corvettes in a few races.

The ultra-lightweight Grand Sport coupes were supposed to be powered by a port-fuel-injected, twin-ignition, 377-cid V-8 with an aluminum block and aluminum "hemi" heads that generated at least 550 hp. They cars weighed only 1,908 pounds. Unfortunately, the Grand Sport program was cancelled in the fall of 1963, after GM management again ordered all of its divisions to stop factory-backed racing efforts, including under-the-counter support. As a result, only five engine-less Grand Sports built during the previous summer ever saw the light of day. By some means (rumors said it was via unmarked trucks) two of the cars got into the hands of a Chevrolet dealer named Dick Doane and a Union Pure Oil executive named Grady Davis.

Doane installed Corvette engines in the two cars and Davis loaned his to Dr. Thompson, who campaigned it for the entire year and won the race at Watkins Glen. An oil executive from Texas named John Mecom borrowed the remaining cars from Chevrolet and took them to Nassau Speedweeks where Roger Penske, Augie Pabst, and Jim Hall drove them. Penske finished third overall and first in the Prototype Class in the Governor's Trophy race. The Grand Sports finished first and third in their class in the Nassau Trophy race and fourth and eighth overall.

In early 1964, GM took the three Grand Sports back

1969 Owens Corning Fiberglas Corvette.

from Mecom with plans to convert them into roadsters for Daytona, but corporate managers clamped down again and transferred them to a warehouse. They sat for three years until 1966, when Roger Penske and George Wintersteen purchased them. Modern collectors consider the 1963 Grand Sports to be among the ultimate Corvette racing models, even though they never really had their day in the sun.

Although the Grand Sports were largely stillborn, Duntov was still quite adamant about giving Corvette enthusiasts the power they needed to battle Shelby's Cobras on the racetracks. In 1964, he added a 327-cid 375-hp fuel-injected V-8 (RPO L84) to the factory options list and everyone knew it wasn't there for weekend shopping trips. In 1965, Duntov upped the ante by releasing the awesome RPO L78 engine. This 396-cid 425-hp monster motor was based on the porcupine-head "NASCAR mystery engine" that Chevrolet had been developing before the 1963-1964 corporate racing ban.

From 1963 to 1966, Corvettes continued to win races and championships. In 1963, in addition to Penske's Prototype Class win at Nassau, Don Yenko took the SCCA B-Production championship again. In 1964, a Grand Sport took first place in the GT Class at the Daytona Continental and Frank Dominianni won the SCCA B-Production championship. Corvette pilot John Martin also took SCCA's Midwest Division A-Production championship in 1965 and Brad Brooker's Corvette won B-Production honors in the same division. Zoltran Petrany's Corvette was B-Production champ in the SCCA's Southwest Division. In 1966, a Corvette co-piloted by Roger Penske, George Wintersteen, Dick Gulstrand and Ben Moore took first place in the GT Class in both the Daytona Continental and the 12 Hours of Sebring.

In 1967, Chevrolet added the RPO L88 engine as a $928 Corvette option. This 427-cid 560-hp big-block transformed the fiberglass sports car into a rocket. Competition-prepped L88s set records at NHRA and IHRA drag strips, in road

GM Photo

1986 Corvette Indy Pace Car

1988 Corvette and Protofab Engineer IMSA GTO racer kit

racing events, and even on NASCAR superspeedways like Daytona. At the Bonneville Salt Flats in Utah, a 1967 L88 Corvette set the Class A Grand Touring record of 192.879 mph. Watching all this with a great sense of satisfaction was the only GM employee who was in charge of a single model car—Corvette chief engineer Zora Arkus-Duntov.

The third-generation Corvette, introduced in 1968, had some early quality-control problems, but still offered a 427-cid 435-hp V-8 that racers could build upon to continue their winning ways. Dave Morgan and Hal Sharp were able to take one of the new models to a first in class at the 12 Hours of Sebring in 1968. Jerry Thompson, Jerry Grant, Tony DeLorenzo and John Greenwood were other familiar names in Corvette racing that year. Actor James Garner also organized his American International Corvettes racing team.

Corvettes returned to their domination of road racing in the late 1960s and early 1970s when they won 16 SCCA national A- and B-Production titles. Jerry Thompson captured Class A honors in 1969, when Allan Barker was Class B champ. The following year, John Greenwood won the Class A title and Barker turned in a repeat performance in Class B. In 1971, Don Yenko and Tony DeLorenzo teamed up to drive a Corvette to a first in GT Class

1988 Corvette race car

1990 Corvette Challenge Series cars.

and fourth overall at the Daytona 24-Hour Sports Car race. At the 12-Hours of Sebring, John Greenwood and entertainer Dickie Smothers won the GT-class checkered flag. Greenwood was Class A-Production champ that year and Allan Barker took the Class B-Production title for the third year in a row. Barker repeated again in 1972, when Jerry Hansen, another Corvette driver, took the Class A-Production title. John Greenwood also put in a strong performance at LeMans that year, holding down first in class until a parts failure forced him out.

The Corvette driving team of John Greenwood and Ron Grable teamed up in 1973 to take a first in class at the 12 Hours of Sebring. Three SCCA national championships also went to Corvette pilots that year with Bill Jobe taking B-Production honors, John Anderson capturing the B-Stock Solo II title, and Craig Johnson winning in the B-Prepared Solo II race series. In 1974, Corvettes put in another strong performance. J.M. Robbins drove his to the A-Production Class title. Bill Jobe's car was 1974's B-Production champion and Corvette pilot Steve Eberman was the points leader in B-Stock Solo II competition.

By 1975, Corvettes were competing in the SCCA's Trans-American Series racing. The competition was formidable, but the Corvettes continued to win and John Greenwood was first overall in national Trans-Am competition. The A-Production Class championship went to Corvette driver Frank Fahey. Championship-winning Corvette drivers for 1976 included Gene Bothello in A-Production, Howard Park in B-Production and Orin Butterick in B-Stock Solo II. The 1977 champions were Steve Anderson in A-Production, Bruce Kalin in B-Stock Solo II, and Jack McDonald in B-Prepared Solo II.

By the end of the 1978 season, Greg Pickett picked up another first overall finish in Trans-Am Category II racing. Five more SCCA championships went to other Corvette drivers including A-Production to Elliott Forbes-Robinson, B-Production to Andy Porterfield, B-Stock Solo II to Dave Wright, B-Prepared Solo II to John Seiler, and B-Stock Ladies Solo II to Sandra Schneider.

In 1975, Zora Arkus-Duntov decided to step aside as chief engineer of the marque. However, Duntov's passion for using racing to refine and sell the car was carried on

1990 Corvette race car

1990 Corvette Challenge Series race car

by Dave McLellan, the new head of engineering. Dave immediately started helping Corvette racers. Along with Doug Robinson, John Heinricy, Jim Minneker, and Scott Allman, he built an endurance racing team that was so dominant that the Sports Car Club of America eventually "outlawed" the Corvette for winning too many races!

For collectors, a notable victory of 1979 was Bob Paterson's win in the first vintage car race at Riverside, California, behind the wheel of his restored No. 003 Corvette Grand Sport. Gene Bothello was first overall in a Corvette in Category I Trans-Am competition that year. Andy Porterfield was B-Production champ, Steve Eberman won in B-Stock Solo II, Larry Park took B-Prepared Solo II honors, and the B-Stock Ladies Solo II title went to Janet Saxton.

In 1980, the IMSA GTP Corvette of Chevy dealer Rick Hendrick reached speeds above 200 mph, thanks to its 1200-hp, turbocharged Chevrolet engine. Also gaining popularity were showroom-stock Corvette racecars that were very close to street-driven production cars. By the mid-80's, when Dave McLellan rolled out the C4 Corvette, it wasn't a question of which car would win, but which Corvette would. Corvettes took 19 of 19 SCCA endurance races from 1985 to 1987.

In 1988, the Corvette Challenge pro racing series was established as a reaction to the expulsion of Corvettes

1996 Callaway SuperNatural Corvette

1998 Indy 500 Pace Car

from Sports Car Club of America showroom stock racing. McLellan and Chevrolet engineers Doug Robinson and Frank Ellis sold the SCCA on the idea of a series of races in which identically prepared Corvettes would compete against each other in a fashion similar to the Camaros used in the IROC racing series. The Corvette Challenge cars were a special order item. Buyers of the cars had to hold an SCCA license. Canadian enthusiast John Powell was appointed director of the Corvette Challenge Series races.

Mid America Designs, Goodyear Tire, and Exxon put up money to create a $1,000,000 prize fund, with each of 10 one-hour sprint races in 1988 paying out $50,000 in prize money and the series championship paying a $500,000 end-of-season purse. A total of 56 cars were built that year. All were identical in a technical sense, with all engines equalized to within 2.5 percent of the stock 245 hp. The hoods of the cars were then sealed so no modifications could be made.

Stuart Hayner of Yorba Linda, California, was the inaugural Corvette Challenge champion in 1988 with a victory at Mosport and nine top-10 finishes. The Challenge Series events were continued in 1989, when 29 additional racing cars were built. Drivers who participated in the races included Johnny Rutherford, Jeff Andretti, Jimmy Vasser, and Jaun Fangio II. The final 1989 Challenge Series race was held in St. Petersburg, Florida, at the St. Pete Grand Prix circuit. The winner of that race was Scott

2001 C5-R race car

Wieck Media

2000 race car unveiling

Lagase of the Texas American Racing Team. Overall, Bill Cooper of the Valley Chevrolet team took the 1989 series title.

The Corvette Challenge series was a step towards the development of Dave McLellan's personal dream Corvette, the ZR-1. This high-performance Corvette was introduced during a press conference at the 1989 Geneva Auto Show. It was soon being called the "King of the Hill" Corvette. On March 2, 1990, driver Tommy Morrison took a stock ZR-1 and a small group of experienced drivers (including three Corvette engineers) to Firestone's test track in Ft. Stockton, Texas. There they shattered three world records, including one set by Ab Jenkins, in a Duesenberg! The hot Corvette established speed and endurance records for 24-

Wieck Media

2001 24 Hours of Daytona

Wieck Media

2001 Sebring 12 Hour Race

hours, 5,000 miles and 5,000 kilometers. C4 Corvettes—including ZR-1s—went on to register many additional wins during the 1990s.

In 1992, Dave McLellan retired and Dave Hill took over as Corvette chief engineer. One of his first accomplishments was the 1997 C5 (fifth-generation) Corvette. Before very long, C5s dominated SCCA racing. Corvette made a long-awaited return to Trans-Am racing in 1998 and a successful one, too. The No. 8 Autolink Corvette driven by veteran road racer Paul Gentilozzi placed first in the season opener at Long Beach, California. In 1999, Hill and his team developed a lightweight Corvette hardtop to enhance the C5's racing potential.

The C5-R Corvette GTS racecar, which employed

Wieck Media

2002 LeMans Racing Team

a high number of production components, also proved competitive in international endurance racing. In 1999—its first season on track—the C5-R ran in six races. It had a third in class win in its first race (the Rolex 24 at Daytona) and went on to capture two class seconds at Sears Point and Laguna Seca. At the 2000 Rolex 24, the C5-R registered a second overall finish. The year 2001 brought a new Z06 Corvette with a competition package for serious enthusiasts. The new ZO6 continues a proud heritage of Corvette racing that Zora Arkus-Duntov started some 45 years ago.

Wieck Media

2003 Sebring 12 Hour Race

Wieck Media

2004 24 Hours of LeMans 2003 Sebring 12 Hour Race

CORVETTES PRICING

The prices listed here represent a sample of British sports cars imported to North America, taken from the 2004 Old Cars Price Guide. If you do not see your car here, check the 2005 edition of Cars and Prices published by Krause Publications or contact the club for your British car.

VEHICLE CONDITION SCALE

1. **Excellent.** Restored to current maximum professional standards of quality in every area or perfect original with components operating and appearing as new. A 95-plus point show car that is not driven.
2. **Fine.** Well-restored or a combination of superior restoration and excellent original parts. An extremely well-maintained original vehicle showing minimal wear.
3. **Very good.** Completely operable original or older restoration. A good amateur restoration, or a combination of well-done restoration and good operable components or partially restored car with parts necessary to complete and/or valuable NOS parts.
4. **Good.** A driveable vehicle needed no work or only minor work to be functional. A deteriorated restoration or poor amateur restoration. All components may need restoration to be "excellent" but the car is useable "as is."
5. **Restorable.** Needs complete restoration of body, chassis, and interior. May or may not be running. Isn't weathered or stripped to the point of being useful only for parts.
6. **Parts car.** May or may not be running but it weathered, wrecked and/or stripped to the point of being useful primarily for parts.

	6	5	4	3	2	1
1953						
6-cyl. Conv	4,480	13,440	22,400	44,800	78,400	112,000
1954						
6-cyl. Conv	2,920	8,760	14,600	29,200	51,100	73,000

NOTE: Add $3,000 & up for access. hardtop.

	6	5	4	3	2	1
1955						
6-cyl. Conv	3,000	9,000	15,000	30,000	52,500	75,000
8-cyl. Conv	3,120	9,360	15,600	31,200	54,600	78,000

NOTE: Add $3,000 & up for access. hardtop.

	6	5	4	3	2	1
1956						
Conv	2,960	8,880	14,800	29,600	51,800	74,000

NOTE: All post-1955 Corvettes are V-8 powered. Add $3,000 & up for removable hardtop. Add 20 percent for two 4 barrel carbs.

	6	5	4	3	2	1
1957						
Conv	3,000	9,000	15,000	30,000	52,500	75,000

NOTE: Add $3,000 for hardtop. Add 50 percent for F.I., 250 hp. Add 75 percent for F.I., 283 hp. Add 25 percent for two 4 barrel carbs, 245 hp. Add 35 percent for two 4 barrel carbs, 270 hp. Add 15 per

Nicky Wright

1953 Corvette Roadster, one of only 300 built

1958

	6	5	4	3	2	1
Conv	2,560	7,680	12,800	25,600	44,800	64,000

NOTE: Add $3,000 for hardtop. Add 25 percent for two 4 barrel carbs, 245 hp. Add 35 percent for two 4 barrel carbs, 270 hp. Add 40 percent for F.I., 250 hp. Add 60 percent for F.I., 290 hp.

1959

	6	5	4	3	2	1
Conv	2,200	6,600	11,000	22,000	38,500	55,000

NOTE: Add $3,000 for hardtop. Add 40 percent for F.I., 250 hp. Add 60 percent for F.I., 290 hp. Add 25 percent for two 4 barrel carbs, 245 hp. Add 35 percent for two 4 barrel carbs, 270 hp.

1960

	6	5	4	3	2	1
Conv	2,200	6,600	11,000	22,000	38,500	55,000

NOTE: Add $3,000 for hardtop. Add 40 percent for F.I., 275 hp. Add 60 percent for F.I., 315 hp. Add 25 percent for two 4 barrel carbs, 245 hp. Add 35 percent for two 4 barrel carbs, 270 hp.

1961

	6	5	4	3	2	1
Conv	2,240	6,720	11,200	22,400	39,200	56,000

NOTE: Add $3,000 for hardtop. Add 40 percent for F.I., 275 hp. Add 60 percent for F.I., 315 hp. Add 25 percent for two 4 barrel carbs, 245 hp. Add 35 percent for two 4 barrel carbs, 270 hp.

1962

	6	5	4	3	2	1
Conv	2,280	6,840	11,400	22,800	39,900	57,000

NOTE: Add $3,000 for hardtop; 30 percent for F.I.

1963

	6	5	4	3	2	1
Spt Cpe	2,100	6,250	10,400	20,800	36,400	52,000
Conv	2,100	6,350	10,600	21,200	37,100	53,000
GS		value not estimable				

NOTE: Add 30 percent for F.I.; $4,500 for A/C. Add $3,000 for hardtop; $3,00 for knock off wheels. Z06 option, value not estimable.

Nicky Wright

1961 Corvette with redesigned grille

1964

	6	5	4	3	2	1
Spt Cpe	1,880	5,640	9,400	18,800	32,900	47,000
Conv	2,100	6,350	10,600	21,200	37,100	53,000

NOTE: Add 30 percent for F.I.; $4,500 for A/C. Add 30 percent for 327 cid, 365 hp. Add $3,000 for hardtop; $3,000 for knock off wheels.

1965

	6	5	4	3	2	1
Spt Cpe	1,900	5,750	9,600	19,200	33,600	48,000
Conv	2,100	6,350	10,600	21,200	37,100	53,000

NOTE: Add 40 percent for F.I.; $4,500 for A/C. Add 60 percent for 396 cid. Add $3,000 for knock off wheels. Add $3,000 for hardtop.

1966

	6	5	4	3	2	1
Spt Cpe	1,960	5,880	9,800	19,600	34,300	49,000
Conv	2,160	6,480	10,800	21,600	37,800	54,000

NOTE: Add $4,500 for A/C.; 20 percent for 427 engine - 390 hp. Add 50 percent for 427 engine - 425 hp (L72 listed by Chevrolet as having 425 hp, but, is believed to have more). Add $3,000 for knock of

1967

	6	5	4	3	2	1
Spt Cpe	2,040	6,120	10,200	20,400	35,700	51,000
Conv	2,240	6,720	11,200	22,400	39,200	56,000

NOTE: Add $4,500 for A/C. L88 & L89 option not estimable, 30 percent for 427 engine - 390 hp. Add 50 percent for 427 engine - 400 hp, 70 percent for 427 engine - 435 hp; $4,000 for aluminum wheels; $3

1968

	6	5	4	3	2	1
Spt Cpe	1,160	3,480	5,800	11,600	20,300	29,000
Conv	1,320	3,960	6,600	13,200	23,100	33,000

NOTE: Add 40 percent for L89 427 - 435 hp aluminum head option. L88 engine option not estimable. Add 40 percent for 427, 400 hp. Add 20 percent for L71 427-435 hp cast head.

1969

	6	5	4	3	2	1
Spt Cpe	1,160	3,480	5,800	11,600	20,300	29,000
Conv	1,320	3,960	6,600	13,200	23,100	33,000

NOTE: Add 40 percent for 427 - 435 hp aluminum head option. L88 engine option not estimable. Add 40 percent for 427, 400 hp. Add 20 percent for L71 427-435 hp cast head.

1970

	6	5	4	3	2	1
Spt Cpe	1,120	3,360	5,600	11,200	19,600	28,000
Conv	1,280	3,840	6,400	12,800	22,400	32,000

NOTE: Add 70 percent for LT-1 option. ZR1 option not estimable. Add 30 percent for LS5 option.

1971

	6	5	4	3	2	1
Spt Cpe	1,080	3,240	5,400	10,800	18,900	27,000
Conv	1,240	3,720	6,200	12,400	21,700	31,000

NOTE: Add 50 percent for LT-1 option; 30 percent for LS5 option; 75 percent for LS6 option.

1972

	6	5	4	3	2	1
Spt Cpe	1,080	3,240	5,400	10,800	18,900	27,000
Conv	1,240	3,720	6,200	12,400	21,700	31,000

NOTE: Add 50 percent for LT-1 option. Add 30 percent for LS5 option. Add 25 percent for air on LT-1.

1973

	6	5	4	3	2	1
Spt Cpe	1,000	3,000	5,000	10,000	17,500	25,000
Conv	1,160	3,480	5,800	11,600	20,300	29,000

NOTE: Add 10 percent for L82. Add 25 percent for LS4.

1968 Corvette convertible, the Sting Ray name was not used this year

1974

	6	5	4	3	2	1
Spt Cpe	880	2,640	4,400	8,800	15,400	22,000
Conv	1,080	3,240	5,400	10,800	18,900	27,000

NOTE: Add 10 percent for L82. Add 25 percent for LS4.

1975

	6	5	4	3	2	1
Spt Cpe	840	2,520	4,200	8,400	14,700	21,000
Conv	1,040	3,120	5,200	10,400	18,200	26,000

NOTE: Add 10 percent for L82.

1976

	6	5	4	3	2	1
Cpe	800	2,400	4,000	8,000	14,000	20,000

NOTE: Add 10 percent for L82.

1977

	6	5	4	3	2	1
Cpe	840	2,520	4,200	8,400	14,700	21,000

NOTE: Add 10 percent for L82.

1978

	6	5	4	3	2	1
Cpe	960	2,880	4,800	9,600	16,800	24,000

NOTE: Add 10 percent for anniversary model. Add 25 percent for Pace Car. Add 10 percent for L82 engine option.

1979

	6	5	4	3	2	1
Cpe	840	2,520	4,200	8,400	14,700	21,000

NOTE: Add 10 percent for L82 engine option.

1980

	6	5	4	3	2	1
Cpe	840	2,520	4,200	8,400	14,700	21,000

NOTE: Add 20 percent for L82 engine option.

1981

	6	5	4	3	2	1
Cpe	840	2,520	4,200	8,400	14,700	21,000

1982

	6	5	4	3	2	1
2d Cpe	880	2,640	4,400	8,800	15,400	22,000

NOTE: Add 20 percent for Collector Edition.

1983

NOTE: None manufactured.

1984

	6	5	4	3	2	1
2d HBk	1,100	3,250	5,400	10,800	18,900	27,000

Nicky Wright

1976 Corvette coupe

	6	5	4	3	2	1
1985						
2d HBk	1,100	3,250	5,400	10,800	18,900	27,000
1986						
2d HBk	1,100	3,350	5,600	11,200	19,600	28,000
Conv Pace Car	1,400	4,200	7,050	14,100	24,600	35,200
1987						
2d HBk	1,100	3,350	5,600	11,200	19,600	28,000
Conv	1,300	3,850	6,400	12,800	22,400	32,000
1988						
2d Cpe	1,100	3,300	5,500	11,000	19,300	27,500
Conv	1,200	3,600	6,000	12,000	21,000	30,000
1989						
2d Cpe	1,100	3,350	5,600	11,200	19,600	28,000
Conv	1,250	3,700	6,200	12,400	21,700	31,000
1990						
2d HBk	1,100	3,250	5,400	10,800	18,900	27,000
Conv	1,250	3,700	6,200	12,400	21,700	31,000
2d HBk ZR1	1,950	5,900	9,800	19,600	34,300	49,000
1991						
2d HBk	1,300	3,950	6,600	13,200	23,100	33,000
Conv	1,450	4,300	7,200	14,400	25,200	36,000
2d HBk ZR1	2,100	6,250	10,400	20,800	36,400	52,000
1992						
2d HBk Cpe	1,350	4,100	6,800	13,600	23,800	34,000
2d Conv	1,500	4,450	7,400	14,800	25,900	37,000
2d ZR1 Cpe	2,100	6,350	10,600	21,200	37,100	53,000

	6	5	4	3	2	1
1993						
2d Cpe	1,400	4,200	7,000	14,000	24,500	35,000
2d ZR1 Cpe	2,150	6,500	10,800	21,600	37,800	54,000
2d Conv	1,500	4,550	7,600	15,200	26,600	38,000

NOTE: Add 10 percent for Anniversary model.

	6	5	4	3	2	1
1994						
2d Cpe	1,400	4,200	7,000	14,000	24,500	35,000
2d Conv	1,550	4,700	7,800	15,600	27,300	39,000
2d ZR1 Cpe	2,200	6,600	11,000	22,000	38,500	55,000
1995						
2d Cpe	1,400	4,200	7,000	14,000	24,500	35,000
2d Conv	1,550	4,700	7,800	15,600	27,300	39,000
2d ZR1 Cpe	2,200	6,600	11,000	22,000	38,500	55,000

NOTE: Add 10 percent for Pace Car.

	6	5	4	3	2	1
1996						
2d Cpe	1,400	4,200	7,000	14,000	24,500	35,000
2d Conv	1,550	4,700	7,800	15,600	27,300	39,000

NOTE: Add 10 percent for Grand Sport/Collector Ed. Add 5 percent for LT4 V-8 in base model.

	6	5	4	3	2	1
1997						
2d Cpe	1,480	4,440	7,400	14,800	25,900	37,000

Jerry Heasley

1997 Corvette